SEMANTICS WITH APPLICATIONS

SEMANTICS WITH APPLICATIONS

A Formal Introduction

Hanne Riis Nielson

and

Flemming Nielson
Aarhus University, Denmark

JOHN WILEY & SONS
Chichester · New York · Brisbane · Toronto · Singapore

Other Wiley Editorial Offices

John Wiley & Sons, Inc., 605 Third Avenue,
New York, NY 10158-0012, USA

Jacaranda Wiley Ltd, G.P.O. Box 859, Brisbane,
Queensland 4001, Australia

John Wiley & Sons (Canada) Ltd, 5353 Dundas Street West, Fourth Floor,
Etobicoke, Ontario M9B 6H8, Canada

John Wiley & Sons (SEA) Pte Ltd, 37 Jalan Pemimpin 05-04,
Block B, Union Industrial Building, Singapore 2057

A catalogue record for this book is available from the British Library

ISBN 0 471 92980 8

Printed in Great Britain by Courier International, East Kilbride

Contents

List of Tables

Preface

Many books on formal semantics begin by explaining that there are three major approaches to semantics, that is

- operational semantics,
- denotational semantics, and
- axiomatic semantics;

but then they go on to study just *one* of these in greater detail. The purpose of this book is to

- present the *fundamental ideas* behind *all* of these approaches,
- to stress their *relationship* by formulating and proving the relevant theorems, and
- to illustrate the *applicability* of formal semantics as a tool in computer science.

This is an ambitious goal and to achieve it, the bulk of the development concentrates on a rather small core language of `while`-programs for which the three approaches are developed to roughly the same level of sophistication. To demonstrate the *applicability* of formal semantics we show

- how to use semantics for validating prototype implementations of programming languages,
- how to use semantics for verifying analyses used in more advanced implementations of programming languages, and
- how to use semantics for verifying useful program properties including information about execution time.

The development is *introductory* as is already reflected in the title. For this reason very many advanced concepts within operational, denotational and axiomatic semantics have had to be omitted. Also we have had to omit treatment of other approaches to semantics, for example Petri-nets and temporal logic. Some pointers to further reading are given in Chapter 7.

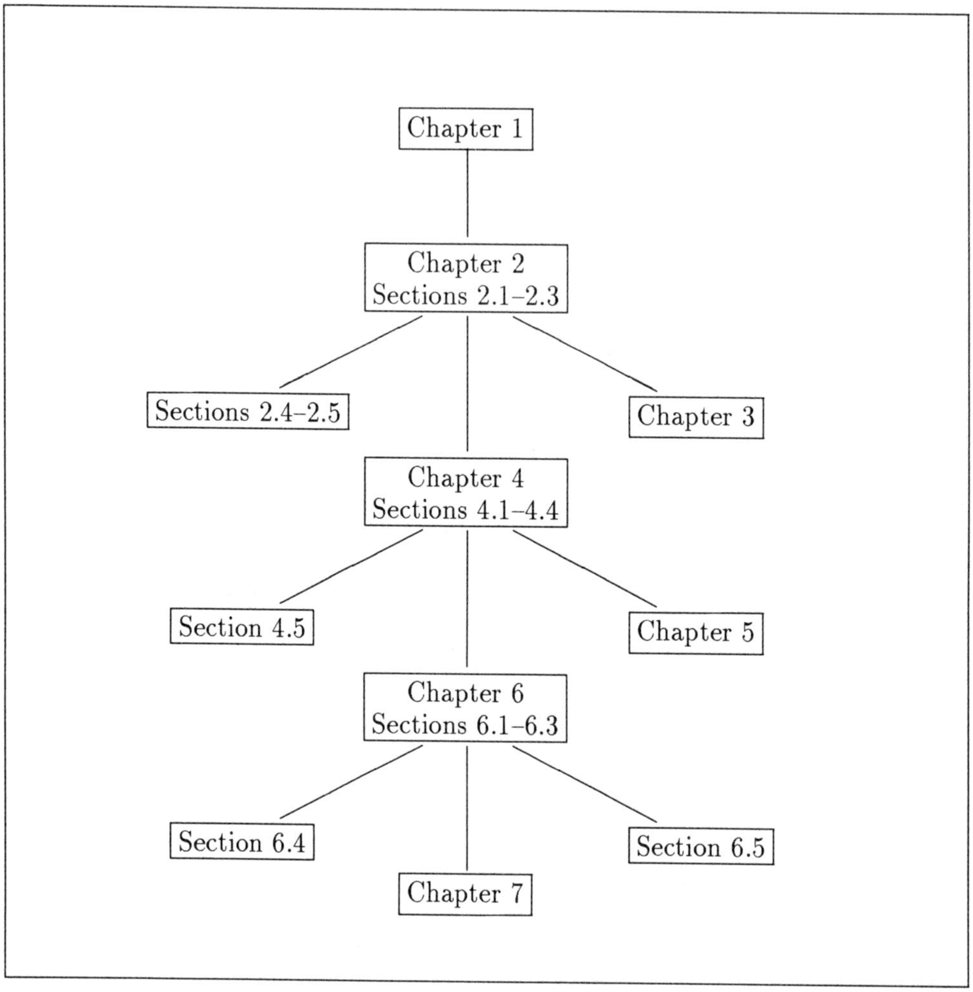

Overview

As is illustrated in the dependency diagram, Chapters 1, 2, 4, 6 and 7 form the core of the book. Chapter 1 introduces the example language of `while`-programs that is used throughout the book. In Chapter 2 we cover two approaches to *operational semantics*, the natural semantics of G. Kahn and the structural operational semantics of G. Plotkin. Chapter 4 develops the *denotational semantics* of D. Scott and C. Strachey including simple fixed point theory. Chapter 6 introduces *program verification* based on operational and denotational semantics and goes on to present the axiomatic approach due to C. A. R. Hoare. Finally, Chapter 7 contains suggestions for further reading.

The first three or four sections of each of the Chapters 2, 4 and 6 are devoted to the language of `while`-programs and covers specification as well as theoretical aspects. In each of the chapters we extend the `while`-language with various other constructs and the emphasis is here on specification rather than theory. In Sections 2.4 and 2.5 we consider extensions with abortion, non-determinism, parallelism, block constructs, dynamic and static procedures, and non-recursive and recursive procedures. In Section 4.5 we consider extensions of the `while`-language with static procedures that may or may not be recursive and we show how to handle exceptions, that is, certain kinds of jumps. Finally, in Section 6.4 we consider an extension with non-recursive and recursive procedures and we also show how total correctness properties are handled. The sections on extending the operational, denotational and axiomatic semantics may be studied in any order.

The applicability of operational, denotational and axiomatic semantics is illustrated in Chapters 3, 5 and 6. In Chapter 3 we show how to prove the correctness of a simple compiler for the `while`-language using the operational semantics. In Chapter 5 we prove an analysis for the `while`-language correct using the denotational semantics. Finally, in Section 6.5 we extend the axiomatic approach so as to obtain information about execution time of `while`-programs.

Appendix A reviews the mathematical notation on which this book is based. It is mostly standard notation but some may find our use of $\hookrightarrow$ and $\diamond$ non-standard. We use $D \hookrightarrow E$ for the set of *partial* functions from D to E; this is because we find that the $D \rightharpoonup E$ notation is too easily overlooked. Also we use $R \diamond S$ for the composition of binary relations R and S; this is because of the different order of composition used for relations and functions. When dealing with axiomatic semantics we use formulae $\{\ P\ \}\ S\ \{\ Q\ \}$ for partial correctness assertions but $\{\ P\ \}\ S\ \{\ \Downarrow Q\ \}$ for total correctness assertions because the explicit occurrence of $\Downarrow$ (for termination) may prevent the student from confusing the two systems.

Appendices B, C and D contain implementations of some of the semantic specifications using the functional language **Miranda**.[1] The intention is that the ability to experiment with semantic definitions enhances the understanding of material that is often regarded as being terse and heavy with formalism. It should be possible to rework these implementations in any functional language but if an eager language (like **Standard ML**) is used, great care must be taken in the implementation of the fixed point combinator. However, no continuity is lost if these appendices are ignored.

Notes for the instructor

The reader should preferably be acquainted with the BNF-style of specifying the syntax of programming languages and should be familiar with most of the mathematical concepts surveyed in Appendix A. To appreciate the prototype implementations of the appendices some experience in functional programming is required.

[1]**Miranda** is a trademark of Research Software Limited, 23 St Augustines Road, Canterbury, Kent CT1 1XP, UK.

We have ourselves used this book for an undergraduate course at Aarhus University in which the required functional programming is introduced "on-the-fly".

We provide two kinds of exercises. One kind helps the student in his/her understanding of the definitions/results/techniques used in the text. In particular there are exercises that ask the student to prove auxiliary results needed for the main results but then the proof techniques will be minor variations of those already explained in the text. We have marked those exercises whose results are needed later by "**(Essential)**". The other kind of exercises are more challenging in that they extend the development, for example by relating it to other approaches. We use a star to mark the more difficult of these exercises. Exercises marked by two stars are rather lengthy and may require insight not otherwise presented in the book. It will not be necessary for students to attempt all the exercises but we do recommend that they read them and try to understand what the exercises are about.

Acknowledgements

In writing this book we have been greatly assisted by the comments and suggestions provided by colleagues and reviewers and by students and instructors at Aarhus University. This includes Anders Gammelgaard, Chris Hankin, Torben Amtoft Hansen, Jens Palsberg Jørgensen, Ernst-Rüdiger Olderog, David A. Schmidt, Kirsten L. Solberg and Bernhard Steffen. Special thanks are due to Steffen Grarup, Jacob Seligmann, and Bettina Blaaberg Sørensen for their enthusiasm and great care in reading preliminary versions.

Aarhus, October 1991

Hanne Riis Nielson

Flemming Nielson

Chapter 1

Introduction

The purpose of this book is

- to describe some of the main ideas and methods used in semantics,
- to illustrate these on interesting applications, and
- to investigate the relationship between the various methods.

Formal semantics is concerned with rigorously specifying the meaning, or behaviour, of programs, pieces of hardware etc. The need for rigour arises because

- it can reveal ambiguities and subtle complexities in apparently crystal clear defining documents (for example programming language manuals), and
- it can form the basis for implementation, analysis and verification (in particular proofs of correctness).

We will use informal set theoretic notation (reviewed in Appendix A) to represent semantic concepts. This will suffice in this book but for other purposes greater notational precision (that is, formality) may be needed, for example when processing semantic descriptions by machine as in semantics directed compiler-compilers or machine assisted proof checkers.

1.1 Semantic description methods

It is customary to distinguish between the syntax and the semantics of a programming language. The *syntax* is concerned with the grammatical structure of programs. So a syntactic analysis of the program

```
z:=x; x:=y; y:=z
```

will realize that it consists of three statements separated by the symbol ';'. Each of these statements has the form of a variable followed by the composite symbol ':=' and an expression which is just a variable.

The *semantics* is concerned with the meaning of grammatically correct programs. So it will express that the meaning of the above program is to exchange the values of the variables **x** and **y** (and setting **z** to the final value of **y**). If we were to explain this in more detail we would look at the grammatical structure of the program and use explanations of the meanings of

- sequences of statements separated by ';', and
- a statement consisting of a variable followed by ':=' and an expression.

The actual explanations can be formalized in different ways. In this book we shall consider three approaches. Very roughly, the ideas are as follows:

Operational semantics: The meaning of a construct is specified by the computation it induces when it is executed on a machine. In particular, it is of interest *how* the effect of a computation is produced.

Denotational semantics: Meanings are modelled by mathematical objects that represent the effect of executing the constructs. Thus *only* the effect is of interest, not how it is obtained.

Axiomatic semantics: Specific properties of the effect of executing the constructs are expressed as *assertions*. Thus there may be aspects of the executions that are ignored.

To get a feeling for their different nature let us see how they express the meaning of the example program above.

Operational semantics (Chapter 2)

An operational explanation of the meaning of a construct will tell how to *execute* it:

- To execute a sequence of statements separated by ';' we execute the individual statements one after the other and from left to right.
- To execute a statement consisting of a variable followed by ':=' and another variable we determine the value of the second variable and assign it to the first variable.

We shall record the execution of the example program in a state where **x** has the value **5**, **y** the value **7** and **z** the value **0** by the following "derivation sequence":

$$\begin{array}{lrl} & \langle \texttt{z:=x; x:=y; y:=z}, & [\texttt{x}{\mapsto}\mathbf{5}, \texttt{y}{\mapsto}\mathbf{7}, \texttt{z}{\mapsto}\mathbf{0}]\rangle \\ \Rightarrow & \langle \texttt{x:=y; y:=z}, & [\texttt{x}{\mapsto}\mathbf{5}, \texttt{y}{\mapsto}\mathbf{7}, \texttt{z}{\mapsto}\mathbf{5}]\rangle \\ \Rightarrow & \langle \texttt{y:=z}, & [\texttt{x}{\mapsto}\mathbf{7}, \texttt{y}{\mapsto}\mathbf{7}, \texttt{z}{\mapsto}\mathbf{5}]\rangle \\ \Rightarrow & & [\texttt{x}{\mapsto}\mathbf{7}, \texttt{y}{\mapsto}\mathbf{5}, \texttt{z}{\mapsto}\mathbf{5}] \end{array}$$

In the first step we execute the statement z:=x and the value of z is changed to **5** whereas those of x and y are unchanged. The remaining program is now x:=y; y:=z. After the second step the value of x is **7** and we are left with the program y:=z. The third and final step of the computation will change the value of y to **5**. Therefore the initial values of x and y have been exchanged, using z as a temporary variable.

This explanation gives an *abstraction* of how the program is executed on a machine. It is important to observe that it is indeed an abstraction: we ignore details like use of registers and addresses for variables. So the operational semantics is rather independent of machine architectures and implementation strategies.

In Chapter 2 we shall formalize this kind of operational semantics which is often called *structural operational semantics* (or small-step semantics). An alternative operational semantics is called *natural semantics* (or big-step semantics) and differs from the structural operational semantics by hiding even more execution details. In the natural semantics the execution of the example program in the same state as before will be represented by the following "derivation tree":

$$\dfrac{\dfrac{\langle \texttt{z:=x}, s_0\rangle \to s_1 \qquad \langle \texttt{x:=y}, s_1\rangle \to s_2}{\langle \texttt{z:=x; x:=y}, s_0\rangle \to s_2} \qquad \langle \texttt{y:=z}, s_2\rangle \to s_3}{\langle \texttt{z:=x; x:=y; y:=z}, s_0\rangle \to s_3}$$

where we have used the abbreviations:

$$\begin{array}{lcl} s_0 & = & [\texttt{x}{\mapsto}\mathbf{5}, \texttt{y}{\mapsto}\mathbf{7}, \texttt{z}{\mapsto}\mathbf{0}] \\ s_1 & = & [\texttt{x}{\mapsto}\mathbf{5}, \texttt{y}{\mapsto}\mathbf{7}, \texttt{z}{\mapsto}\mathbf{5}] \\ s_2 & = & [\texttt{x}{\mapsto}\mathbf{7}, \texttt{y}{\mapsto}\mathbf{7}, \texttt{z}{\mapsto}\mathbf{5}] \\ s_3 & = & [\texttt{x}{\mapsto}\mathbf{7}, \texttt{y}{\mapsto}\mathbf{5}, \texttt{z}{\mapsto}\mathbf{5}] \end{array}$$

This is to be read as follows: The execution of z:=x in the state s_0 will result in the state s_1 and the execution of x:=y in state s_1 will result in state s_2. Therefore the execution of z:=x; x:=y in state s_0 will give state s_2. Furthermore, execution of y:=z in state s_2 will give state s_3 so in total the execution of the program in state s_0 will give the resulting state s_3. This is expressed by

$$\langle \texttt{z:=x; x:=y; y:=z}, s_0\rangle \to s_3$$

but now we have hidden the above explanation of how it was actually obtained.

In Chapter 3 we shall use the natural semantics as the basis for proving the correctness of an implementation of a simple programming language.

Denotational semantics (Chapter 4)

In the denotational semantics we concentrate on the *effect* of executing the programs and we shall model this by mathematical functions:

- The effect of a sequence of statements separated by ';' is the functional composition of the effects of the individual statements.
- The effect of a statement consisting of a variable followed by ':=' and another variable is the function that given a state will produce a new state: it is as the original one except that the value of the first variable of the statement is equal to that of the second variable.

For the example program we obtain functions written $\mathcal{S}[\![\texttt{z:=x}]\!]$, $\mathcal{S}[\![\texttt{x:=y}]\!]$, and $\mathcal{S}[\![\texttt{y:=z}]\!]$ for each of the assignment statements and for the overall program we get the function

$$\mathcal{S}[\![\texttt{z:=x; x:=y; y:=z}]\!] = \mathcal{S}[\![\texttt{y:=z}]\!] \circ \mathcal{S}[\![\texttt{x:=y}]\!] \circ \mathcal{S}[\![\texttt{z:=x}]\!]$$

Note that the *order* of the statements have changed because we use the usual notation for function composition where $(f \circ g)\ s$ means $f\ (g\ s)$. If we want to determine the effect of executing the program on a particular state then we can *apply* the function to that state and *calculate* the resulting state as follows:

$$\begin{aligned}
&\mathcal{S}[\![\texttt{z:=x; x:=y; y:=z}]\!]([\texttt{x}\mapsto\mathbf{5},\ \texttt{y}\mapsto\mathbf{7},\ \texttt{z}\mapsto\mathbf{0}])\\
&\quad= (\mathcal{S}[\![\texttt{y:=z}]\!] \circ \mathcal{S}[\![\texttt{x:=y}]\!] \circ \mathcal{S}[\![\texttt{z:=x}]\!])([\texttt{x}\mapsto\mathbf{5},\ \texttt{y}\mapsto\mathbf{7},\ \texttt{z}\mapsto\mathbf{0}])\\
&\quad= \mathcal{S}[\![\texttt{y:=z}]\!](\mathcal{S}[\![\texttt{x:=y}]\!](\mathcal{S}[\![\texttt{z:=x}]\!]([\texttt{x}\mapsto\mathbf{5},\ \texttt{y}\mapsto\mathbf{7},\ \texttt{z}\mapsto\mathbf{0}])))\\
&\quad= \mathcal{S}[\![\texttt{y:=z}]\!](\mathcal{S}[\![\texttt{x:=y}]\!]([\texttt{x}\mapsto\mathbf{5},\ \texttt{y}\mapsto\mathbf{7},\ \texttt{z}\mapsto\mathbf{5}]))\\
&\quad= \mathcal{S}[\![\texttt{y:=z}]\!]([\texttt{x}\mapsto\mathbf{7},\ \texttt{y}\mapsto\mathbf{7},\ \texttt{z}\mapsto\mathbf{5}])\\
&\quad= [\texttt{x}\mapsto\mathbf{7},\ \texttt{y}\mapsto\mathbf{5},\ \texttt{z}\mapsto\mathbf{5}]
\end{aligned}$$

Note that we are only manipulating mathematical objects; we are not concerned with executing programs. The difference may seem small for a program with only assignment and sequencing statements but for programs with more sophisticated constructs it is substantial. The benefits of the denotational approach are mainly due to the fact that it abstracts away from how programs are executed. Therefore it becomes easier to reason about programs as it simply amounts to reasoning about mathematical objects. However, a prerequisite for doing so is to establish a firm mathematical basis for denotational semantics and this task turns out not to be entirely trivial.

The denotational approach can easily be adapted to express other sorts of properties of programs. Some examples are:

- Determine whether all variables are initialized before they are used — if not a warning may be appropriate.
- Determine whether a certain expression in the program always evaluates to a constant — if so one can replace the expression by the constant.
- Determine whether all parts of the program are reachable — if not they could as well be removed or a warning might be appropriate.

In Chapter 5 we develop an example of this.

While we prefer the denotational approach when reasoning about programs we may prefer an operational approach when implementing the language. It is therefore of interest whether a denotational definition is *equivalent* to an operational definition and this is studied in Section 4.3.

Axiomatic semantics (Chapter 6)

Often one is interested in *partial correctness properties* of programs: A program is partially correct, with respect to a precondition and a postcondition, if whenever the initial state fulfils the precondition and the program terminates, then the final state is guaranteed to fulfil the postcondition. For our example program we have the partial correctness property:

$$\{ \texttt{x=n} \land \texttt{y=m} \}\ \texttt{z:=x; x:=y; y:=z}\ \{ \texttt{y=n} \land \texttt{x=m} \}$$

where $\texttt{x=n} \land \texttt{y=m}$ is the precondition and $\texttt{y=n} \land \texttt{x=m}$ is the postcondition. The names n and m are used to "remember" the initial values of x and y, respectively. The state [x↦**5**, y↦**7**, z↦**0**] satisfies the precondition by taking n=**5** and m=**7** and when we have *proved* the partial correctness property we can deduce that *if* the program terminates *then* it will do so in a state where y is **5** and x is **7**. However, the partial correctness property does not ensure that the program *will* terminate although this is clearly the case for the example program.

The axiomatic semantics provides a *logical system* for proving partial correctness properties of individual programs. A proof of the above partial correctness property may be expressed by the following "proof tree":

$$\dfrac{\dfrac{\{ p_0 \}\ \texttt{z:=x}\ \{ p_1 \} \qquad \{ p_1 \}\ \texttt{x:=y}\ \{ p_2 \}}{\{ p_0 \}\ \texttt{z:=x; x:=y}\ \{ p_2 \}} \qquad \{ p_2 \}\ \texttt{y:=z}\ \{ p_3 \}}{\{ p_0 \}\ \texttt{z:=x; x:=y; y:=z}\ \{ p_3 \}}$$

where we have used the abbreviations

$$p_0 = \texttt{x=n} \wedge \texttt{y=m}$$

$$p_1 = \texttt{z=n} \wedge \texttt{y=m}$$

$$p_2 = \texttt{z=n} \wedge \texttt{x=m}$$

$$p_3 = \texttt{y=n} \wedge \texttt{x=m}$$

We may view the logical system as a specification of only certain aspects of the semantics. It usually does not capture all aspects for the simple reason that all the partial correctness properties listed below can be proved using the logical system but certainly we would not regard the programs as behaving in the same way:

{ x=n ∧ y=m } z:=x; x:=y; y:=z { y=n ∧ x=m }

{ x=n ∧ y=m } `if x=y then skip else` (z:=x; x:=y; y:=z) { y=n ∧ x=m }

{ x=n ∧ y=m } `while true do skip` { y=n ∧ x=m }

The benefits of the axiomatic approach are that the logical systems provide an easy way of proving properties of programs — and to a large extent it has been possible to automate it. Of course this is only worthwhile if the axiomatic semantics is faithful to the "more general" (denotational or operational) semantics we have in mind and we shall discuss this in Section 6.3.

The complementary view

It is important to note that these kinds of semantics are *not* rival approaches, but are different techniques appropriate for different purposes and — to some extent — for different programming languages. To stress this, the development will address the following issues:

- It will develop each of the approaches for a simple language of `while`-programs.
- It will illustrate the power and weakness of each of the approaches by extending the `while`-language with other programming constructs.
- It will prove the relationship between the approaches for the `while`-language.
- It will give examples of applications of the semantic descriptions in order to illustrate their merits.

1.2 The example language While

This book illustrates the various forms of semantics on a very simple imperative programming language called **While**. As a first step we must specify its syntax.

The syntactic notation we use is based on BNF. First we list the various *syntactic categories* and give a meta-variable that will be used to range over *constructs* of each category. For our language the meta-variables and categories are as follows:

n will range over numerals, **Num**,

x will range over variables, **Var**,

a will range over arithmetic expressions, **Aexp**,

b will range over boolean expressions, **Bexp**, and

S will range over statements, **Stm**.

The meta-variables can be primed or subscripted. So, for example, n, n', n_1, n_2 all stand for numerals.

We assume that the structure of numerals and variables is given elsewhere; for example numerals might be strings of digits, and variables strings of letters and digits starting with a letter. The structure of the other constructs is:

$$
\begin{array}{lcl}
a & ::= & n \mid x \mid a_1 + a_2 \mid a_1 \star a_2 \mid a_1 - a_2 \\
b & ::= & \texttt{true} \mid \texttt{false} \mid a_1 = a_2 \mid a_1 \leq a_2 \mid \neg b \mid b_1 \wedge b_2 \\
S & ::= & x := a \mid \texttt{skip} \mid S_1 \; ; \; S_2 \mid \texttt{if } b \texttt{ then } S_1 \texttt{ else } S_2 \\
 & \mid & \texttt{while } b \texttt{ do } S
\end{array}
$$

Thus, a boolean expression b can only have one of six forms. It is called a *basis element* if it is `true` or `false` or has the form $a_1 = a_2$ or $a_1 \leq a_2$ where a_1 and a_2 are arithmetic expressions. It is called a *composite element* if it has the form $\neg b$ where b is a boolean expression, or the form $b_1 \wedge b_2$ where b_1 and b_2 are boolean expressions. Similar remarks apply to arithmetic expressions and statements.

The specification above defines the *abstract syntax* of **While** in that it simply says how to build arithmetic expressions, boolean expressions and statements in the language. One way to think of the abstract syntax is as specifying the parse trees of the language and it will then be the purpose of the *concrete syntax* to provide sufficient information that enable unique parse trees to be constructed.

So given the string of characters:

```
z:=x; x:=y; y:=z
```

the concrete syntax of the language must be able to resolve which of the two abstract syntax trees below it is intended to represent:

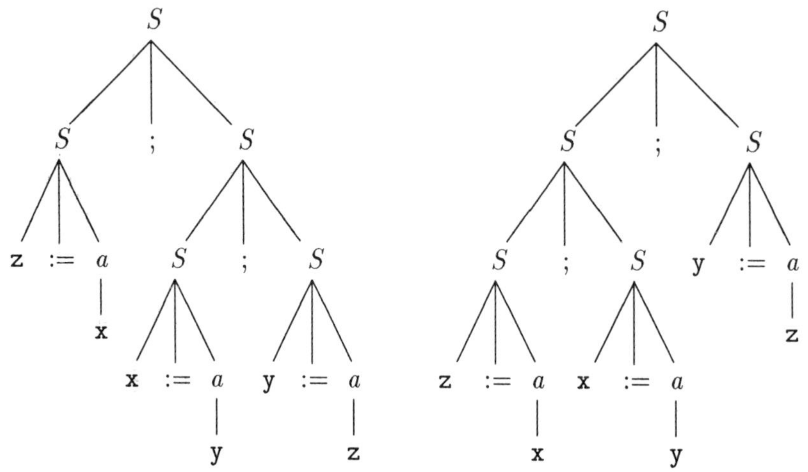

In this book we shall *not* be concerned with concrete syntax. Whenever we talk about syntactic entities such as arithmetic expressions, boolean expressions or statements we will always be talking about the abstract syntax so there is no ambiguity with respect to the form of the entity. In particular, the two trees above are both elements of the syntactic category **Stm**.

It is rather cumbersome to use the graphical representation of abstract syntax and we shall therefore use a linear notation. So we shall write

z:=x; (x:=y; y:=z)

for the leftmost syntax tree and

(z:=x; x:=y); y:=z

for the rightmost one. For statements one often writes the brackets as `begin` ⋯ **end** but we shall feel free to use (⋯) in this book. Similarly, we use brackets (⋯) to resolve ambiguities for elements in the other syntactic categories. To cut down on the number of brackets needed we shall allow to use the familiar relative binding powers (precedences) of +, ⋆ and − etc. and so write 1+x⋆2 for 1+(x⋆2) but not for (1+x)⋆2.

Exercise 1.1 The following statement is in **While**:

y:=1; while ¬(x=1) do (y:=y⋆x; x:=x−1)

It computes the factorial of the initial value bound to x (provided that it is positive) and the result will be the final value of y. Draw a graphical representation of the abstract syntax tree. □

Exercise 1.2 Assume that the initial value of the variable x is n and that the initial value of y is m. Write a statement in **While** that assigns z the value of n to the power of m, that is

$$\underbrace{n \star \cdots \star n}_{m \text{ times}}$$

Give a linear as well as a graphical representation of the abstract syntax. □

The semantics of **While** is given by defining so-called *semantic functions* for each of the syntactic categories. The idea is that a semantic function takes a syntactic entity as argument and returns its meaning. The operational, denotational and axiomatic approaches mentioned earlier will be used to specify semantic functions for the statements of **While**. For numerals, arithmetic expressions and boolean expressions the semantic functions are specified once and for all below.

1.3 Semantics of expressions

Before embarking on specifying the semantics of the arithmetic and boolean expressions of **While** let us have a brief look at the numerals; this will present the main ingredients of the approach in a very simple setting. So assume for the moment that the numerals are in the *binary* system. Their abstract syntax could then be specified by:

$$n ::= \mathtt{0} \mid \mathtt{1} \mid n\ \mathtt{0} \mid n\ \mathtt{1}$$

In order to determine the number represented by a numeral we shall define a function

$$\mathcal{N}: \mathbf{Num} \rightarrow \mathbf{Z}$$

This is called a *semantic function* as it defines the semantics of the numerals. We want $\mathcal{N}$ to be a *total function* because we want to determine a unique number for each numeral of **Num**. If $n \in \mathbf{Num}$ then we write $\mathcal{N}[\![n]\!]$ for the application of $\mathcal{N}$ to n, that is for the corresponding numeral. In general, the application of a semantic function to a syntactic entity will be written within the "syntactic" brackets '$[\![$' and '$]\!]$' rather than the more usual '(' and ')'. These brackets have no special meaning but throughout this book we shall enclose syntactic arguments to semantic functions using the "syntactic" brackets whereas we use ordinary brackets (or juxtapositioning) in all other cases.

The semantic function $\mathcal{N}$ is defined by the following *semantic clauses* (or *equations*):

$$\begin{aligned}
\mathcal{N}[\![\mathtt{0}]\!] &= \mathbf{0}\\
\mathcal{N}[\![\mathtt{1}]\!] &= \mathbf{1}\\
\mathcal{N}[\![n\ \mathtt{0}]\!] &= \mathbf{2} \star \mathcal{N}[\![n]\!]\\
\mathcal{N}[\![n\ \mathtt{1}]\!] &= \mathbf{2} \star \mathcal{N}[\![n]\!] + \mathbf{1}
\end{aligned}$$

Here $\mathbf{0}$ and $\mathbf{1}$ are numbers, that is elements of $\mathbf{Z}$. Furthermore, $\star$ and $+$ are the usual arithmetic operations on numbers. The above definition is an example of a *compositional* definition; this means that for each possible way of constructing a numeral it tells how the corresponding number is obtained from the meanings of the *sub*constructs.

Example 1.3 We can calculate the number $\mathcal{N}[\![\mathtt{101}]\!]$ corresponding to the numeral `101` as follows:

$$\begin{aligned}
\mathcal{N}[\![\mathtt{101}]\!] &= \mathbf{2} \star \mathcal{N}[\![\mathtt{10}]\!] + \mathbf{1}\\
&= \mathbf{2} \star (\mathbf{2} \star \mathcal{N}[\![\mathtt{1}]\!]) + \mathbf{1}\\
&= \mathbf{2} \star (\mathbf{2} \star \mathbf{1}) + \mathbf{1}\\
&= \mathbf{5}
\end{aligned}$$

Note that the string `101` is decomposed according to the syntax for numerals. □

So far we have only *claimed* that the definition of $\mathcal{N}$ gives rise to a well-defined total function. We shall now present a *formal proof* showing that this is indeed the case.

Fact 1.4 The above equations for $\mathcal{N}$, define a total function $\mathcal{N}$: **Num** $\rightarrow$ **Z**.

Proof: We have a total function $\mathcal{N}$, if for all arguments $n \in$ **Num**

$$\text{there is exactly one number } \mathbf{n} \in \mathbf{Z} \text{ such that } \mathcal{N}[\![n]\!] = \mathbf{n} \qquad (*)$$

Given a numeral n it can have one of four forms: it can be a basis element and then it is equal to `0` or `1`, or it can be a composite element and then it is equal to $n'\mathtt{0}$ or $n'\mathtt{1}$ for some other numeral n'. So, in order to prove (*) we have to consider all four possibilities.

The proof will be conducted by *induction* on the *structure* of the numeral n. In the *base case* we prove (*) for the basis elements of **Num**, that is for the cases where n is `0` or `1`. In the *induction step* we consider the composite elements of **Num**, that is the cases where n is $n'\mathtt{0}$ or $n'\mathtt{1}$. The induction hypothesis will then allow us to assume that (*) holds for the immediate constituent of n, that is n'. We shall then prove that (*) holds for n. It then follows that (*) holds for all numerals n because any numeral n can be constructed in that way.

The case $n = \mathtt{0}$: Only one of the semantic clauses defining $\mathcal{N}$ can be used and it gives $\mathcal{N}[\![n]\!] = \mathbf{0}$. So clearly there is exactly one number $\mathbf{n}$ in $\mathbf{Z}$ (namely $\mathbf{0}$) such that $\mathcal{N}[\![n]\!] = \mathbf{n}$.

The case $n = \mathtt{1}$ is similar and we omit the details.

The case $n = n'\mathtt{0}$: Inspection of the clauses defining $\mathcal{N}$ shows that only one of the clauses is applicable and we have $\mathcal{N}[\![n]\!] = \mathbf{2} \star \mathcal{N}[\![n']\!]$. We can now apply the induction hypothesis to n' and get that there is exactly one number $\mathbf{n}'$ such that $\mathcal{N}[\![n']\!] = \mathbf{n}'$. But then it is clear that there is exactly one number $\mathbf{n}$ (namely $\mathbf{2} \star \mathbf{n}'$) such that $\mathcal{N}[\![n]\!] = \mathbf{n}$.

The case $n = n'\mathtt{1}$ is similar and we omit the details. □

The general technique that we have applied in the definition of the syntax and semantics of numerals can be summarized as follows:

Compositional Definitions

1: The syntactic category is specified by an abstract syntax giving the *basis elements* and the *composite elements*. The composite elements have a unique decomposition into their immediate constituents.

2: The semantics is defined by *compositional* definitions of a function: There is a *semantic clause* for each of the basis elements of the syntactic category and one for each of the methods for constructing composite elements. The clauses for composite elements are defined in terms of the semantics of the immediate constituents of the elements.

The proof technique we have applied is closely connected with the approach to defining semantic functions. It can be summarized as follows:

Structural Induction

1: Prove that the property holds for all the *basis* elements of the syntactic category.

2: Prove that the property holds for all the *composite* elements of the syntactic category: Assume that the property holds for all the immediate constituents of the element (this is called the *induction hypothesis*) and prove that it also holds for the element itself.

In the remainder of this book we shall assume that numerals are in decimal notation and have their normal meanings (so for example $\mathcal{N}[\![\mathtt{137}]\!] = \mathbf{137} \in \mathbf{Z}$). It is important to understand, however, that there is a distinction between numerals (which are syntactic) and numbers (which are semantic), even in decimal notation.

Semantic functions

The meaning of an expression depends on the values bound to the variables that occur in it. For example, if `x` is bound to **3** then the arithmetic expression `x+1` evaluates to **4** but if `x` is bound to **2** then the expression evaluates to **3**. We shall therefore introduce the concept of a *state*: to each variable the state will associate its current value. We shall represent a state as a function from variables to values, that is an element of the set

$$\mathbf{State} = \mathbf{Var} \to \mathbf{Z}$$

Each state s specifies a value, written $s\ x$, for each variable x of **Var**. Thus if $s\ \mathtt{x} = \mathbf{3}$ then the value of `x+1` in state s is **4**.

Actually, this is just one of several representations of the state. Some other possibilities are to use a table:

x	5
y	7
z	0

or a "list" of the form

$$[\mathtt{x}\mapsto\mathbf{5},\ \mathtt{y}\mapsto\mathbf{7},\ \mathtt{z}\mapsto\mathbf{0}]$$

(as in Section 1.1). In all cases we must ensure that exactly one value is associated with each variable. By requiring a state to be a function this is trivially fulfilled whereas for the alternative representations above extra restrictions have to be enforced.

Given an arithmetic expression a and a state s we can determine the value of the expression. Therefore we shall define the meaning of arithmetic expressions as a total function $\mathcal{A}$ that takes two arguments: the syntactic construct *and* the state. The functionality of $\mathcal{A}$ is

$$\mathcal{A}\colon \mathbf{Aexp} \to (\mathbf{State} \to \mathbf{Z})$$

This means that $\mathcal{A}$ takes its parameters *one at a time*. So we may supply $\mathcal{A}$ with its first parameter, say `x+1`, and study the function $\mathcal{A}[\![\mathtt{x+1}]\!]$. It has functionality **State** $\to$ **Z** and only when we supply it with a state (which happens to be a function but that does not matter) do we obtain the value of the expression `x+1`.

Assuming the existence of the function $\mathcal{N}$ defining the meaning of numerals, we can define the function $\mathcal{A}$ by defining its value $\mathcal{A}[\![a]\!]s$ on each arithmetic expression

$$\begin{array}{lcl}
\mathcal{A}[\![n]\!]s & = & \mathcal{N}[\![n]\!] \\
\mathcal{A}[\![x]\!]s & = & s\ x \\
\mathcal{A}[\![a_1 + a_2]\!]s & = & \mathcal{A}[\![a_1]\!]s + \mathcal{A}[\![a_2]\!]s \\
\mathcal{A}[\![a_1 \star a_2]\!]s & = & \mathcal{A}[\![a_1]\!]s \star \mathcal{A}[\![a_2]\!]s \\
\mathcal{A}[\![a_1 - a_2]\!]s & = & \mathcal{A}[\![a_1]\!]s - \mathcal{A}[\![a_2]\!]s
\end{array}$$

Table 1.1: The semantics of arithmetic expressions

a and state s. The definition of $\mathcal{A}$ is given in Table 1.1. The clause for n reflects that the value of n in any state is $\mathcal{N}[\![n]\!]$. The value of a variable x in state s is the value bound to x in s, that is $s\ x$. The value of the composite expression a_1+a_2 in s is the sum of the values of a_1 and a_2 in s. Similarly, the value of $a_1 \star a_2$ in s is the product of the values of a_1 and a_2 in s, and the value of $a_1 - a_2$ in s is the difference between the values of a_1 and a_2 in s. Note that $+$, $\star$ and $-$ occurring on the right of these equations are the usual arithmetic operations, whilst on the left they are just pieces of syntax; this is analogous to the distinction between numerals and numbers but we shall not bother to use different symbols.

Example 1.5 Suppose that $s\ \mathtt{x} = \mathbf{3}$. Then:

$$\begin{array}{lcl}
\mathcal{A}[\![\mathtt{x}+\mathtt{1}]\!]s & = & \mathcal{A}[\![\mathtt{x}]\!]s + \mathcal{A}[\![\mathtt{1}]\!]s \\
& = & (s\ \mathtt{x}) + \mathcal{N}[\![\mathtt{1}]\!] \\
& = & \mathbf{3} + \mathbf{1} \\
& = & \mathbf{4}
\end{array}$$

Note that here $\mathtt{1}$ is a numeral (enclosed in the brackets '$[\![$' and '$]\!]$') whereas $\mathbf{1}$ is a number. □

Example 1.6 Suppose we add the arithmetic expression $-\ a$ to our language. An acceptable semantic clause for this construct would be

$$\mathcal{A}[\![-\ a]\!]s = \mathbf{0} - \mathcal{A}[\![a]\!]s$$

whereas the alternative clause $\mathcal{A}[\![-\ a]\!]s = \mathcal{A}[\![\mathtt{0} - a]\!]s$ would contradict the compositionality requirement. □

Exercise 1.7 Prove that the equations of Table 1.1 define a total function $\mathcal{A}$ in $\mathbf{Aexp} \to (\mathbf{State} \to \mathbf{Z})$: First argue that it is sufficient to prove that for each $a \in \mathbf{Aexp}$ and each $s \in \mathbf{State}$ there is exactly one value $\mathbf{v} \in \mathbf{Z}$ such that $\mathcal{A}[\![a]\!]s = \mathbf{v}$. Next use structural induction on the arithmetic expressions to prove that this is indeed the case. □

$$
\begin{array}{lcl}
\mathcal{B}[\![\texttt{true}]\!]s & = & \mathbf{tt} \\
\mathcal{B}[\![\texttt{false}]\!]s & = & \mathbf{ff} \\
\mathcal{B}[\![a_1 = a_2]\!]s & = & \begin{cases} \mathbf{tt} & \text{if } \mathcal{A}[\![a_1]\!]s = \mathcal{A}[\![a_2]\!]s \\ \mathbf{ff} & \text{if } \mathcal{A}[\![a_1]\!]s \neq \mathcal{A}[\![a_2]\!]s \end{cases} \\
\mathcal{B}[\![a_1 \leq a_2]\!]s & = & \begin{cases} \mathbf{tt} & \text{if } \mathcal{A}[\![a_1]\!]s \leq \mathcal{A}[\![a_2]\!]s \\ \mathbf{ff} & \text{if } \mathcal{A}[\![a_1]\!]s > \mathcal{A}[\![a_2]\!]s \end{cases} \\
\mathcal{B}[\![\neg\, b]\!]s & = & \begin{cases} \mathbf{tt} & \text{if } \mathcal{B}[\![b]\!]s = \mathbf{ff} \\ \mathbf{ff} & \text{if } \mathcal{B}[\![b]\!]s = \mathbf{tt} \end{cases} \\
\mathcal{B}[\![b_1 \wedge b_2]\!]s & = & \begin{cases} \mathbf{tt} & \text{if } \mathcal{B}[\![b_1]\!]s = \mathbf{tt} \text{ and } \mathcal{B}[\![b_2]\!]s = \mathbf{tt} \\ \mathbf{ff} & \text{if } \mathcal{B}[\![b_1]\!]s = \mathbf{ff} \text{ or } \mathcal{B}[\![b_2]\!]s = \mathbf{ff} \end{cases}
\end{array}
$$

Table 1.2: The semantics of boolean expressions

The values of boolean expressions are truth values so in a similar way we shall define their meanings by a (total) function from **State** to **T**:

$$\mathcal{B}\text{: } \mathbf{Bexp} \to (\mathbf{State} \to \mathbf{T})$$

Here **T** consists of the truth values **tt** (for true) and **ff** (for false).

Using $\mathcal{A}$ we can define $\mathcal{B}$ by the semantic clauses of Table 1.2. Again we have the distinction between syntax (e.g. $\leq$ on the left-hand side) and semantics (e.g. $\leq$ on the right-hand side).

Exercise 1.8 Assume that $s\ \texttt{x} = \mathbf{3}$ and determine $\mathcal{B}[\![\neg(\texttt{x} = \texttt{1})]\!]s$. □

Exercise 1.9 Prove that the equations of Table 1.2 define a total function $\mathcal{B}$ in **Bexp** → (**State** → **T**). □

Exercise 1.10 The syntactic category **Bexp′** is defined as the following extension of **Bexp**:

$$
\begin{array}{lcl}
b & ::= & \texttt{true} \mid \texttt{false} \mid a_1 = a_2 \mid a_1 \neq a_2 \mid a_1 \leq a_2 \mid a_1 \geq a_2 \\
 & \mid & a_1 < a_2 \mid a_1 > a_2 \mid \neg b \mid b_1 \wedge b_2 \mid b_1 \vee b_2 \\
 & \mid & b_1 \Rightarrow b_2 \mid b_1 \Leftrightarrow b_2
\end{array}
$$

Give a *compositional* extension of the semantic function $\mathcal{B}$ of Table 1.2.

Two boolean expressions b_1 and b_2 are *equivalent* if for all states s,

$$\mathcal{B}[\![b_1]\!]s = \mathcal{B}[\![b_2]\!]s$$

Show that for each b' of **Bexp′** there exists a boolean expression b of **Bexp** such that b' and b are equivalent. □

1.4 Properties of the semantics

Later in the book we shall be interested in two kinds of properties for expressions. One is that their values do not depend on values of variables that do not occur in them. The other is that if we replace a variable with an expression then we could as well have made a similar change in the state. We shall formalize these properties below and prove that they do hold.

Free variables

The *free variables* of an arithmetic expression a is defined to be the set of variables occurring in it. Formally, we may give a compositional definition of the subset $\mathrm{FV}(a)$ of **Var**:

$$\begin{aligned}
\mathrm{FV}(n) &= \emptyset \\
\mathrm{FV}(x) &= \{\, x \,\} \\
\mathrm{FV}(a_1 + a_2) &= \mathrm{FV}(a_1) \cup \mathrm{FV}(a_2) \\
\mathrm{FV}(a_1 \star a_2) &= \mathrm{FV}(a_1) \cup \mathrm{FV}(a_2) \\
\mathrm{FV}(a_1 - a_2) &= \mathrm{FV}(a_1) \cup \mathrm{FV}(a_2)
\end{aligned}$$

As an example $\mathrm{FV}(\mathtt{x+1}) = \{\, \mathtt{x} \,\}$ and $\mathrm{FV}(\mathtt{x+y{\star}x}) = \{\, \mathtt{x}, \mathtt{y} \,\}$. It should be obvious that only the variables in $\mathrm{FV}(a)$ may influence the value of a. This is formally expressed by:

Lemma 1.11 Let s and s' be two states satisfying that $s\ x = s'\ x$ for all x in $\mathrm{FV}(a)$. Then $\mathcal{A}[\![a]\!]s = \mathcal{A}[\![a]\!]s'$.

Proof: We shall give a fairly detailed proof of the lemma using structural induction on the arithmetic expressions. We shall first consider the basis elements of **Aexp**:

The case n: From Table 1.1 we have $\mathcal{A}[\![n]\!]s = \mathcal{N}[\![n]\!]$ as well as $\mathcal{A}[\![n]\!]s' = \mathcal{N}[\![n]\!]$. So $\mathcal{A}[\![n]\!]s = \mathcal{A}[\![n]\!]s'$ and clearly the lemma holds in this case.

The case x: From Table 1.1 we have $\mathcal{A}[\![x]\!]s = s\ x$ as well as $\mathcal{A}[\![x]\!]s' = s'\ x$. From the assumptions of the lemma we get $s\ x = s'\ x$ because $x \in \mathrm{FV}(x)$ so clearly the lemma holds in this case.

Next we turn to the composite elements of **Aexp**:

The case $a_1 + a_2$: From Table 1.1 we have $\mathcal{A}[\![a_1 + a_2]\!]s = \mathcal{A}[\![a_1]\!]s + \mathcal{A}[\![s_2]\!]s$ and similarly $\mathcal{A}[\![a_1 + a_2]\!]s' = \mathcal{A}[\![a_1]\!]s' + \mathcal{A}[\![s_2]\!]s'$. Since a_i (for i = 1,2) is an immediate subexpression of $a_1 + a_2$ and $\mathrm{FV}(a_i) \subseteq \mathrm{FV}(a_1 + a_2)$ we can apply the induction hypothesis (that is the lemma) to a_i and get $\mathcal{A}[\![a_i]\!]s = \mathcal{A}[\![a_i]\!]s'$. It is now easy to see that the lemma holds for $a_1 + a_2$ as well.

The cases $a_1 - a_2$ and $a_1 \star a_2$ follow the same pattern and are omitted. This completes the proof. □

In a similar way we may define the set $\text{FV}(b)$ of free variables in a boolean expression b by

$$
\begin{array}{lcl}
\text{FV}(\texttt{true}) & = & \emptyset \\
\text{FV}(\texttt{false}) & = & \emptyset \\
\text{FV}(a_1 = a_2) & = & \text{FV}(a_1) \cup \text{FV}(a_2) \\
\text{FV}(a_1 \leq a_2) & = & \text{FV}(a_1) \cup \text{FV}(a_2) \\
\text{FV}(\neg b) & = & \text{FV}(b) \\
\text{FV}(b_1 \land b_2) & = & \text{FV}(b_1) \cup \text{FV}(b_2)
\end{array}
$$

Exercise 1.12 (Essential) Let s and s' be two states satisfying that $s\ x = s'\ x$ for all x in $\text{FV}(b)$. Prove that $\mathcal{B}[\![b]\!]s = \mathcal{B}[\![b]\!]s'$. □

Substitutions

We shall later be interested in replacing each occurrence of a variable y in an arithmetic expression a with another arithmetic expression a_0. This is called *substitution* and we write $a[y \mapsto a_0]$ for the arithmetic expression so obtained. The formal definition is as follows:

$$
\begin{array}{lcl}
n[y \mapsto a_0] & = & n \\
x[y \mapsto a_0] & = & \begin{cases} a_0 & \text{if } x = y \\ x & \text{if } x \neq y \end{cases} \\
(a_1 + a_2)[y \mapsto a_0] & = & (a_1[y \mapsto a_0]) + (a_2[y \mapsto a_0]) \\
(a_1 \star a_2)[y \mapsto a_0] & = & (a_1[y \mapsto a_0]) \star (a_2[y \mapsto a_0]) \\
(a_1 - a_2)[y \mapsto a_0] & = & (a_1[y \mapsto a_0]) - (a_2[y \mapsto a_0])
\end{array}
$$

As an example $(\texttt{x+1})[\texttt{x} \mapsto 3] = \texttt{3+1}$ and $(\texttt{x+y}\star\texttt{x})[\texttt{x} \mapsto \texttt{y-5}] = (\texttt{y-5})\texttt{+y}\star(\texttt{y-5})$.

We also have a notion of substitution (or updating) for states. We define $s[y \mapsto v]$ to be the state that is as s except that the value bound to y is v, that is

$$
(s[y \mapsto v])\ x = \begin{cases} v & \text{if } x = y \\ s\ x & \text{if } x \neq y \end{cases}
$$

The relationship between the two concepts is shown in the following exercise:

Exercise 1.13 (Essential) Prove that $\mathcal{A}[\![a[y\mapsto a_0]]\!]s = \mathcal{A}[\![a]\!](s[y\mapsto\mathcal{A}[\![a_0]\!]s])$ for all states s. □

Exercise 1.14 (Essential) Define substitution for boolean expressions: $b[y\mapsto a_0]$ is to be the boolean expression that is as b except that all occurrences of the variable y are replaced by the arithmetic expression a_0. Prove that your definition satisfies

$$\mathcal{B}[\![b[y\mapsto a_0]]\!]s = \mathcal{B}[\![b]\!](s[y\mapsto\mathcal{A}[\![a_0]\!]s])$$

for all states s. □

Chapter 2

Operational Semantics

The role of a statement in **While** is to change the state. For example, if $\mathbf{x}$ is bound to **3** in s and we execute the statement $\mathtt{x} := \mathtt{x} + 1$ then we get a new state where $\mathbf{x}$ is bound to **4**. So while the semantics of arithmetic and boolean expressions only *inspect* the state in order to determine the value of the expression, the semantics of statements will *modify* the state as well.

In an operational semantics we are concerned with *how* to execute programs and not merely what the results of execution are. More precisely, we are interested in how the states are modified during the execution of the statement. We shall consider two different approaches to operational semantics:

- *Natural semantics*: its purpose is to describe how the *overall* results of executions are obtained.
- *Structural operational semantics*: its purpose is to describe how the *individual steps* of the computations take place.

We shall see that for the language **While** we can easily specify both kinds of semantics and that they will be "equivalent" in a sense to be made clear later. However, we shall also give examples of programming constructs where one of the approaches is superior to the other.

For both kinds of operational semantics, the meaning of statements will be specified by a *transition system*. It will have two types of configurations:

$\langle S, s\rangle$	representing that the statement S is to be executed from the state s, and
s	representing a terminal (that is final) state.

The *terminal configurations* will be those of the latter form. The *transition relation* will then describe how the execution takes place. The difference between the two approaches to operational semantics amounts to different ways of specifying the transition relation.

[ass$_{\text{ns}}$]	$\langle x := a,\ s\rangle \rightarrow s[x\mapsto\mathcal{A}[\![a]\!]s]$
[skip$_{\text{ns}}$]	$\langle \texttt{skip},\ s\rangle \rightarrow s$
[comp$_{\text{ns}}$]	$\dfrac{\langle S_1,\ s\rangle \rightarrow s',\ \langle S_2,\ s'\rangle \rightarrow s''}{\langle S_1;S_2,\ s\rangle \rightarrow s''}$
[if$^{\text{tt}}_{\text{ns}}$]	$\dfrac{\langle S_1,\ s\rangle \rightarrow s'}{\langle \texttt{if}\ b\ \texttt{then}\ S_1\ \texttt{else}\ S_2,\ s\rangle \rightarrow s'}$ if $\mathcal{B}[\![b]\!]s = \mathbf{tt}$
[if$^{\text{ff}}_{\text{ns}}$]	$\dfrac{\langle S_2,\ s\rangle \rightarrow s'}{\langle \texttt{if}\ b\ \texttt{then}\ S_1\ \texttt{else}\ S_2,\ s\rangle \rightarrow s'}$ if $\mathcal{B}[\![b]\!]s = \mathbf{ff}$
[while$^{\text{tt}}_{\text{ns}}$]	$\dfrac{\langle S,\ s\rangle \rightarrow s',\ \langle \texttt{while}\ b\ \texttt{do}\ S,\ s'\rangle \rightarrow s''}{\langle \texttt{while}\ b\ \texttt{do}\ S,\ s\rangle \rightarrow s''}$ if $\mathcal{B}[\![b]\!]s = \mathbf{tt}$
[while$^{\text{ff}}_{\text{ns}}$]	$\langle \texttt{while}\ b\ \texttt{do}\ S,\ s\rangle \rightarrow s$ if $\mathcal{B}[\![b]\!]s = \mathbf{ff}$

Table 2.1: Natural semantics for **While**

2.1 Natural semantics

In a natural semantics we are concerned with the relationship between the *initial* and the *final* state of an execution. Therefore the transition relation will specify the relationship between the initial state and the final state for each statement. We shall write a transition as

$$\langle S,\ s\rangle \rightarrow s'$$

Intuitively this means that the execution of S from s will terminate and the resulting state will be s'.

The definition of $\rightarrow$ is given by the rules of Table 2.1. A *rule* has the general form

$$\frac{\langle S_1,\ s_1\rangle \rightarrow s'_1,\ \cdots,\ \langle S_n,\ s_n\rangle \rightarrow s'_n}{\langle S,\ s\rangle \rightarrow s'}\ \text{if}\ \cdots$$

where S_1, $\cdots$, S_n are *immediate constituents* of S or are statements *constructed from* the immediate constituents of S. A rule has a number of *premises* (written above the solid line) and one *conclusion* (written below the solid line). A rule may also have a number of *conditions* (written to the right of the solid line) that have to be fulfilled whenever the rule is applied. Rules with an empty set of premises are called *axioms* and the solid line is then omitted.

Intuitively, the axiom [ass$_{\text{ns}}$] says that in a state s, $x := a$ is executed to yield a final state $s[x\mapsto\mathcal{A}[\![a]\!]s]$ which is as s except that x has the value $\mathcal{A}[\![a]\!]s$. This is really an *axiom schema* because x, a and s are meta-variables standing for arbitrary variables, arithmetic expressions and states but we shall simply use the term axiom for this. We obtain an *instance* of the axiom by selecting particular variables, arithmetic expressions and states. As an example, if s_0 is the state that assigns the value $\mathbf{0}$ to all variables then

$$\langle \texttt{x := x+1},\ s_0\rangle \to s_0[\texttt{x}\mapsto\mathbf{1}]$$

is an instance of [ass_{ns}] because x is instantiated to **x**, a to **x+1**, s to s_0, and the value $\mathcal{A}[\![\texttt{x+1}]\!]s_0$ is determined to be **1**.

Similarly [skip_{ns}] is an axiom and, intuitively, it says that **skip** does not change the state. Letting s_0 be as above we obtain

$$\langle \texttt{skip},\ s_0\rangle \to s_0$$

as an instance of the axiom [skip_{ns}].

Intuitively, the rule [comp_{ns}] says that to execute $S_1;S_2$ from state s we must first execute S_1 from s. Assuming that this yields a final state s' we shall then execute S_2 from s'. The premises of the rule are concerned with the two statements S_1 and S_2 whereas the conclusion expresses a property of the composite statement itself. The following is an *instance* of the rule:

$$\frac{\langle \texttt{skip},\ s_0\rangle \to s_0,\ \langle \texttt{x := x+1},\ s_0\rangle \to s_0[\texttt{x}\mapsto\mathbf{1}]}{\langle \texttt{skip; x := x+1},\ s_0\rangle \to s_0[\texttt{x}\mapsto\mathbf{1}]}$$

Here S_1 is instantiated to **skip**, S_2 to **x := x + 1**, s and s' are both instantiated to s_0 and s'' is instantiated to $s_0[\texttt{x}\mapsto\mathbf{1}]$. Similarly

$$\frac{\langle \texttt{skip},\ s_0\rangle \to s_0[\texttt{x}\mapsto\mathbf{5}],\ \langle \texttt{x := x+1},\ s_0[\texttt{x}\mapsto\mathbf{5}]\rangle \to s_0}{\langle \texttt{skip; x := x+1},\ s_0\rangle \to s_0}$$

is an instance of [comp_{ns}] although it is less interesting because its premises can never be derived from the axioms and rules of Table 2.1.

For the **if**-construct we have two rules. The first one, [$\text{if}^{\text{tt}}_{\text{ns}}$], says that to execute **if** b **then** S_1 **else** S_2 we simply execute S_1 provided that b evaluates to **tt** in the state. The other rule, [$\text{if}^{\text{ff}}_{\text{ns}}$], says that if b evaluates to **ff** then to execute **if** b **then** S_1 **else** S_2 we just execute S_2. Taking s_0 **x** = **0** the following is an instance of the rule [$\text{if}^{\text{tt}}_{\text{ns}}$]:

$$\frac{\langle \texttt{skip},\ s_0\rangle \to s_0}{\langle \texttt{if x = 0 then skip else x := x+1},\ s_0\rangle \to s_0}$$

because $\mathcal{B}[\![\texttt{x = 0}]\!]s_0 = \texttt{tt}$. However, had it been the case that s_0 **x** $\neq$ **0** then it would not be an instance of the rule [$\text{if}^{\text{tt}}_{\text{ns}}$] because then $\mathcal{B}[\![\texttt{x = 0}]\!]s_0$ would amount to **ff**. Furthermore it would not be an instance of the rule [$\text{if}^{\text{ff}}_{\text{ns}}$] because the premise has the wrong form.

Finally, we have one rule and one axiom expressing how to execute the **while**-construct. Intuitively, the meaning of the construct **while** b **do** S in the state s can be explained as follows:

- If the test b evaluates to true in the state s then we first execute the body of the loop and then continue with the loop itself from the state so obtained.

- If the test b evaluates to false in the state s then the execution of the loop terminates.

The rule [$\text{while}_{\text{ns}}^{\text{tt}}$] formalizes the first case where b evaluates to **tt** and it says that then we have to execute S followed by **while** b **do** S again. The axiom [$\text{while}_{\text{ns}}^{\text{ff}}$] formalizes the second possibility and states that if b evaluates to **ff** then we terminate the execution of the **while**-construct leaving the state unchanged. Note that the rule [$\text{while}_{\text{ns}}^{\text{tt}}$] specifies the meaning of the **while**-construct in terms of the meaning of the very same construct so that we do *not* have a compositional definition of the semantics of statements.

When we use the axioms and rules to derive a transition $\langle S, s\rangle \to s'$ we obtain a *derivation tree*. The *root* of the derivation tree is $\langle S, s\rangle \to s'$ and the *leaves* are instances of axioms. The *internal nodes* are conclusions of instantiated rules and they have the corresponding premises as their immediate sons. We request that all the instantiated conditions of axioms and rules must be satisfied. When displaying a derivation tree it is common to have the root at the bottom rather than at the top; hence the son is *above* its father. A derivation tree is called *simple* if it is an instance of an axiom, otherwise it is called *composite*.

Example 2.1 Let us first consider the statement of Chapter 1:

(z:=x; x:=y); y:=z

Let s_0 be the state that maps all variables except x and y to **0** and has s_0 x = **5** and s_0 y = **7**. Then the following is an example of a derivation tree:

$$\cfrac{\cfrac{\langle \texttt{z:=x}, s_0\rangle \to s_1 \qquad \langle \texttt{x:=y}, s_1\rangle \to s_2}{\langle \texttt{z:=x; x:=y}, s_0\rangle \to s_2} \qquad \langle \texttt{y:=z}, s_2\rangle \to s_3}{\langle (\texttt{z:=x; x:=y}); \texttt{y:=z}, s_0\rangle \to s_3}$$

where we have used the abbreviations:

$$\begin{aligned} s_1 &= s_0[\texttt{z}\mapsto\mathbf{5}] \\ s_2 &= s_1[\texttt{x}\mapsto\mathbf{7}] \\ s_3 &= s_2[\texttt{y}\mapsto\mathbf{5}] \end{aligned}$$

The derivation tree has three leaves denoted $\langle \texttt{z:=x},\ s_0\rangle \to s_1$, $\langle \texttt{x:=y},\ s_1\rangle \to s_2$, and $\langle \texttt{y:=z},\ s_2\rangle \to s_3$, corresponding to three applications of the axiom [ass$_{\text{ns}}$]. The rule [comp$_{\text{ns}}$] has been applied twice. One instance is

$$\frac{\langle \texttt{z:=x},\ s_0\rangle \to s_1,\ \langle \texttt{x:=y},\ s_1\rangle \to s_2}{\langle \texttt{z:=x; x:=y},\ s_0\rangle \to s_2}$$

which has been used to combine the leaves $\langle \texttt{z:=x},\ s_0\rangle \to s_1$ and $\langle \texttt{x:=y},\ s_1\rangle \to s_2$ with the internal node labelled $\langle \texttt{z:=x; x:=y},\ s_0\rangle \to s_2$. The other instance is

$$\frac{\langle \texttt{z:=x; x:=y},\ s_0\rangle \to s_2,\ \langle \texttt{y:=z},\ s_2\rangle \to s_3}{\langle (\texttt{z:=x; x:=y}); \texttt{y:=z},\ s_0\rangle \to s_3}$$

which has been used to combine the internal node $\langle \texttt{z:=x; x:=y},\ s_0\rangle \to s_2$ and the leaf $\langle \texttt{y:=z},\ s_2\rangle \to s_3$ with the root $\langle (\texttt{z:=x; x:=y}); \texttt{y:=z},\ s_0\rangle \to s_3$. □

Consider now the problem of constructing a derivation tree for a given statement S and state s. The best way to approach this is to try to construct the tree from the root upwards. So we will start by finding an axiom or rule with a conclusion where the left-hand side matches the configuration $\langle S,\ s\rangle$. There are two cases:

- If it is an *axiom* and if the conditions of the axiom are satisfied then we can determine the final state and the construction of the derivation tree is completed.
- If it is a *rule* then the next step is to try to construct derivation trees for the premises of the rule. When this has been done, it must be checked that the conditions of the rule are fulfilled, and only then can we determine the final state corresponding to $\langle S,\ s\rangle$.

Often there will be more than one axiom or rule that matches a given configuration and then the various possibilities have to be inspected in order to find a derivation tree. We shall see later that for **While** there will be at most one derivation tree for each transition $\langle S,\ s\rangle \to s'$ but that this need not hold in extensions of **While**.

Example 2.2 Consider the factorial statement:

$$\texttt{y:=1; while}\ \neg(\texttt{x=1})\ \texttt{do (y:=y} \star \texttt{x; x:-x-1)}$$

and let s be a state with $s\ \texttt{x} = \mathbf{3}$. In this example we shall show that

$$\langle \texttt{y:=1; while}\ \neg(\texttt{x=1})\ \texttt{do (y:=y} \star \texttt{x; x:=x-1)},\ s\rangle \to s[\texttt{y}\mapsto\mathbf{6}][\texttt{x}\mapsto\mathbf{1}] \qquad (*)$$

To do so we shall show that (*) can be obtained from the transition system of Table 2.1. This is done by constructing a derivation tree with the transition (*) as its root.

Rather than presenting the complete derivation tree T in one go, we shall build it in an upwards manner. Initially, we only know that the root of T is of the form:

$$\langle \texttt{y:=1; while } \neg(\texttt{x=1}) \texttt{ do (y:=y} \star \texttt{x; x:=x}-1\texttt{)}, s\rangle \to s_{61}$$

However, the statement

$$\texttt{y:=1; while } \neg(\texttt{x=1}) \texttt{ do (y:=y} \star \texttt{x; x:=x}-1\texttt{)}$$

is of the form S_1; S_2 so the only rule that could have been used to produce the root of T is [comp$_{ns}$]. Therefore T must have the form:

$$\frac{\langle \texttt{y:=1}, s\rangle \to s_{13} \qquad\qquad T_1}{\langle \texttt{y:=1; while } \neg(\texttt{x=1}) \texttt{ do (y:=y}\star\texttt{x; x:=x}-1\texttt{)}, s\rangle \to s_{61}}$$

for some state s_{13} and some derivation tree T_1 which has root

$$\langle \texttt{while } \neg(\texttt{x=1}) \texttt{ do (y:=y}\star\texttt{x; x:=x}-1\texttt{)}, s_{13}\rangle \to s_{61} \qquad (**)$$

Since $\langle \texttt{y:=1}, s\rangle \to s_{13}$ has to be an instance of the axiom [ass$_{ns}$] we get that $s_{13} = s[\texttt{y}\mapsto\mathbf{1}]$.

The missing part T_1 of T is a derivation tree with root (**). Since the statement of (**) has the form **while** b **do** S the derivation tree T_1 must have been constructed by applying either the rule [while$^{tt}_{ns}$] or the axiom [while$^{ff}_{ns}$]. Since $\mathcal{B}[\![\neg(\texttt{x=1})]\!]s_{13} = \textbf{tt}$ we see that only the rule [while$^{tt}_{ns}$] could have been applied so T_1 will have the form:

$$\frac{T_2 \qquad\qquad T_3}{\langle \texttt{while } \neg(\texttt{x=1}) \texttt{ do (y:=y}\star\texttt{x; x:=x}-1\texttt{)}, s_{13}\rangle \to s_{61}}$$

where T_2 is a derivation tree with root

$$\langle \texttt{y:=y}\star\texttt{x; x:=x}-1, s_{13}\rangle \to s_{32}$$

and T_3 is a derivation tree with root

$$\langle \texttt{while } \neg(\texttt{x=1}) \texttt{ do (y:=y}\star\texttt{x; x:=x}-1\texttt{)}, s_{32}\rangle \to s_{61} \qquad (***)$$

for some state s_{32}.

Using that the form of the statement y:=y⋆x; x:=x−1 is S_1;S_2 it is now easy to see that the derivation tree T_2 is

$$\frac{\langle \texttt{y:=y}\star\texttt{x}, s_{13}\rangle \to s_{33} \qquad \langle \texttt{x:=x}-1, s_{33}\rangle \to s_{32}}{\langle \texttt{y:=y}\star\texttt{x; x:=x}-1, s_{13}\rangle \to s_{32}}$$

where $s_{33} = s[\texttt{y}\mapsto\mathbf{3}]$ and $s_{32} = s[\texttt{y}\mapsto\mathbf{3}][\texttt{x}\mapsto\mathbf{2}]$. The leaves of T_2 are instances of [ass$_{ns}$] and they are combined using [comp$_{ns}$]. So now T_2 is fully constructed.

In a similar way we can construct the derivation tree T_3 with root (***) and we get:

$$\dfrac{\dfrac{\langle \mathtt{y:=y\star x},\ s_{32}\rangle \rightarrow s_{62} \qquad \langle \mathtt{x:=x-1},\ s_{62}\rangle \rightarrow s_{61}}{\langle \mathtt{y:=y\star x;\ x:=x-1},\ s_{32}\rangle \rightarrow s_{61}} \qquad T_4}{\langle \mathtt{while}\ \neg(\mathtt{x=1})\ \mathtt{do}\ (\mathtt{y:=y\star x;\ x:=x-1}),\ s_{32}\rangle \rightarrow s_{61}}$$

where $s_{62} = s[\mathtt{y}{\mapsto}\mathbf{6}][\mathtt{x}{\mapsto}\mathbf{2}]$, $s_{61} = s[\mathtt{y}{\mapsto}\mathbf{6}][\mathtt{x}{\mapsto}\mathbf{1}]$ and T_4 is a derivation tree with root

$$\langle \mathtt{while}\ \neg(\mathtt{x=1})\ \mathtt{do}\ (\mathtt{y:=y\star x;\ x:=x-1}),\ s_{61}\rangle \rightarrow s_{61}$$

Finally, we see that the derivation tree T_4 is an instance of the axiom $[\text{while}^{\text{ff}}_{\text{ns}}]$ because $\mathcal{B}[\![\neg(\mathtt{x=1})]\!]s_{61} = \mathbf{ff}$. This completes the construction of the derivation tree T for (*). □

Exercise 2.3 Consider the statement

$$\mathtt{z:=0;\ while\ y\leq x\ do\ (z:=z+1;\ x:=x-y)}$$

Construct a derivation tree for this statement when executed in a state where `x` has the value **17** and `y` has the value **5**. □

We shall introduce the following terminology: The execution of a statement S on a state s

- *terminates* if and only if there is a state s' such that $\langle S, s\rangle \rightarrow s'$, and
- *loops* if and only if there is *no* state s' such that $\langle S, s\rangle \rightarrow s'$.

We shall say that a statement S *always terminates* if its execution on a state s terminates for all choices of s, and *always loops* if its execution on a state s loops for all choices of s.

Exercise 2.4 Consider the following statements

- $\mathtt{while}\ \neg(\mathtt{x=1})\ \mathtt{do}\ (\mathtt{y:=y\star x;\ x:=x-1})$
- $\mathtt{while\ 1\leq x\ do\ (y:=y\star x;\ x:=x-1)}$
- `while true do skip`

For each statement determine whether or not it always terminates and whether or not it always loops. Try to argue for your answers using the axioms and rules of Table 2.1. □

Properties of the semantics

The transition system gives us a way of arguing about statements and their properties. As an example we may be interested in whether two statements S_1 and S_2 are *semantically equivalent*; by this we mean that for all states s and s'

$$\langle S_1,\ s\rangle \to s' \text{ if and only if } \langle S_2,\ s\rangle \to s'$$

Lemma 2.5 The statement

$$\texttt{while}\ b\ \texttt{do}\ S$$

is semantically equivalent to

$$\texttt{if}\ b\ \texttt{then}\ (S;\ \texttt{while}\ b\ \texttt{do}\ S)\ \texttt{else skip}.$$

Proof: The proof is in two stages. We shall first prove that if

$$\langle\texttt{while}\ b\ \texttt{do}\ S,\ s\rangle \to s'' \qquad (*)$$

then

$$\langle\texttt{if}\ b\ \texttt{then}\ (S;\ \texttt{while}\ b\ \texttt{do}\ S)\ \texttt{else skip},\ s\rangle \to s'' \qquad (**)$$

Thus, if the execution of the loop terminates then so does its one-level unfolding. Later we shall show that if the unfolded loop terminates then so will the loop itself; the conjunction of these results then prove the lemma.

Because (*) holds we know that we have a derivation tree T for it. It can have one of two forms depending on whether it has been constructed using the rule [$\text{while}^{\text{tt}}_{\text{ns}}$] or the axiom [$\text{while}^{\text{ff}}_{\text{ns}}$]. In the first case the derivation tree T has the form:

$$\frac{T_1 \qquad T_2}{\langle\texttt{while}\ b\ \texttt{do}\ S,\ s\rangle \to s''}$$

where T_1 is a derivation tree with root $\langle S,\ s\rangle{\to}s'$ and T_2 is a derivation tree with root $\langle\texttt{while}\ b\ \texttt{do}\ S,\ s'\rangle{\to}s''$. Furthermore, $\mathcal{B}[\![b]\!]s = \mathbf{tt}$. Using the derivation trees T_1 and T_2 as the premises for the rules [comp_{ns}] we can construct the derivation tree:

$$\frac{T_1 \qquad T_2}{\langle S;\ \texttt{while}\ b\ \texttt{do}\ S,\ s\rangle \to s''}$$

Using that $\mathcal{B}[\![b]\!]s = \mathbf{tt}$ we can use the rule [$\text{if}^{\text{tt}}_{\text{ns}}$] to construct the derivation tree

$$\frac{\dfrac{T_1 \qquad\qquad T_2}{\langle S;\ \texttt{while}\ b\ \texttt{do}\ S,\ s\rangle \to s''}}{\langle \texttt{if}\ b\ \texttt{then}\ (S;\ \texttt{while}\ b\ \texttt{do}\ S)\ \texttt{else skip},\ s\rangle \to s''}$$

thereby showing that (**) holds.

Alternatively, the derivation tree T is an instance of [$\text{while}^{\text{ff}}_{\text{ns}}$]. Then $\mathcal{B}[\![b]\!]s = \mathbf{ff}$ and we must have that $s''=s$. So T simply is

$$\langle \texttt{while}\ b\ \texttt{do}\ S,\ s\rangle \to s$$

Using the axiom [skip_{ns}] we get a derivation tree

$$\langle \texttt{skip},\ s\rangle \to s''$$

and we can now apply the rule [$\text{if}^{\text{ff}}_{\text{ns}}$] to construct a derivation tree for (**):

$$\frac{\langle \texttt{skip},\ s\rangle \to s''}{\langle \texttt{if}\ b\ \texttt{then}\ (S;\ \texttt{while}\ b\ \texttt{do}\ S)\ \texttt{else skip},\ s\rangle \to s''}$$

This completes the first part of the proof.

For the second stage of the proof we assume that (**) holds and shall prove that (*) holds. So we have a derivation tree T for (**) and must construct one for (*). Only two rules could give rise to the derivation tree T for (**), namely [$\text{if}^{\text{tt}}_{\text{ns}}$] or [$\text{if}^{\text{ff}}_{\text{ns}}$]. In the first case, $\mathcal{B}[\![b]\!]s = \mathbf{tt}$ and we have a derivation tree T_1 with root

$$\langle S;\ \texttt{while}\ b\ \texttt{do}\ S,\ s\rangle \to s''$$

The statement has the general form $S_1;\ S_2$ and the only rule that could give this is [comp_{ns}]. Therefore there are derivation trees T_2 and T_3 for

$\langle S,\ s\rangle \to s'$, and

$\langle \texttt{while}\ b\ \texttt{do}\ S,\ s'\rangle \to s''$

for some state s'. It is now straightforward to use the rule [$\text{while}^{\text{tt}}_{\text{ns}}$] to combine T_2 and T_3 to a derivation tree for (*).

In the second case, $\mathcal{B}[\![b]\!]s = \mathbf{ff}$ and T is constructed using the rule [$\text{if}^{\text{ff}}_{\text{ns}}$]. This means that we have a derivation tree for

$$\langle \texttt{skip},\ s\rangle \to s''$$

and according to axiom [skip_{ns}] it must be the case that $s=s''$. But then we can use the axiom [$\text{while}^{\text{ff}}_{\text{ns}}$] to construct a derivation tree for (*). This completes the proof. □

Exercise 2.6 Prove that the two statements S_1;(S_2;S_3) and (S_1;S_2);S_3 are semantically equivalent. Construct a statement showing that S_1;S_2 is not, in general, semantically equivalent to S_2;S_1. □

Exercise 2.7 Extend the language **While** with the statement

`repeat` S `until` b

and define the relation → for it. (The semantics of the `repeat`-construct is not allowed to rely on the existence of a `while`-construct in the language.) Prove that `repeat` S `until` b and S; `if` b `then skip else` (`repeat` S `until` b) are semantically equivalent. □

Exercise 2.8 Another iterative construct is

`for` x := a_1 `to` a_2 `do` S

Extend the language **While** with this statement and define the relation → for it. Evaluate the statement

`y:=1; for z:=1 to x do (y:=y ⋆ x; x:=x−1)`

according to your definition. Hint: You may need to assume that you have an "inverse" to $\mathcal{N}$, so that there is a numeral for each number that may arise during the computation. (The semantics of the `for`-construct is not allowed to rely on the existence of a `while`-construct in the language.) □

In the above proof we used Table 2.1 to inspect the structure of the derivation tree for a certain transition known to hold. In the proof of the next result we shall combine this with an *induction on the shape of the derivation tree.* The idea can be summarized as follows:

Induction on the Shape of Derivation Trees	
1:	Prove that the property holds for all the simple derivation trees by showing that it holds for the *axioms* of the transition system.
2:	Prove that the property holds for all composite derivation trees: For each *rule* assume that the property holds for its premises (this is called the *induction hypothesis*) and prove that it also holds for the conclusion of the rule provided that the conditions of the rule are satisfied.

To formulate the theorem we shall say that the semantics of Table 2.1 is *deterministic* if for all choices of S, s, s' and s'' we have that

$\langle S, s\rangle \rightarrow s'$ and $\langle S, s\rangle \rightarrow s''$ imply $s' = s''$

This means that for every statement S and initial state s we can uniquely determine a final state s' if (and only if) the execution of S terminates.

Theorem 2.9 The natural semantics of Table 2.1 is deterministic.

Proof: We assume that $\langle S,\ s\rangle \rightarrow s'$ and shall prove that

$$\text{if } \langle S,\ s\rangle \rightarrow s'' \text{ then } s' = s''.$$

We shall proceed by induction on the shape of the derivation tree for $\langle S,\ s\rangle \rightarrow s'$.

The case $[\text{ass}_{\text{ns}}]$: Then S is $x{:=}a$ and s' is $s[x \mapsto \mathcal{A}[\![a]\!]s]$. The only axiom or rule that could be used to give $\langle x{:=}a,\ s\rangle \rightarrow s''$ is $[\text{ass}_{\text{ns}}]$ so it follows that s'' must be $s[x \mapsto \mathcal{A}[\![a]\!]s]$ and thereby $s' = s''$.

The case $[\text{skip}_{\text{ns}}]$: Analogous.

The case $[\text{comp}_{\text{ns}}]$: Assume that

$$\langle S_1;S_2,\ s\rangle \rightarrow s'$$

holds because

$$\langle S_1,\ s\rangle \rightarrow s_0 \text{ and } \langle S_2,\ s_0\rangle \rightarrow s'$$

for some s_0. The only rule that could be applied to give $\langle S_1;S_2,\ s\rangle \rightarrow s''$ is $[\text{comp}_{\text{ns}}]$ so there is a state s_1 such that

$$\langle S_1,\ s\rangle \rightarrow s_1 \text{ and } \langle S_2,\ s_1\rangle \rightarrow s''$$

The induction hypothesis can be applied to the premise $\langle S_1,\ s\rangle \rightarrow s_0$ and from $\langle S_1,\ s\rangle \rightarrow s_1$ we get $s_0 = s_1$. Similarly, the induction hypothesis can be applied to the premise $\langle S_2,\ s_0\rangle \rightarrow s'$ and from $\langle S_2,\ s_0\rangle \rightarrow s''$ we get $s' = s''$ as required.

The case $[\text{if}_{\text{ns}}^{\text{tt}}]$: Assume that

$$\langle \texttt{if}\ b\ \texttt{then}\ S_1\ \texttt{else}\ S_2,\ s\rangle \rightarrow s'$$

holds because

$$\mathcal{B}[\![b]\!]s = \mathbf{tt} \text{ and } \langle S_1,\ s\rangle \rightarrow s'$$

From $\mathcal{B}[\![b]\!]s = \mathbf{tt}$ we get that the only rule that could be applied to give the alternative $\langle \texttt{if}\ b\ \texttt{then}\ S_1\ \texttt{else}\ S_2,\ s\rangle \rightarrow s''$ is $[\text{if}_{\text{ns}}^{\text{tt}}]$. So it must be the case that

$$\langle S_1,\ s\rangle \rightarrow s''$$

But then the induction hypothesis can be applied to the premise $\langle S_1, s\rangle \to s'$ and from $\langle S_1, s\rangle \to s''$ we get $s' = s''$.

The case $[\text{if}^{\text{ff}}_{\text{ns}}]$: Analogous.

The case $[\text{while}^{\text{tt}}_{\text{ns}}]$: Assume that

$$\langle \texttt{while}\ b\ \texttt{do}\ S,\ s\rangle \to s'$$

because

$$\mathcal{B}[\![b]\!]s = \mathbf{tt},\ \langle S,\ s\rangle \to s_0 \text{ and } \langle \texttt{while}\ b\ \texttt{do}\ S,\ s_0\rangle \to s'$$

The only rule that could be applied to give $\langle \texttt{while}\ b\ \texttt{do}\ S,\ s\rangle \to s''$ is $[\text{while}^{\text{tt}}_{\text{ns}}]$ because $\mathcal{B}[\![b]\!]s = \mathbf{tt}$ and this means that

$$\langle S,\ s\rangle \to s_1 \text{ and } \langle \texttt{while}\ b\ \texttt{do}\ S,\ s_1\rangle \to s''$$

must hold for some s_1. Again the induction hypothesis can be applied to the premise $\langle S, s\rangle \to s_0$ and from $\langle S, s\rangle \to s_1$ we get $s_0 = s_1$. Thus we have

$$\langle \texttt{while}\ b\ \texttt{do}\ S,\ s_0\rangle \to s' \text{ and } \langle \texttt{while}\ b\ \texttt{do}\ S,\ s_0\rangle \to s''$$

Since $\langle \texttt{while}\ b\ \texttt{do}\ S,\ s_0\rangle \to s'$ is a premise of (the instance of) $[\text{while}^{\text{tt}}_{\text{ns}}]$ we can apply the induction hypothesis to it. From $\langle \texttt{while}\ b\ \texttt{do}\ S,\ s_0\rangle \to s''$ we therefore get $s' = s''$ as required.

The case $[\text{while}^{\text{ff}}_{\text{ns}}]$: Straightforward. □

Exercise 2.10 * Prove that `repeat` S `until` b (as defined in Exercise 2.7) is semantically equivalent to S; `while` $\neg b$ `do` S. Argue that this means that the extended semantics is deterministic. □

It is worth observing that we could not prove Theorem 2.9 using structural induction on the statement S. The reason is that the rule $[\text{while}^{\text{tt}}_{\text{ns}}]$ defines the semantics of `while` b `do` S in terms of itself. Structural induction works fine when the semantics is defined *compositionally* (as e.g. $\mathcal{A}$ and $\mathcal{B}$ in Chapter 1). But the natural semantics of Table 2.1 is *not* defined compositionally because of the rule $[\text{while}^{\text{tt}}_{\text{ns}}]$.

Basically, induction on the shape of derivation trees is a kind of structural induction on the derivation trees: In the *base case* we show that the property holds for the simple derivation trees. In the *induction step* we assume that the property holds for the immediate constituents of a derivation tree and show that it also holds for the composite derivation tree.

The semantic function $\mathcal{S}_{\text{ns}}$

The *meaning* of statements can now be summarized as a (partial) function from **State** to **State**. We define

$$\mathcal{S}_{\text{ns}}\text{: } \mathbf{Stm} \to (\mathbf{State} \hookrightarrow \mathbf{State})$$

and this means that for every statement S we have a partial function

$$\mathcal{S}_{\text{ns}}[\![S]\!] \in \mathbf{State} \hookrightarrow \mathbf{State}.$$

It is given by

$$\mathcal{S}_{\text{ns}}[\![S]\!]s = \begin{cases} s' & \text{if } \langle S,\ s\rangle \to s' \\ \underline{\text{undef}} & \text{otherwise} \end{cases}$$

Note that $\mathcal{S}_{\text{ns}}$ is a well-defined partial function because of Theorem 2.9. The need for partiality is demonstrated by the statement `while true do skip` that always loops (see Exercise 2.4); we then have

$$\mathcal{S}_{\text{ns}}[\![\texttt{while true do skip}]\!]\ s = \underline{\text{undef}}$$

for all states s.

Exercise 2.11 The semantics of arithmetic expressions is given by the function $\mathcal{A}$. We can also use an operational approach and define a natural semantics for the arithmetic expressions. It will have two kinds of configurations:

$\langle a,\ s\rangle$ denoting that a has to be evaluated in state s, and

z denoting the final value (an element of $\mathbf{Z}$).

The transition relation $\to_{\text{Aexp}}$ has the form

$$\langle a,\ s\rangle \to_{\text{Aexp}} z$$

where the idea is that a evaluates to z in state s. Some example axioms and rules are

$$\langle n,\ s\rangle \to_{\text{Aexp}} \mathcal{N}[\![n]\!]$$

$$\langle x,\ s\rangle \to_{\text{Aexp}} s\ x$$

$$\frac{\langle a_1,\ s\rangle \to_{\text{Aexp}} z_1,\ \langle a_2,\ s\rangle \to_{\text{Aexp}} z_2}{\langle a_1 + a_2,\ s\rangle \to_{\text{Aexp}} z} \quad \text{where } z = z_1 + z_2$$

Complete the specification of the transition system. Use structural induction on **Aexp** to prove that the meaning of a defined by this relation is the same as that defined by $\mathcal{A}$. □

Exercise 2.12 In a similar way we can specify a natural semantics for the boolean expressions. The transitions will have the form

$$\langle b, s\rangle \to_{\text{Bexp}} t$$

where $t \in \mathbf{T}$. Specify the transition system and prove that the meaning of b defined in this way is the same as that defined by $\mathcal{B}$. □

Exercise 2.13 Determine whether or not semantic equivalence of S_1 and S_2 amounts to $\mathcal{S}_{\text{ns}}[\![S_1]\!] = \mathcal{S}_{\text{ns}}[\![S_2]\!]$. □

2.2 Structural operational semantics

In structural operational semantics the emphasis is on the *individual steps* of the execution, that is the execution of assignments and tests. The transition relation has the form

$$\langle S, s\rangle \Rightarrow \gamma$$

where γ either is of the form $\langle S', s'\rangle$ or of the form s'. The transition expresses the *first* step of the execution of S from state s. There are two possible outcomes:

- If γ is of the form $\langle S', s'\rangle$ then the execution of S from s is *not* completed and the remaining computation is expressed by the intermediate configuration $\langle S', s'\rangle$.

- If γ is of the form s' then the execution of S from s *has* terminated and the final state is s'.

We shall say that $\langle S, s\rangle$ is *stuck* if there is no γ such that $\langle S, s\rangle \Rightarrow \gamma$.

The definition of $\Rightarrow$ is given by the axioms and rules of Table 2.2 and the general form of these are as in the previous section. Axioms [ass_{sos}] and [skip_{sos}] have not changed at all because the assignment and `skip` statements are fully executed in one step.

The rules [$\text{comp}^1_{\text{sos}}$] and [$\text{comp}^2_{\text{sos}}$] express that to execute $S_1;S_2$ in state s we first execute S_1 one step from s. Then there are two possible outcomes:

- If the execution of S_1 has not been completed we have to complete it before embarking on the execution of S_2.

- If the execution of S_1 has been completed we can start on the execution of S_2.

$[\text{ass}_{\text{sos}}]$	$\langle x := a,\ s\rangle \Rightarrow s[x\mapsto\mathcal{A}[\![a]\!]s]$
$[\text{skip}_{\text{sos}}]$	$\langle \texttt{skip},\ s\rangle \Rightarrow s$
$[\text{comp}^1_{\text{sos}}]$	$\dfrac{\langle S_1,\ s\rangle \Rightarrow \langle S_1',\ s'\rangle}{\langle S_1;S_2,\ s\rangle \Rightarrow \langle S_1';S_2,\ s'\rangle}$
$[\text{comp}^2_{\text{sos}}]$	$\dfrac{\langle S_1,\ s\rangle \Rightarrow s'}{\langle S_1;S_2,\ s\rangle \Rightarrow \langle S_2,\ s'\rangle}$
$[\text{if}^{\text{tt}}_{\text{sos}}]$	$\langle \texttt{if}\ b\ \texttt{then}\ S_1\ \texttt{else}\ S_2,\ s\rangle \Rightarrow \langle S_1,\ s\rangle$ if $\mathcal{B}[\![b]\!]s = \mathbf{tt}$
$[\text{if}^{\text{ff}}_{\text{sos}}]$	$\langle \texttt{if}\ b\ \texttt{then}\ S_1\ \texttt{else}\ S_2,\ s\rangle \Rightarrow \langle S_2,\ s\rangle$ if $\mathcal{B}[\![b]\!]s = \mathbf{ff}$
$[\text{while}_{\text{sos}}]$	$\langle \texttt{while}\ b\ \texttt{do}\ S,\ s\rangle \Rightarrow$ $\langle \texttt{if}\ b\ \texttt{then}\ (S;\ \texttt{while}\ b\ \texttt{do}\ S)\ \texttt{else skip},\ s\rangle$

Table 2.2: Structural operational semantics for **While**

The first case is captured by the rule $[\text{comp}^1_{\text{sos}}]$: If the result of executing the first step of $\langle S,\ s\rangle$ is an intermediate configuration $\langle S_1',\ s'\rangle$ then the next configuration is $\langle S_1';S_2,\ s'\rangle$ showing that we have to complete the execution of S_1 before we can start on S_2. The second case above is captured by the rule $[\text{comp}^2_{\text{sos}}]$: If the result of executing S_1 from s is a final state s' then the next configuration is $\langle S_2,\ s'\rangle$, so that we can now start on S_2.

From the axioms $[\text{if}^{\text{tt}}_{\text{sos}}]$ and $[\text{if}^{\text{ff}}_{\text{sos}}]$ we see that the first step in executing a conditional is to perform the test and to select the appropriate branch. Finally, the axiom $[\text{while}_{\text{sos}}]$ shows that the first step in the execution of the `while`-construct is to unfold it one level, that is to rewrite it as a conditional. The test will therefore be performed in the second step of the execution (where one of the axioms for the `if`-construct is applied). We shall see an example of this shortly.

A *derivation sequence* of a statement S starting in state s is either

- a *finite* sequence

  $$\gamma_0,\ \gamma_1,\ \gamma_2,\ \cdots,\ \gamma_k$$

  of configurations satisfying $\gamma_0 = \langle S,\ s\rangle$, $\gamma_i \Rightarrow \gamma_{i+1}$ for $0\leq i<k$, $k\geq 0$, and where γ_k is either a terminal configuration or a stuck configuration, or it is

- an *infinite* sequence

  $$\gamma_0,\ \gamma_1,\ \gamma_2,\ \cdots$$

  of configurations satisfying $\gamma_0 = \langle S,\ s\rangle$ and $\gamma_i \Rightarrow \gamma_{i+1}$ for $0\leq i$

We shall write $\gamma_0 \Rightarrow^{\text{i}} \gamma_{\text{i}}$ to indicate that there are i steps in the execution from γ_0 to γ_{i} and we write $\gamma_0 \Rightarrow^* \gamma_{\text{i}}$ to indicate that there is a finite number of steps. Note that $\gamma_0 \Rightarrow^{\text{i}} \gamma_{\text{i}}$ and $\gamma_0 \Rightarrow^* \gamma_{\text{i}}$ need *not* be derivation sequences: they will be so if and only if γ_{i} is either a terminal configuration or a stuck configuration.

Example 2.14 Consider the statement

$$(\texttt{z := x; x := y}); \texttt{ y := z}$$

of Chapter 1 and let s_0 be the state that maps all variables except x and y to **0** and that has s_0 x = **5** and s_0 y = **7**. We then have the derivation sequence:

$$\begin{aligned}
&\langle(\texttt{z := x; x := y}); \texttt{ y := z}, s_0\rangle \\
&\qquad\Rightarrow \langle\texttt{x := y; y := z}, s_0[\texttt{z}\mapsto\mathbf{5}]\rangle \\
&\qquad\Rightarrow \langle\texttt{y := z}, (s_0[\texttt{z}\mapsto\mathbf{5}])[\texttt{x}\mapsto\mathbf{7}]\rangle \\
&\qquad\Rightarrow ((s_0[\texttt{z}\mapsto\mathbf{5}])[\texttt{x}\mapsto\mathbf{7}])[\texttt{y}\mapsto\mathbf{5}]
\end{aligned}$$

Corresponding to *each* of these steps we have *derivation trees* explaining why they take place. For the first step

$$\langle(\texttt{z := x; x := y}); \texttt{ y := z}, s_0\rangle \Rightarrow \langle\texttt{x := y; y := z}, s_0[\texttt{z}\mapsto\mathbf{5}]\rangle$$

the derivation tree is

$$\cfrac{\cfrac{\langle\texttt{z := x}, s_0\rangle \Rightarrow s_0[\texttt{z}\mapsto\mathbf{5}]}{\langle\texttt{z := x; x := y}, s_0\rangle \Rightarrow \langle\texttt{x := y}, s_0[\texttt{z}\mapsto\mathbf{5}]\rangle}}{\langle(\texttt{z := x; x := y}); \texttt{ y := z}, s_0\rangle \Rightarrow \langle\texttt{x := y; y := z}, s_0[\texttt{z}\mapsto\mathbf{5}]\rangle}$$

and it has been constructed from the axiom $[\text{ass}_{\text{sos}}]$ and the rules $[\text{comp}^1_{\text{sos}}]$ and $[\text{comp}^2_{\text{sos}}]$. The derivation tree for the second step is constructed in a similar way using only $[\text{ass}_{\text{sos}}]$ and $[\text{comp}^2_{\text{sos}}]$ and for the third step it simply is an instance of $[\text{ass}_{\text{sos}}]$. □

Example 2.15 Assume that s x = **3**. The first step of execution from the configuration

$$\langle\texttt{y:=1; while } \neg(\texttt{x=1}) \texttt{ do } (\texttt{y:=y} \star \texttt{x; x:=x}-1), s\rangle$$

will give the configuration

$$\langle\texttt{while } \neg(\texttt{x=1}) \texttt{ do } (\texttt{y:=y} \star \texttt{x; x:=x}-1), s[\texttt{y}\mapsto\mathbf{1}]\rangle$$

This is achieved using the axiom $[\text{ass}_{\text{sos}}]$ and the rule $[\text{comp}^2_{\text{sos}}]$ as shown by the derivation tree:

$$\frac{\dfrac{}{\langle \mathtt{y{:=}1},\ s\rangle \Rightarrow s[\mathtt{y}\mapsto\mathbf{1}]}}{\langle \mathtt{y{:=}1;\ while\ \neg(x{=}1)\ do\ (y{:=}y{\star}x;\ x{:=}x{-}1)},\ s\rangle \Rightarrow \langle \mathtt{while\ \neg(x{=}1)\ do\ (y{:=}y{\star}x;\ x{:=}x{-}1)},\ s[\mathtt{y}\mapsto\mathbf{1}]\rangle}$$

The next step of the execution will rewrite the loop as a conditional using the axiom [$\text{while}_{\text{sos}}$] so we get the configuration

$$\langle \mathtt{if\ \neg(x{=}1)\ then\ ((y{:=}y{\star}x;\ x{:=}x{-}1);\ while\ \neg(x{=}1)\ do\ (y{:=}y{\star}x;\ x{:=}x{-}1))\ else\ skip},\ s[\mathtt{y}\mapsto\mathbf{1}]\rangle$$

The following step will perform the test and yields (according to [$\text{if}^{\text{tt}}_{\text{sos}}$]) the configuration

$$\langle \mathtt{(y{:=}y{\star}x;\ x{:=}x{-}1);\ while\ \neg(x{=}1)\ do\ (y{:=}y\ \star\ x;\ x{:=}x{-}1)},\ s[\mathtt{y}\mapsto\mathbf{1}]\rangle$$

We can then use [ass_{sos}], [$\text{comp}^2_{\text{sos}}$] and [$\text{comp}^1_{\text{sos}}$] to obtain the configuration

$$\langle \mathtt{x{:=}x{-}1;\ while\ \neg(x{=}1)\ do\ (y{:=}y\ \star\ x;\ x{:=}x{-}1)},\ s[\mathtt{y}\mapsto\mathbf{3}]\rangle$$

as is verified by the derivation tree:

$$\frac{\dfrac{\langle \mathtt{y{:=}y{\star}x},\ s[\mathtt{y}\mapsto\mathbf{1}]\rangle \Rightarrow s[\mathtt{y}\mapsto\mathbf{3}]}{\langle \mathtt{y{:=}y{\star}x;\ x{:=}x{-}1},\ s[\mathtt{y}\mapsto\mathbf{1}]\rangle \Rightarrow \langle \mathtt{x{:=}x{-}1},\ s[\mathtt{y}\mapsto\mathbf{3}]\rangle}}{\langle \mathtt{(y{:=}y{\star}x;\ x{:=}x{-}1);\ while\ \neg(x{=}1)\ do\ (y{:=}y{\star}x;\ x{:=}x{-}1)},\ s[\mathtt{y}\mapsto\mathbf{1}]\rangle \Rightarrow \langle \mathtt{x{:=}x{-}1;\ while\ \neg(x{=}1)\ do\ (y{:=}y\ \star\ x;\ x{:=}x{-}1)},\ s[\mathtt{y}\mapsto\mathbf{3}]\rangle}$$

Using [ass_{sos}] and [$\text{comp}^2_{\text{sos}}$] the next configuration will then be

$$\langle \mathtt{while\ \neg(x{=}1)\ do\ (y{:=}y\ \star\ x;\ x{:=}x{-}1)},\ s[\mathtt{y}\mapsto\mathbf{3}][\mathtt{x}\mapsto\mathbf{2}]\rangle$$

Continuing in this way we eventually reach the final state $s[\mathtt{y}\mapsto\mathbf{6}][\mathtt{x}\mapsto\mathbf{1}]$. □

Exercise 2.16 Construct a derivation sequence for the statement

$$\mathtt{z{:=}0;\ while\ y{\le}x\ do\ (z{:=}z{+}1;\ x{:=}x{-}y)}$$

when executed in a state where $\mathtt{x}$ has the value $\mathbf{17}$ and $\mathtt{y}$ has the value $\mathbf{5}$. Determine a state s such that the derivation sequence obtained for the above statement and s is infinite. □

Given a statement S in the language **While** and a state s it is always possible to find *at least one* derivation sequence that starts in the configuration $\langle S, s\rangle$: simply apply axioms and rules forever or until a terminal or stuck configuration is reached. Inspection of Table 2.2 shows that there are no stuck configurations in **While** and Exercise 2.22 below will show that there is in fact only one derivation sequence that starts with $\langle S, s\rangle$. However, some of the constructs considered in Section 2.4 that extend **While** will have configurations that are stuck or more than one derivation sequence that starts in a given configuration.

In analogy with the terminology of the previous section we shall say that the execution of a statement S on a state s

- *terminates* if and only if there is a finite derivation sequence starting with $\langle S, s\rangle$, and

- *loops* if and only if there is an infinite derivation sequence starting with $\langle S, s\rangle$.

We shall say that the execution of S on s *terminates successfully* if $\langle S, s\rangle \Rightarrow^* s'$ for some state s'; in **While** an execution terminates successfully if and only if it terminates because there are no stuck configurations. Finally, we shall say that a statement S *always terminates* if it terminates on all states, and *always loops* if it loops on all states.

Exercise 2.17 Extend **While** with the construct `repeat` S `until` b and specify the structural operational semantics for it. (The semantics for the `repeat`-construct is not allowed to rely on the existence of a `while`-construct.) □

Exercise 2.18 Extend **While** with the construct `for` x := a_1 `to` a_2 `do` S and specify the structural operational semantics for it. Hint: You may need to assume that you have an "inverse" to $\mathcal{N}$, so that there is a numeral for each number that may arise during the computation. (The semantics for the `for`-construct is not allowed to rely on the existence of a `while`-construct.) □

Properties of the semantics

For structural operational semantics it is often useful to conduct proofs by induction on the *length* of the derivation sequences. The proof technique may be summarized as follows:

Induction on the Length of Derivation Sequences	
1:	Prove that the property holds for all derivation sequences of length 0.
2:	Prove that the property holds for all other derivation sequences: Assume that the property holds for all derivation sequences of length at most k (this is called the *induction hypothesis*) and show that it holds for derivation sequences of length k+1.

The induction step of a proof following this principle will often be done by inspecting either

- the structure of the syntactic element, or
- the derivation tree validating the first transition of the derivation sequence.

Note that the proof technique is a simple application of mathematical induction.

To illustrate the use of the proof technique we shall prove the following lemma (to be used in the next section). Intuitively, the lemma expresses that the execution of a composite construct $S_1;S_2$ can be split into two parts, one corresponding to S_1 and the other corresponding to S_2.

Lemma 2.19 If $\langle S_1;S_2,\ s\rangle \Rightarrow^{\mathrm{k}} s''$ then there exists a state s' and natural numbers k_1 and k_2 such that $\langle S_1,\ s\rangle \Rightarrow^{\mathrm{k}_1} s'$ and $\langle S_2,\ s'\rangle \Rightarrow^{\mathrm{k}_2} s''$ where $\mathrm{k} = \mathrm{k}_1+\mathrm{k}_2$.

Proof: The proof is by induction on the number k, that is by induction on the length of the derivation sequence $\langle S_1;S_2,\ s\rangle \Rightarrow^{\mathrm{k}} s''$.

If $\mathrm{k} = 0$ then the result holds vacuously.

For the induction step we assume that the lemma holds for $\mathrm{k} \leq \mathrm{k}_0$ and we shall prove it for k_0+1. So assume that

$$\langle S_1;S_2,\ s\rangle \Rightarrow^{\mathrm{k}_0+1} s''$$

This means that the derivation sequence can be written as

$$\langle S_1;S_2,\ s\rangle \Rightarrow \gamma \Rightarrow^{\mathrm{k}_0} s''$$

for some configuration γ. Now one of two cases applies depending on which of the two rules [$\mathrm{comp}^1_{\mathrm{sos}}$] and [$\mathrm{comp}^2_{\mathrm{sos}}$] was used to obtain $\langle S_1;S_2,\ s\rangle \Rightarrow \gamma$.

In the first case where [$\mathrm{comp}^1_{\mathrm{sos}}$] is used we have

$$\langle S_1;S_2,\ s\rangle \Rightarrow \langle S_1';S_2,\ s'\rangle$$

because

$$\langle S_1,\ s\rangle \Rightarrow \langle S_1',\ s'\rangle$$

We therefore have

$$\langle S_1';S_2,\ s'\rangle \Rightarrow^{k_0} s''$$

and the induction hypothesis can be applied to this derivation sequence because it is shorter than the one we started with. This means that there is a state s_0 and natural numbers k_1 and k_2 such that

$$\langle S_1',\ s'\rangle \Rightarrow^{k_1} s_0 \text{ and } \langle S_2,\ s_0\rangle \Rightarrow^{k_2} s''$$

where $k_1+k_2=k_0$. Using that $\langle S_1,\ s\rangle \Rightarrow \langle S_1',\ s'\rangle$ and $\langle S_1',\ s'\rangle \Rightarrow^{k_1} s_0$ we get

$$\langle S_1,\ s\rangle \Rightarrow^{k_1+1} s_0$$

We have already seen that $\langle S_2,\ s_0\rangle \Rightarrow^{k_2} s''$ and since $(k_1+1)+k_2 = k_0+1$ we have proved the required result.

The second possibility is that [$\text{comp}^2_{\text{sos}}$] has been used to obtain the derivation $\langle S_1;S_2,\ s\rangle \Rightarrow \gamma$. Then we have

$$\langle S_1,\ s\rangle \Rightarrow s'$$

and γ is $\langle S_2,\ s'\rangle$ so that

$$\langle S_2,\ s'\rangle \Rightarrow^{k_0} s''$$

The result now follows by choosing $k_1=1$ and $k_2=k_0$. □

Exercise 2.20 Suppose that $\langle S_1;S_2,\ s\rangle \Rightarrow^* \langle S_2,\ s'\rangle$. Show that it is *not* necessarily the case that $\langle S_1,\ s\rangle \Rightarrow^* s'$. □

Exercise 2.21 (Essential) Prove that

$$\text{if } \langle S_1,\ s\rangle \Rightarrow^{k} s' \text{ then } \langle S_1;S_2,\ s\rangle \Rightarrow^{k} \langle S_2,\ s'\rangle$$

that is the execution of S_1 is not influenced by the statement following it. □

In the previous section we defined a notion of determinism based on the natural semantics. For the structural operational semantics we define the similar notion as follows. The semantics of Table 2.2 is *deterministic* if for all choices of S, s, γ and γ' we have that

$$\langle S,\ s\rangle \Rightarrow \gamma \text{ and } \langle S,\ s\rangle \Rightarrow \gamma' \text{ imply } \gamma = \gamma'$$

Exercise 2.22 (Essential) Show that the structural operational semantics of Table 2.2 is deterministic. Deduce that there is exactly one derivation sequence starting in a configuration $\langle S, s\rangle$. Argue that a statement S of **While** cannot both terminate and loop on a state s and hence it cannot both be always terminating and always looping. □

In the previous section we defined a notion of two statements S_1 and S_2 being semantically equivalent. The similar notion can be defined based on the structural operational semantics: S_1 and S_2 are *semantically equivalent* if for all states s

- $\langle S_1, s\rangle \Rightarrow^* \gamma$ if and only if $\langle S_2, s\rangle \Rightarrow^* \gamma$, whenever γ is a configuration that is either stuck or terminal, and
- there is an infinite derivation sequence starting in $\langle S_1, s\rangle$ if and only if there is one starting in $\langle S_2, s\rangle$.

Note that in the first case the length of the two derivation sequences may be different.

Exercise 2.23 Show that the following statements of **While** are semantically equivalent in the above sense:

- S;`skip` and S
- `while` b `do` S and `if` b `then` (S; `while` b `do` S) `else skip`
- S_1;(S_2;S_3) and (S_1;S_2);S_3

You may use the result of Exercise 2.22. Discuss to what extent the notion of semantic equivalence introduced above is the same as that defined from the natural semantics. □

Exercise 2.24 Prove that `repeat` S `until` b (as defined in Exercise 2.17) is semantically equivalent to S; `while` $\neg$ b `do` S. □

The semantic function $\mathcal{S}_{\text{sos}}$

As in the previous section the *meaning* of statements can be summarized by a (partial) function from **State** to **State**:

$$\mathcal{S}_{\text{sos}}\text{: } \mathbf{Stm} \to (\mathbf{State} \hookrightarrow \mathbf{State})$$

It is given by

$$\mathcal{S}_{\text{sos}}[\![S]\!]s = \begin{cases} s' & \text{if } \langle S, s\rangle \Rightarrow^* s' \\ \underline{\text{undef}} & \text{otherwise} \end{cases}$$

The well-definedness of the definition follows from Exercise 2.22.

Exercise 2.25 Determine whether or not semantic equivalence of S_1 and S_2 amounts to $\mathcal{S}_{\text{sos}}[\![S_1]\!] = \mathcal{S}_{\text{sos}}[\![S_2]\!]$. □

2.3 An equivalence result

We have given two definitions of the semantics of **While** and we shall now address the question of their equivalence.

Theorem 2.26 For every statement S of **While** we have $\mathcal{S}_{\text{ns}}[\![S]\!] = \mathcal{S}_{\text{sos}}[\![S]\!]$.

This result expresses two properties:

- If the execution of S from some state terminates in one of the semantics then it also terminates in the other and the resulting states will be equal.
- If the execution of S from some state loops in one of the semantics then it will also loop in the other.

It should be fairly obvious that the first property follows from the theorem because there are no stuck configurations in the structural operational semantics of **While**. For the other property suppose that the execution of S on state s loops in one of the semantics. If it terminates in the other semantics we have a contradiction with the first property because both semantics are deterministic (Theorem 2.9 and Exercise 2.22). Hence S will have to loop on state s also in the other semantics.

The theorem is proved in two stages as expressed by Lemma 2.27 and Lemma 2.28 below. We shall first prove:

Lemma 2.27 For every statement S of **While** and states s and s' we have

$$\langle S,\ s\rangle \to s' \text{ implies } \langle S,\ s\rangle \Rightarrow^* s'.$$

So if the execution of S from s terminates in the natural semantics then it will terminate in the same state in the structural operational semantics.

Proof: The proof proceeds by induction on the shape of the derivation tree for $\langle S,\ s\rangle \to s'$.

The case [ass_{ns}]: We assume that

$$\langle x := a,\ s\rangle \to s[x \mapsto \mathcal{A}[\![a]\!]s]$$

From [ass_{sos}] we get the required

$$\langle x := a,\ s\rangle \Rightarrow s[x \mapsto \mathcal{A}[\![a]\!]s]$$

The case [skip_{ns}]: Analogous.

The case [comp_{ns}]: Assume that

$$\langle S_1;S_2,\ s\rangle \to s''$$

because

$$\langle S_1,\ s\rangle \to s' \text{ and } \langle S_2,\ s'\rangle \to s''$$

The induction hypothesis can be applied to both of the premises $\langle S_1,\ s\rangle \to s'$ and $\langle S_2,\ s'\rangle \to s''$ and gives

$$\langle S_1,\ s\rangle \Rightarrow^* s' \text{ and } \langle S_2,\ s'\rangle \Rightarrow^* s''$$

From Exercise 2.21 we get

$$\langle S_1;S_2,\ s\rangle \Rightarrow^* \langle S_2,\ s'\rangle$$

and thereby $\langle S_1;S_2,\ s\rangle \Rightarrow^* s''$.

The case $[\text{if}_{\text{ns}}^{\text{tt}}]$: Assume that

$$\langle \texttt{if}\ b\ \texttt{then}\ S_1\ \texttt{else}\ S_2,\ s\rangle \to s'$$

because

$$\mathcal{B}[\![b]\!]s = \mathbf{tt} \text{ and } \langle S_1,\ s\rangle \to s'$$

Since $\mathcal{B}[\![b]\!]s = \mathbf{tt}$ we get

$$\langle \texttt{if}\ b\ \texttt{then}\ S_1\ \texttt{else}\ S_2,\ s\rangle \Rightarrow \langle S_1,\ s\rangle \Rightarrow^* s'$$

where the first relationship comes from $[\text{if}_{\text{sos}}^{\text{tt}}]$ and the second from the induction hypothesis applied to the premise $\langle S_1,\ s\rangle \to s'$.

The case $[\text{if}_{\text{ns}}^{\text{ff}}]$: Analogous.

The case $[\text{while}_{\text{ns}}^{\text{tt}}]$: Assume that

$$\langle \texttt{while}\ b\ \texttt{do}\ S,\ s\rangle \to s''$$

because

$$\mathcal{B}[\![b]\!]s = \mathbf{tt},\ \langle S,\ s\rangle \to s' \text{ and } \langle \texttt{while}\ b\ \texttt{do}\ S,\ s'\rangle \to s''$$

The induction hypothesis can be applied to both of the premises $\langle S,\ s\rangle \to s'$ and $\langle \texttt{while}\ b\ \texttt{do}\ S,\ s'\rangle \to s''$ and gives

$$\langle S,\ s\rangle \Rightarrow^* s' \text{ and } \langle \texttt{while}\ b\ \texttt{do}\ S,\ s'\rangle \Rightarrow^* s''$$

Using Exercise 2.21 we get

$$\langle S;\ \texttt{while}\ b\ \texttt{do}\ S,\ s\rangle \Rightarrow^* s''$$

Using $[\text{while}_{\text{sos}}]$ and $[\text{if}_{\text{sos}}^{\text{tt}}]$ (with $\mathcal{B}[\![b]\!]s = \mathbf{tt}$) we get the first two steps of

$$\begin{aligned}&\langle \texttt{while}\ b\ \texttt{do}\ S,\ s\rangle\\ &\qquad \Rightarrow \langle \texttt{if}\ b\ \texttt{then}\ (S;\ \texttt{while}\ b\ \texttt{do}\ S)\ \texttt{else skip},\ s\rangle\\ &\qquad \Rightarrow \langle S;\ \texttt{while}\ b\ \texttt{do}\ S,\ s\rangle\\ &\qquad \Rightarrow^{*} s''\end{aligned}$$

and we have already argued for the last part.

The case [$\text{while}^{\text{ff}}_{\text{ns}}$]: Straightforward. □

This completes the proof of Lemma 2.27. The second part of the theorem follows from:

Lemma 2.28 For every statement S of **While**, states s and s' and natural number k we have that

$$\langle S,\ s\rangle \Rightarrow^{\text{k}} s' \text{ implies } \langle S,\ s\rangle \to s'.$$

So if the execution of S from s terminates in the structural operational semantics then it will terminate in the same state in the natural semantics.

Proof: The proof proceeds by induction on the length of the derivation sequence $\langle S,\ s\rangle \Rightarrow^{\text{k}} s'$, that is by induction on k.

If k=0 then the result holds vacuously.

To prove the induction step we assume that the lemma holds for $\text{k} \leq \text{k}_0$ and we shall then prove that it holds for k_0+1. We proceed by cases on how the first step of $\langle S,\ s\rangle \Rightarrow^{\text{k}_0+1} s'$ is obtained, that is by inspecting the derivation tree for the first step of computation in the structural operational semantics.

The case [ass_{sos}]: Straightforward (and $\text{k}_0 = 0$).

The case [skip_{sos}]: Straightforward (and $\text{k}_0 = 0$).

The cases [$\text{comp}^{1}_{\text{sos}}$] and [$\text{comp}^{2}_{\text{sos}}$]: In both cases we assume that

$$\langle S_1;S_2,\ s\rangle \Rightarrow^{\text{k}_0+1} s''$$

We can now apply Lemma 2.19 and get that there exists a state s' and natural numbers k_1 and k_2 such that

$$\langle S_1,\ s\rangle \Rightarrow^{\text{k}_1} s' \text{ and } \langle S_2,\ s'\rangle \Rightarrow^{\text{k}_2} s''$$

where $\text{k}_1+\text{k}_2=\text{k}_0+1$. The induction hypothesis can now be applied to each of these derivation sequences because $\text{k}_1 \leq \text{k}_0$ and $\text{k}_2 \leq \text{k}_0$. So we get

$$\langle S_1,\ s\rangle \to s' \text{ and } \langle S_2,\ s'\rangle \to s''$$

Using [comp$_{\text{ns}}$] we now get the required $\langle S_1;S_2,\ s\rangle \rightarrow s''$.

The case [if$^{\text{tt}}_{\text{sos}}$]: Assume that $\mathcal{B}[\![b]\!]s = \mathbf{tt}$ and that

$$\langle \texttt{if}\ b\ \texttt{then}\ S_1\ \texttt{else}\ S_2,\ s\rangle \Rightarrow \langle S_1,\ s\rangle \Rightarrow^{\mathrm{k_0}} s'$$

The induction hypothesis can be applied to the derivation sequence $\langle S_1,\ s\rangle \Rightarrow^{\mathrm{k_0}} s'$ and gives

$$\langle S_1,\ s\rangle \rightarrow s'$$

The result now follows using [if$^{\text{tt}}_{\text{ns}}$].

The case [if$^{\text{ff}}_{\text{sos}}$]: Analogous.

The case [while$_{\text{sos}}$]: We have

$$\begin{aligned}&\langle \texttt{while}\ b\ \texttt{do}\ S,\ s\rangle\\ &\qquad\Rightarrow \langle \texttt{if}\ b\ \texttt{then}\ (S;\ \texttt{while}\ b\ \texttt{do}\ S)\ \texttt{else skip},\ s\rangle\\ &\qquad\Rightarrow^{\mathrm{k_0}} s''\end{aligned}$$

The induction hypothesis can be applied to the $\mathrm{k_0}$ last steps of the derivation sequence and gives

$$\langle \texttt{if}\ b\ \texttt{then}\ (S;\ \texttt{while}\ b\ \texttt{do}\ S)\ \texttt{else skip},\ s\rangle \rightarrow s''$$

and from Lemma 2.5 we get the required

$$\langle \texttt{while}\ b\ \texttt{do}\ S,\ s\rangle \rightarrow s''$$ □

Proof of Theorem 2.26: For an arbitrary statement S and state s it follows from Lemmas 2.27 and 2.28 that if $\mathcal{S}_{\text{ns}}[\![S]\!]s = s'$ then $\mathcal{S}_{\text{sos}}[\![S]\!]s = s'$ and vice versa. This suffices for showing that the functions $\mathcal{S}_{\text{ns}}[\![S]\!]$ and $\mathcal{S}_{\text{sos}}[\![S]\!]$ must be equal: if one is defined on a state s then so is the other, and therefore, if one is not defined on a state s then neither is the other. □

Exercise 2.29 Consider the extension of the language **While** with the statement `repeat` S `until` b. The natural semantics of the construct was considered in Exercise 2.7 and the structural operational semantics in Exercise 2.17. Modify the proof of Theorem 2.26 so that the theorem applies to the extended language. □

Exercise 2.30 Consider the extension of the language **While** with the statement `for` $x := a_1$ `to` a_2 `do` S. The natural semantics of the construct was considered in Exercise 2.8 and the structural operational semantics in Exercise 2.18. Modify the proof of Theorem 2.26 so that the theorem applies to the extended language. □

The proof technique employed in the proof of Theorem 2.26 may be summarized as follows:

Proof Summary for While:	
Equivalence of two Operational Semantics	
1:	Prove by *induction on the shape of derivation trees* that for each derivation tree in the natural semantics there is a corresponding finite derivation sequence in the structural operational semantics.
2:	Prove by *induction on the length of derivation sequences* that for each finite derivation sequence in the structural operational semantics there is a corresponding derivation tree in the natural semantics.

When proving the equivalence of two operational semantics for a language with additional programming constructs one may need to amend the above proof technique. One reason is that the equivalence result may have to be expressed differently from that of Theorem 2.26 (as will be the case if the extended language is non-deterministic). Also one might want to consider only some of the finite derivation sequences, for example those ending in a terminal configuration.

2.4 Extensions of While

In order to illustrate the power and weakness of the two approaches to operational semantics we shall consider various extensions of the language **While**. For each extension we shall show how to modify the operational semantics.

Abortion

We first extend **While** with the simple statement `abort`. The idea is that `abort` *stops* the execution of the complete program. This means that `abort` behaves differently from `while true do skip` in that it causes the execution to stop rather than loop. Also `abort` behaves differently from `skip` because a statement following `abort` will never be executed whereas one following `skip` certainly will.

Formally, the new syntax of statements is given by:

$$
\begin{array}{rcl}
S & ::= & x := a \mid \texttt{skip} \mid S_1 \texttt{ ; } S_2 \mid \texttt{if } b \texttt{ then } S_1 \texttt{ else } S_2 \\
 & \mid & \texttt{while } b \texttt{ do } S \mid \texttt{abort}
\end{array}
$$

We shall not repeat the definitions of the sets of configurations but tacitly assume that they are modified so as to correspond to the extended syntax. The task that remains, therefore, is to define the new transition relations $\rightarrow$ and $\Rightarrow$.

The fact that `abort` stops the execution of the program is modelled by ensuring that the configurations of the form $\langle$`abort`, $s\rangle$ are *stuck*. Therefore the *natural semantics* of the extended language is still defined by the transition relation $\rightarrow$ of Table 2.1. So although the language and thereby the set of configurations have been extended we do not modify the definition of the transition relation. Similarly, the *structural operational semantics* of the extended language is still defined by Table 2.2.

From the structural operational semantics point of view it is clear now that `abort` and `skip` cannot be semantically equivalent. This is because

$$\langle \texttt{skip}, s\rangle \Rightarrow s$$

is the only derivation sequence for `skip` starting in s and

$$\langle \texttt{abort}, s\rangle$$

is the only derivation sequence for `abort` starting in s. Similarly, `abort` cannot be semantically equivalent to `while true do skip` because

$$\begin{aligned}
&\langle \texttt{while true do skip}, s\rangle \\
&\qquad \Rightarrow \langle \texttt{if true then (skip; while true do skip) else skip}, s\rangle \\
&\qquad \Rightarrow \langle \texttt{skip; while true do skip}, s\rangle \\
&\qquad \Rightarrow \langle \texttt{while true do skip}, s\rangle \\
&\qquad \Rightarrow \cdots
\end{aligned}$$

is an infinite derivation sequence for `while true do skip` whereas `abort` has none. Thus we shall claim that the structural operational semantics captures the informal explanation given earlier.

From the natural semantics point of view it is also clear that `skip` and `abort` cannot be semantically equivalent. However, it turns out that `while true do skip` and `abort` *are* semantically equivalent! The reason is that in the natural semantics we are only concerned with executions that terminate properly. So if we do not have a derivation tree for $\langle S, s\rangle \rightarrow s'$ then we cannot tell whether it is because we entered a stuck configuration or a looping execution. We can summarize this as follows:

Natural Semantics versus Structural Operational Semantics
• In a natural semantics we cannot distinguish between *looping* and *abnormal termination*. • In a structural operational semantics *looping* is reflected by infinite derivation sequences and *abnormal termination* by finite derivation sequences ending in a stuck configuration.

We should note, however, that if abnormal termination is modelled by "normal termination" in a special error configuration (included in the set of terminal configurations) then we can distinguish between the three statements in both semantic styles.

Exercise 2.31 Theorem 2.26 expresses that the natural semantics and the structural operational semantics of **While** are equivalent. Discuss whether or not a similar result holds for **While** extended with `abort`. □

Exercise 2.32 Extend **While** with the statement

$\texttt{assert}\ b\ \texttt{before}\ S$

The idea is that if b evaluates to true then we execute S and otherwise the execution of the complete program aborts. Extend the structural operational semantics of Table 2.2 to express this (without assuming that **While** contains the `abort`-statement). Show that $\texttt{assert true before}\ S$ is semantically equivalent to S but that $\texttt{assert false before}\ S$ neither is equivalent to `while true do skip` nor `skip`. □

Non-determinism

The second extension of **While** has statements given by

$$\begin{array}{rcl} S & ::= & x := a \mid \texttt{skip} \mid S_1\ ;\ S_2 \mid \texttt{if}\ b\ \texttt{then}\ S_1\ \texttt{else}\ S_2 \\ & \mid & \texttt{while}\ b\ \texttt{do}\ S \mid S_1\ \texttt{or}\ S_2 \end{array}$$

The idea is here that in $S_1\ \texttt{or}\ S_2$ we can non-deterministically choose to execute either S_1 or S_2. So we shall expect that execution of the statement

$\texttt{x := 1 or (x := 2; x := x + 2)}$

could result in a state where `x` has the value **1**, but it could as well result in a state where `x` has the value **4**.

When specifying the *natural semantics* we extend Table 2.1 with the two rules:

$$[\mathrm{or}^1_{\mathrm{ns}}] \qquad \frac{\langle S_1, s\rangle \to s'}{\langle S_1\ \texttt{or}\ S_2, s\rangle \to s'}$$

$$[\mathrm{or}^2_{\mathrm{ns}}] \qquad \frac{\langle S_2, s\rangle \to s'}{\langle S_1\ \texttt{or}\ S_2, s\rangle \to s'}$$

Corresponding to the configuration $\langle \texttt{x := 1 or (x := 2; x := x+2)}, s\rangle$ we have derivation trees for

$$\langle \texttt{x := 1 or (x := 2; x := x+2)}, s\rangle \to s[\texttt{x}\mapsto\mathbf{1}]$$

as well as

$$\langle \texttt{x := 1 or (x := 2; x := x+2)}, s\rangle \rightarrow s[\texttt{x}\mapsto\mathbf{4}]$$

It is important to note that if we replace `x := 1` by `while true do skip` in the above statement then we will only have one derivation tree, namely that for

$$\langle \texttt{(while true do skip) or (x := 2; x := x+2)}, s\rangle \rightarrow s[\texttt{x}\mapsto\mathbf{4}]$$

Turning to the *structural operational semantics* we shall extend Table 2.2 with the two axioms:

$$[\text{or}^1_{\text{sos}}] \qquad \langle S_1 \texttt{ or } S_2, s\rangle \Rightarrow \langle S_1, s\rangle$$

$$[\text{or}^2_{\text{sos}}] \qquad \langle S_1 \texttt{ or } S_2, s\rangle \Rightarrow \langle S_2, s\rangle$$

For the statement `x := 1 or (x := 2; x := x+2)` we have two derivation sequences:

$$\langle \texttt{x := 1 or (x := 2; x := x+2)}, s\rangle \Rightarrow^* s[\texttt{x}\mapsto\mathbf{1}]$$

and

$$\langle \texttt{x := 1 or (x := 2; x := x+2)}, s\rangle \Rightarrow^* s[\texttt{x}\mapsto\mathbf{4}]$$

If we replace `x := 1` by `while true do skip` in the above statement then we still have two derivation sequences. One is infinite

$$\begin{aligned} &\langle \texttt{(while true do skip) or (x := 2; x := x+2)}, s\rangle \\ &\qquad \Rightarrow \langle \texttt{while true do skip}, s\rangle \\ &\qquad \Rightarrow^3 \langle \texttt{while true do skip}, s\rangle \\ &\qquad \Rightarrow \cdots \end{aligned}$$

and the other is finite

$$\langle \texttt{(while true do skip) or (x := 2; x := x+2)}, s\rangle \Rightarrow^* s[\texttt{x}\mapsto\mathbf{4}]$$

Comparing the natural semantics and the structural operational semantics we see that the latter can choose the "wrong" branch of the `or`-statement whereas the first always chooses the "right" branch. This is summarized as follows:

Natural Semantics versus Structural Operational Semantics
• In a natural semantics *non-determinism will suppress looping*, if possible. • In a structural operational semantics *non-determinism does not suppress looping.*

Exercise 2.33 Consider the statement

$$\texttt{x := -1; while x}\leq\texttt{0 do (x := x-1 or x := (-1)}\star\texttt{x)}$$

Given a state s describe the set of final states that may result according to the natural semantics. Further describe the set of derivation sequences that are specified by the structural operational semantics. Based on this discuss whether or not you would regard the natural semantics as being equivalent to the structural operational semantics for this particular statement. □

Exercise 2.34 We shall now extend **While** with the statement

$$\texttt{random}(x)$$

and the idea is that its execution will change the value of x to be any positive natural number. Extend the natural semantics as well as the structural operational semantics to express this. Discuss whether $\texttt{random}(x)$ is a superfluous construct in the case where **While** is also extended with the `or` construct. □

Parallelism

We shall now consider an extension of **While** with a parallel construct. So now the syntax of expressions is given by

$$\begin{array}{rcl} S & ::= & x := a \mid \texttt{skip} \mid S_1 \,;\, S_2 \mid \texttt{if } b \texttt{ then } S_1 \texttt{ else } S_2 \\ & \mid & \texttt{while } b \texttt{ do } S \mid S_1 \texttt{ par } S_2 \end{array}$$

The idea is that both statements of S_1 `par` S_2 have to be executed but that the execution can be *interleaved*. This means that a statement like

$$\texttt{x := 1 par (x := 2; x := x+2)}$$

can give three different results for `x`, namely **4**, **1** and **3**: If we first execute `x := 1` and then `x := 2; x := x+2` we get the final value **4**. Alternatively, if we first execute `x := 2; x := x+2` and then `x := 1` we get the final value **1**. Finally, we have the possibility of first executing `x := 2`, then `x := 1` and lastly `x := x+2` and we then get the final value **3**.

To express this in the *structural operational semantics* we extend Table 2.2 with the following rules:

$$[\text{par}^1_{\text{sos}}] \qquad \frac{\langle S_1,\, s\rangle \Rightarrow \langle S_1',\, s'\rangle}{\langle S_1 \texttt{ par } S_2,\, s\rangle \Rightarrow \langle S_1' \texttt{ par } S_2,\, s'\rangle}$$

$$[\text{par}^2_{\text{sos}}] \qquad \frac{\langle S_1,\, s\rangle \Rightarrow s'}{\langle S_1 \texttt{ par } S_2,\, s\rangle \Rightarrow \langle S_2,\, s'\rangle}$$

$$[\text{par}^3_{\text{sos}}] \qquad \frac{\langle S_2,\ s\rangle \Rightarrow \langle S'_2,\ s'\rangle}{\langle S_1\ \texttt{par}\ S_2,\ s\rangle \Rightarrow \langle S_1\ \texttt{par}\ S'_2,\ s'\rangle}$$

$$[\text{par}^4_{\text{sos}}] \qquad \frac{\langle S_2,\ s\rangle \Rightarrow s'}{\langle S_1\ \texttt{par}\ S_2,\ s\rangle \Rightarrow \langle S_1,\ s'\rangle}$$

The first two rules take account of the case where we begin by executing the first step of statement S_1. If the execution of S_1 is not fully completed we modify the configuration so as to remember how far we have reached. Otherwise only S_2 has to be executed and we update the configuration accordingly. The last two rules are similar but for the case where we begin by executing the first step of S_2.

Using these rules we get the following derivation sequences for the example statement:

$$\begin{aligned}\langle \texttt{x} := \texttt{1 par (x := 2; x := x+2)},\ s\rangle &\Rightarrow \langle \texttt{x := 2; x := x+2},\ s[\texttt{x}\mapsto\mathbf{1}]\rangle\\ &\Rightarrow \langle \texttt{x := x+2},\ s[\texttt{x}\mapsto\mathbf{2}]\rangle\\ &\Rightarrow s[\texttt{x}\mapsto\mathbf{4}]\end{aligned}$$

$$\begin{aligned}\langle \texttt{x} := \texttt{1 par (x := 2; x := x+2)},\ s\rangle &\Rightarrow \langle \texttt{x := 1 par x := x+2},\ s[\texttt{x}\mapsto\mathbf{2}]\rangle\\ &\Rightarrow \langle \texttt{x := 1},\ s[\texttt{x}\mapsto\mathbf{4}]\rangle\\ &\Rightarrow s[\texttt{x}\mapsto\mathbf{1}]\end{aligned}$$

and

$$\begin{aligned}\langle \texttt{x} := \texttt{1 par (x := 2; x := x+2)},\ s\rangle &\Rightarrow \langle \texttt{x := 1 par x := x+2},\ s[\texttt{x}\mapsto\mathbf{2}]\rangle\\ &\Rightarrow \langle \texttt{x := x+2},\ s[\texttt{x}\mapsto\mathbf{1}]\rangle\\ &\Rightarrow s[\texttt{x}\mapsto\mathbf{3}]\end{aligned}$$

Turning to the *natural semantics* we might start by extending Table 2.1 with the two rules:

$$\frac{\langle S_1,\ s\rangle \to s',\ \langle S_2,\ s'\rangle \to s''}{\langle S_1\ \texttt{par}\ S_2,\ s\rangle \to s''}$$

$$\frac{\langle S_2,\ s\rangle \to s',\ \langle S_1,\ s'\rangle \to s''}{\langle S_1\ \texttt{par}\ S_2,\ s\rangle \to s''}$$

However, it is easy to see that this will not do because the rules only express that either S_1 is executed before S_2 or vice versa. This means that we have lost the ability to *interleave* the execution of two statements. Furthermore, it seems impossible to be able to express this in the natural semantics because we consider the execution of a statement as an atomic entity that cannot be split into smaller pieces. This may be summarized as follows:

Natural Semantics versus Structural Operational Semantics
• In a natural semantics the execution of the immediate constituents is an *atomic entity* so we cannot express interleaving of computations.
• In a structural operational semantics we concentrate on the *small steps* of the computation so we can easily express interleaving.

Exercise 2.35 Consider an extension of **While** that in addition to the `par`-construct also contains the construct

`protect` S `end`

The idea is that the statement S has to be executed as an atomic entity so that for example

`x := 1 par protect (x := 2; x := x+2) end`

only have two possible outcomes namely **1** and **4**. Extend the structural operational semantics to express this. Can you specify a natural semantics for the extended language? □

Exercise 2.36 Specify a structural operational semantics for arithmetic expressions where the individual parts of an expression may be computed in parallel. Try to prove that you still obtain the result that was specified by $\mathcal{A}$. □

2.5 Blocks and procedures

We now extend the language **While** with blocks containing declarations of variables and procedures. In doing so we introduce a couple of important concepts:

- variable and procedure environments, and
- locations and stores.

We shall concentrate on the natural semantics and will consider dynamic as well as static scope and non-recursive as well as recursive procedures.

Blocks and simple declarations

We first extend the language **While** with blocks containing declarations of local variables. The new language is called **Block** and its syntax is

$$\begin{array}{lcl} S & ::= & x := a \mid \texttt{skip} \mid S_1 \;;\; S_2 \mid \texttt{if}\ b\ \texttt{then}\ S_1\ \texttt{else}\ S_2 \\ & \mid & \texttt{while}\ b\ \texttt{do}\ S \mid \texttt{begin}\ D_V\ S\ \texttt{end} \end{array}$$

where D_V is a meta-variable ranging over the syntactic category $\mathbf{Dec}_V$ of *variable declarations*. The syntax of variable declarations is given by:

$$D_V \;::=\; \texttt{var}\ x := a;\ D_V \mid \varepsilon$$

where ε is the empty declaration. The idea is that the variables declared inside a block `begin` D_V S `end` are *local* to it. So in a statement like

```
begin var y := 1;
        (x := 1;
         begin var x := 2; y := x+1 end;
         x := y+x)
end
```

the `x` in `y := x+1` relates to the local variable `x` introduced by `var x := 2`, whereas the `x` in `x := y+x` relates to the global variable `x` that is also used in the statement `x := 1`. In both cases the `y` refers to the `y` declared in the outer block. Therefore, the statement `y := x+1` assigns `y` the value **3**, rather than **2**, and the statement `x := y+x` assigns `x` the value **4**, rather than **5**.

Before going into the details of how to specify the semantics we shall define the set $\mathrm{DV}(D_V)$ of variables declared in D_V:

$$\begin{array}{lcl} \mathrm{DV}(\texttt{var}\ x := a;\ D_V) & = & \{x\} \cup \mathrm{DV}(D_V) \\ \mathrm{DV}(\varepsilon) & = & \emptyset \end{array}$$

We next define the *natural semantics*. The idea will be to have one transition system for *each* of the syntactic categories **Stm** and $\mathbf{Dec}_V$. For statements the transition system is as in Table 2.1 but extended with the rule of Table 2.3. The transition system for variable declarations has configurations of the two forms $\langle D_V, s\rangle$ and s and the idea is that the transition relation $\to_D$ specifies the relationship between initial and final states as before:

$$\langle D_V, s\rangle \to_D s'$$

The relation $\to_D$ for variable declarations is given in Table 2.4. We generalize the substitution operation on states and write $s'[X{\longmapsto}s]$ for the state that is as s' except for variables in the set X where it is as specified by s. Formally,

[block$_{ns}$]	$$\frac{\langle D_V,\ s\rangle \rightarrow_D s',\ \langle S,\ s'\rangle \rightarrow s''}{\langle \texttt{begin}\ D_V\ S\ \texttt{end},\ s\rangle \rightarrow s''[\mathrm{DV}(D_V)\longmapsto s]}$$

Table 2.3: Natural semantics for statements of **Block**

[var$_{ns}$]	$$\frac{\langle D_V,\ s[x\mapsto\mathcal{A}[\![a]\!]s]\rangle \rightarrow_D s'}{\langle \texttt{var}\ x\ :=\ a;\ D_V,\ s\rangle \rightarrow_D s'}$$
[none$_{ns}$]	$\langle \varepsilon,\ s\rangle \rightarrow_D s$

Table 2.4: Natural semantics for variable declarations

$$(s'[X\longmapsto s])\ x = \begin{cases} s\ x & \text{if } x \in X \\ s'\ x & \text{if } x \notin X \end{cases}$$

This operation will ensure that local variables are restored to their previous values when the block is left.

Exercise 2.37 Use the natural semantics of Table 2.3 to show that execution of the statement

```
begin var y := 1;
      (x := 1;
      begin var x := 2; y := x+1 end;
      x := y+x)
end
```

will lead to a state where **x** has the value **4**. □

It is somewhat harder to specify a *structural operational semantics* for the extended language. One approach is to replace states with a structure that is similar to the run-time stacks used in the implementation of block structured languages. Another is to extend the statements with fragments of the state. However, we shall not go further into this.

Procedures

We shall now extend the language **Block** with procedure declarations. The syntax of the language **Proc** is:

$$
\begin{array}{lcl}
S & ::= & x := a \mid \texttt{skip} \mid S_1 \; ; \; S_2 \mid \texttt{if } b \texttt{ then } S_1 \texttt{ else } S_2 \\
 & \mid & \texttt{while } b \texttt{ do } S \mid \texttt{begin } D_V \; D_P \; S \texttt{ end} \mid \texttt{call } p \\
D_V & ::= & \texttt{var } x := a; D_V \mid \varepsilon \\
D_P & ::= & \texttt{proc } p \texttt{ is } S; D_P \mid \varepsilon
\end{array}
$$

Here p is a meta-variable ranging over the syntactic category **Pname** of procedure names; in the concrete syntax there need not be any difference between procedure names and variable names but in the abstract syntax it is convenient to be able to distinguish between the two. Furthermore, D_P is a meta-variable ranging over the syntactic category **Dec**$_{\text{P}}$ of *procedure declarations.*

We shall give three different semantics of this language. They differ in their choice of scope rules for variables and procedures:

- dynamic scope for variables as well as procedures,
- dynamic scope for variables but static scope for procedures, and
- static scope for variables as well as procedures.

To illustrate the difference consider the statement

```
begin var x := 0;
      proc p is x := x ⋆ 2;
      proc q is call p;
      begin var x := 5;
            proc p is x := x + 1;
            call q; y := x
      end
end
```

If *dynamic scope* is used for variables as well as procedures then the final value of `y` is **6**. The reason is that `call q` will call the *local* procedure `p` which will update the *local* variable `x`. If we use dynamic scope for variables but *static scope* for procedures then `y` gets the value **10**. The reason is that now `call q` will call the *global* procedure `p` and it will update the *local* variable `x`. Finally, if we use static scope for variables as well as procedures then `y` gets the value **5**. The reason is that `call q` now will call the *global* procedure `p` which will update the *global* variable `x` so the local variable `x` is unchanged.

Dynamic scope rules for variables and procedures

The general idea is that to execute the statement `call` p we shall execute the body of the procedure. This means that we have to keep track of the association of procedure names with procedure bodies. To facilitate this we shall introduce the notion of a *procedure environment*. Given a procedure name the procedure environment env_P will return the statement that is its body. So env_P is an element of

$$\mathbf{Env_P} = \mathbf{Pname} \hookrightarrow \mathbf{Stm}$$

The next step will be to extend the natural semantics to take the environment into account. We shall extend the transition system for statements to have transitions of the form

$$env_P \vdash \langle S,\ s\rangle \rightarrow s'$$

The presence of the environment means that we can always access it and therefore get hold of the bodies of declared procedures. The result of modifying Table 2.1 to incorporate this extra information is shown in Table 2.5.

Concerning the rule for `begin` D_V D_P S `end` the idea is that we update the procedure environment so that the procedures declared in D_P will be available when executing S. Given a global environment env_P and a declaration D_P, the updated procedure environment, $\text{upd}_P(D_P,\ env_P)$, is specified by:

$$\text{upd}_P(\texttt{proc}\ p\ \texttt{is}\ S;\ D_P,\ env_P) = \text{upd}_P(D_P,\ env_P[p \mapsto S])$$
$$\text{upd}_P(\varepsilon,\ env_P) = env_P$$

As the variable declarations do not need to access the procedure environment it is not necessary to extend the transition system for declarations with the extra component. So for variable declarations we still have transitions of the form

$$\langle D,\ s\rangle \rightarrow_D s'$$

The relation is defined as for the language **Block**, that is by Table 2.4.

We can now complete the specification of the semantics of blocks and procedure calls. Note that in the rule [block_{ns}] of Table 2.5 we use the updated environment when executing the body of the block. In the rule [$\text{call}_{\text{ns}}^{\text{rec}}$] for procedure calls we make use of the information provided by the environment. It follows that procedures will *always* be recursive.

Exercise 2.38 Consider the following statement of **Proc**:

[ass$_{ns}$]	$env_P \vdash \langle x := a,\ s\rangle \to s[x \mapsto \mathcal{A}[\![a]\!]s]$
[skip$_{ns}$]	$env_P \vdash \langle \texttt{skip},\ s\rangle \to s$
[comp$_{ns}$]	$\dfrac{env_P \vdash \langle S_1,\ s\rangle \to s',\ env_P \vdash \langle S_2,\ s'\rangle \to s''}{env_P \vdash \langle S_1;S_2,\ s\rangle \to s''}$
[if$^{tt}_{ns}$]	$\dfrac{env_P \vdash \langle S_1,\ s\rangle \to s'}{env_P \vdash \langle \texttt{if}\ b\ \texttt{then}\ S_1\ \texttt{else}\ S_2,\ s\rangle \to s'}$ if $\mathcal{B}[\![b]\!]s = \mathbf{tt}$
[if$^{ff}_{ns}$]	$\dfrac{env_P \vdash \langle S_2,\ s\rangle \to s'}{env_P \vdash \langle \texttt{if}\ b\ \texttt{then}\ S_1\ \texttt{else}\ S_2,\ s\rangle \to s'}$ if $\mathcal{B}[\![b]\!]s = \mathbf{ff}$
[while$^{tt}_{ns}$]	$\dfrac{env_P \vdash \langle S,\ s\rangle \to s',\ env_P \vdash \langle \texttt{while}\ b\ \texttt{do}\ S,\ s'\rangle \to s''}{env_P \vdash \langle \texttt{while}\ b\ \texttt{do}\ S,\ s\rangle \to s''}$ if $\mathcal{B}[\![b]\!]s = \mathbf{tt}$
[while$^{ff}_{ns}$]	$env_P \vdash \langle \texttt{while}\ b\ \texttt{do}\ S,\ s\rangle \to s$ if $\mathcal{B}[\![b]\!]s = \mathbf{ff}$
[block$_{ns}$]	$\dfrac{\langle D_V,\ s\rangle \to_D s',\ \mathrm{upd_P}(D_P,\ env_P) \vdash \langle S,\ s'\rangle \to s''}{env_P \vdash \langle \texttt{begin}\ D_V\ D_P\ S\ \texttt{end},\ s\rangle \to s''[\mathrm{DV}(D_V) \longmapsto s]}$
[call$^{rec}_{ns}$]	$\dfrac{env_P \vdash \langle S,\ s\rangle \to s'}{env_P \vdash \langle \texttt{call}\ p,\ s\rangle \to s'}$ where $env_P\ p = S$

Table 2.5: Natural semantics for **Proc** with dynamic scope rules

```
begin proc fac is begin var z := x;
                        if x = 1 then skip
                        else (x := x−1; call fac; y := z⋆y)
                  end;
      (y := 1; call fac)
end
```

Construct a derivation tree for the execution of this statement from a state s where $s\ \texttt{x} = \mathbf{3}$. □

Exercise 2.39 Use the semantics to verify that the statement

```
begin var x := 0;
      proc p is x := x ⋆ 2;
      proc q is call p;
      begin var x := 5;
            proc p is x := x + 1;
            call q; y := x
      end
end
```

considered earlier does indeed assign the expected value to y. □

Static scope rules for procedures

We shall now modify the semantics of **Proc** to specify static scope rules for procedures. The first step will be to extend the procedure environment env_P so that procedure names are associated with their body as well as the procedure environment at the point of declaration. To this end we define

$$\mathbf{Env_P} = \mathbf{Pname} \hookrightarrow \mathbf{Stm} \times \mathbf{Env_P}$$

This definition may seem problematic because $\mathbf{Env_P}$ is defined in terms of itself. However, this is not really a problem because a concrete procedure environment always will be built from smaller environments starting with the empty procedure environment. The function $\mathrm{upd_P}$ updating the procedure environment can then be redefined as:

$$\mathrm{upd_P}(\texttt{proc}\ p\ \texttt{is}\ S;\ D_P,\ env_P) = \mathrm{upd_P}(D_P,\ env_P[p \mapsto (S,\ env_P)])$$

$$\mathrm{upd_P}(\varepsilon,\ env_P) = env_P$$

The semantics of variable declarations are unaffected and so is the semantics of most of the statements. Compared with Table 2.5 we shall only need to modify the rules for procedure calls. In the case where the procedures of **Proc** are assumed to be *non-recursive* we simply consult the procedure environment to determine the body of the procedure and the environment at the point of declaration. This is expressed by the rule $[\mathrm{call_{ns}}]$ of Table 2.6. In the case where the procedures of **Proc** are assumed to be *recursive* we have to make sure that occurrences of `call` p inside the body of p refer to the procedure itself. We shall therefore update the procedure environment to contain that information. This is expressed by the rule $[\mathrm{call_{ns}^{rec}}]$ of Table 2.6. The remaining axioms and rules are as in Tables 2.5 (without $[\mathrm{call_{ns}^{rec}}]$) and 2.4.

[call$_{ns}$]	$$\frac{env'_P \vdash \langle S,\ s\rangle \rightarrow s'}{env_P \vdash \langle \texttt{call}\ p,\ s\rangle \rightarrow s'}$$ where $env_P\ p = (S,\ env'_P)$
[call$_{ns}^{rec}$]	$$\frac{env'_P[p\mapsto(S,\ env'_P)] \vdash \langle S,\ s\rangle \rightarrow s'}{env_P \vdash \langle \texttt{call}\ p,\ s\rangle \rightarrow s'}$$ where $env_P\ p = (S,\ env'_P)$

Table 2.6: Procedure calls in case of mixed scope rules

Exercise 2.40 Construct a statement that illustrates the difference between the two rules for procedure call given in Table 2.6. Validate your claim by constructing derivation trees for the executions of the statement from a suitable state. □

Exercise 2.41 Use the semantics to verify that the statement of Exercise 2.39 assigns the expected value to y. □

Static scope rules for variables

We shall now modify the semantics of **Proc** to specify static scope rules for variables as well as procedures. To achieve this we shall replace the states with two mappings: a *variable environment* that associates a *location* with each variable and a *store* that associates a value with each location. Formally, we define a variable environment env_V as an element of

$$\mathbf{Env_V} = \mathbf{Var} \rightarrow \mathbf{Loc}$$

where **Loc** is a set of locations. For the sake of simplicity we shall take $\mathbf{Loc} = \mathbf{Z}$. A store *sto* is an element of

$$\mathbf{Store} = \mathbf{Loc} \cup \{\ \text{next}\ \} \rightarrow \mathbf{Z}$$

where 'next' is a special token used to hold the next free location. We shall need a function

$$\text{new: } \mathbf{Loc} \rightarrow \mathbf{Loc}$$

that given a location will produce the next one. In our case where **Loc** is **Z** we take 'new' to be the successor function on the integers.

So rather than having a single mapping s from variables to values we have split it into two mappings env_V and *sto* and the idea is that $s = sto \circ env_V$. To determine the value of a variable x we shall first

- determine the location $l = env_V\ x$ associated with x and then

[var$_{ns}$]	$$\frac{\langle D_V,\ env_V[x\mapsto l],\ sto[l\mapsto v][\text{next}\mapsto \text{new } l]\rangle \to_D (env'_V,\ sto')}{\langle \texttt{var}\ x := a;\ D_V,\ env_V,\ sto\rangle \to_D (env'_V,\ sto')}$$ where $v = \mathcal{A}[\![a]\!](sto \circ env_V)$ and $l = sto$ next
[none$_{ns}$]	$\langle \varepsilon,\ env_V,\ sto\rangle \to_D (env_V,\ sto)$

Table 2.7: Natural semantics for variable declarations using locations

- determine the value $sto\ l$ associated with the location l.

Similarly, to assign a value v to a variable x we shall first

- determine the location $l = env_V\ x$ associated with x and then
- update the store to have $sto\ l = v$.

The initial variable environment could for example map all variables to the location **0** and the initial store could for example map 'next' to **1**. The variable environment (and the store) is updated by the variable declarations. The transition system for variable declarations is therefore modified to have the form

$$\langle D_V,\ env_V,\ sto\rangle \to_D (env'_V,\ sto')$$

because a variable declaration will modify the variable environment as well as the store. The relation is defined in Table 2.7. Note that we use '*sto* next' to determine the location l to be associated with x in the variable environment. Also the store is updated to hold the correct value for l as well as 'next'. Finally note that the declared variables will get positive locations.

To obtain static scoping for variables we shall extend the procedure environment to hold the variable environment at the point of declaration. Therefore env_P will now be an element of

$$\mathbf{Env_P} = \mathbf{Pname} \hookrightarrow \mathbf{Stm} \times \mathbf{Env_V} \times \mathbf{Env_P}$$

The procedure environment is updated by the procedure declarations as before, the only difference being that the current variable environment is supplied as an additional parameter. The function upd$_P$ is now defined by:

$$\text{upd}_P(\texttt{proc}\ p\ \texttt{is}\ S;\ D_P,\ env_V,\ env_P) =$$
$$\quad \text{upd}_P(D_P,\ env_V,\ env_P[p\mapsto(S,\ env_V,\ env_P)])$$
$$\text{upd}_P(\varepsilon,\ env_V,\ env_P) = env_P$$

Finally, the transition system for statements will have the form:

$$env_V,\ env_P \vdash \langle S,\ sto\rangle \to sto'$$

$$[\text{ass}_{\text{ns}}] \quad env_V,\ env_P \vdash \langle x := a,\ sto\rangle \to sto[l \mapsto v]$$
$$\text{where } l = env_V\ x \text{ and } v = \mathcal{A}[\![a]\!](sto \circ env_V)$$

$$[\text{skip}_{\text{ns}}] \quad env_V,\ env_P \vdash \langle \texttt{skip},\ sto\rangle \to sto$$

$$[\text{comp}_{\text{ns}}] \quad \frac{env_V,\ env_P \vdash \langle S_1,\ sto\rangle \to sto',\quad env_V,\ env_P \vdash \langle S_2,\ sto'\rangle \to sto''}{env_V,\ env_P \vdash \langle S_1;S_2,\ sto\rangle \to sto''}$$

$$[\text{if}^{\text{tt}}_{\text{ns}}] \quad \frac{env_V,\ env_P \vdash \langle S_1,\ sto\rangle \to sto'}{env_V,\ env_P \vdash \langle \texttt{if}\ b\ \texttt{then}\ S_1\ \texttt{else}\ S_2,\ sto\rangle \to sto'}$$
$$\text{if } \mathcal{B}[\![b]\!](sto \circ env_V) = \mathbf{tt}$$

$$[\text{if}^{\text{ff}}_{\text{ns}}] \quad \frac{env_V,\ env_P \vdash \langle S_2,\ sto\rangle \to sto'}{env_V,\ env_P \vdash \langle \texttt{if}\ b\ \texttt{then}\ S_1\ \texttt{else}\ S_2,\ sto\rangle \to sto'}$$
$$\text{if } \mathcal{B}[\![b]\!](sto \circ env_V) = \mathbf{ff}$$

$$[\text{while}^{\text{tt}}_{\text{ns}}] \quad \frac{\begin{array}{c} env_V,\ env_P \vdash \langle S,\ sto\rangle \to sto', \\ env_V,\ env_P \vdash \langle \texttt{while}\ b\ \texttt{do}\ S,\ sto'\rangle \to sto'' \end{array}}{env_V,\ env_P \vdash \langle \texttt{while}\ b\ \texttt{do}\ S,\ sto\rangle \to sto''}$$
$$\text{if } \mathcal{B}[\![b]\!](sto \circ env_V) = \mathbf{tt}$$

$$[\text{while}^{\text{ff}}_{\text{ns}}] \quad env_V,\ env_P \vdash \langle \texttt{while}\ b\ \texttt{do}\ S,\ sto\rangle \to sto$$
$$\text{if } \mathcal{B}[\![b]\!](sto \circ env_V) = \mathbf{ff}$$

$$[\text{block}_{\text{ns}}] \quad \frac{\begin{array}{c} \langle D_V,\ env_V,\ sto\rangle \to_D (env'_V,\ sto'), \\ env'_V,\ env'_P \vdash \langle S,\ sto'\rangle \to sto'' \end{array}}{env_V,\ env_P \vdash \langle \texttt{begin}\ D_V\ D_P\ S\ \texttt{end},\ sto\rangle \to sto''}$$
$$\text{where } env'_P = \text{upd}_P(D_P,\ env'_V,\ env_P)$$

$$[\text{call}_{\text{ns}}] \quad \frac{env'_V,\ env'_P \vdash \langle S,\ sto\rangle \to sto'}{env_V,\ env_P \vdash \langle \texttt{call}\ p,\ sto\rangle \to sto'}$$
$$\text{where } env_P\ p = (S,\ env'_V,\ env'_P)$$

$$[\text{call}^{\text{rec}}_{\text{ns}}] \quad \frac{env'_V,\ env'_P[p \mapsto (S,\ env'_V,\ env'_P)] \vdash \langle S,\ sto\rangle \to sto'}{env_V,\ env_P \vdash \langle \texttt{call}\ p,\ sto\rangle \to sto'}$$
$$\text{where } env_P\ p = (S,\ env'_V,\ env'_P)$$

Table 2.8: Natural semantics for **Proc** with static scope rules

so given a variable environment and a procedure environment we get a relationship between an initial store and a final store. The modification of Tables 2.5 and 2.6 is rather straightforward and is given in Table 2.8. Note that in the new rule for blocks there is no analogue of $s''[\mathrm{DV}(D_V)\longmapsto s]$ as the values of variable only can be obtained by accessing the environment.

Exercise 2.42 Apply the natural semantics of Table 2.8 to the factorial statement of Exercise 2.38 and a store where the location for **x** has the value **3**. □

Exercise 2.43 Verify that the semantics applied to the statement of Exercise 2.39 gives the expected result. □

Exercise 2.44 * An alternative semantics of the language **While** is defined by the axioms and rules $[\mathrm{ass}_{\mathrm{ns}}]$, $[\mathrm{skip}_{\mathrm{ns}}]$, $[\mathrm{comp}_{\mathrm{ns}}]$, $[\mathrm{if}^{\mathrm{tt}}_{\mathrm{ns}}]$, $[\mathrm{if}^{\mathrm{ff}}_{\mathrm{ns}}]$, $[\mathrm{while}^{\mathrm{tt}}_{\mathrm{ns}}]$ and $[\mathrm{while}^{\mathrm{ff}}_{\mathrm{ns}}]$ of Table 2.8. Formulate and prove the equivalence between this semantics and that of Table 2.1. □

Exercise 2.45 Modify the syntax of procedure declarations so that procedures take two *call-by-value* parameters:

$$D_P ::= \texttt{proc}\ p(x_1,x_2)\ \texttt{is}\ S;\ D_P \mid \varepsilon$$

$$S ::= \cdots \mid \texttt{call}\ p(a_1,a_2)$$

Procedure environments will now be elements of

$$\mathbf{Env_P} = \mathbf{Pname} \hookrightarrow \mathbf{Var} \times \mathbf{Var} \times \mathbf{Stm} \times \mathbf{Env_V} \times \mathbf{Env_P}$$

Modify the semantics given above to handle this language. In particular, provide new rules for procedure calls: one for non-recursive procedures and another for recursive procedures. Construct statements that illustrate how the new rules are used. □

Exercise 2.46 Now consider the language **Proc** and the task of achieving *mutual recursion*. The procedure environment is now defined to be an element of

$$\mathbf{Env_P} = \mathbf{Pname} \hookrightarrow \mathbf{Stm} \times \mathbf{Env_V} \times \mathbf{Env_P} \times \mathcal{P}(\mathbf{Pname})$$

The idea is that if $env_P\ p = (S,\ env'_V,\ env'_P,\ P)$ then P is the set of procedure names that are defined in the same block as p. Define upd'_P by

$$\mathrm{upd}'_P(\texttt{proc}\ p\ \texttt{is}\ S;\ D_P,\ env_V,\ env_P,\ P) =$$

$$\qquad \mathrm{upd}'_P(D_P,\ env_V,\ env_P[p\mapsto(S,\ env_V,\ env_P,P)],\ P)$$

$$\mathrm{upd}'_P(\varepsilon,\ env_V,\ env_P,\ P) = env_P$$

Next redefine upd_P by

$$\text{upd}_P(D_P,\ env_V,\ env_P) = \text{upd}'_P(D_P,\ env_V,\ env_P,\ \text{DP}(D_P))$$

where $\text{DP}(D_P)$ is the set of procedures declared in D_P, that is

$$\begin{aligned} \text{DP}(\texttt{proc}\ p\ \texttt{is}\ S;\ D_P) &= \{p\} \cup \text{DP}(D_P) \\ \text{DP}(\varepsilon) &= \emptyset \end{aligned}$$

Modify the semantics of **Proc** so as to obtain mutual recursion among procedures defined in the same block. Illustrate how the new rules are used on a statement of your choice. □

Exercise 2.47 We shall consider a variant of the semantics where we use the variable environment rather than the store to hold the next free location. So assume that

$$\mathbf{Env_V} = \mathbf{Var} \cup \{\ \text{next}\ \} \to \mathbf{Loc}$$

and

$$\mathbf{Store} = \mathbf{Loc} \to \mathbf{Z}$$

As before we shall write $sto \circ env_V$ for the state obtained by first using env_V to find the location of the variable and then sto to find the value of the location. The clauses of Table 2.7 are now replaced by

$$\frac{\langle D_V,\ env_V[x \mapsto l][\text{next} \mapsto \text{new}\ l],\ sto[l \mapsto v]\rangle \to_D (env'_V,\ sto')}{\langle \texttt{var}\ x := a;\ D_V,\ env_V,\ sto\rangle \to_D (env'_V,\ sto')}$$
where $v = \mathcal{A}[\![a]\!](sto \circ env_V)$ and $l = env_V\ \text{next}$

$$\langle \varepsilon,\ env_V,\ sto\rangle \to_D (env_V,\ sto)$$

Construct a statement that computes different results under the two variants of the semantics. Validate your claim by constructing derivation trees for the executions of the statement from a suitable state. □

Chapter 3

Provably Correct Implementation

A formal specification of the semantics of a programming language is useful when implementing it. In particular, it becomes possible to argue about the correctness of the implementation. We shall illustrate this by showing how to translate the language **While** into a structured form of assembler code for an abstract machine and we shall then prove that the translation is correct. The idea is that we first define the *meaning* of the abstract machine instructions by an operational semantics. Then we define *translation functions* that will map expressions and statements in the **While** language into sequences of such instructions. The correctness result will then state that if we

- translate a program into code, and
- execute the code on the abstract machine,

then we get the same result as was specified by the semantic functions $\mathcal{S}_{\mathrm{ns}}$ and $\mathcal{S}_{\mathrm{sos}}$ of the previous chapter.

3.1 The abstract machine

When specifying the abstract machine it is convenient first to present its configurations and next its instructions and their meanings.

The abstract machine **AM** has configurations of the form $\langle c,\ e,\ s\rangle$ where

- c is the sequence of instructions (or code) to be executed,
- e is the evaluation stack, and
- s is the storage.

We use the *evaluation stack* to evaluate arithmetic and boolean expressions. Formally, it is a list of values, so writing

$$\mathbf{Stack} = (\mathbf{Z} \cup \mathbf{T})^{\star}$$

we have $e \in \mathbf{Stack}$. For the sake of simplicity we shall assume that the *storage* is similar to the state, that is $s \in \mathbf{State}$, and it is used to hold the values of variables.

The *instructions* of **AM** are given by the abstract syntax

$$\begin{array}{lll} inst & ::= & \text{PUSH-}n \mid \text{ADD} \mid \text{MULT} \mid \text{SUB} \\ & \mid & \text{TRUE} \mid \text{FALSE} \mid \text{EQ} \mid \text{LE} \mid \text{AND} \mid \text{NEG} \\ & \mid & \text{FETCH-}x \mid \text{STORE-}x \\ & \mid & \text{NOOP} \mid \text{BRANCH}(c,\ c) \mid \text{LOOP}(c,\ c) \\ c & ::= & \varepsilon \mid inst{:}c \end{array}$$

where ε is the empty sequence. We shall write **Code** for the syntactic category of *sequences of instructions*, so c is a meta-variable ranging over **Code**. Therefore we have

$$\langle c,\ e,\ s\rangle \in \mathbf{Code} \times \mathbf{Stack} \times \mathbf{State}$$

A configuration is a *terminal* (or final) configuration if its code component is the empty sequence, that is if it has the form $\langle \varepsilon,\ e,\ s\rangle$.

The semantics of the instructions of the abstract machine is given by an *operational semantics*. As in the previous chapter it will be specified by a transition system. The configurations have the form $\langle c,\ e,\ s\rangle$ as described above and the transition relation $\triangleright$ specifies how to execute the instructions:

$$\langle c,\ e,\ s\rangle \ \triangleright\ \langle c',\ e',\ s'\rangle$$

The idea is that *one step of execution* will transform the configuration $\langle c,\ e,\ s\rangle$ into $\langle c',\ e',\ s'\rangle$. The relation is defined by the axioms of Table 3.1 where we (ambiguously) use the notation ':' both for appending two instruction sequences and for prepending an element to a sequence. The evaluation stack is represented as a sequence of elements. It has the top of the stack to the left and we shall write ε for the empty sequence.

In addition to the usual arithmetic and boolean operations we have six instructions that modify the evaluation stack: The operation PUSH-n pushes a constant value n onto the stack and TRUE and FALSE push the constants **tt** and **ff**, respectively, onto the stack. The operation FETCH-x pushes the value bound to x onto the stack whereas STORE-x pops the topmost element off the stack and updates the storage so that the popped value is bound to x. The instruction BRANCH(c_1, c_2) will also change the flow of control: If the top of the stack is the value **tt** (that is

$\langle \text{PUSH-}n{:}c,\ e,\ s\rangle$	$\triangleright$	$\langle c,\ \mathcal{N}[\![n]\!]{:}e,\ s\rangle$	
$\langle \text{ADD}{:}c,\ z_1{:}z_2{:}e,\ s\rangle$	$\triangleright$	$\langle c,\ (z_1{+}z_2){:}e,\ s\rangle$	if $z_1,\ z_2 \in \mathbf{Z}$
$\langle \text{MULT}{:}c,\ z_1{:}z_2{:}e,\ s\rangle$	$\triangleright$	$\langle c,\ (z_1{\star}z_2){:}e,\ s\rangle$	if $z_1,\ z_2 \in \mathbf{Z}$
$\langle \text{SUB}{:}c,\ z_1{:}z_2{:}e,\ s\rangle$	$\triangleright$	$\langle c,\ (z_1{-}z_2){:}e,\ s\rangle$	if $z_1,\ z_2 \in \mathbf{Z}$
$\langle \text{TRUE}{:}c,\ e,\ s\rangle$	$\triangleright$	$\langle c,\ \mathbf{tt}{:}e,\ s\rangle$	
$\langle \text{FALSE}{:}c,\ e,\ s\rangle$	$\triangleright$	$\langle c,\ \mathbf{ff}{:}e,\ s\rangle$	
$\langle \text{EQ}{:}c,\ z_1{:}z_2{:}e,\ s\rangle$	$\triangleright$	$\langle c,\ (z_1{=}z_2){:}e,\ s\rangle$	if $z_1,\ z_2 \in \mathbf{Z}$
$\langle \text{LE}{:}c,\ z_1{:}z_2{:}e,\ s\rangle$	$\triangleright$	$\langle c,\ (z_1{\leq}z_2){:}e,\ s\rangle$	if $z_1,\ z_2 \in \mathbf{Z}$
$\langle \text{AND}{:}c,\ t_1{:}t_2{:}e,\ s\rangle$	$\triangleright$	$\begin{cases} \langle c, \mathbf{tt} : e, s\rangle & \text{if } t_1{=}\mathbf{tt} \text{ and } t_2{=}\mathbf{tt} \\ \langle c, \mathbf{ff} : e, s\rangle & \text{if } t_1{=}\mathbf{ff} \text{ or } t_2{=}\mathbf{ff},\ t_1,\ t_2 \in \mathbf{T} \end{cases}$	
$\langle \text{NEG}{:}c,\ t{:}e,\ s\rangle$	$\triangleright$	$\begin{cases} \langle c, \mathbf{ff} : e, s\rangle & \text{if } t{=}\mathbf{tt} \\ \langle c, \mathbf{tt} : e, s\rangle & \text{if } t{=}\mathbf{ff} \end{cases}$	
$\langle \text{FETCH-}x{:}c,\ e,\ s\rangle$	$\triangleright$	$\langle c,\ (s\ x){:}e,\ s\rangle$	
$\langle \text{STORE-}x{:}c,\ z{:}e,\ s\rangle$	$\triangleright$	$\langle c,\ e,\ s[x{\mapsto}z]\rangle$	if $z \in \mathbf{Z}$
$\langle \text{NOOP}{:}c,\ e,\ s\rangle$	$\triangleright$	$\langle c,\ e,\ s\rangle$	
$\langle \text{BRANCH}(c_1,\ c_2){:}c,\ t{:}e,\ s\rangle$	$\triangleright$	$\begin{cases} \langle c_1 : c, e, s\rangle & \text{if } t{=}\mathbf{tt} \\ \langle c_2 : c, e, s\rangle & \text{if } t{=}\mathbf{ff} \end{cases}$	
$\langle \text{LOOP}(c_1,\ c_2){:}c,\ e,\ s\rangle$	$\triangleright$	$\langle c_1{:}\text{BRANCH}(c_2{:}\text{LOOP}(c_1,\ c_2),\ \text{NOOP}){:}c,\ e,\ s\rangle$	

Table 3.1: Operational semantics for **AM**

some boolean expression has been evaluated to true) then the stack is popped and c_1 is to be executed next. Otherwise, if the top element of the stack is **ff** then it will be popped and c_2 will be executed next.

There are two instructions that change the flow of control. The instruction BRANCH(c_1, c_2) will be used to implement the conditional: as described above it will choose the code component c_1 or c_2 depending on the current value on top of the stack. If the top of the stack is not a truth value the machine will halt as there is no next configuration (since the meaning of BRANCH($\cdots$,$\cdots$) is not defined in that case). A looping construct such as the `while`-construct of **While** can be implemented using the instruction LOOP(c_1, c_2). The semantics of this instruction is defined by rewriting it to a combination of other constructs including the BRANCH-instruction and itself. We shall see shortly how this can be used.

The operational semantics of Table 3.1 is indeed a structural operational semantics for **AM**. Corresponding to the derivation sequences of Chapter 2 we shall define a *computation sequence* for **AM**. Given a sequence c of instructions and a storage s, a computation sequence for c and s is either

- a *finite* sequence

  $$\gamma_0, \gamma_1, \gamma_2, \cdots, \gamma_k$$

  of configurations satisfying $\gamma_0 = \langle c, \varepsilon, s\rangle$ and $\gamma_i \rhd \gamma_{i+1}$ for $0 \leq i < k$, $k \geq 0$, and where there is no γ such that $\gamma_k \rhd \gamma$, or it is

- an *infinite* sequence

  $$\gamma_0, \gamma_1, \gamma_2, \cdots$$

  of configurations satisfying $\gamma_0 = \langle c, \varepsilon, s\rangle$ and $\gamma_i \rhd \gamma_{i+1}$ for $0 \leq i$.

Note that initial configurations always have an *empty* evaluation stack. A computation sequence is

- *terminating* if and only if it is finite, and
- *looping* if and only if it is infinite.

A terminating computation sequence may end in a terminal configuration (that is a configuration with an empty code component) or in a stuck configuration (for example $\langle$ADD, ε, $s\rangle$).

Example 3.1 Consider the instruction sequence

PUSH-1:FETCH-**x**:ADD:STORE-**x**

Assuming that the initial storage s has s **x** = **3** we get

$$\begin{aligned}&\langle \text{PUSH-1:FETCH-}\mathbf{x}\text{:ADD:STORE-}\mathbf{x}, \varepsilon, s\rangle\\ &\qquad \rhd \langle \text{FETCH-}\mathbf{x}\text{:ADD:STORE-}\mathbf{x}, \mathbf{1}, s\rangle\\ &\qquad \rhd \langle \text{ADD:STORE-}\mathbf{x}, \mathbf{3{:}1}, s\rangle\\ &\qquad \rhd \langle \text{STORE-}\mathbf{x}, \mathbf{4}, s\rangle\\ &\qquad \rhd \langle \varepsilon, \varepsilon, s[\mathbf{x}\mapsto\mathbf{4}]\rangle\end{aligned}$$

The computation now stops because there is no next step. This is an example of a terminating computation sequence. □

Example 3.2 Consider the code

LOOP(TRUE, NOOP)

We have

$\langle$LOOP(TRUE, NOOP), ε, $s\rangle$

$\triangleright$ $\langle$TRUE:BRANCH(NOOP:LOOP(TRUE, NOOP), NOOP), ε, $s\rangle$

$\triangleright$ $\langle$BRANCH(NOOP:LOOP(TRUE, NOOP), NOOP), **tt**, $s\rangle$

$\triangleright$ $\langle$NOOP:LOOP(TRUE, NOOP), ε, $s\rangle$

$\triangleright$ $\langle$LOOP(TRUE, NOOP), ε, $s\rangle$

$\triangleright$ $\cdots$

and the unfolding of the LOOP-instruction is repeated. This is an example of a looping computation sequence. □

Exercise 3.3 Consider the code

```
PUSH-0:STORE-z:FETCH-x:STORE-r:
LOOP(FETCH-r:FETCH-y:LE,
     FETCH-y:FETCH-r:SUB:STORE-r:
     PUSH-1:FETCH-z:ADD:STORE-z)
```

Determine the function computed by this code. □

Properties of AM

The semantics we have specified for the abstract machine is concerned with the execution of individual instructions and is therefore close in spirit to the structural operational semantics studied in Chapter 2. When proving the correctness of the code generation we shall need a few results analogous to those holding for the structural operational semantics. As their proofs follow the same lines as those for the structural operational semantics we shall leave them as exercises and only *reformulate* the proof technique from Section 2.2:

Induction on the Length of Computation Sequences	
1:	Prove that the property holds for all computation sequences of length 0.
2:	Prove that the property holds for all other computation sequences: Assume that the property holds for all computation sequences of length at most k (this is called the *induction hypothesis*) and show that it holds for computation sequences of length k+1.

The induction step of a proof following this technique will often be done by a case analysis on the first instruction of the code component of the configuration.

Exercise 3.4 (Essential) By analogy with Exercise 2.21 prove that

$$\text{if } \langle c_1,\ e_1,\ s\rangle \ \triangleright^{\mathrm{k}} \langle c',\ e',\ s'\rangle \text{ then } \langle c_1{:}c_2,\ e_1{:}e_2,\ s\rangle \ \triangleright^{\mathrm{k}} \langle c'{:}c_2,\ e'{:}e_2,\ s'\rangle$$

This means that we can extend the code component as well as the stack component without changing the behaviour of the machine. □

Exercise 3.5 (Essential) By analogy with Lemma 2.19 prove that if

$$\langle c_1{:}c_2,\ e,\ s\rangle \ \triangleright^{\mathrm{k}} \langle \varepsilon,\ e'',\ s''\rangle$$

then there exists a configuration $\langle \varepsilon,\ e',\ s'\rangle$ and natural numbers k_1 and k_2 with $\mathrm{k}_1+\mathrm{k}_2=\mathrm{k}$ such that

$$\langle c_1,\ e,\ s\rangle \ \triangleright^{\mathrm{k}_1} \langle \varepsilon,\ e',\ s'\rangle \text{ and } \langle c_2,\ e',\ s'\rangle \ \triangleright^{\mathrm{k}_2} \langle \varepsilon,\ e'',\ s''\rangle$$

This means that the execution of a composite sequence of instructions can be split into two pieces. □

The notion of determinism is defined as for the structural operational semantics. So the semantics of an abstract machine is *deterministic* if for all choices of γ, γ' and γ'':

$$\gamma \ \triangleright \gamma' \text{ and } \gamma \ \triangleright \gamma'' \text{ imply } \gamma' = \gamma''$$

Exercise 3.6 (Essential) Show that the machine semantics of Table 3.1 is deterministic. Deduce that there is exactly one computation sequence starting in a configuration $\langle c,\ e,\ s\rangle$. □

The execution function $\mathcal{M}$

We shall define the *meaning* of a sequence of instructions as a (partial) function from **State** to **State**:

$$\mathcal{M}\text{: } \mathbf{Code} \rightarrow (\mathbf{State} \hookrightarrow \mathbf{State})$$

It is given by

$$\mathcal{M}[\![c]\!]\ s = \begin{cases} s' & \text{if } \langle c,\ \varepsilon,\ s\rangle \ \triangleright^{*} \langle \varepsilon,\ e,\ s'\rangle \\ \underline{\text{undef}} & \text{otherwise} \end{cases}$$

The function is well-defined because of Exercise 3.6. Note that the definition does not require the stack component of the terminal configuration to be empty but it does require the code component to be so.

The abstract machine **AM** may seem far removed from more traditional machine architectures. In the next few exercises we shall gradually bridge this gap.

Exercise 3.7 **AM** refers to variables by their *name* rather than by their *address*. The abstract machine $\mathbf{AM}_1$ differs from **AM** in that

- the configurations have the form $\langle c,\ e,\ m\rangle$ where c and e are as in **AM** and m, the *memory*, is a (finite) list of values, that is $m \in \mathbf{Z}^\star$, and
- the instructions FETCH-x and STORE-x are replaced by instructions GET-n and PUT-n where n is a natural number (an address).

Specify the operational semantics of the machine. You may write $m[n]$ to select the nth value in the list m (when n is positive but less than or equal to the length of m). What happens if we reference an address that is outside the memory? □

Exercise 3.8 The next step is to get rid of the operations BRANCH($\cdots$,$\cdots$) and LOOP($\cdots$,$\cdots$). The idea is to introduce instructions for *defining labels* and for *jumping to labels*. The abstract machine $\mathbf{AM}_2$ differs from $\mathbf{AM}_1$ (of Exercise 3.7) in that

- the configurations have the form $\langle pc,\ c,\ e,\ m\rangle$ where c, e and m are as before and pc is the program counter (a natural number) pointing to an instruction in c, and
- the instructions BRANCH($\cdots$,$\cdots$) and LOOP($\cdots$,$\cdots$) are replaced by the instructions LABEL-l, JUMP-l and JUMPFALSE-l where l is a label (a natural number).

The idea is that we will execute the instruction in c that pc points to and in most cases this will cause the program counter to be incremented by 1. The instruction LABEL-l has no effect except updating the program counter. The instruction JUMP-l will move the program counter to the unique instruction LABEL-l (if it exists). The instruction JUMPFALSE-l will only move the program counter to the instruction LABEL-l if the value on top of the stack is **ff**; if it is **tt** the program counter will be incremented by 1.

Specify an operational semantics for $\mathbf{AM}_2$. You may write $c[pc]$ for the instruction in c pointed to by pc (if pc is positive and less than or equal to the length of c). What happens if the same label is defined more than once? □

Exercise 3.9 Finally, we shall consider an abstract machine $\mathbf{AM}_3$ where the labels of the instructions JUMP-l and JUMPFALSE-l of Exercise 3.8 are *absolute addresses*; so JUMP-7 means jump to the 7th instruction of the code (rather than to the instruction LABEL-7). Specify the operational semantics of the machine. What happens if we jump to an instruction that is not in the code? □

3.2 Specification of the translation

We shall now study how to generate code for the abstract machine.

Expressions

Arithmetic and boolean expressions will be evaluated on the evaluation stack of the machine and the code to be generated must effect this. This is accomplished by the (total) functions

$$\mathcal{CA}\text{: } \mathbf{Aexp} \to \mathbf{Code}$$

and

$$\mathcal{CB}\text{: } \mathbf{Bexp} \to \mathbf{Code}$$

specified in Table 3.2. Note that the code generated for binary expressions consists

$\mathcal{CA}[\![n]\!]$	=	PUSH-n
$\mathcal{CA}[\![x]\!]$	=	FETCH-x
$\mathcal{CA}[\![a_1+a_2]\!]$	=	$\mathcal{CA}[\![a_2]\!]$:$\mathcal{CA}[\![a_1]\!]$:ADD
$\mathcal{CA}[\![a_1 \star a_2]\!]$	=	$\mathcal{CA}[\![a_2]\!]$:$\mathcal{CA}[\![a_1]\!]$:MULT
$\mathcal{CA}[\![a_1-a_2]\!]$	=	$\mathcal{CA}[\![a_2]\!]$:$\mathcal{CA}[\![a_1]\!]$:SUB
$\mathcal{CB}[\![\texttt{true}]\!]$	=	TRUE
$\mathcal{CB}[\![\texttt{false}]\!]$	=	FALSE
$\mathcal{CB}[\![a_1 = a_2]\!]$	=	$\mathcal{CA}[\![a_2]\!]$:$\mathcal{CA}[\![a_1]\!]$:EQ
$\mathcal{CB}[\![a_1 \leq a_2]\!]$	=	$\mathcal{CA}[\![a_2]\!]$:$\mathcal{CA}[\![a_1]\!]$:LE
$\mathcal{CB}[\![\neg b]\!]$	=	$\mathcal{CB}[\![b]\!]$:NEG
$\mathcal{CB}[\![b_1 \wedge b_2]\!]$	=	$\mathcal{CB}[\![b_2]\!]$:$\mathcal{CB}[\![b_1]\!]$:AND

Table 3.2: Translation of expressions

of the code for the *right* argument followed by that for the *left* argument and finally the appropriate instruction for the operator. In this way it is ensured that the arguments appear on the evaluation stack in the order required by the instructions (in Table 3.1). Note that $\mathcal{CA}$ and $\mathcal{CB}$ are defined compositionally.

Example 3.10 For the arithmetic expression `x+1` we calculate the code as follows:

$$\mathcal{CA}[\![\texttt{x+1}]\!] = \mathcal{CA}[\![\texttt{1}]\!]\text{:}\mathcal{CA}[\![\texttt{x}]\!]\text{:ADD} = \text{PUSH-1:FETCH-}x\text{:ADD}$$ □

Exercise 3.11 It is clear that $\mathcal{A}[\![(a_1+a_2)+a_3]\!]$ equals $\mathcal{A}[\![a_1+(a_2+a_3)]\!]$. Show that it is *not* the case that $\mathcal{CA}[\![(a_1+a_2)+a_3]\!]$ equals $\mathcal{CA}[\![a_1+(a_2+a_3)]\!]$. Nonetheless, show that $\mathcal{CA}[\![(a_1+a_2)+a_3]\!]$ and $\mathcal{CA}[\![a_1+(a_2+a_3)]\!]$ do in fact *behave* similar to one another. □

Statements

The translation of statements into abstract machine code is given by the (total) function

$\mathcal{CS}$: **Stm** → **Code**

specified in Table 3.3. The code generated for an arithmetic expression a ensures

$\mathcal{CS}[\![x := a]\!]$	$=$	$\mathcal{CA}[\![a]\!]$:STORE-x
$\mathcal{CS}[\![$`skip`$]\!]$	$=$	NOOP
$\mathcal{CS}[\![S_1;S_2]\!]$	$=$	$\mathcal{CS}[\![S_1]\!]$:$\mathcal{CS}[\![S_2]\!]$
$\mathcal{CS}[\![$`if` b `then` S_1 `else` $S_2]\!]$	$=$	$\mathcal{CB}[\![b]\!]$:BRANCH($\mathcal{CS}[\![S_1]\!]$,$\mathcal{CS}[\![S_2]\!]$)
$\mathcal{CS}[\![$`while` b `do` $S]\!]$	$=$	LOOP($\mathcal{CB}[\![b]\!]$,$\mathcal{CS}[\![S]\!]$)

Table 3.3: Translation of statements in **While**

that the value of the expression is on top of the evaluation stack when it has been computed. So in the code for $x := a$ it suffices to append the code for a with the instruction STORE-x. This instruction assigns x the appropriate value and additionally pops the stack. For the `skip`-statement we generate the NOOP-instruction. For sequencing of statements we just concatenate the two instruction sequences. When generating code for the conditional, the code for the boolean expression will ensure that a truth value will be placed on top of the evaluation stack and the BRANCH-instruction will then inspect (and pop) that value and select the appropriate piece of code. Finally, the code for the `while`-construct uses the LOOP-instruction. Again we may note that $\mathcal{CS}$ is defined in a compositional manner.

Example 3.12 The code generated for the factorial statement considered earlier is as follows:

$\mathcal{CS}[\![$y:=1; `while` ¬(x=1) `do` (y:=y ⋆ x; x:=x−1)$]\!]$

= $\mathcal{CS}[\![$y:=1$]\!]$:$\mathcal{CS}[\![$`while` ¬(x=1) `do` (y:=y ⋆ x; x:=x−1)$]\!]$

= $\mathcal{CA}[\![$1$]\!]$:STORE-y:LOOP($\mathcal{CB}[\![$¬(x=1)$]\!]$,$\mathcal{CS}[\![$y:=y ⋆ x; x:=x−1$]\!]$)

= PUSH-1:STORE-y:LOOP($\mathcal{CB}[\![$x=1$]\!]$:NEG,$\mathcal{CS}[\![$y:=y ⋆ x$]\!]$:$\mathcal{CS}[\![$x:=x−1$]\!]$)

⋮

= PUSH-1:STORE-y:LOOP(PUSH-1:FETCH-x:EQ:NEG,

FETCH-x:FETCH-y:MULT:STORE-y:

PUSH-1:FETCH-x:SUB:STORE-x) □

Exercise 3.13 Use $\mathcal{CS}$ to generate code for the statement

`z:=0; while y≤x do (z:=z+1; x:=x−y)`

Trace the computation of the code starting from a storage where **x** is **17** and **y** is **5**. □

Exercise 3.14 Extend **While** with the construct `repeat` S `until` b and specify how to generate code for it. Note that the definition has to be compositional and that it is *not* necessary to extend the instruction set of the abstract machine. □

Exercise 3.15 Extend **While** with the construct `for` x := a_1 `to` a_2 `do` S and specify how to generate code for it. As in Exercise 3.14 the definition has to be compositional but you may have to introduce an instruction COPY that duplicates the element on top of the evaluation stack. □

The semantic function $\mathcal{S}_{\mathrm{am}}$

The meaning of a statement S can now be obtained by first translating it into code for **AM** and next executing the code on the abstract machine. The effect of this is expressed by the function

$$\mathcal{S}_{\mathrm{am}}\colon \mathbf{Stm} \to (\mathbf{State} \hookrightarrow \mathbf{State})$$

defined by

$$\mathcal{S}_{\mathrm{am}}[\![S]\!] = (\mathcal{M} \circ \mathcal{CS})[\![S]\!]$$

Exercise 3.16 Modify the code generation so as to translate **While** into code for the abstract machine $\mathbf{AM}_1$ of Exercise 3.7. You may assume the existence of a function

$$env\colon \mathbf{Var} \to \mathbf{N}$$

that maps variables to their addresses. Apply the code generation function to the factorial statement of Example 1.1 and execute the code so obtained starting from a storage where **x** is **3**. □

Exercise 3.17 Modify the code generation so as to translate **While** into code for the abstract machine $\mathbf{AM}_2$ of Exercise 3.8. Be careful to generate unique labels, for example by having "the next unused label" as an additional parameter to the code generation functions. Apply the code generation function to the factorial statement and execute the code so obtained starting from a storage where **x** has the value **3**. □

3.3 Correctness

The correctness of the implementation amounts to showing that, if we first translate a statement into code for **AM** and then execute that code, then we must obtain the same result as specified by the operational semantics of **While**.

Expressions

The correctness of the implementation of arithmetic expressions is expressed by the following lemma:

Lemma 3.18 For all arithmetic expressions a we have

$$\langle \mathcal{CA}[\![a]\!],\ \varepsilon,\ s\rangle \ \rhd^* \langle \varepsilon,\ \mathcal{A}[\![a]\!]s,\ s\rangle$$

Furthermore, all intermediate configurations of this computation sequence will have a non-empty evaluation stack.

Proof: The proof is by structural induction on a. Below we shall give the proof for three illustrative cases, leaving the remaining ones as an exercise.

The case n: We have $\mathcal{CA}[\![n]\!] = \text{PUSH-}n$ and from Table 3.1 we get

$$\langle \text{PUSH-}n,\ \varepsilon,\ s\rangle \ \rhd \langle \varepsilon,\ \mathcal{N}[\![n]\!],\ s\rangle$$

Since $\mathcal{A}[\![n]\!]s = \mathcal{N}[\![n]\!]$ (see Table 1.1) we have completed the proof in this case.

The case x: We have $\mathcal{CA}[\![x]\!] = \text{FETCH-}x$ and from Table 3.1 we get

$$\langle \text{FETCH-}x,\ \varepsilon,\ s\rangle \ \rhd \langle \varepsilon,\ (s\ x),\ s\rangle$$

Since $\mathcal{A}[\![x]\!]s = s\ x$ this is the required result.

The case a_1+a_2: We have $\mathcal{CA}[\![a_1+a_2]\!] = \mathcal{CA}[\![a_2]\!]{:}\mathcal{CA}[\![a_1]\!]{:}\text{ADD}$. The induction hypothesis applied to a_1 and a_2 gives that

$$\langle \mathcal{CA}[\![a_1]\!],\ \varepsilon,\ s\rangle \ \rhd^* \langle \varepsilon,\ \mathcal{A}[\![a_1]\!]s,\ s\rangle$$

and

$$\langle \mathcal{CA}[\![a_2]\!],\ \varepsilon,\ s\rangle \ \rhd^* \langle \varepsilon,\ \mathcal{A}[\![a_2]\!]s,\ s\rangle$$

In both cases all intermediate configurations will have a non-empty evaluation stack. Using Exercise 3.4 we get that

$$\langle \mathcal{CA}[\![a_2]\!]{:}\mathcal{CA}[\![a_1]\!]{:}\text{ADD},\ \varepsilon,\ s\rangle \ \rhd^* \langle \mathcal{CA}[\![a_1]\!]{:}\text{ADD},\ \mathcal{A}[\![a_2]\!]s,\ s\rangle$$

Applying the exercise once more we get that

$$\langle \mathcal{CA}[\![a_1]\!]\text{:ADD},\ \mathcal{A}[\![a_2]\!]s,\ s\rangle \ \triangleright^*\ \langle \text{ADD},\ (\mathcal{A}[\![a_1]\!]s)\text{:}(\mathcal{A}[\![a_2]\!]s),\ s\rangle$$

Using the transition relation for ADD given in Table 3.1 we get

$$\langle \text{ADD},\ (\mathcal{A}[\![a_1]\!]s)\text{:}(\mathcal{A}[\![a_2]\!]s),\ s\rangle \ \triangleright\ \langle \varepsilon,\ \mathcal{A}[\![a_1]\!]s+\mathcal{A}[\![a_2]\!]s,\ s\rangle$$

It is easy to check that all intermediate configurations have a non-empty evaluation stack. Since $\mathcal{A}[\![a_1+a_2]\!]s = \mathcal{A}[\![a_1]\!]s + \mathcal{A}[\![a_2]\!]s$ we have the desired result. □

We have a similar result for boolean expressions:

Exercise 3.19 (Essential) Show that for all boolean expressions b we have

$$\langle \mathcal{CB}[\![b]\!],\ \varepsilon,\ s\rangle \ \triangleright^*\ \langle \varepsilon,\ \mathcal{B}[\![b]\!]s,\ s\rangle$$

Furthermore, show that all intermediate configurations of this computation sequence will have a non-empty evaluation stack. □

Statements

When formulating the correctness of the result for statements we have a choice between using

- the natural semantics, or
- the structural operational semantics.

Here we shall use the natural semantics but in the next section we sketch the proof in the case where the structural operational semantics is used.

The correctness of the translation of statements is expressed by the following theorem:

Theorem 3.20 For every statement S of **While** we have $\mathcal{S}_{\mathrm{ns}}[\![S]\!] = \mathcal{S}_{\mathrm{am}}[\![S]\!]$.

This theorem relates the behaviour of a statement under the natural semantics with the behaviour of the code on the abstract machine under its operational semantics. In analogy with Theorem 2.26 it expresses two properties:

- If the execution of S from some state terminates in one of the semantics then it also terminates in the other and the resulting states will be equal.
- Furthermore, if the execution of S from some state loops in one of the semantics then it will also loop in the other.

The theorem is proved in two stages as expressed by Lemmas 3.21 and 3.22 below. We shall first prove:

Lemma 3.21 For every statement S of **While** and states s and s', we have that

$$\text{if } \langle S,\ s\rangle \to s' \text{ then } \langle \mathcal{CS}[\![S]\!],\ \varepsilon,\ s\rangle \ \rhd^* \ \langle \varepsilon,\ \varepsilon,\ s'\rangle$$

So if the execution of S from s terminates in the natural semantics then the execution of the code for S from storage s will terminate and the resulting states and storages will be equal.

Proof: We proceed by induction on the shape of the derivation tree for $\langle S,\ s\rangle \to s'$.

The case [ass$_{\text{ns}}$]: We assume that

$$\langle x{:=}a,\ s\rangle \to s'$$

where $s'{=}s[x{\mapsto}\mathcal{A}[\![a]\!]s]$. From Table 3.3 we have

$$\mathcal{CS}[\![x{:=}a]\!] = \mathcal{CA}[\![a]\!]{:}\text{STORE-}x$$

From Lemma 3.18 applied to a we get

$$\langle \mathcal{CA}[\![a]\!],\ \varepsilon,\ s\rangle \ \rhd^* \ \langle \varepsilon,\ \mathcal{A}[\![a]\!]s,\ s\rangle$$

and then Exercise 3.4 gives the first part of

$$\begin{aligned}\langle \mathcal{CA}[\![a]\!]{:}\text{STORE-}x,\ \varepsilon,\ s\rangle \ &\rhd^* \ \langle \text{STORE-}x,\ (\mathcal{A}[\![a]\!]s),\ s\rangle\\ &\rhd \ \langle \varepsilon,\ \varepsilon,\ s[x{\mapsto}\mathcal{A}[\![a]\!]s]\rangle\end{aligned}$$

and the second part follows from the operational semantics for STORE-x given in Table 3.1. Since $s' = s[x{\mapsto}\mathcal{A}[\![a]\!]s]$ this completes the proof.

The case [skip$_{\text{ns}}$]: Straightforward.

The case [comp$_{\text{ns}}$]: Assume that

$$\langle S_1{;}S_2,\ s\rangle \to s''$$

holds because

$$\langle S_1,\ s\rangle \to s' \text{ and } \langle S_2,\ s'\rangle \to s''$$

From Table 3.3 we have

$$\mathcal{CS}[\![S_1{;}S_2]\!] = \mathcal{CS}[\![S_1]\!]{:}\mathcal{CS}[\![S_2]\!]$$

We shall now apply the induction hypothesis to the premises $\langle S_1,\ s\rangle \to s'$ and $\langle S_2,\ s'\rangle \to s''$ and we get

$$\langle \mathcal{CS}[\![S_1]\!],\ \varepsilon,\ s\rangle \ \rhd^* \ \langle \varepsilon,\ \varepsilon,\ s'\rangle$$

and

$$\langle \mathcal{CS}[\![S_2]\!],\ \varepsilon,\ s'\rangle \ \triangleright^* \ \langle \varepsilon,\ \varepsilon,\ s''\rangle$$

Using Exercise 3.4 we then have

$$\langle \mathcal{CS}[\![S_1]\!]{:}\mathcal{CS}[\![S_2]\!],\ \varepsilon,\ s\rangle \ \triangleright^* \ \langle \mathcal{CS}[\![S_2]\!],\ \varepsilon,\ s'\rangle \ \triangleright^* \ \langle \varepsilon,\ \varepsilon,\ s''\rangle$$

and the result follows.

The case $[\text{if}_{\text{ns}}^{\text{tt}}]$: Assume that

$$\langle \texttt{if } b \texttt{ then } S_1 \texttt{ else } S_2,\ s\rangle \to s'$$

because $\mathcal{B}[\![b]\!]s = \mathbf{tt}$ and

$$\langle S_1,\ s\rangle \to s'$$

From Table 3.3 we get that

$$\mathcal{CS}[\![\texttt{if } b \texttt{ then } S_1 \texttt{ else } S_2]\!] = \mathcal{CB}[\![b]\!]{:}\text{BRANCH}(\mathcal{CS}[\![S_1]\!],\ \mathcal{CS}[\![S_2]\!])$$

Using Exercises 3.19 and 3.4 we get the first part of

$$\begin{aligned}
&\langle \mathcal{CB}[\![b]\!]{:}\text{BRANCH}(\mathcal{CS}[\![S_1]\!],\ \mathcal{CS}[\![S_2]\!]),\ \varepsilon,\ s\rangle\\
&\qquad \triangleright^* \ \langle \text{BRANCH}(\mathcal{CS}[\![S_1]\!],\ \mathcal{CS}[\![S_2]\!]),\ (\mathcal{B}[\![b]\!]s),\ s\rangle\\
&\qquad \triangleright \ \langle \mathcal{CS}[\![S_1]\!],\ \varepsilon,\ s\rangle\\
&\qquad \triangleright^* \ \langle \varepsilon,\ \varepsilon,\ s'\rangle
\end{aligned}$$

The second part follows from the definition of the meaning of the instruction BRANCH in the case where the element on top of the evaluation stack is **tt** (which is the value of $\mathcal{B}[\![b]\!]s$). The third part of the computation sequence comes from applying the induction hypothesis to the premise $\langle S_1,\ s\rangle \to s'$.

The case $[\text{if}_{\text{ns}}^{\text{ff}}]$: Analogous.

The case $[\text{while}_{\text{ns}}^{\text{tt}}]$: Assume that

$$\langle \texttt{while } b \texttt{ do } S,\ s\rangle \to s''$$

because $\mathcal{B}[\![b]\!]s = \mathbf{tt}$,

$$\langle S,\ s\rangle \to s' \text{ and } \langle \texttt{while } b \texttt{ do } S,\ s'\rangle \to s''$$

From Table 3.3 we have

$$\mathcal{CS}[\![\texttt{while } b \texttt{ do } S]\!] = \text{LOOP}(\mathcal{CB}[\![b]\!],\ \mathcal{CS}[\![S]\!])$$

and get

$$\begin{aligned}&\langle \text{LOOP}(\mathcal{CB}[\![b]\!], \mathcal{CS}[\![S]\!]), \varepsilon, s\rangle\\ &\quad\rhd \langle \mathcal{CB}[\![b]\!]{:}\text{BRANCH}(\mathcal{CS}[\![S]\!]{:}\text{LOOP}(\mathcal{CB}[\![b]\!], \mathcal{CS}[\![S]\!]), \text{NOOP}), \varepsilon, s\rangle\\ &\quad\rhd^* \langle \text{BRANCH}(\mathcal{CS}[\![S]\!]{:}\text{LOOP}(\mathcal{CB}[\![b]\!], \mathcal{CS}[\![S]\!]), \text{NOOP}), (\mathcal{B}[\![b]\!]s), s\rangle\\ &\quad\rhd \langle \mathcal{CS}[\![S]\!]{:}\text{LOOP}(\mathcal{CB}[\![b]\!], \mathcal{CS}[\![S]\!]), \varepsilon, s\rangle\end{aligned}$$

Here the first part follows from the meaning of the LOOP-instruction (see Table 3.1) and the second part from Exercises 3.19 and 3.4. Since $\mathcal{B}[\![b]\!]s = \mathbf{tt}$ the third part follows from the meaning of the BRANCH-instruction. The induction hypothesis can now be applied to the premises $\langle S, s\rangle \to s'$ and $\langle \texttt{while}\ b\ \texttt{do}\ S, s'\rangle \to s''$ and gives

$$\begin{aligned}&\langle \mathcal{CS}[\![S]\!], \varepsilon, s\rangle \ \rhd^* \langle \varepsilon, \varepsilon, s'\rangle\\ &\langle \text{LOOP}(\mathcal{CB}[\![b]\!], \mathcal{CS}[\![S]\!]), \varepsilon, s'\rangle \ \rhd^* \langle \varepsilon, \varepsilon, s''\rangle\end{aligned}$$

so using Exercise 3.4 we get

$$\begin{aligned}&\langle \mathcal{CS}[\![S]\!]{:}\text{LOOP}(\mathcal{CB}[\![b]\!], \mathcal{CS}[\![S]\!]), \varepsilon, s\rangle\\ &\quad\rhd^* \langle \text{LOOP}(\mathcal{CB}[\![b]\!], \mathcal{CS}[\![S]\!]), \varepsilon, s'\rangle\\ &\quad\rhd^* \langle \varepsilon, \varepsilon, s''\rangle\end{aligned}$$

The case [while$^{\text{ff}}_{\text{ns}}$]: Assume that $\langle \texttt{while}\ b\ \texttt{do}\ S, s\rangle \to s'$ holds because $\mathcal{B}[\![b]\!]s = \mathbf{ff}$ and then $s = s'$. We have

$$\begin{aligned}&\langle \text{LOOP}(\mathcal{CB}[\![b]\!], \mathcal{CS}[\![S]\!]), \varepsilon, s\rangle\\ &\quad\rhd \langle \mathcal{CB}[\![b]\!]{:}\text{BRANCH}(\mathcal{CS}[\![S]\!]{:}\text{LOOP}(\mathcal{CB}[\![b]\!], \mathcal{CS}[\![S]\!]), \text{NOOP}), \varepsilon, s\rangle\\ &\quad\rhd^* \langle \text{BRANCH}(\mathcal{CS}[\![S]\!]{:}\text{LOOP}(\mathcal{CB}[\![b]\!], \mathcal{CS}[\![S]\!]), \text{NOOP}), (\mathcal{B}[\![b]\!]s), s\rangle\\ &\quad\rhd \langle \text{NOOP}, \varepsilon, s\rangle\\ &\quad\rhd \langle \varepsilon, \varepsilon, s\rangle\end{aligned}$$

using the definitions of the LOOP-, BRANCH- and NOOP-instructions in Table 3.1 together with Exercises 3.19 and 3.4. □

This proves Lemma 3.21. The second part of the theorem follows from:

Lemma 3.22 For every statement S of **While** and states s and s', we have that

$$\text{if } \langle \mathcal{CS}[\![S]\!], \varepsilon, s\rangle \ \rhd^k \langle \varepsilon, e, s'\rangle \text{ then } \langle S, s\rangle \to s' \text{ and } e = \varepsilon$$

So if the execution of the code for S from a storage s terminates then the natural semantics of S from s will terminate in a state being equal to the storage of the terminal configuration.

Proof: We shall proceed by induction on the length k of the computation sequence of the abstract machine. If $k = 0$ the result holds vacuously because $\mathcal{CS}[\![S]\!] = \varepsilon$ cannot occur. So assume that it holds for $k \leq k_0$ and we shall prove that it holds for $k = k_0+1$. We proceed by cases on the statement S.

The case $x{:=}a$: We then have $\mathcal{CS}[\![x := a]\!] = \mathcal{CA}[\![a]\!]{:}\text{STORE-}x$ so assume that

$$\langle \mathcal{CA}[\![a]\!]{:}\text{STORE-}x,\ \varepsilon,\ s\rangle \rhd^{k_0+1} \langle \varepsilon,\ e,\ s'\rangle$$

Then by Exercise 3.5 there must be a configuration of the form $\langle \varepsilon,\ e'',\ s''\rangle$ such that

$$\langle \mathcal{CA}[\![a]\!],\ \varepsilon,\ s\rangle \rhd^{k_1} \langle \varepsilon,\ e'',\ s''\rangle$$
$$\langle \text{STORE-}x,\ e'',\ s''\rangle \rhd^{k_2} \langle \varepsilon,\ e,\ s'\rangle$$

where $k_1 + k_2 = k_0 + 1$. From Lemma 3.18 and Exercise 3.6 we get that e'' must be $(\mathcal{A}[\![a]\!]s)$ and s'' must be s. Using the semantics of STORE-x we therefore see that s' is $s[x \mapsto \mathcal{A}[\![a]\!]s]$ and e is ε. It now follows from [ass$_{ns}$] that $\langle x{:=}a,\ s\rangle \to s'$.

The case skip: Straightforward.

The case $S_1;S_2$: Assume that

$$\langle \mathcal{CS}[\![S_1]\!]{:}\mathcal{CS}[\![S_2]\!],\ \varepsilon,\ s\rangle \rhd^{k_0+1} \langle \varepsilon,\ e,\ s''\rangle$$

Then by Exercise 3.5 there must be a configuration of the form $\langle \varepsilon,\ e',\ s'\rangle$ such that

$$\langle \mathcal{CS}[\![S_1]\!],\ \varepsilon,\ s\rangle \rhd^{k_1} \langle \varepsilon,\ e',\ s'\rangle$$
$$\langle \mathcal{CS}[\![S_2]\!],\ e',\ s'\rangle \rhd^{k_2} \langle \varepsilon,\ e,\ s''\rangle$$

where $k_1 + k_2 = k_0 + 1$. The induction hypothesis can now be applied to the first of these computation sequences because $k_1 \leq k_0$ and gives

$$\langle S_1,\ s\rangle \to s' \text{ and } e' = \varepsilon$$

Thus we have $\langle \mathcal{CS}[\![S_2]\!],\ \varepsilon,\ s'\rangle \rhd^{k_2} \langle \varepsilon,\ e,\ s''\rangle$ and since $k_2 \leq k_0$ the induction hypothesis can be applied to this computation sequence and gives

$$\langle S_2,\ s'\rangle \to s'' \text{ and } e = \varepsilon$$

The rule [comp$_{ns}$] now gives $\langle S_1;S_2,\ s\rangle \to s''$ as required.

The case `if` b `then` S_1 `else` S_2: The code generated for the conditional is

$$\mathcal{CB}[\![b]\!]{:}\text{BRANCH}(\mathcal{CS}[\![S_1]\!],\ \mathcal{CS}[\![S_2]\!])$$

so we assume that

$$\langle \mathcal{CB}[\![b]\!]{:}\text{BRANCH}(\mathcal{CS}[\![S_1]\!],\ \mathcal{CS}[\![S_2]\!]),\ \varepsilon,\ s\rangle \rhd^{k_0+1} \langle \varepsilon,\ e,\ s'\rangle$$

Then by Exercise 3.5 there must be a configuration of the form $\langle \varepsilon,\ e'',\ s'' \rangle$ such that

$$\langle \mathcal{CB}[\![b]\!],\ \varepsilon,\ s \rangle \ \triangleright^{\mathrm{k}_1}\ \langle \varepsilon,\ e'',\ s'' \rangle$$

and

$$\langle \mathrm{BRANCH}(\mathcal{CS}[\![S_1]\!],\ \mathcal{CS}[\![S_2]\!]),\ e'',\ s'' \rangle \ \triangleright^{\mathrm{k}_2}\ \langle \varepsilon,\ e,\ s' \rangle$$

where $\mathrm{k}_1 + \mathrm{k}_2 = \mathrm{k}_0 + 1$. From Exercises 3.19 and 3.6 we get that e'' must be $\mathcal{B}[\![b]\!]s$ and s'' must be s. We shall now assume that $\mathcal{B}[\![b]\!]s = \mathbf{tt}$. Then there must be a configuration $\langle \mathcal{CS}[\![S_1]\!],\ \varepsilon,\ s \rangle$ such that

$$\langle \mathcal{CS}[\![S_1]\!],\ \varepsilon,\ s \rangle \ \triangleright^{\mathrm{k}_2 - 1}\ \langle \varepsilon,\ e,\ s' \rangle$$

The induction hypothesis can now be applied to this computation sequence because $\mathrm{k}_2 - 1 \leq \mathrm{k}_0$ and we get

$$\langle S_1,\ s \rangle \to s' \text{ and } e = \varepsilon$$

The rule $[\mathrm{if}^{\mathrm{tt}}_{\mathrm{ns}}]$ gives the required $\langle \texttt{if}\ b\ \texttt{then}\ S_1\ \texttt{else}\ S_2,\ s \rangle \to s'$. The case where $\mathcal{B}[\![b]\!]s = \mathbf{ff}$ is similar.

The case `while` b `do` S: The code for the `while`-loop is $\mathrm{LOOP}(\mathcal{CB}[\![b]\!],\ \mathcal{CS}[\![S]\!])$ and we therefore assume that

$$\langle \mathrm{LOOP}(\mathcal{CB}[\![b]\!],\ \mathcal{CS}[\![S]\!]),\ \varepsilon,\ s \rangle \ \triangleright^{\mathrm{k}_0 + 1}\ \langle \varepsilon,\ e,\ s'' \rangle$$

Using the definition of the LOOP-instruction this means that the computation sequence can be rewritten as

$$\begin{aligned} &\langle \mathrm{LOOP}(\mathcal{CB}[\![b]\!],\ \mathcal{CS}[\![S]\!]),\ \varepsilon,\ s \rangle \\ &\quad \triangleright\ \langle \mathcal{CB}[\![b]\!]{:}\mathrm{BRANCH}(\mathcal{CS}[\![S]\!]{:}\mathrm{LOOP}(\mathcal{CB}[\![b]\!],\ \mathcal{CS}[\![S]\!]),\ \mathrm{NOOP}),\ \varepsilon,\ s \rangle \\ &\quad \triangleright^{\mathrm{k}_0}\ \langle \varepsilon,\ e,\ s'' \rangle \end{aligned}$$

According to Exercise 3.5 there will then be a configuration $\langle \varepsilon,\ e',\ s' \rangle$ such that

$$\langle \mathcal{CB}[\![b]\!],\ \varepsilon,\ s \rangle \ \triangleright^{\mathrm{k}_1}\ \langle \varepsilon,\ e',\ s' \rangle$$

and

$$\langle \mathrm{BRANCH}(\mathcal{CS}[\![S]\!]{:}\mathrm{LOOP}(\mathcal{CB}[\![b]\!],\ \mathcal{CS}[\![S]\!]),\ \mathrm{NOOP}),\ e',\ s' \rangle \ \triangleright^{\mathrm{k}_2}\ \langle \varepsilon,\ e,\ s'' \rangle$$

where $\mathrm{k}_1 + \mathrm{k}_2 = \mathrm{k}_0$. From Exercises 3.19 and 3.6 we get $e' = \mathcal{B}[\![b]\!]s$ and $s' = s$. We now have two cases.

In the first case assume that $\mathcal{B}[\![b]\!]s = \mathbf{ff}$. We then have

$$\begin{aligned}&\langle \text{BRANCH}(\mathcal{CS}[\![S]\!]{:}\text{LOOP}(\mathcal{CB}[\![b]\!], \mathcal{CS}[\![S]\!]), \text{NOOP}), \mathcal{B}[\![b]\!]s, s\rangle\\ &\qquad \rhd \langle \text{NOOP}, \varepsilon, s\rangle\\ &\qquad \rhd \langle \varepsilon, \varepsilon, s\rangle\end{aligned}$$

so $e = \varepsilon$ and $s = s''$. Using rule [while$^{\text{ff}}_{\text{ns}}$] we get $\langle \texttt{while}\ b\ \texttt{do}\ S, s\rangle \to s''$ as required.

In the second case assume that $\mathcal{B}[\![b]\!]s = \mathbf{tt}$. Then we have

$$\begin{aligned}&\langle \text{BRANCH}(\mathcal{CS}[\![S]\!]{:}\text{LOOP}(\mathcal{CB}[\![b]\!], \mathcal{CS}[\![S]\!]), \text{NOOP}), \mathcal{B}[\![b]\!]s, s\rangle\\ &\qquad \rhd \quad \langle \mathcal{CS}[\![S]\!]{:}\text{LOOP}(\mathcal{CB}[\![b]\!], \mathcal{CS}[\![S]\!]), \varepsilon, s\rangle\\ &\qquad \rhd^{\text{k}_2-1} \langle \varepsilon, e, s''\rangle\end{aligned}$$

We then proceed very much as in the case of the composition statement and get a configuration $\langle \varepsilon, e', s'\rangle$ such that

$$\begin{aligned}&\langle \mathcal{CS}[\![S]\!], \varepsilon, s\rangle \rhd^{\text{k}_3} \langle \varepsilon, e', s'\rangle\\ &\langle \text{LOOP}(\mathcal{CB}[\![b]\!], \mathcal{CS}[\![S]\!]), e', s'\rangle \rhd^{\text{k}_4} \langle \varepsilon, e, s''\rangle\end{aligned}$$

where $\text{k}_3 + \text{k}_4 = \text{k}_2 - 1$. Since $\text{k}_3 \le \text{k}_0$ we can apply the induction hypothesis to the first of these computation sequences and get

$$\langle S, s\rangle \to s' \text{ and } e' = \varepsilon$$

We can then use that $\text{k}_4 \le \text{k}_0$ and apply the induction hypothesis to the computation sequence $\langle \text{LOOP}(\mathcal{CB}[\![b]\!], \mathcal{CS}[\![S]\!]), \varepsilon, s'\rangle \rhd^{\text{k}_4} \langle \varepsilon, e, s''\rangle$ and get

$$\langle \texttt{while}\ b\ \texttt{do}\ S, s'\rangle \to s'' \text{ and } e = \varepsilon$$

Using rule [while$^{\text{tt}}_{\text{ns}}$] we then get $\langle \texttt{while}\ b\ \texttt{do}\ S, s\rangle \to s''$ as required. This completes the proof of the lemma. □

The proof technique employed in the above proof may be summarized as follows:

Proof Summary for While:

Correctness of Implementation

1: Prove by *induction on the shape of derivation trees* that for each derivation tree in the natural semantics there is a corresponding finite computation sequence on the abstract machine.

2: Prove by *induction on the length of computation sequences* that for each finite computation sequence obtained from executing a statement of **While** on the abstract machine there is a corresponding derivation tree in the natural semantics.

Note the *similarities* between this proof technique and that for showing the equivalence of two operational semantics (see Section 2.3). Again one has to be careful when adapting this approach to a language with additional programming constructs or a different machine language.

Exercise 3.23 Consider the "optimized" code generation function $\mathcal{CS}'$ that is as $\mathcal{CS}$ except of Table 3.3 except that $\mathcal{CS}'[\![\texttt{skip}]\!] = \varepsilon$. Would this complicate the proof of Theorem 3.20? □

Exercise 3.24 Extend the proof of Theorem 3.20 to hold for the **While** language extended with `repeat` S `until` b. The code generated for this construct was studied in Exercise 3.14 and its natural semantics in Exercise 2.7. □

Exercise 3.25 Prove that the code generated for $\mathbf{AM}_1$ in Exercise 3.16 is correct. What assumptions do you need to make about *env*? □

3.4 An alternative proof technique

In Theorem 3.20 we proved the correctness of the implementation with respect to the natural semantics. It is obvious that the implementation will also be correct with respect to the structural operational semantics, that is

$$\mathcal{S}_{\text{sos}}[\![S]\!] = \mathcal{S}_{\text{am}}[\![S]\!] \text{ for all statements } S \text{ of } \mathbf{While}$$

because we showed in Theorem 2.26 that the natural semantics is equivalent to the structural operational semantics. However, one might argue that it would be easier to give a direct proof of the correctness of the implementation with respect to the structural operational semantics, because both approaches are based on the idea of specifying the individual steps of the computation. We shall comment upon this shortly.

A direct proof of the correctness result with respect to the structural operational semantics could proceed as follows. We shall define a *bisimulation* relation $\approx$ between the configurations of the structural operational semantics and those of the operational semantics for **AM**. It is defined by

$$\begin{aligned} \langle S, s\rangle &\approx \langle \mathcal{CS}[\![S]\!], \varepsilon, s\rangle \\ s &\approx \langle \varepsilon, \varepsilon, s\rangle \end{aligned}$$

for all statements S and states s. The first stage will then be to prove that whenever *one* step of the structural operational semantics *changes* the configuration then there is a *sequence* of steps in the semantics of **AM** that will make a *similar change* in the configuration of the abstract machine:

Exercise 3.26 * Show that if

$$\gamma_{\text{sos}} \approx \gamma_{\text{am}} \text{ and } \gamma_{\text{sos}} \Rightarrow \gamma'_{\text{sos}}$$

then there exists a configuration γ'_{am} such that

$$\gamma_{\text{am}} \rhd^{+} \gamma'_{\text{am}} \text{ and } \gamma'_{\text{sos}} \approx \gamma'_{\text{am}}$$

Argue that this means that if $\langle S,\ s\rangle \Rightarrow^{*} s'$ then $\langle \mathcal{CS}[\![S]\!],\ \varepsilon,\ s\rangle \rhd^{*} \langle \varepsilon,\ \varepsilon,\ s'\rangle$. □

The second part of the proof is to show that whenever **AM** makes a sequence of moves from a configuration with an *empty* evaluation stack to another configuration with an *empty* evaluation stack, then the structural operational semantics can make a similar change of configurations. Note that **AM** may have to make more than one step to arrive at a configuration with an empty stack, due to the way it evaluates expressions; in the structural operational semantics, however, expressions are evaluated as part of a single step.

Exercise 3.27 ** Assume that $\gamma_{\text{sos}} \approx \gamma^{1}_{\text{am}}$ and

$$\gamma^{1}_{\text{am}} \rhd \gamma^{2}_{\text{am}} \rhd \cdots \rhd \gamma^{k}_{\text{am}}$$

where k>1 and only γ^{1}_{am} and γ^{k}_{am} have empty evaluation stacks (that is, are of the form $\langle c,\ \varepsilon,\ s\rangle$). Show that there exists a configuration γ'_{sos} such that

$$\gamma_{\text{sos}} \Rightarrow \gamma'_{\text{sos}} \text{ and } \gamma'_{\text{sos}} \approx \gamma^{k}_{\text{am}}$$

Argue that this means that if $\langle \mathcal{CS}[\![S]\!],\ \varepsilon,\ s\rangle \rhd^{*} \langle \varepsilon,\ \varepsilon,\ s'\rangle$ then $\langle S,\ s\rangle \Rightarrow^{*} s'$. □

Exercise 3.28 Show that Exercises 3.26 and 3.27 together constitute a direct proof of $\mathcal{S}_{\text{sos}}[\![S]\!] = \mathcal{S}_{\text{am}}[\![S]\!]$, for all statements S of **While**. □

The success of this approach relies on the two semantics proceeding in *lock-step*: that one is able to find configurations in the two derivation sequences that correspond to one another (as specified by the bisimulation relation). Often this is not possible and then one has to raise the level of abstraction for one of the semantics. This is exactly what happens when the structural operational semantics is replaced by the natural semantics: we do not care about the individual steps of the execution but only on the result.

The proof technique employed in the above sketch of proof may be summarized as follows:

Proof Summary for While:	
Correctness of Implementation using Bisimulation	
1:	Prove that one step in the structural operational semantics can be simulated by a non-empty sequence of steps on the abstract machine. Show that this extends to sequences of steps in the structural operational semantics.
2:	Prove that a carefully selected non-empty sequence of steps on the abstract machine can be simulated by a step in the structural operational semantics. Show that this extends to more general sequences of steps on the abstract machine.

Again, this method needs to be modified when considering a programming language with additional constructs or a different abstract machine.

Exercise 3.29 * Consider the following, seemingly innocent, modification of the structural operational semantics of Table 2.2 in which [while$_{\text{sos}}$] is replaced by the two axioms:

$$\langle \texttt{while}\ b\ \texttt{do}\ S,\ s\rangle \Rightarrow \langle S;\ \texttt{while}\ b\ \texttt{do}\ S,\ s\rangle \text{ if } \mathcal{B}[\![b]\!]s = \mathbf{tt}$$

$$\langle \texttt{while}\ b\ \texttt{do}\ S,\ s\rangle \Rightarrow s \qquad\qquad \text{ if } \mathcal{B}[\![b]\!]s = \mathbf{ff}$$

Show that the modified semantic function, $\mathcal{S}'_{\text{sos}}$, satisfies

$$\mathcal{S}_{\text{sos}}[\![S]\!] = \mathcal{S}'_{\text{sos}}[\![S]\!] \text{ for all statements } S \text{ of } \mathbf{While}$$

Investigate whether or not this complicates the proofs of (analogues of) Exercises 3.26 and 3.27. □

Chapter 4

Denotational Semantics

In the operational approach we were interested in *how* a program is executed. This is contrary to the denotational approach where we are merely interested in the *effect* of executing a program. By effect we here mean an association between initial states and final states. The idea then is to define a *semantic function* for each *syntactic category*. It maps each *syntactic construct* to a *mathematical object*, often a function, that describes the effect of executing that construct.

The hallmark of denotational semantics is that semantic functions are defined *compositionally*, that is

- there is a semantic clause for each of the basis elements of the syntactic category, and
- for each method of constructing a composite element (in the syntactic category) there is a semantic clause defined in terms of the semantic function applied to the immediate constituents of the composite element.

The functions $\mathcal{A}$ and $\mathcal{B}$ defined in Chapter 1 are examples of denotational definitions: the mathematical objects associated with arithmetic expressions are functions in **State** $\rightarrow$ **Z** and those associated with boolean expressions are functions in **State** $\rightarrow$ **T**. The functions $\mathcal{S}_{\mathrm{ns}}$ and $\mathcal{S}_{\mathrm{sos}}$ associate mathematical objects with each statement, namely partial functions in **State** $\hookrightarrow$ **State**. However, they are *not* examples of denotational definitions because they are *not* defined compositionally.

4.1 Direct style semantics: specification

The effect of executing a statement S is to change the state so we shall define the meaning of S to be a partial function on states:

$$\mathcal{S}_{\mathrm{ds}}\colon \mathbf{Stm} \rightarrow (\mathbf{State} \hookrightarrow \mathbf{State})$$

$$\mathcal{S}_{\rm ds}[\![x := a]\!]s = s[x \mapsto \mathcal{A}[\![a]\!]s]$$

$$\mathcal{S}_{\rm ds}[\![\texttt{skip}]\!] = \text{id}$$

$$\mathcal{S}_{\rm ds}[\![S_1 \,;\, S_2]\!] = \mathcal{S}_{\rm ds}[\![S_2]\!] \circ \mathcal{S}_{\rm ds}[\![S_1]\!]$$

$$\mathcal{S}_{\rm ds}[\![\texttt{if } b \texttt{ then } S_1 \texttt{ else } S_2]\!] = \text{cond}(\mathcal{B}[\![b]\!], \mathcal{S}_{\rm ds}[\![S_1]\!], \mathcal{S}_{\rm ds}[\![S_2]\!])$$

$$\mathcal{S}_{\rm ds}[\![\texttt{while } b \texttt{ do } S]\!] = \text{FIX } F$$
$$\text{where } F\ g = \text{cond}(\mathcal{B}[\![b]\!], g \circ \mathcal{S}_{\rm ds}[\![S]\!], \text{id})$$

Table 4.1: Denotational semantics for **While**

This is also the functionality of $\mathcal{S}_{\rm ns}$ and $\mathcal{S}_{\rm sos}$ and the need for partiality is again demonstrated by the statement `while true do skip`. The definition is summarized in Table 4.1 and we explain it in detail below; in particular, we shall define the *auxiliary functions* 'cond' and FIX.

For assignment the clause

$$\mathcal{S}_{\rm ds}[\![x := a]\!]s = s[x \mapsto \mathcal{A}[\![a]\!]s]$$

ensures that if $\mathcal{S}_{\rm ds}[\![x := a]\!]s = s'$ then $s'\ x = \mathcal{A}[\![a]\!]s$ and $s'\ y = s\ y$ for $y \neq x$. The clause for `skip` expresses that no state change takes place: the function id is the identity function on **State** so $\mathcal{S}_{\rm ds}[\![\texttt{skip}]\!]s = s$.

For sequencing the clause is

$$\mathcal{S}_{\rm ds}[\![S_1 \,;\, S_2]\!] = \mathcal{S}_{\rm ds}[\![S_2]\!] \circ \mathcal{S}_{\rm ds}[\![S_1]\!]$$

So the effect of executing $S_1 \,;\, S_2$ is the functional composition of the effect of executing S_1 and that of executing S_2. Functional composition is defined such that if one of the functions is undefined on a given argument then their composition is undefined as well. Given a state s, we therefore have

$$
\begin{aligned}
&\mathcal{S}_{\rm ds}[\![S_1 \,;\, S_2]\!]s \\
&\quad= (\mathcal{S}_{\rm ds}[\![S_2]\!] \circ \mathcal{S}_{\rm ds}[\![S_1]\!])s \\
&\quad= \begin{cases} s'' & \text{if there exists } s' \text{ such that } \mathcal{S}_{\rm ds}[\![S_1]\!]s = s' \\ & \text{and } \mathcal{S}_{\rm ds}[\![S_2]\!]s' = s'' \\ \underline{\text{undef}} & \text{if } \mathcal{S}_{\rm ds}[\![S_1]\!]s = \underline{\text{undef}} \\ & \text{or if there exists } s' \text{ such that } \mathcal{S}_{\rm ds}[\![S_1]\!]s = s' \\ & \text{but } \mathcal{S}_{\rm ds}[\![S_2]\!]s' = \underline{\text{undef}} \end{cases}
\end{aligned}
$$

It follows that the sequencing construct will only give a defined result if both components do.

For conditional the clause is

$$\mathcal{S}_{ds}[\![\texttt{if } b \texttt{ then } S_1 \texttt{ else } S_2]\!] = \text{cond}(\mathcal{B}[\![b]\!], \mathcal{S}_{ds}[\![S_1]\!], \mathcal{S}_{ds}[\![S_2]\!])$$

and the auxiliary function 'cond' has functionality

$$\begin{aligned}\text{cond: } & (\textbf{State} \to \textbf{T}) \times (\textbf{State} \hookrightarrow \textbf{State}) \times (\textbf{State} \hookrightarrow \textbf{State}) \\ & \to (\textbf{State} \hookrightarrow \textbf{State})\end{aligned}$$

and is defined by

$$\text{cond}(p, g_1, g_2)\ s = \begin{cases} g_1\ s & \text{if } p\ s = \textbf{tt} \\ g_2\ s & \text{if } p\ s = \textbf{ff} \end{cases}$$

The first parameter to 'cond' is a function that, when supplied with an argument, will select either the second or the third parameter of 'cond' and then supply that parameter with the same argument. Thus we have

$$\begin{aligned} & \mathcal{S}_{ds}[\![\texttt{if } b \texttt{ then } S_1 \texttt{ else } S_2]\!]\ s \\ = \ & \text{cond}(\mathcal{B}[\![b]\!], \mathcal{S}_{ds}[\![S_1]\!], \mathcal{S}_{ds}[\![S_2]\!])\ s \\ = \ & \begin{cases} s' & \text{if } \mathcal{B}[\![b]\!]s = \textbf{tt} \text{ and } \mathcal{S}_{ds}[\![S_1]\!]s = s' \\ & \text{or if } \mathcal{B}[\![b]\!]s = \textbf{ff} \text{ and } \mathcal{S}_{ds}[\![S_2]\!]s = s' \\ \underline{\text{undef}} & \text{if } \mathcal{B}[\![b]\!]s = \textbf{tt} \text{ and } \mathcal{S}_{ds}[\![S_1]\!]s = \underline{\text{undef}} \\ & \text{or if } \mathcal{B}[\![b]\!]s = \textbf{ff} \text{ and } \mathcal{S}_{ds}[\![S_2]\!]s = \underline{\text{undef}} \end{cases}\end{aligned}$$

So if the selected branch gives a defined result then so does the conditional. Note that since $\mathcal{B}[\![b]\!]$ is a total function, $\mathcal{B}[\![b]\!]s$ cannot be undef.

Defining the effect of `while` b `do` S is a major task. To motivate the actual definition we first observe that the effect of `while` b `do` S must equal that of

`if` b `then` (S; `while` b `do` S) `else skip`

Using the parts of $\mathcal{S}_{ds}$ that have already been defined, this gives

$$\mathcal{S}_{ds}[\![\texttt{while } b \texttt{ do } S]\!] = \text{cond}(\mathcal{B}[\![b]\!], \mathcal{S}_{ds}[\![\texttt{while } b \texttt{ do } S]\!] \circ \mathcal{S}_{ds}[\![S]\!], \text{id}) \qquad (*)$$

Note that we cannot use (*) as the definition of $\mathcal{S}_{ds}[\![\texttt{while } b \texttt{ do } S]\!]$ because then $\mathcal{S}_{ds}$ would *not* be a compositional definition. However, (*) expresses that

$\mathcal{S}_{ds}[\![\texttt{while } b \texttt{ do } S]\!]$ must be a *fixed point* of the functional F defined by

$$F\ g = \text{cond}(\mathcal{B}[\![b]\!], g \circ \mathcal{S}_{ds}[\![S]\!], \text{id})$$

that is $\mathcal{S}_{ds}[\![\texttt{while } b \texttt{ do } S]\!] = F\ (\mathcal{S}_{ds}[\![\texttt{while } b \texttt{ do } S]\!])$. In this way we will get a compositional definition of $\mathcal{S}_{ds}$ because when defining F we only apply $\mathcal{S}_{ds}$ to the immediate constituents of `while` b `do` S and not to the construct itself. Thus we write

$$\mathcal{S}_{\rm ds}[\![\texttt{while}\ b\ \texttt{do}\ S]\!] = \text{FIX}\ F$$
$$\text{where}\ F\ g = \text{cond}(\mathcal{B}[\![b]\!],\ g \circ \mathcal{S}_{\rm ds}[\![S]\!],\ \text{id})$$

to indicate that $\mathcal{S}_{\rm ds}[\![\texttt{while}\ b\ \texttt{do}\ S]\!]$ is a fixed point of F. The functionality of the auxiliary function FIX is

$$\text{FIX: } ((\textbf{State} \hookrightarrow \textbf{State}) \to (\textbf{State} \hookrightarrow \textbf{State})) \to (\textbf{State} \hookrightarrow \textbf{State})$$

Example 4.1 Consider the statement

`while` $\neg(\texttt{x} = 0)$ `do skip`

It is easy to verify that the corresponding functional F' is defined by

$$(F'\ g)\ s = \begin{cases} g\ s & \text{if } s\ \texttt{x} \neq \mathbf{0} \\ s & \text{if } s\ \texttt{x} = \mathbf{0} \end{cases}$$

The function g_1 defined by

$$g_1\ s = \begin{cases} \underline{\text{undef}} & \text{if } s\ \texttt{x} \neq \mathbf{0} \\ s & \text{if } s\ \texttt{x} = \mathbf{0} \end{cases}$$

is a fixed point of F' because

$$\begin{aligned} (F'\ g_1)\ s &= \begin{cases} g_1\ s & \text{if } s\ \texttt{x} \neq \mathbf{0} \\ s & \text{if } s\ \texttt{x} = \mathbf{0} \end{cases} \\ &= \begin{cases} \underline{\text{undef}} & \text{if } s\ \texttt{x} \neq \mathbf{0} \\ s & \text{if } s\ \texttt{x} = \mathbf{0} \end{cases} \\ &= g_1\ s \end{aligned}$$

Next we claim that the function g_2 defined by

$$g_2\ s = \underline{\text{undef}} \text{ for all } s$$

cannot be a fixed point for F'. The reason is that if s' is a state with $s'\ \texttt{x} = \mathbf{0}$ then $(F'\ g_2)\ s' = s'$ whereas $g_2\ s' = \underline{\text{undef}}$. □

Unfortunately, this does *not* suffice for defining $\mathcal{S}_{\rm ds}[\![\texttt{while}\ b\ \texttt{do}\ S]\!]$. We face two problems:

- there are functionals that have *more than one fixed point*, and
- there are functionals that have *no fixed point* at all.

The functional F' of Example 4.1 has more than one fixed point. In fact, *any* function g' of **State** $\hookrightarrow$ **State** satisfying $g'\ s = s$ if $s\ \mathtt{x} = \mathbf{0}$ will be a fixed point of F'.

To give an example of a functional that has no fixed points consider F_1 defined by

$$F_1\ g = \begin{cases} g_1 & \text{if } g = g_2 \\ g_2 & \text{otherwise} \end{cases}$$

If $g_1 \neq g_2$ then clearly there will be no function g_0 such that $F_1\ g_0 = g_0$. Thus F_1 has no fixed points at all.

Exercise 4.2 Determine the functional F associated with the statement

```
while ¬(x=0) do x := x−1
```

using the semantic equations of Table 4.1. Consider the following partial functions of **State** $\hookrightarrow$ **State**:

$$g_1\ s = \underline{\text{undef}} \text{ for all } s$$

$$g_2\ s = \begin{cases} s[\mathtt{x}\mapsto\mathbf{0}] & \text{if } s\ \mathtt{x} \geq \mathbf{0} \\ \underline{\text{undef}} & \text{if } s\ \mathtt{x} < \mathbf{0} \end{cases}$$

$$g_3\ s = \begin{cases} s[\mathtt{x}\mapsto\mathbf{0}] & \text{if } s\ \mathtt{x} \geq \mathbf{0} \\ s & \text{if } s\ \mathtt{x} < \mathbf{0} \end{cases}$$

$$g_4\ s = s[\mathtt{x}\mapsto\mathbf{0}] \text{ for all } s$$

$$g_5\ s = s \text{ for all } s$$

Determine which of these functions are fixed points of F. □

Exercise 4.3 Consider the following fragment of the factorial statement

```
while ¬(x=1) do (y := y⋆x; x := x−1)
```

Determine the functional F associated with this statement. Determine at least two different fixed points for F. □

Requirements on the fixed point

Our solution to the two problems listed above will be to develop a framework where

- we impose requirements on the fixed points and show that there is at most one fixed point fulfilling these requirements, and

- all functionals originating from statements in **While** do have a fixed point that satisfies these requirements.

To motivate our choice of requirements let us consider the execution of a statement `while` b `do` S from a state s_0. There are three possible outcomes:

A: it *terminates*,

B: it *loops locally*, that is there is a construct in S that loops, or

C: it *loops globally*, that is the outer `while`-construct loops.

We shall now investigate what can be said about the functional F and its fixed points in each of the three cases.

The case A: In this case the execution of `while` b `do` S from s_0 terminates. This means that there are states $s_1, \cdots, s_n$ such that

$$\mathcal{B}[\![b]\!]\ s_i = \begin{cases} \mathbf{tt} & \text{if } i<n \\ \mathbf{ff} & \text{if } i=n \end{cases}$$

and

$$\mathcal{S}_{ds}[\![S]\!]\ s_i = s_{i+1} \quad \text{for } i<n$$

An example of a statement and a state satisfying these conditions is the statement

```
while 0≤x do x := x−1
```

and any state where `x` has a non-negative value.

Let g_0 be any fixed point of F, that is assume that $F\ g_0 = g_0$. In the case where i<n we calculate

$$\begin{aligned} g_0\ s_i &= (F\ g_0)\ s_i \\ &= \text{cond}(\mathcal{B}[\![b]\!],\ g_0 \circ \mathcal{S}_{ds}[\![S]\!],\ \text{id})\ s_i \\ &= g_0\ (\mathcal{S}_{ds}[\![S]\!]\ s_i) \\ &= g_0\ s_{i+1} \end{aligned}$$

In the case where i=n we get

$$\begin{aligned} g_0\ s_n &= (F\ g_0)\ s_n \\ &= \text{cond}(\mathcal{B}[\![b]\!],\ g_0 \circ \mathcal{S}_{ds}[\![S]\!],\ \text{id})\ s_n \\ &= \text{id}\ s_n \\ &= s_n \end{aligned}$$

Thus *any* fixed point g_0 of F will satisfy

$$g_0\ s_0 = s_n$$

so in this case we do not obtain any additional requirements that will help us to choose one of the fixed points as the preferred one.

The case B: In this case the execution of `while` b `do` S from s_0 loops *locally*. This means that there are states $s_1, \cdots, s_n$ such that

$$\mathcal{B}[\![b]\!]s_i = \mathbf{tt} \text{ for } i \leq n$$

and

$$\mathcal{S}_{ds}[\![S]\!]s_i = \begin{cases} s_{i+1} & \text{for } i<n \\ \underline{\text{undef}} & \text{for } i=n \end{cases}$$

An example of a statement and a state satisfying these conditions is the statement

```
while 0≤x do (if x=0 then (while true do skip)
                      else x := x−1)
```

and any state where `x` has a non-negative value.

Let g_0 be any fixed point of F, that is $F\ g_0 = g_0$. In the case where i<n we obtain

$$g_0\ s_i = g_0\ s_{i+1}$$

just as in the previous case. However, in the case where i=n we get

$$\begin{aligned} g_0\ s_n &= (F\ g_0)\ s_n \\ &= \text{cond}(\mathcal{B}[\![b]\!],\ g_0 \circ \mathcal{S}_{ds}[\![S]\!],\ \text{id})\ s_n \\ &= (g_0 \circ \mathcal{S}_{ds}[\![S]\!])\ s_n \\ &= \underline{\text{undef}} \end{aligned}$$

Thus *any* fixed point g_0 of F will satisfy

$$g_0\ s_0 = \underline{\text{undef}}$$

so, again, in this case we do not obtain any additional requirements that will help us to choose one of the fixed points as the preferred one.

The case C: The potential difference between fixed points comes to light when we consider the possibility that the execution of `while` b `do` S from s_0 loops *globally*. This means that there are infinitely many states $s_1, \cdots$ such that

$$\mathcal{B}[\![b]\!]s_i = \mathbf{tt} \text{ for all } i$$

and

$$\mathcal{S}_{\text{ds}}[\![S]\!]s_{\text{i}} = s_{\text{i+1}} \text{ for all i.}$$

An example of a statement and a state satisfying these conditions is the statement

```
while ¬(x=0) do skip
```

and any state where **x** is not equal to **0**.

Let g_0 be any fixed point of F, that is $F\ g_0 = g_0$. As in the previous cases we get

$$g_0\ s_{\text{i}} = g_0\ s_{\text{i+1}}$$

for all i≥0. Thus we have

$$g_0\ s_0 = g_0\ s_{\text{i}} \text{ for all i}$$

and we cannot determine the value of $g_0\ s_0$ in this way. This is the situation in which the various fixed points of F may differ.

This is not surprising because the statement `while ¬(x=0) do skip` of Example 4.1 has the functional F' given by

$$(F'\ g)\ s = \begin{cases} g\ s & \text{if } s\ \mathtt{x} \neq \mathbf{0} \\ s & \text{if } s\ \mathtt{x} = \mathbf{0} \end{cases}$$

and *any* partial function g of **State** $\hookrightarrow$ **State** satisfying $g\ s = s$ if $s\ \mathtt{x} = \mathbf{0}$ will indeed be a fixed point of F'. However, our computational experience tells us that we want

$$\mathcal{S}_{\text{ds}}[\![\mathtt{while}\ \neg(\mathtt{x}=0)\ \mathtt{do\ skip}]\!]s_0 = \begin{cases} \underline{\text{undef}} & \text{if } s_0\ \mathtt{x} \neq \mathbf{0} \\ s_0 & \text{if } s_0\ \mathtt{x} = \mathbf{0} \end{cases}$$

in order to record the looping. Thus our preferred fixed point of F' is the function g_0 defined by

$$g_0\ s = \begin{cases} \underline{\text{undef}} & \text{if } s\ \mathtt{x} \neq \mathbf{0} \\ s & \text{if } s\ \mathtt{x} = \mathbf{0} \end{cases}$$

The property that distinguishes g_0 from some other fixed point g' of F' is that whenever $g_0\ s = s'$ then we also have $g'\ s = s'$ but not vice versa.

Generalizing this experience leads to the following requirement: the desired fixed point FIX F should be some partial function g_0: **State** $\hookrightarrow$ **State** such that

- g_0 is a fixed point of F, that is $F\ g_0 = g_0$, and
- if g is another fixed point of F, that is $F\ g = g$, then

  $$g_0\ s = s' \text{ implies } g\ s = s'$$

for all choices of s and s'.

Note that if $g_0\ s = \underline{\text{undef}}$ then there are no requirements on $g\ s$.

Exercise 4.4 Determine which of the fixed points considered in Exercise 4.2 is the desired fixed point, if any. □

Exercise 4.5 Determine the desired fixed point of the functional constructed in Exercise 4.3. □

4.2 Fixed point theory

To prepare for a framework that guarantees the existence of the desired fixed point FIX F we shall reformulate the requirements to FIX F in a slightly more formal way. The first step will be to formalize the requirement that FIX F shares its results with all other fixed points. To do so we define an *ordering* $\sqsubseteq$ on partial functions of **State** $\hookrightarrow$ **State**. We set

$$g_1 \sqsubseteq g_2$$

when the partial function g_1: **State** $\hookrightarrow$ **State** *shares its results* with the partial function g_2: **State** $\hookrightarrow$ **State** in the sense that

$$\text{if } g_1\ s = s' \text{ then } g_2\ s = s'$$

for all choices of s and s'.

Example 4.6 Let g_1, g_2, g_3 and g_4 be partial functions in **State** $\hookrightarrow$ **State** defined as follows:

$$g_1\ s = s \text{ for all } s$$

$$g_2\ s = \begin{cases} s & \text{if } s\ \mathbf{x} \geq \mathbf{0} \\ \underline{\text{undef}} & \text{otherwise} \end{cases}$$

$$g_3\ s = \begin{cases} s & \text{if } s\ \mathbf{x} = \mathbf{0} \\ \underline{\text{undef}} & \text{otherwise} \end{cases}$$

$$g_4\ s = \begin{cases} s & \text{if } s\ \mathbf{x} \leq \mathbf{0} \\ \underline{\text{undef}} & \text{otherwise} \end{cases}$$

Then we have

$g_1 \sqsubseteq g_1$,

$g_2 \sqsubseteq g_1$, $g_2 \sqsubseteq g_2$,

$g_3 \sqsubseteq g_1$, $g_3 \sqsubseteq g_2$, $g_3 \sqsubseteq g_3$, $g_3 \sqsubseteq g_4$, and

$g_4 \sqsubseteq g_1$, $g_4 \sqsubseteq g_4$.

It is neither the case that $g_2 \sqsubseteq g_4$ nor that $g_4 \sqsubseteq g_2$. Pictorially, the ordering may be expressed as follows[1]:

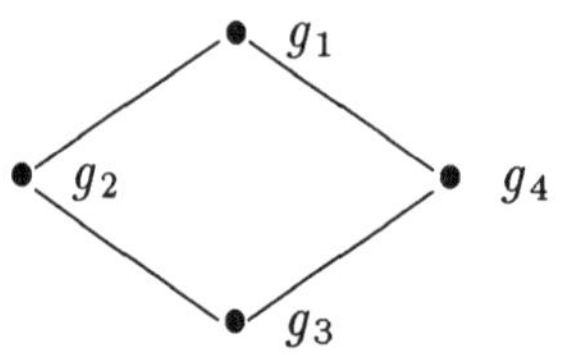

The idea is that the smaller elements are at the bottom of the picture and that the lines indicate the order between the elements. However, we shall not draw lines when there already is a "broken line", so the fact that $g_3 \sqsubseteq g_1$ is left implicit in the picture. □

Exercise 4.7 Let g_1, g_2 and g_3 be defined as follows:

$$g_1\ s = \begin{cases} s & \text{if } s\ \mathbf{x} \text{ is even} \\ \underline{\text{undef}} & \text{otherwise} \end{cases}$$

$$g_2\ s = \begin{cases} s & \text{if } s\ \mathbf{x} \text{ is a prime} \\ \underline{\text{undef}} & \text{otherwise} \end{cases}$$

$$g_3\ s = s$$

First, determine the ordering among these partial functions. Next, determine a partial function g_4 such that $g_4 \sqsubseteq g_1$, $g_4 \sqsubseteq g_2$ and $g_4 \sqsubseteq g_3$. Finally, determine a partial function g_5 such that $g_1 \sqsubseteq g_5$, $g_2 \sqsubseteq g_5$ and $g_5 \sqsubseteq g_3$ but g_5 is neither equal to g_1, g_2 nor g_3. □

Exercise 4.8 (Essential) An alternative characterization of the ordering $\sqsubseteq$ on **State** $\hookrightarrow$ **State** is

$$g_1 \sqsubseteq g_2 \text{ if and only if graph}(g_1) \subseteq \text{graph}(g_2) \qquad (*)$$

where graph(g) is the graph of the partial function g as defined in Appendix A. Prove that (*) is indeed correct. □

[1]Such a diagram is sometimes called a Hasse diagram.

The set **State** $\hookrightarrow$ **State** equipped with the ordering $\sqsubseteq$ is an example of a partially ordered set as we shall see in Lemma 4.13 below. In general, a *partially ordered set* is a pair $(D, \sqsubseteq_D)$ where D is a set and $\sqsubseteq_D$ is a relation on D satisfying

$d \sqsubseteq_D d$	(reflexivity)
$d_1 \sqsubseteq_D d_2$ and $d_2 \sqsubseteq_D d_3$ imply $d_1 \sqsubseteq_D d_3$	(transitivity)
$d_1 \sqsubseteq_D d_2$ and $d_2 \sqsubseteq_D d_1$ imply $d_1 = d_2$	(anti-symmetry)

The relation $\sqsubseteq_D$ is said to be a *partial order* on D and we shall often omit the subscript D of $\sqsubseteq_D$ and write $\sqsubseteq$. Occasionally, we may write $d_1 \sqsupseteq d_2$ instead of $d_2 \sqsubseteq d_1$ and we shall say that d_2 *shares its information with* d_1. An element d of D satisfying

$$d \sqsubseteq d' \text{ for all } d' \text{ of } D$$

is called *a least element* of D and we shall say that it contains *no information.*

Fact 4.9 If a partially ordered set $(D, \sqsubseteq)$ has a least element d then d is unique.

Proof: Assume that D has two least elements d_1 and d_2. Since d_1 is a least element we have $d_1 \sqsubseteq d_2$. Since d_2 is a least element we also have $d_2 \sqsubseteq d_1$. The anti-symmetry of the ordering $\sqsubseteq$ then gives that $d_1 = d_2$. □

This fact permits us to talk about *the* least element of D, if one exists, and we shall denote it by $\bot_D$ or simply $\bot$ (pronounced "bottom").

Example 4.10 Let S be a non-empty set and define

$$\mathcal{P}(S) = \{\, K \mid K \subseteq S \,\}$$

Then $(\mathcal{P}(S), \subseteq)$ is a partially ordered set because

- $\subseteq$ is reflexive: $K \subseteq K$
- $\subseteq$ is transitive: if $K_1 \subseteq K_2$ and $K_2 \subseteq K_3$ then $K_1 \subseteq K_3$
- $\subseteq$ is anti-symmetric: if $K_1 \subseteq K_2$ and $K_2 \subseteq K_1$ then $K_1 = K_2$

In the case where S = {a,b,c} the ordering can be depicted as follows:

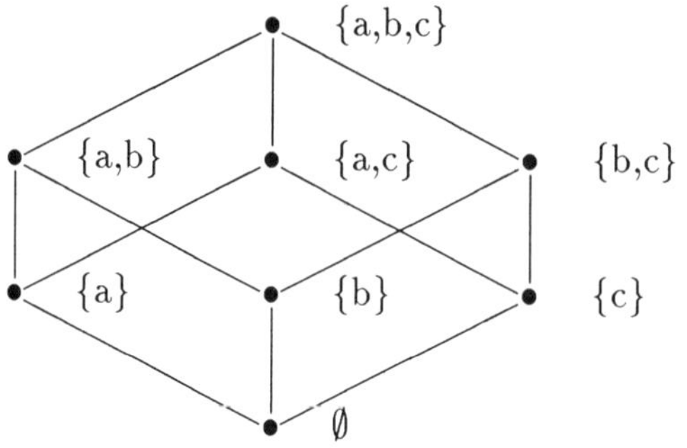

Also, $(\mathcal{P}(S), \subseteq)$ has a least element, namely $\emptyset$. □

Exercise 4.11 Show that $(\mathcal{P}(S), \supseteq)$ is a partially ordered set and determine the least element. Draw a picture of the ordering when $S = \{a,b,c\}$. □

Exercise 4.12 Let S be a non-empty set and define

$$\mathcal{P}_{\mathsf{fin}}(S) = \{\ K \mid K \text{ is finite and } K \subseteq S\ \}$$

Verify that $(\mathcal{P}_{\mathsf{fin}}(S), \subseteq)$ and $(\mathcal{P}_{\mathsf{fin}}(S), \supseteq)$ are partially ordered sets. Do both partially ordered sets have a least element for all choices of S? □

Lemma 4.13 (**State** $\hookrightarrow$ **State**, $\sqsubseteq$) is a partially ordered set. The partial function $\bot$: **State** $\hookrightarrow$ **State** defined by

$$\bot\ s = \underline{\text{undef}} \text{ for all } s$$

is the least element of **State** $\hookrightarrow$ **State**.

Proof: We shall first prove that $\sqsubseteq$ fulfils the three requirements to a partial order: Clearly, $g \sqsubseteq g$ holds because $g\ s = s'$ trivially implies that $g\ s = s'$ so $\sqsubseteq$ is a *reflexive* ordering.

To see that it is a *transitive* ordering assume that $g_1 \sqsubseteq g_2$ and $g_2 \sqsubseteq g_3$ and we shall prove that $g_1 \sqsubseteq g_3$. Assume that $g_1\ s = s'$. From $g_1 \sqsubseteq g_2$ we get $g_2\ s = s'$ and then $g_2 \sqsubseteq g_3$ gives that $g_3\ s = s'$.

To see that it is an *anti-symmetric* ordering assume that $g_1 \sqsubseteq g_2$ and $g_2 \sqsubseteq g_1$ and we shall then prove that $g_1 = g_2$. Assume that $g_1\ s = s'$. Then $g_2\ s = s'$ follows from $g_1 \sqsubseteq g_2$ so g_1 and g_2 are equal on s. If $g_1\ s = \underline{\text{undef}}$ then it must be the case that $g_2\ s = \underline{\text{undef}}$ since otherwise $g_2\ s = s'$ and the assumption $g_2 \sqsubseteq g_1$ then gives $g_1\ s = s'$ which is a contradiction. Thus g_1 and g_2 will be equal on s.

Finally, we shall prove that $\perp$ is the *least element* of **State** $\hookrightarrow$ **State**. It is easy to see that $\perp$ is indeed an element of **State** $\hookrightarrow$ **State** and it is also obvious that $\perp \sqsubseteq g$ holds for all g since $\perp\ s = s'$ vacuously implies that $g\ s = s'$. □

Having introduced an ordering on the partial functions we can now give a more precise statement of the requirements to FIX F:

- FIX F is a *fixed point* of F, that is $F(\text{FIX } F) = \text{FIX } F$, and
- FIX F is a *least* fixed point of F, that is

  if $F\ g = g$ then FIX $F \sqsubseteq g$.

Exercise 4.14 By analogy with Fact 4.9 show that if F has a least fixed point g_0 then g_0 is unique. □

The next task will be to ensure that all functionals F that may arise do indeed have least fixed points. We shall do so by developing a general theory that gives more structure to the partially ordered sets and that imposes restrictions on the functionals so that they have least fixed points.

Exercise 4.15 Determine the least fixed points of the functionals considered in Exercises 4.2 and 4.3. Compare with Exercises 4.4 and 4.5. □

Complete partially ordered sets

Consider a partially ordered set $(D, \sqsubseteq)$ and assume that we have a subset Y of D. We shall be interested in an element of D that summarizes all the information of Y and this is called an *upper bound* of Y; formally, it is an element d of D such that

$$\forall d' \in Y.\ d' \sqsubseteq d$$

An upper bound d of Y is a *least upper bound* if and only if

d' is an upper bound of Y implies that $d \sqsubseteq d'$

Thus a least upper bound of Y will add as little extra information as possible to that already present in the elements of Y.

Exercise 4.16 By analogy with Fact 4.9 show that if Y has a least upper bound d then d is unique. □

If Y has a (necessarily unique) least upper bound we shall denote it by $\bigsqcup Y$. Finally, a subset Y is called a *chain* if it is consistent in the sense that if we take any two elements of Y then one will share its information with the other; formally, this is expressed by

$$\forall d_1, d_2 \in Y.\ d_1 \sqsubseteq d_2 \text{ or } d_2 \sqsubseteq d_1$$

Example 4.17 Consider the partially ordered set $(\mathcal{P}(\{a,b,c\}), \subseteq)$ of Example 4.10. Then the subset

$$Y_0 = \{\ \emptyset, \{a\}, \{a,c\}\ \}$$

is a chain. Both {a,b,c} and {a,c} are upper bounds of Y_0 and {a,c} is the least upper bound. The element {a,b} is *not* an upper bound because $\{a,c\} \not\subseteq \{a,b\}$. In general, the least upper bound of a non-empty chain in $\mathcal{P}(\{a,b,c\})$ will be the largest element of the chain.

The subset $\{\ \emptyset, \{a\}, \{c\}, \{a,c\}\ \}$ is *not* a chain because {a} and {c} are unrelated by the ordering. However, it does have a least upper bound, namely {a,c}.

The *subset* $\emptyset$ of $\mathcal{P}(\{a,b,c\})$ is a chain and it has any element of $\mathcal{P}(\{a,b,c\})$ as an upper bound. Its least upper bound is the *element* $\emptyset$. □

Exercise 4.18 Let S be a non-empty set and consider the partially ordered set $(\mathcal{P}(S), \subseteq)$. Show that every subset of $\mathcal{P}(S)$ has a least upper bound. Repeat the exercise for the partially ordered set $(\mathcal{P}(S), \supseteq)$. □

Exercise 4.19 Let S be a non-empty set and consider the partially ordered set $(\mathcal{P}_{\mathrm{fin}}(S), \subseteq)$ as defined in Exercise 4.12. Show by means of an example that there are choices of S such that $(\mathcal{P}_{\mathrm{fin}}(S), \subseteq)$ has a chain with no upper bound and therefore no least upper bound. □

Example 4.20 Let g_{n}: **State** $\hookrightarrow$ **State** be defined by

$$g_{\mathrm{n}}\ s = \begin{cases} \underline{\text{undef}} & \text{if } s\ \mathbf{x} > \mathrm{n} \\ s[\mathbf{x}\mapsto\mathbf{-1}] & \text{if } \mathbf{0} \le s\ \mathbf{x} \text{ and } s\ \mathbf{x} \le \mathrm{n} \\ s & \text{if } s\ \mathbf{x} < \mathbf{0} \end{cases}$$

It is straightforward to verify that $g_{\mathrm{n}} \sqsubseteq g_{\mathrm{m}}$ whenever $\mathrm{n} \le \mathrm{m}$ because g_{n} will be undefined for more states than g_{m}. Now define Y_0 to be

$$Y_0 = \{\ g_{\mathrm{n}} \mid \mathrm{n} \ge 0\ \}$$

Then Y_0 is a chain because $g_{\mathrm{n}} \sqsubseteq g_{\mathrm{m}}$ whenever $\mathrm{n} \le \mathrm{m}$. The partial function

$$g\ s = \begin{cases} s[\mathbf{x}\mapsto\mathbf{-1}] & \text{if } \mathbf{0} \le s\ \mathbf{x} \\ s & \text{if } s\ \mathbf{x} < \mathbf{0} \end{cases}$$

is the least upper bound of Y. □

Exercise 4.21 Construct a subset Y of **State** $\hookrightarrow$ **State** such that Y has no upper bound and hence no least upper bound. □

Exercise 4.22 Let g_n be the partial function defined by

$$g_n\ s = \begin{cases} s[y \mapsto (s\ \mathbf{x})!][\mathbf{x} \mapsto \mathbf{1}] & \text{if } \mathbf{0} < s\ \mathbf{x} \text{ and } s\ \mathbf{x} \leq n \\ \underline{\text{undef}} & \text{if } s\ \mathbf{x} \leq \mathbf{0} \text{ or } s\ \mathbf{x} > n \end{cases}$$

Define $Y_0 = \{\ g_n \mid n \geq 0\ \}$ and show that it is a chain. Characterize the upper bounds of Y_0 and determine the least upper bound. □

A partially ordered set $(D, \sqsubseteq)$ is called a *chain complete* partially ordered set (abbreviated *ccpo*) whenever $\bigsqcup Y$ exists for all chains Y. It is a *complete lattice* if $\bigsqcup Y$ exists for all subsets Y of D.

Example 4.23 Exercise 4.18 shows that $(\mathcal{P}(S), \subseteq)$ and $(\mathcal{P}(S), \supseteq)$ are complete lattices, and hence ccpo's, for all non-empty sets S. Exercise 4.19 shows that $(\mathcal{P}_{\text{fin}}(S), \subseteq)$ need not be a complete lattice nor a ccpo. □

Fact 4.24 If $(D, \sqsubseteq)$ is a ccpo then it has a least element $\bot$ given by $\bot = \bigsqcup\emptyset$.

Proof: It is straightforward to check that $\emptyset$ is a chain and since $(D, \sqsubseteq)$ is a ccpo we get that $\bigsqcup\emptyset$ exists. Using the definition of $\bigsqcup\emptyset$ we see that for any element d of D we have $\bigsqcup\emptyset \sqsubseteq d$. This means that $\bigsqcup\emptyset$ is the least element of D. □

Exercise 4.21 shows that **State** $\hookrightarrow$ **State** is not a complete lattice. Fortunately, we have

---

Lemma 4.25 (**State** $\hookrightarrow$ **State**, $\sqsubseteq$) is a ccpo. The least upper bound $\bigsqcup Y$ of a chain Y is given by

$$\text{graph}(\bigsqcup Y) = \bigcup\{\ \text{graph}(g) \mid g \in Y\ \}$$

that is $(\bigsqcup Y)s = s'$ if and only if $g\ s = s'$ for some $g \in Y$.

Proof: The proof is in three stages: First we prove that

$$\bigcup\{\ \text{graph}(g) \mid g \in Y\ \} \qquad (*)$$

is indeed a graph of a partial function in **State** $\hookrightarrow$ **State**. Secondly, we prove that this function will be an upper bound of Y and thirdly that it is less than any other upper bound of Y, that is it is the least upper bound of Y.

To verify that (*) specifies a *partial function* we only need to show that if $\langle s, s'\rangle$ and $\langle s, s''\rangle$ are elements of

$$X = \bigcup\{ \text{graph}(g) \mid g \in Y \}$$

then $s' = s''$. When $\langle s, s' \rangle \in X$ there will be a partial function $g \in Y$ such that $g\ s = s'$. Similarly, when $\langle s, s'' \rangle \in X$ then there will be a partial function $g' \in Y$ such that $g'\ s = s''$. Since Y is a chain we will have that either $g \sqsubseteq g'$ or $g' \sqsubseteq g$. In any case we get $g\ s = g'\ s$ and this means that $s' = s''$ as required. This completes the first part of the proof.

In the second part of the proof we define the partial function g_0 by

$$\text{graph}(g_0) = \bigcup\{ \text{graph}(g) \mid g \in Y \}$$

To show that g_0 is an upper bound of Y let g be an element of Y. Then we have $\text{graph}(g) \subseteq \text{graph}(g_0)$ and using the result of Exercise 4.8 we see that $g \sqsubseteq g_0$ as required and we have completed the second part of the proof.

In the third part of the proof we show that g_0 is the least upper bound of Y. So let g_1 be some upper bound of Y. Using the definition of an upper bound we get that $g \sqsubseteq g_1$ must hold for all $g \in Y$. Exercise 4.8 gives that $\text{graph}(g) \subseteq \text{graph}(g_1)$. Hence it must be the case that

$$\bigcup\{ \text{graph}(g) \mid g \in Y \} \subseteq \text{graph}(g_1)$$

But this is the same as $\text{graph}(g_0) \subseteq \text{graph}(g_1)$ and Exercise 4.8 gives that $g_0 \sqsubseteq g_1$. This shows that g_0 is the least upper bound of Y and thereby we have completed the proof. □

Continuous functions

Let $(D, \sqsubseteq)$ and $(D', \sqsubseteq')$ be ccpo's and consider a (total) function $f\colon D \to D'$. If $d_1 \sqsubseteq d_2$ then the intuition is that d_1 shares its information with d_2. So when the function f has been applied to the two elements d_1 and d_2 then we shall expect that a similar relationship holds between the results. That is we shall expect that $f\ d_1 \sqsubseteq' f\ d_2$ and when this is the case we say that f is *monotone*. Formally, f is monotone if and only if

$$d_1 \sqsubseteq d_2 \text{ implies } f\ d_1 \sqsubseteq' f\ d_2$$

for all choices of d_1 and d_2.

Example 4.26 Consider the ccpo's $(\mathcal{P}(\{a,b,c\}), \subseteq)$ and $(\mathcal{P}(\{d,e\}), \subseteq)$. The function $f_1\colon \mathcal{P}(\{a,b,c\}) \to \mathcal{P}(\{d,e\})$ defined by the table

X	{a,b,c}	{a,b}	{a,c}	{b,c}	{a}	{b}	{c}	∅
$f_1\ X$	{d,e}	{d}	{d,e}	{d,e}	{d}	{d}	{e}	∅

is monotone: it simply changes a's and b's to d's and c's to e's.

The function f_2: $\mathcal{P}(\{a,b,c\}) \to \mathcal{P}(\{d,e\})$ defined by the table

X	{a,b,c}	{a,b}	{a,c}	{b,c}	{a}	{b}	{c}	$\emptyset$
$f_2\ X$	{d}	{d}	{d}	{e}	{d}	{e}	{e}	{e}

is *not* monotone because $\{b,c\} \subseteq \{a,b,c\}$ but $f_2\ \{b,c\} \not\subseteq f_2\ \{a,b,c\}$. Intuitively, all sets that contain an a are mapped to {d} whereas the others are mapped to {e} and since the elements {d} and {e} are incomparable this does not give a monotone function. However, if we change the definition such that sets with an a are mapped to {d} and all other sets to $\emptyset$ then the function will be monotone. □

Exercise 4.27 Consider the ccpo $(\mathcal{P}(\mathbf{N}), \subseteq)$. Determine which of the following functions in $\mathcal{P}(\mathbf{N}) \to \mathcal{P}(\mathbf{N})$ are monotone:

- $f_1\ X = \mathbf{N} \setminus X$
- $f_2\ X = X \cup \{\mathbf{27}\}$
- $f_3\ X = X \cap \{\mathbf{7}, \mathbf{9}, \mathbf{13}\}$
- $f_4\ X = \{\ n \in X \mid n \text{ is a prime }\}$
- $f_5\ X = \{\ \mathbf{2} \star n \mid n \in X\ \}$ □

Exercise 4.28 Determine which of the following functionals of

$$(\textbf{State} \hookrightarrow \textbf{State}) \to (\textbf{State} \hookrightarrow \textbf{State})$$

are monotone:

- $F_0\ g = g$
- $F_1\ g = \begin{cases} g_1 & \text{if } g = g_2 \\ g_2 & \text{otherwise} \end{cases}$ where $g_1 \neq g_2$
- $(F'\ g)\ s = \begin{cases} g\ s & \text{if } s\ \mathtt{x} \neq \mathbf{0} \\ s & \text{if } s\ \mathtt{x} = \mathbf{0} \end{cases}$ □

The monotone functions have a couple of interesting properties. First we prove that the composition of two monotone functions is a monotone function.

Fact 4.29 Let $(D, \sqsubseteq)$, $(D', \sqsubseteq')$ and $(D'', \sqsubseteq'')$ be ccpo's and let f: $D \to D'$ and f': $D' \to D''$ be monotone functions. Then $f' \circ f$: $D \to D''$ is a monotone function.

Proof: Assume that $d_1 \sqsubseteq d_2$. The monotonicity of f gives that $f\ d_1 \sqsubseteq' f\ d_2$. The monotonicity of f' then gives $f'\ (f\ d_1) \sqsubseteq'' f'\ (f\ d_2)$ as required. □

Next we prove that the image of a chain under a monotone function is itself a chain.

Lemma 4.30 Let $(D, \sqsubseteq)$ and $(D', \sqsubseteq')$ be ccpo's and let f: $D \to D'$ be a monotone function. If Y is a chain in D then $\{\ f\ d \mid d \in Y\ \}$ is a chain in D'. Furthermore,

$$\bigsqcup'\{\ f\ d \mid d \in Y\ \} \sqsubseteq' f(\bigsqcup Y)$$

Proof: If $Y = \emptyset$ then the result holds immediately since $\bot' \sqsubseteq' f\ \bot$. So assume that $Y \neq \emptyset$. We shall first prove that $\{\ f\ d \mid d \in Y\ \}$ is a chain in D'. So let d_1' and d_2' be two elements of $\{\ f\ d \mid d \in Y\ \}$. Then there are elements d_1 and d_2 in Y such that $d_1' = f\ d_1$ and $d_2' = f\ d_2$. Since Y is a chain we have that either $d_1 \sqsubseteq d_2$ or $d_2 \sqsubseteq d_1$. In either case we get that the same order holds between d_1' and d_2' because of the monotonicity of f. This proves that $\{\ f\ d \mid d \in Y\ \}$ is a chain.

To prove the second part of the lemma consider an arbitrary element d of Y. Then it will be the case that $d \sqsubseteq \bigsqcup Y$. The monotonicity of f gives that $f\ d \sqsubseteq' f(\bigsqcup Y)$. Since this holds for all $d \in Y$ we get that $f(\bigsqcup Y)$ is an upper bound on $\{\ f\ d \mid d \in Y\ \}$, that is $\bigsqcup'\ \{\ f\ d \mid d \in Y\ \} \sqsubseteq' f(\bigsqcup Y)$. □

In general we cannot expect that a monotone function preserves least upper bounds on chains, that is $\bigsqcup'\ \{\ f\ d \mid d \in Y\ \} = f(\bigsqcup Y)$. This is illustrated by the following example:

Example 4.31 From Example 4.23 we get that $(\mathcal{P}(\mathbf{N} \cup \{\mathrm{a}\}), \subseteq)$ is a ccpo. Now consider the function f: $\mathcal{P}(\mathbf{N} \cup \{\mathrm{a}\}) \to \mathcal{P}(\mathbf{N} \cup \{\mathrm{a}\})$ defined by

$$f\ X = \begin{cases} X & \text{if } X \text{ is finite} \\ X \cup \{\mathrm{a}\} & \text{if } X \text{ is infinite} \end{cases}$$

Clearly, f is a monotone function: if $X_1 \subseteq X_2$ then also $f\ X_1 \subseteq f\ X_2$. However, f does not preserve the least upper bounds of chains. To see this consider the set

$$Y = \{\ \{0,1,\cdots,\mathrm{n}\} \mid \mathrm{n} \geq 0\ \}$$

It consists of the elements {0}, {0,1}, {0,1,2}, $\cdots$ and it is straightforward to verify that it is a chain with **N** as its least upper bound, that is $\bigsqcup Y = \mathbf{N}$. When we apply f to the elements of Y we get

$$\bigsqcup \{ f\ X \mid X \in Y \} = \bigsqcup Y = \mathbf{N}$$

However, we also have

$$f\ (\bigsqcup Y) = f\ \mathbf{N} = \mathbf{N} \cup \{\mathrm{a}\}$$

showing that f does not preserve the least upper bounds of chains. □

We shall be interested in functions that preserve least upper bounds of chains, that is functions f that satisfy

$$\bigsqcup'\{ f\ d \mid d \in Y \} = f(\bigsqcup Y)$$

Intuitively, this means that we obtain the same information independently of whether we determine the least upper bound before or after applying the function f.

We shall say that a function f: $D \to D'$ defined on ccpo's $(D, \sqsubseteq)$ and $(D', \sqsubseteq')$ is *continuous* if it is monotone and

$$\bigsqcup'\{ f\ d \mid d \in Y \} = f(\bigsqcup Y)$$

holds for all *non-empty* chains Y. If $\bigsqcup\{ f\ d \mid d \in Y \} = f(\bigsqcup Y)$ holds for the empty chain, that is $\bot = f\ \bot$, then we shall say that f is *strict.*

Example 4.32 The function f_1 of Example 4.26 is also continuous. To see this consider a non-empty chain Y of $\mathcal{P}(\{\mathrm{a,b,c}\})$. The least upper bound of Y will be the largest element, say X_0, of Y (see Example 4.17). Therefore we have

$$\begin{array}{rcll} f_1\ (\bigsqcup Y) & = & f_1\ X_0 & \text{because } X_0 = \bigsqcup Y \\ & \subseteq & \bigsqcup\{ f_1\ X \mid X \in Y \} & \text{because } X_0 \in Y \end{array}$$

Using that f_1 is monotone we get from Lemma 4.30 that $\bigsqcup\{ f_1\ X \mid X \in Y \} \subseteq f_1\ (\bigsqcup Y)$. It follows that f_1 is continuous. Also, f_1 is a strict function because $f_1\ \emptyset = \emptyset$.

The function f of Example 4.31 is *not* a continuous function because there is a chain for which it does not preserve the least upper bound. □

Exercise 4.33 Show that the functional F' of Example 4.1 is continuous. □

Exercise 4.34 Assume that $(D, \sqsubseteq)$ and $(D', \sqsubseteq')$ are ccpo's and that f: $D \to D'$ satisfies

$$\bigsqcup'\{ f\ d \mid d \in Y \} = f(\bigsqcup Y)$$

for all *non-empty* chains Y of D. Show that f is monotone. □

We can extend the result of Lemma 4.29 to show that the composition of two continuous functions will also be continuous:

Lemma 4.35 Let $(D, \sqsubseteq)$, $(D', \sqsubseteq')$ and $(D'', \sqsubseteq'')$ be ccpo's and let f: $D \to D'$ and f': $D' \to D''$ be continuous functions. Then $f' \circ f$: $D \to D''$ is a continuous function.

Proof: From Lemma 4.29 we get that $f' \circ f$ is monotone. To prove that it is continuous let Y be a non-empty chain in D. The continuity of f gives

$$\bigsqcup'\{\, f\ d \mid d \in Y \,\} = f\ (\bigsqcup Y)$$

Since $\{\, f\ d \mid d \in Y \,\}$ is a (non-empty) chain in D' we can use the continuity of f' and get

$$\bigsqcup''\{\, f'\ d' \mid d' \in \{\, f\ d \mid d \in Y \,\} \,\} = f'\ (\bigsqcup'\{\, f\ d \mid d \in Y \,\})$$

which is equivalent to

$$\bigsqcup''\{\, f'\ (f\ d) \mid d \in Y \,\} = f'\ (f\ (\bigsqcup Y))$$

This proves the result. □

Exercise 4.36 Prove that if f and f' are strict functions then so is $f' \circ f$. □

We can now define the required fixed point operator FIX:

Theorem 4.37 Let f: $D \to D$ be a continuous function on the ccpo $(D, \sqsubseteq)$ with least element $\bot$. Then

$$\text{FIX}\ f = \bigsqcup\{\, f^{\text{n}}\ \bot \mid \text{n}{\geq}0 \,\}$$

defines an element of D and this element is the least fixed point of f.

Here we have used that

$$f^0 = \text{id, and}$$

$$f^{\text{n}+1} = f \circ f^{\text{n}} \text{ for n}{\geq}0$$

Proof: We first show the *well-definedness* of FIX f. Note that $f^0\ \bot = \bot$ and that $\bot \sqsubseteq d$ for all $d \in D$. By induction on n one may show that

$$f^n \perp \sqsubseteq f^n\ d$$

for all $d \in D$ since f is monotone. It follows that $f^n \perp \sqsubseteq f^m \perp$ whenever n≤m. Hence $\{ f^n \perp \mid n \geq 0 \}$ is a (non-empty) chain in D and FIX f exists because D is a ccpo.

We next show that FIX f is a *fixed point*, that is f (FIX f) = FIX f. We calculate:

$$
\begin{array}{rcll}
f\ (\text{FIX}\ f) & = & f\ (\bigsqcup\{ f^n \perp \mid n\geq 0 \}) & (\text{definition of FIX}\ f) \\
& = & \bigsqcup\{ f(f^n \perp) \mid n\geq 0 \} & (\text{continuity of}\ f) \\
& = & \bigsqcup\{ f^n \perp \mid n\geq 1 \} & \\
& = & \bigsqcup(\{ f^n \perp \mid n\geq 1 \} \cup \{\perp\}) & (\bigsqcup(Y \cup \{\perp\}) = \bigsqcup Y \\
& & & \text{for all chains}\ Y) \\
& = & \bigsqcup\{ f^n \perp \mid n\geq 0 \} & (f^0 \perp = \perp) \\
& = & \text{FIX}\ f & (\text{definition of FIX}\ f)
\end{array}
$$

To see that FIX f is the *least* fixed point assume that d is some other fixed point. Clearly $\perp \sqsubseteq d$ so the monotonicity of f gives $f^n \perp \sqsubseteq f^n\ d$ for n≥0 and as d was a fixed point we obtain $f^n \perp \sqsubseteq d$ for all n≥0. Hence d is an upper bound of the chain $\{ f^n \perp \mid n\geq 0 \}$ and using that FIX f is the least upper bound we have FIX $f \sqsubseteq d$. □

Example 4.38 Consider the function F' of Example 4.1:

$$
(F'\ g)\ s = \begin{cases} g\ s & \text{if}\ s\ \mathtt{x} \neq \mathbf{0} \\ s & \text{if}\ s\ \mathtt{x} = \mathbf{0} \end{cases}
$$

We shall determine its least fixed point using the approach of Theorem 4.37. The least element $\perp$ of **State** ↪ **State** is given by Lemma 4.13 and has $\perp\ s$ = <u>undef</u> for all s. We then determine the elements of the set $\{ F'^n \perp \mid n\geq 0 \}$ as follows:

$$
\begin{array}{rcll}
(F'^0 \perp)\ s & = & (\text{id}\ \perp)\ s & (\text{definition of}\ F'^0 \perp) \\
& = & \underline{\text{undef}} & (\text{definition of id and}\ \perp) \\
(F'^1 \perp)\ s & = & (F'\ \perp)\ s & (\text{definition of}\ F'^1 \perp) \\
& = & \begin{cases} \perp\ s & \text{if}\ s\ \mathtt{x} \neq \mathbf{0} \\ s & \text{if}\ s\ \mathtt{x} = \mathbf{0} \end{cases} & (\text{definition of}\ F'\ \perp) \\
& = & \begin{cases} \underline{\text{undef}} & \text{if}\ s\ \mathtt{x} \neq \mathbf{0} \\ s & \text{if}\ s\ \mathtt{x} = \mathbf{0} \end{cases} & (\text{definition of}\ \perp)
\end{array}
$$

$$
\begin{aligned}
(F'^2 \perp)\ s &= F'\ (F'^1 \perp)\ s && \text{(definition of } F'^2 \perp\text{)}\\
&= \begin{cases} (F'^1 \perp)\ s & \text{if } s\ \mathbf{x} \neq \mathbf{0}\\ s & \text{if } s\ \mathbf{x} = \mathbf{0}\end{cases} && \text{(definition of } F'\text{)}\\
&= \begin{cases} \underline{\text{undef}} & \text{if } s\ \mathbf{x} \neq \mathbf{0}\\ s & \text{if } s\ \mathbf{x} = \mathbf{0}\end{cases} && \text{(definition of } F'^1 \perp\text{)}\\
&\vdots
\end{aligned}
$$

In general we have $F'^n \perp = F'^{n+1} \perp$ for n > 0. Therefore

$$\bigsqcup\{\ F'^n \perp \mid n{\geq}0\ \} = \bigsqcup\ \{F'^0 \perp,\ F'^1 \perp\} = F'^1 \perp$$

because $F'^0 \perp = \perp$. Thus the least fixed point of F' will be the function

$$g_1\ s = \begin{cases} \underline{\text{undef}} & \text{if } s\ \mathbf{x} \neq \mathbf{0}\\ s & \text{if } s\ \mathbf{x} = \mathbf{0}\end{cases}$$ □

Exercise 4.39 Redo Exercise 4.15 using the approach of Theorem 4.37, that is deduce the general form of the iterands, $F^n \perp$, for the functional, F, of Exercises 4.2 and 4.3. □

Exercise 4.40 (Essential) Let f: $D \to D$ be a continuous function on a ccpo $(D, \sqsubseteq)$ and let $d{\in}D$ satisfy $f\ d \sqsubseteq d$. Show that FIX $f \sqsubseteq d$. □

The table below summarizes the development we have performed in order to demonstrate the existence of least fixed points:

Fixed Point Theory	
1:	We restrict ourselves to *chain complete partially ordered sets* — ccpo's.
2:	We restrict ourselves to *continuous functions* on ccpo's.
3:	We show that continuous functions on ccpo's always have *least fixed points* (Theorem 4.37).

Exercise 4.41 * Let $(D, \sqsubseteq)$ be a ccpo and define the ccpo $(D{\to}D, \sqsubseteq')$ by setting

$$f_1 \sqsubseteq' f_2 \text{ if and only if } f_1\ d \sqsubseteq f_2\ d \text{ for all } d \in D$$

Show that FIX is "continuous" in the sense that

$$\text{FIX}\ (\bigsqcup'\ \mathcal{F}) = \bigsqcup\{\ \text{FIX}\ f \mid f \in \mathcal{F}\ \}$$

holds for all non-empty chains $\mathcal{F} \subseteq D{\to}D$ of continuous functions. □

Exercise 4.42 ** (For mathematicians) Given a ccpo $(D, \sqsubseteq)$ we define an *open set* of D to be a subset Y of D satisfying

(1) if $d_1 \in Y$ and $d_1 \sqsubseteq d_2$ then $d_2 \in Y$, and

(2) if Y' is a non-empty chain satisfying $\bigsqcup Y' \in Y$ then there exists an element d of Y' which also is an element of Y.

The set of open sets of D is denoted $\mathcal{O}_D$. Show that this is indeed a *topology* on D, that is show that

- $\emptyset$ and D are members of $\mathcal{O}_D$, and
- the intersection of two open sets is an open set, and
- the union of any collection of open sets is an open set.

Let $(D, \sqsubseteq)$ and $(D', \sqsubseteq')$ be ccpo's. A function $f{:}D \rightarrow D'$ is *topologically-continuous* if and only if the function f^{-1}: $\mathcal{P}(D') \rightarrow \mathcal{P}(D)$ defined by

$$f^{-1}(Y') = \{\ d \in D \mid f\ d \in Y'\ \}$$

maps open sets to open sets, that is specializes to f^{-1}: $\mathcal{O}_{D'} \rightarrow \mathcal{O}_D$. Show that f is a continuous function between D and D' if and only if it is a topologically-continuous function between D and D'. □

4.3 Direct style semantics: existence

We have now obtained the mathematical foundations needed to prove that the semantic clauses of Table 4.1 do indeed define a function. So consider once again the clause

$$\begin{aligned} \mathcal{S}_{\text{ds}}[\![\texttt{while}\ b\ \texttt{do}\ S]\!] &= \text{FIX}\ F \\ \text{where}\ F\ g &= \text{cond}(\mathcal{B}[\![b]\!],\ g \circ \mathcal{S}_{\text{ds}}[\![S]\!],\ \text{id}) \end{aligned}$$

For this to make sense we must show that F is continuous. To do so we first observe that

$$F\ g = F_1\ (F_2\ g)$$

where

$$\begin{aligned} F_1\ g &= \text{cond}(\mathcal{B}[\![b]\!],\ g,\ \text{id}) \\ F_2\ g &= g \circ \mathcal{S}_{\text{ds}}[\![S]\!] \end{aligned}$$

Using Lemma 4.35 we then obtain the continuity of F by showing that F_1 and F_2 are continuous. We shall first prove that F_1 is continuous:

Lemma 4.43 Let g_0: **State** $\hookrightarrow$ **State**, p: **State** $\to$ **T** and define

$$F\ g = \text{cond}(p,\ g,\ g_0)$$

Then F is continuous.

Proof: We shall first prove that F is *monotone*. So assume that $g_1 \sqsubseteq g_2$ and we shall show that $F\ g_1 \sqsubseteq F\ g_2$. It suffices to consider an arbitrary state s and show that

$$(F\ g_1)\ s = s' \text{ implies } (F\ g_2)\ s = s'$$

If $p\ s = \mathbf{tt}$ then $(F\ g_1)\ s = g_1\ s$ and from $g_1 \sqsubseteq g_2$ we get that $g_1\ s = s'$ implies $g_2\ s = s'$. Since $(F\ g_2)\ s = g_2\ s$ we have proved the result. So consider the case where $p\ s = \mathbf{ff}$. Then $(F\ g_1)\ s = g_0\ s$ and similarly $(F\ g_2)\ s = g_0\ s$ and the result is immediate.

To prove that F is *continuous* let Y be a non-empty chain in **State** $\hookrightarrow$ **State**. We must show that

$$F\ (\bigsqcup Y) \sqsubseteq \bigsqcup\{\ F\ g \mid g \in Y\ \}$$

since $F\ (\bigsqcup Y) \sqsupseteq \bigsqcup\{\ F\ g \mid g \in Y\ \}$ follows from the monotonicity of F (see Lemma 4.30). Thus we have to show that

$$\text{graph}(F(\bigsqcup Y)) \subseteq \bigcup\{\ \text{graph}(F\ g) \mid g \in Y\ \}$$

using the characterization of least upper bounds of chains in **State** $\hookrightarrow$ **State** given in Lemma 4.25. So assume that $(F\ (\bigsqcup Y))\ s = s'$ and let us determine $g \in Y$ such that $(F\ g)\ s = s'$. If $p\ s = \mathbf{ff}$ we have $F\ (\bigsqcup Y)\ s = g_0\ s = s'$ and clearly, for every element g of the non-empty set Y we have $(F\ g)\ s = g_0\ s = s'$. If $p\ s = \mathbf{tt}$ then we get $(F\ (\bigsqcup Y))\ s = (\bigsqcup Y)\ s = s'$ so $\langle s,\ s'\rangle \in \text{graph}(\bigsqcup Y)$. Since

$$\text{graph}(\bigsqcup Y) = \bigcup\{\ \text{graph}(g) \mid g \in Y\ \}$$

(according to Lemma 4.25) we therefore have $g \in Y$ such that $g\ s = s'$ and it follows that $(F\ g)\ s = s'$. This proves the result. □

Exercise 4.44 (Essential) Prove that F defined by $F\ g = \text{cond}(p,\ g_0,\ g)$ is continuous, that is 'cond' is continuous in its second and third arguments. □

Lemma 4.45 Let g_0: **State** $\hookrightarrow$ **State** and define

$$F\ g = g \circ g_0$$

Then F is continuous.

Proof: We shall first prove that F is monotone. If $g_1 \sqsubseteq g_2$ then graph(g_1) $\subseteq$ graph(g_2) according to Exercise 4.8 so that

$$\text{graph}(g_0) \diamond \text{graph}(g_1) \subseteq \text{graph}(g_0) \diamond \text{graph}(g_2)$$

and this shows that $F\ g_1 \sqsubseteq F\ g_2$. Next we shall prove that F is continuous. If Y is a non-empty chain then

$$\begin{aligned}\text{graph}(F(\bigsqcup Y)) &= \text{graph}((\bigsqcup Y) \circ g_0)\\ &= \text{graph}(g_0) \diamond \text{graph}(\bigsqcup Y)\\ &= \text{graph}(g_0) \diamond \bigcup\{\text{graph}(g) \mid g{\in}Y\}\\ &= \bigcup\{\text{graph}(g_0) \diamond \text{graph}(g) \mid g{\in}Y\}\\ &= \text{graph}(\bigsqcup\{F\ g \mid g{\in}Y\})\end{aligned}$$

where we have used Lemma 4.25 twice. Thus $F\ (\bigsqcup Y) = \bigsqcup\{F\ g \mid g{\in}\text{Y}\}$. □

Exercise 4.46 (Essential) Prove that F defined by $F\ g = g_0 \circ g$ is continuous, that is $\circ$ is continuous in both arguments. □

We have now established the results needed to show that the equations of Table 4.1 define a function $\mathcal{S}_{\text{ds}}$:

Proposition 4.47 The semantic equations of Table 4.1 define a total function $\mathcal{S}_{\text{ds}}$ in **Stm** $\rightarrow$ (**State** $\hookrightarrow$ **State**).

Proof: The proof is by structural induction on the statement S.

The case $x := a$: Clearly the function that maps a state s to the state $s[x{\mapsto}\mathcal{A}[\![a]\!]s]$ is well-defined.

The case `skip`: Clearly the function id is well-defined.

The case $S_1;S_2$: The induction hypothesis gives that $\mathcal{S}_{\text{ds}}[\![S_1]\!]$ and $\mathcal{S}_{\text{ds}}[\![S_2]\!]$ are well-defined and clearly their composition will be well-defined.

The case `if` b `then` S_1 `else` S_2: The induction hypothesis gives that $\mathcal{S}_{\text{ds}}[\![S_1]\!]$

and $\mathcal{S}_{\mathrm{ds}}[\![S_2]\!]$ are well-defined functions and clearly this property is preserved by the function 'cond'.

The case `while` b `do` S: The induction hypothesis gives that $\mathcal{S}_{\mathrm{ds}}[\![S]\!]$ is well-defined. The functions F_1 and F_2 defined by

$$F_1\ g = \mathrm{cond}(\mathcal{B}[\![b]\!],\ g,\ \mathrm{id})$$

$$F_2\ g = g \circ \mathcal{S}_{\mathrm{ds}}[\![S]\!]$$

are continuous according to Lemmas 4.43 and 4.45. Thus Lemma 4.35 gives that $F\ g = F_1\ (F_2\ g)$ is continuous. From Theorem 4.37 we then have that FIX F is well-defined and thereby that $\mathcal{S}_{\mathrm{ds}}[\![\texttt{while}\ b\ \texttt{do}\ S]\!]$ is well-defined. This completes the proof. □

Example 4.48 Consider the denotational semantics of the factorial statement:

$$\mathcal{S}_{\mathrm{ds}}[\![\mathtt{y} := \mathtt{1};\ \texttt{while}\ \neg(\mathtt{x}=\mathtt{1})\ \texttt{do}\ (\mathtt{y}:=\mathtt{y}\star\mathtt{x};\ \mathtt{x}:=\mathtt{x}-\mathtt{1})]\!]$$

We shall be interested in applying this function to a state s_0 where $\mathtt{x}$ has the value **3**. To do that we shall first apply the clauses of Table 4.1 and we then get that

$$\begin{aligned}&\mathcal{S}_{\mathrm{ds}}[\![\mathtt{y} := \mathtt{1};\ \texttt{while}\ \neg(\mathtt{x}=\mathtt{1})\ \texttt{do}\ (\mathtt{y}:=\mathtt{y}\star\mathtt{x};\ \mathtt{x}:=\mathtt{x}-\mathtt{1})]\!]\ s_0\\ &\qquad= (\mathrm{FIX}\ F)\ s_0[\mathtt{y}\mapsto\mathbf{1}]\end{aligned}$$

where

$$F\ g\ s = \begin{cases} g\ (\mathcal{S}_{\mathrm{ds}}[\![\mathtt{y}:=\ \mathtt{y}\star\mathtt{x};\ \mathtt{x}:=\mathtt{x}-\mathtt{1}]\!]\ s) & \text{if } \mathcal{B}[\![\neg(\mathtt{x}=\mathtt{1})]\!]\ s = \mathbf{tt}\\ s & \text{if } \mathcal{B}[\![\neg(\mathtt{x}=\mathtt{1})]\!]\ s = \mathbf{ff}\end{cases}$$

or, equivalently,

$$F\ g\ s = \begin{cases} g\ (s[\mathtt{y}\mapsto(s\ \mathtt{y})\star(s\ \mathtt{x})][\mathtt{x}\mapsto(s\ \mathtt{x})-\mathbf{1}]) & \text{if } s\ \mathtt{x} \neq \mathbf{1}\\ s & \text{if } s\ \mathtt{x} = \mathbf{1}\end{cases}$$

We can now calculate the various functions $F^n\ \bot$ used in the definition of FIX F in Theorem 4.37:

$$(F^0\ \bot)\ s = \underline{\mathrm{undef}}$$

$$(F^1\ \bot)\ s = \begin{cases} \underline{\mathrm{undef}} & \text{if } s\ \mathtt{x} \neq \mathbf{1}\\ s & \text{if } s\ \mathtt{x} = \mathbf{1}\end{cases}$$

$$(F^2\ \bot)\ s = \begin{cases} \underline{\mathrm{undef}} & \text{if } s\ \mathtt{x} \neq \mathbf{1} \text{ and } s\ \mathtt{x} \neq \mathbf{2}\\ s[\mathtt{y}\mapsto(s\ \mathtt{y})\star\mathbf{2}][\mathtt{x}\mapsto\mathbf{1}] & \text{if } s\ \mathtt{x} = \mathbf{2}\\ s & \text{if } s\ \mathtt{x} = \mathbf{1}\end{cases}$$

Thus if $\mathtt{x}$ is $\mathbf{1}$ or $\mathbf{2}$ then the $F^2 \perp$ will give the correct value for y and for all other values of $\mathtt{x}$ the result is undefined. This is a general pattern: the nth *iterand* $F^{\mathrm{n}} \perp$ will determine the correct value if it can be computed with *at most* n *unfoldings* of the `while`-loop (that is n evaluations of the boolean condition). The general formula is

$$(F^{\mathrm{n}} \perp)\ s = \begin{cases} \underline{\text{undef}} & \text{if } s\ \mathtt{x} < \mathbf{1} \text{ or } s\ \mathtt{x} > \mathrm{n} \\ s[\mathtt{y}{\mapsto}(s\ \mathtt{y}){\star}j{\cdots}{\star}\mathbf{2}{\star}\mathbf{1}][\mathtt{x}{\mapsto}\mathbf{1}] & \text{if } s\ \mathtt{x} = j \text{ and } \mathbf{1}{\leq}j \text{ and } j{\leq}\mathrm{n} \end{cases}$$

We then have

$$(\mathrm{FIX}\ F)\ s = \begin{cases} \underline{\text{undef}} & \text{if } s\ \mathtt{x} < \mathbf{1} \\ s[\mathtt{y}{\mapsto}(s\ \mathtt{y}){\star}n{\cdots}{\star}\mathbf{2}{\star}\mathbf{1}][\mathtt{x}{\mapsto}\mathbf{1}] & \text{if } s\ \mathtt{x} = n \text{ and } n{\geq}\mathbf{1} \end{cases}$$

So in the state s_0 where $\mathtt{x}$ has the value $\mathbf{3}$ we get that the value computed by the factorial statement is

$$(\mathrm{FIX}\ F)\ (s_0[\mathtt{y}{\mapsto}\mathbf{1}])\ \mathtt{x} = \mathbf{1} \star \mathbf{3} \star \mathbf{2} \star \mathbf{1} = \mathbf{6}$$

as expected. □

Exercise 4.49 Consider the statement

```
z:=0; while y≤x do (z:=z+1; x:=x−y)
```

and perform a development analogous to that of Example 4.48. □

Exercise 4.50 Show that $\mathcal{S}_{\mathrm{ds}}[\![$`while true do skip`$]\!]$ is the totally undefined function $\perp$. □

Exercise 4.51 Extend the language with the statement `repeat` S `until` b and give the new (compositional) clause for $\mathcal{S}_{\mathrm{ds}}$. Validate the well-definedness of the extended version of $\mathcal{S}_{\mathrm{ds}}$. □

Exercise 4.52 Extend the language with the statement `for` x := a_1 `to` a_2 `do` S and give the new (compositional) clause for $\mathcal{S}_{\mathrm{ds}}$. Validate the well-definedness of the extended version of $\mathcal{S}_{\mathrm{ds}}$. □

To summarize, the well-definedness of $\mathcal{S}_{\mathrm{ds}}$ relies on the following results established above:

Proof Summary for While: Well-definedness of Denotational Semantics	
1:	The set **State** $\hookrightarrow$ **State** equipped with an appropriate order $\sqsubseteq$ is a ccpo (Lemmas 4.13 and 4.25).
2:	Certain functions Ψ: (**State** $\hookrightarrow$ **State**) $\rightarrow$ (**State** $\hookrightarrow$ **State**) are continuous (Lemmas 4.43 and 4.45).
3:	In the definition of $\mathcal{S}_{\mathrm{ds}}$ we only apply the fixed point operation to continuous functions (Proposition 4.47).

Properties of the semantics

In the operational semantics we defined a notion of two statements being semantically equivalent. A similar notion can be defined based on the denotational semantics: S_1 and S_2 are *semantically equivalent* if and only if

$$\mathcal{S}_{\mathrm{ds}}[\![S_1]\!] = \mathcal{S}_{\mathrm{ds}}[\![S_2]\!]$$

Exercise 4.53 Show that the following statements of **While** are semantically equivalent in the above sense:

- S;`skip` and S
- S_1;(S_2;S_3) and (S_1;S_2);S_3
- `while` b `do` S and `if` b `then` (S; `while` b `do` S) `else skip` □

Exercise 4.54 * Prove that `repeat` S `until` b and S; `while` $\neg b$ `do` S are semantically equivalent using the denotational approach. The semantics of the `repeat`-construct is given in Exercise 4.51. □

4.4 An equivalence result

Having produced yet another semantics of the language **While** we shall be interested in its relation to the operational semantics and for this we shall focus on the structural operational semantics.

Theorem 4.55 For every statement S of **While** we have $\mathcal{S}_{\mathrm{sos}}[\![S]\!] = \mathcal{S}_{\mathrm{ds}}[\![S]\!]$.

Both $\mathcal{S}_{\rm ds}[\![S]\!]$ and $\mathcal{S}_{\rm sos}[\![S]\!]$ are functions in **State** $\hookrightarrow$ **State**, that is they are elements of a partially ordered set. To prove that two elements d_1 and d_2 of a partially ordered set are equal it is sufficient to prove that $d_1 \sqsubseteq d_2$ and that $d_2 \sqsubseteq d_1$. Thus to prove Theorem 4.55 we shall show that

- $\mathcal{S}_{\rm sos}[\![S]\!] \sqsubseteq \mathcal{S}_{\rm ds}[\![S]\!]$, and
- $\mathcal{S}_{\rm ds}[\![S]\!] \sqsubseteq \mathcal{S}_{\rm sos}[\![S]\!]$.

The first result is expressed by the following lemma:

Lemma 4.56 For every statement S of **While** we have $\mathcal{S}_{\rm sos}[\![S]\!] \sqsubseteq \mathcal{S}_{\rm ds}[\![S]\!]$.

Proof: It is sufficient to prove that for all states s and s'

$$\langle S,\ s\rangle \Rightarrow^* s' \text{ implies } \mathcal{S}_{\rm ds}[\![S]\!]s = s' \qquad (*)$$

To do so we shall need to establish the following property

$$\begin{array}{lll} \langle S,\ s\rangle \Rightarrow s' & \text{implies} & \mathcal{S}_{\rm ds}[\![S]\!]s = s' \\ \langle S,\ s\rangle \Rightarrow \langle S',\ s'\rangle & \text{implies} & \mathcal{S}_{\rm ds}[\![S]\!]s = \mathcal{S}_{\rm ds}[\![S']\!]s' \end{array} \qquad (**)$$

Assuming that (**) holds the proof of (*) is a straightforward induction on the length k of the derivation sequence $\langle S,\ s\rangle \Rightarrow^{\rm k} s'$ (see Section 2.2).

We now turn to the proof of (**) and for this we shall use induction on the shape of the derivation tree for $\langle S,\ s\rangle \Rightarrow s'$ or $\langle S,\ s\rangle \Rightarrow \langle S',\ s'\rangle$.

The case [ass$_{\rm sos}$]: We have

$$\langle x := a,\ s\rangle \Rightarrow s[x\mapsto\mathcal{A}[\![a]\!]s]$$

and since $\mathcal{S}_{\rm ds}[\![x := a]\!]s = s[x\mapsto\mathcal{A}[\![a]\!]s]$ the result follows.

The case [skip$_{\rm sos}$]: Analogous.

The case [comp$^1_{\rm sos}$]: Assume that

$$\langle S_1;S_2,\ s\rangle \Rightarrow \langle S_1';S_2,\ s'\rangle$$

because $\langle S_1,\ s\rangle \Rightarrow \langle S_1',\ s'\rangle$. Then the induction hypothesis applied to the latter transition gives $\mathcal{S}_{\rm ds}[\![S_1]\!]s = \mathcal{S}_{\rm ds}[\![S_1']\!]s'$ and we get

$$\begin{aligned} \mathcal{S}_{\rm ds}[\![S_1;S_2]\!]\ s &= \mathcal{S}_{\rm ds}[\![S_2]\!](\mathcal{S}_{\rm ds}[\![S_1]\!]s) \\ &= \mathcal{S}_{\rm ds}[\![S_2]\!](\mathcal{S}_{\rm ds}[\![S_1']\!]s') \\ &= \mathcal{S}_{\rm ds}[\![S_1';S_2]\!]s' \end{aligned}$$

as required.

The case [comp$^2_{\rm sos}$]: Assume that

$$\langle S_1;S_2,\ s\rangle \Rightarrow \langle S_2,\ s'\rangle$$

because $\langle S_1,\ s\rangle \Rightarrow s'$. Then the induction hypothesis applied to that transition gives $\mathcal{S}_{\text{ds}}[\![S_1]\!]s = s'$ and we get

$$\mathcal{S}_{\text{ds}}[\![S_1;S_2]\!]s = \mathcal{S}_{\text{ds}}[\![S_2]\!](\mathcal{S}_{\text{ds}}[\![S_1]\!]s) = \mathcal{S}_{\text{ds}}[\![S_2]\!]s'$$

where the first equality comes from the definition of $\mathcal{S}_{\text{ds}}$ and we just argued for the second equality. This proves the result.

The case $[\text{if}^{\text{tt}}_{\text{sos}}]$: Assume that

$$\langle \texttt{if}\ b\ \texttt{then}\ S_1\ \texttt{else}\ S_2,\ s\rangle \Rightarrow \langle S_1,\ s\rangle$$

because $\mathcal{B}[\![b]\!]\ s = \mathbf{tt}$. Then

$$\mathcal{S}_{\text{ds}}[\![\texttt{if}\ b\ \texttt{then}\ S_1\ \texttt{else}\ S_2]\!]s = \text{cond}(\mathcal{B}[\![b]\!],\ \mathcal{S}_{\text{ds}}[\![S_1]\!],\ \mathcal{S}_{\text{ds}}[\![S_2]\!])s = \mathcal{S}_{\text{ds}}[\![S_1]\!]s$$

as required.

The case $[\text{if}^{\text{ff}}_{\text{sos}}]$: Analogous.

The case $[\text{while}_{\text{sos}}]$: Assume that

$$\langle \texttt{while}\ b\ \texttt{do}\ S,\ s\rangle \Rightarrow \langle \texttt{if}\ b\ \texttt{then}\ (S;\ \texttt{while}\ b\ \texttt{do}\ S)\ \texttt{else skip},\ s\rangle$$

From the definition of $\mathcal{S}_{\text{ds}}$ we have $\mathcal{S}_{\text{ds}}[\![\texttt{while}\ b\ \texttt{do}\ S]\!] = \text{FIX}\ F$ where $F\ g = \text{cond}(\mathcal{B}[\![b]\!],\ g \circ \mathcal{S}_{\text{ds}}[\![S]\!],\ \text{id})$. We therefore get

$$\begin{aligned}
\mathcal{S}_{\text{ds}}[\![\texttt{while}\ b\ \texttt{do}\ S]\!] &= (\text{FIX}\ F) \\
&= F\ (\text{FIX}\ F) \\
&= \text{cond}(\mathcal{B}[\![b]\!],\ \mathcal{S}_{\text{ds}}[\![\texttt{while}\ b\ \texttt{do}\ S]\!] \circ \mathcal{S}_{\text{ds}}[\![S]\!],\ \text{id}) \\
&= \text{cond}(\mathcal{B}[\![b]\!],\ \mathcal{S}_{\text{ds}}[\![S;\ \texttt{while}\ b\ \texttt{do}\ S]\!],\ \mathcal{S}_{\text{ds}}[\![\texttt{skip}]\!]) \\
&= \mathcal{S}_{\text{ds}}[\![\texttt{if}\ b\ \texttt{then}\ (S;\ \texttt{while}\ b\ \texttt{do}\ S)\ \texttt{else skip}]\!]
\end{aligned}$$

as required. This completes the proof of (**). □

Note that (*) does *not* imply that $\mathcal{S}_{\text{sos}}[\![S]\!] = \mathcal{S}_{\text{ds}}[\![S]\!]$ as we have only proved that *if* $\mathcal{S}_{\text{sos}}[\![S]\!]s \neq \underline{\text{undef}}$ *then* $\mathcal{S}_{\text{sos}}[\![S]\!]s = \mathcal{S}_{\text{ds}}[\![S]\!]s$. Still there is the possibility that $\mathcal{S}_{\text{ds}}[\![S]\!]$ may be defined for more arguments than $\mathcal{S}_{\text{sos}}[\![S]\!]$. However this is ruled out by the following lemma:

Lemma 4.57 For every statement S of **While** we have $\mathcal{S}_{\text{ds}}[\![S]\!] \sqsubseteq \mathcal{S}_{\text{sos}}[\![S]\!]$.

Both $\mathcal{S}_{ds}[\![S]\!]$ and $\mathcal{S}_{sos}[\![S]\!]$ are functions in **State** $\hookrightarrow$ **State**, that is they are elements of a partially ordered set. To prove that two elements d_1 and d_2 of a partially ordered set are equal it is sufficient to prove that $d_1 \sqsubseteq d_2$ and that $d_2 \sqsubseteq d_1$. Thus to prove Theorem 4.55 we shall show that

- $\mathcal{S}_{sos}[\![S]\!] \sqsubseteq \mathcal{S}_{ds}[\![S]\!]$, and
- $\mathcal{S}_{ds}[\![S]\!] \sqsubseteq \mathcal{S}_{sos}[\![S]\!]$.

The first result is expressed by the following lemma:

Lemma 4.56 For every statement S of **While** we have $\mathcal{S}_{sos}[\![S]\!] \sqsubseteq \mathcal{S}_{ds}[\![S]\!]$.

Proof: It is sufficient to prove that for all states s and s'

$$\langle S,\ s\rangle \Rightarrow^* s' \text{ implies } \mathcal{S}_{ds}[\![S]\!]s = s' \qquad (*)$$

To do so we shall need to establish the following property

$$\begin{array}{lll} \langle S,\ s\rangle \Rightarrow s' & \text{implies} & \mathcal{S}_{ds}[\![S]\!]s = s' \\ \langle S,\ s\rangle \Rightarrow \langle S',\ s'\rangle & \text{implies} & \mathcal{S}_{ds}[\![S]\!]s = \mathcal{S}_{ds}[\![S']\!]s' \end{array} \qquad (**)$$

Assuming that (**) holds the proof of (*) is a straightforward induction on the length k of the derivation sequence $\langle S,\ s\rangle \Rightarrow^{\mathrm{k}} s'$ (see Section 2.2).

We now turn to the proof of (**) and for this we shall use induction on the shape of the derivation tree for $\langle S,\ s\rangle \Rightarrow s'$ or $\langle S,\ s\rangle \Rightarrow \langle S',\ s'\rangle$.

The case [ass$_{sos}$]: We have

$$\langle x := a,\ s\rangle \Rightarrow s[x \mapsto \mathcal{A}[\![a]\!]s]$$

and since $\mathcal{S}_{ds}[\![x := a]\!]s = s[x \mapsto \mathcal{A}[\![a]\!]s]$ the result follows.

The case [skip$_{sos}$]: Analogous.

The case [comp$^1_{sos}$]: Assume that

$$\langle S_1;S_2,\ s\rangle \Rightarrow \langle S_1';S_2,\ s'\rangle$$

because $\langle S_1,\ s\rangle \Rightarrow \langle S_1',\ s'\rangle$. Then the induction hypothesis applied to the latter transition gives $\mathcal{S}_{ds}[\![S_1]\!]s = \mathcal{S}_{ds}[\![S_1']\!]s'$ and we get

$$\begin{aligned} \mathcal{S}_{ds}[\![S_1;S_2]\!]\ s &= \mathcal{S}_{ds}[\![S_2]\!](\mathcal{S}_{ds}[\![S_1]\!]s) \\ &= \mathcal{S}_{ds}[\![S_2]\!](\mathcal{S}_{ds}[\![S_1']\!]s') \\ &= \mathcal{S}_{ds}[\![S_1';S_2]\!]s' \end{aligned}$$

as required.

The case [comp$^2_{sos}$]: Assume that

$$\langle S_1;S_2,\ s\rangle \Rightarrow \langle S_2,\ s'\rangle$$

because $\langle S_1,\ s\rangle \Rightarrow s'$. Then the induction hypothesis applied to that transition gives $\mathcal{S}_{\mathrm{ds}}[\![S_1]\!]s = s'$ and we get

$$\mathcal{S}_{\mathrm{ds}}[\![S_1;S_2]\!]s = \mathcal{S}_{\mathrm{ds}}[\![S_2]\!](\mathcal{S}_{\mathrm{ds}}[\![S_1]\!]s) = \mathcal{S}_{\mathrm{ds}}[\![S_2]\!]s'$$

where the first equality comes from the definition of $\mathcal{S}_{\mathrm{ds}}$ and we just argued for the second equality. This proves the result.

The case $[\mathrm{if}^{\mathrm{tt}}_{\mathrm{sos}}]$: Assume that

$$\langle \texttt{if}\ b\ \texttt{then}\ S_1\ \texttt{else}\ S_2,\ s\rangle \Rightarrow \langle S_1,\ s\rangle$$

because $\mathcal{B}[\![b]\!]\ s = \mathbf{tt}$. Then

$$\mathcal{S}_{\mathrm{ds}}[\![\texttt{if}\ b\ \texttt{then}\ S_1\ \texttt{else}\ S_2]\!]s = \mathrm{cond}(\mathcal{B}[\![b]\!],\ \mathcal{S}_{\mathrm{ds}}[\![S_1]\!],\ \mathcal{S}_{\mathrm{ds}}[\![S_2]\!])s = \mathcal{S}_{\mathrm{ds}}[\![S_1]\!]s$$

as required.

The case $[\mathrm{if}^{\mathrm{ff}}_{\mathrm{sos}}]$: Analogous.

The case $[\mathrm{while}_{\mathrm{sos}}]$: Assume that

$$\langle \texttt{while}\ b\ \texttt{do}\ S,\ s\rangle \Rightarrow \langle \texttt{if}\ b\ \texttt{then}\ (S;\ \texttt{while}\ b\ \texttt{do}\ S)\ \texttt{else skip},\ s\rangle$$

From the definition of $\mathcal{S}_{\mathrm{ds}}$ we have $\mathcal{S}_{\mathrm{ds}}[\![\texttt{while}\ b\ \texttt{do}\ S]\!] = \mathrm{FIX}\ F$ where $F\ g = \mathrm{cond}(\mathcal{B}[\![b]\!],\ g \circ \mathcal{S}_{\mathrm{ds}}[\![S]\!],\ \mathrm{id})$. We therefore get

$$\begin{aligned}
\mathcal{S}_{\mathrm{ds}}[\![\texttt{while}\ b\ \texttt{do}\ S]\!] &= (\mathrm{FIX}\ F)\\
&= F\ (\mathrm{FIX}\ F)\\
&= \mathrm{cond}(\mathcal{B}[\![b]\!],\ \mathcal{S}_{\mathrm{ds}}[\![\texttt{while}\ b\ \texttt{do}\ S]\!] \circ \mathcal{S}_{\mathrm{ds}}[\![S]\!],\ \mathrm{id})\\
&= \mathrm{cond}(\mathcal{B}[\![b]\!],\ \mathcal{S}_{\mathrm{ds}}[\![S;\ \texttt{while}\ b\ \texttt{do}\ S]\!],\ \mathcal{S}_{\mathrm{ds}}[\![\texttt{skip}]\!])\\
&= \mathcal{S}_{\mathrm{ds}}[\![\texttt{if}\ b\ \texttt{then}\ (S;\ \texttt{while}\ b\ \texttt{do}\ S)\ \texttt{else skip}]\!]
\end{aligned}$$

as required. This completes the proof of (**). □

Note that (*) does *not* imply that $\mathcal{S}_{\mathrm{sos}}[\![S]\!] = \mathcal{S}_{\mathrm{ds}}[\![S]\!]$ as we have only proved that *if* $\mathcal{S}_{\mathrm{sos}}[\![S]\!]s \neq \underline{\mathrm{undef}}$ *then* $\mathcal{S}_{\mathrm{sos}}[\![S]\!]s = \mathcal{S}_{\mathrm{ds}}[\![S]\!]s$. Still there is the possibility that $\mathcal{S}_{\mathrm{ds}}[\![S]\!]$ may be defined for more arguments than $\mathcal{S}_{\mathrm{sos}}[\![S]\!]$. However this is ruled out by the following lemma:

Lemma 4.57 For every statement S of **While** we have $\mathcal{S}_{\mathrm{ds}}[\![S]\!] \sqsubseteq \mathcal{S}_{\mathrm{sos}}[\![S]\!]$.

Proof: We proceed by structural induction on the statement S.

The case $x := a$: Clearly $\mathcal{S}_{\rm ds}[\![x := a]\!]s = \mathcal{S}_{\rm sos}[\![x := a]\!]s$. Note that this means that $\mathcal{S}_{\rm sos}$ satisfies the clause defining $\mathcal{S}_{\rm ds}$ in Table 4.1.

The case `skip`: Clearly $\mathcal{S}_{\rm ds}[\![\texttt{skip}]\!]s = \mathcal{S}_{\rm sos}[\![\texttt{skip}]\!]s$.

The case S_1 ; S_2: Recall that $\circ$ is monotone in both arguments (Lemma 4.45 and Exercise 4.46). We then have

$$\begin{aligned}\mathcal{S}_{\rm ds}[\![S_1 \,;\, S_2]\!] &= \mathcal{S}_{\rm ds}[\![S_2]\!] \circ \mathcal{S}_{\rm ds}[\![S_1]\!] \\ &\sqsubseteq \mathcal{S}_{\rm sos}[\![S_2]\!] \circ \mathcal{S}_{\rm sos}[\![S_1]\!]\end{aligned}$$

because the induction hypothesis applied to S_1 and S_2 gives $\mathcal{S}_{\rm ds}[\![S_1]\!] \sqsubseteq \mathcal{S}_{\rm sos}[\![S_1]\!]$ and $\mathcal{S}_{\rm ds}[\![S_2]\!] \sqsubseteq \mathcal{S}_{\rm sos}[\![S_2]\!]$. Furthermore, Exercise 2.21 gives that if $\langle S_1, s\rangle \Rightarrow^* s'$ then $\langle S_1 \,;\, S_2, s\rangle \Rightarrow^* \langle S_2, s'\rangle$ and hence

$$\mathcal{S}_{\rm sos}[\![S_2]\!] \circ \mathcal{S}_{\rm sos}[\![S_1]\!] \sqsubseteq \mathcal{S}_{\rm sos}[\![S_1 \,;\, S_2]\!]$$

and this proves the result. Note that in this case $\mathcal{S}_{\rm sos}$ fulfils a weaker version of the clause defining $\mathcal{S}_{\rm ds}$ in Table 4.1.

The case `if` b `then` S_1 `else` S_2: Recall that 'cond' is monotone in its second and third argument (Lemma 4.43 and Exercise 4.44). We then have

$$\begin{aligned}\mathcal{S}_{\rm ds}[\![\texttt{if}\ b\ \texttt{then}\ S_1\ \texttt{else}\ S_2]\!] &= \text{cond}(\mathcal{B}[\![b]\!], \mathcal{S}_{\rm ds}[\![S_1]\!], \mathcal{S}_{\rm ds}[\![S_2]\!]) \\ &\sqsubseteq \text{cond}(\mathcal{B}[\![b]\!], \mathcal{S}_{\rm sos}[\![S_1]\!], \mathcal{S}_{\rm sos}[\![S_2]\!])\end{aligned}$$

because the induction hypothesis applied to S_1 and S_2 gives $\mathcal{S}_{\rm ds}[\![S_1]\!] \sqsubseteq \mathcal{S}_{\rm sos}[\![S_1]\!]$ and $\mathcal{S}_{\rm ds}[\![S_2]\!] \sqsubseteq \mathcal{S}_{\rm sos}[\![S_2]\!]$. Furthermore, it follows from $[\text{if}^{\rm tt}_{\rm sos}]$ and $[\text{if}^{\rm ff}_{\rm sos}]$ that

$$\mathcal{S}_{\rm sos}[\![\texttt{if}\ b\ \texttt{then}\ S_1\ \texttt{else}\ S_2]\!]s = \mathcal{S}_{\rm sos}[\![S_1]\!]s \quad \text{if } \mathcal{B}[\![b]\!]s = \mathbf{tt}$$

$$\mathcal{S}_{\rm sos}[\![\texttt{if}\ b\ \texttt{then}\ S_1\ \texttt{else}\ S_2]\!]s = \mathcal{S}_{\rm sos}[\![S_2]\!]s \quad \text{if } \mathcal{B}[\![b]\!]s = \mathbf{ff}$$

so that

$$\text{cond}(\mathcal{B}[\![b]\!], \mathcal{S}_{\rm sos}[\![S_1]\!], \mathcal{S}_{\rm sos}[\![S_2]\!]) = \mathcal{S}_{\rm sos}[\![\texttt{if}\ b\ \texttt{then}\ S_1\ \texttt{else}\ S_2]\!]$$

and this proves the result. Note that in this case $\mathcal{S}_{\rm sos}$ fulfils the clause defining $\mathcal{S}_{\rm ds}$ in Table 4.1.

The case `while` b `do` S: We have

$$\mathcal{S}_{\rm ds}[\![\texttt{while}\ b\ \texttt{do}\ S]\!] = \text{FIX } F$$

where $F\ g = \text{cond}(\mathcal{B}[\![b]\!], g \circ \mathcal{S}_{\rm ds}[\![S]\!], \text{id})$ and we recall that F is continuous. It is sufficient to prove that

$$F(\mathcal{S}_{\rm sos}[\![\texttt{while}\ b\ \texttt{do}\ S]\!]) \sqsubseteq \mathcal{S}_{\rm sos}[\![\texttt{while}\ b\ \texttt{do}\ S]\!]$$

because then Exercise 4.40 gives FIX $F \sqsubseteq \mathcal{S}_{\mathrm{sos}}[\![\texttt{while}\ b\ \texttt{do}\ S]\!]$ as required. From Exercise 2.21 we get

$$\begin{aligned}\mathcal{S}_{\mathrm{sos}}[\![\texttt{while}\ b\ \texttt{do}\ S]\!] &= \mathrm{cond}(\mathcal{B}[\![b]\!], \mathcal{S}_{\mathrm{sos}}[\![S\ ;\ \texttt{while}\ b\ \texttt{do}\ S]\!], \mathrm{id}) \\ &\sqsupseteq \mathrm{cond}(\mathcal{B}[\![b]\!], \mathcal{S}_{\mathrm{sos}}[\![\texttt{while}\ b\ \texttt{do}\ S]\!] \circ \mathcal{S}_{\mathrm{sos}}[\![S]\!], \mathrm{id})\end{aligned}$$

The induction hypothesis applied to S gives $\mathcal{S}_{\mathrm{ds}}[\![S]\!] \sqsubseteq \mathcal{S}_{\mathrm{sos}}[\![S]\!]$ so using the monotonicity of $\circ$ and 'cond' we get

$$\begin{aligned}\mathcal{S}_{\mathrm{sos}}[\![\texttt{while}\ b\ \texttt{do}\ S]\!] &\sqsupseteq \mathrm{cond}(\mathcal{B}[\![b]\!], \mathcal{S}_{\mathrm{sos}}[\![\texttt{while}\ b\ \texttt{do}\ S]\!] \circ \mathcal{S}_{\mathrm{sos}}[\![S]\!], \mathrm{id}) \\ &\sqsupseteq \mathrm{cond}(\mathcal{B}[\![b]\!], \mathcal{S}_{\mathrm{sos}}[\![\texttt{while}\ b\ \texttt{do}\ S]\!] \circ \mathcal{S}_{\mathrm{ds}}[\![S]\!], \mathrm{id}) \\ &= F(\mathcal{S}_{\mathrm{sos}}[\![\texttt{while}\ b\ \texttt{do}\ S]\!])\end{aligned}$$

Note that in this case $\mathcal{S}_{\mathrm{sos}}$ also fulfils a weaker version of the clause defining $\mathcal{S}_{\mathrm{ds}}$ in Table 4.1. □

The key technique used in the proof can be summarized as follows:

Proof Summary for While:

Equivalence of Operational Semantics and Denotational Semantics

1: Prove that $\mathcal{S}_{\mathrm{sos}}[\![S]\!] \sqsubseteq \mathcal{S}_{\mathrm{ds}}[\![S]\!]$ by first using *induction on the shape of derivation trees* to show that

- if a statement is executed *one step* in the structural operational semantics and does not terminate then this does not change the meaning in the denotational semantics, and
- if a statement is executed *one step* in the structural operational semantics and does terminate, then the same result is obtained in the denotational semantics.

and secondly by using *induction on the length of derivation sequences.*

2: Prove that $\mathcal{S}_{\mathrm{ds}}[\![S]\!] \sqsubseteq \mathcal{S}_{\mathrm{sos}}[\![S]\!]$ by showing that

- $\mathcal{S}_{\mathrm{sos}}$ fulfils slightly weaker versions of the clauses defining $\mathcal{S}_{\mathrm{ds}}$ in Table 4.1, that is if

  $$\mathcal{S}_{\mathrm{ds}}[\![S]\!] = \Psi(\cdots\ \mathcal{S}_{\mathrm{ds}}[\![S']\!]\ \cdots)$$

  then $\mathcal{S}_{\mathrm{sos}}[\![S]\!] \sqsupseteq \Psi(\cdots\ \mathcal{S}_{\mathrm{sos}}[\![S']\!]\ \cdots)$

A proof by *structural induction* then gives that $\mathcal{S}_{\mathrm{ds}}[\![S]\!] \sqsubseteq \mathcal{S}_{\mathrm{sos}}[\![S]\!]$.

Exercise 4.58 Give a detailed argument showing that

$$\mathcal{S}_{\text{sos}}[\![\texttt{while } b \texttt{ do } S]\!] \sqsupseteq \text{cond}(\mathcal{B}[\![b]\!], \mathcal{S}_{\text{sos}}[\![\texttt{while } b \texttt{ do } S]\!] \circ \mathcal{S}_{\text{sos}}[\![S]\!], \text{id}). \qquad \square$$

Exercise 4.59 Extend the proof of Theorem 4.55 so that it applies to the language when augmented with `repeat` S `until` b. □

Exercise 4.60 Extend the proof of Theorem 4.55 so that it applies to the language when augmented with `for` $x{:=}a_1$ `to` a_2 `do` S. □

Exercise 4.61 Combining the results of Theorem 2.26 and Theorem 4.55 we get that $\mathcal{S}_{\text{ns}}[\![S]\!] = \mathcal{S}_{\text{ds}}[\![S]\!]$ holds for every statement S of **While**. Give a direct proof of this (that is without using the two theorems). □

4.5 Extensions of While

We shall conclude this chapter by considering a couple of extensions of the language **While**. The extensions have been chosen so as to illustrate two of the most important concepts of denotational semantics:

- *locations*, and
- *continuations*.

In the first case **While** is extended with blocks and procedures and in the second case with exceptions. In both cases we shall show how to modify the semantics of Table 4.1.

The concept of locations

We shall first extend **While** with blocks declaring local variables and procedures. The new language is called **Proc** and its syntax is

$$\begin{array}{lcl} S & ::= & x := a \mid \texttt{skip} \mid S_1 \,;\, S_2 \mid \texttt{if } b \texttt{ then } S_1 \texttt{ else } S_2 \\ & \mid & \texttt{while } b \texttt{ do } S \mid \texttt{begin } D_V\ D_P\ S \texttt{ end} \mid \texttt{call } p \\ D_V & ::= & \texttt{var } x := a;\ D_V \mid \varepsilon \\ D_P & ::= & \texttt{proc } p \texttt{ is } S;\ D_P \mid \varepsilon \end{array}$$

where D_V and D_P are meta-variables ranging over the syntactic categories $\mathbf{Dec}_V$ of variable declarations and $\mathbf{Dec}_P$ of procedure declarations, respectively, and p is a meta-variable ranging over the syntactic category **Pname** of procedure names. The idea is that variables and procedures are only known inside the block where they are declared. Procedures may or may not be recursive and we shall emphasize the differences in the semantics to be specified below.

We shall adopt *static scope rules* rather than dynamic scope rules. Consider the following statement:

```
begin var x := 7; proc p is x := 0;
        begin var x := 5; call p end
end
```

Using static scope rules the effect of executing `call p` in the inner block will be to modify the *global* variable `x`. Using dynamic scope rules the effect will be to modify the *local* variable `x`.

To obtain static scope rules we shall introduce the notion of *locations*: to each variable we associate a uniquc location and to each location we associate a value. This is in contrast to what we did in Table 4.1 where we employed a direct association between variables and values. The idea then is that whenever a new variable is declared it is associated with a new unused location and that it is the value of this location that is changed by assignment to the variable. With respect to the above statement this means that the global variable `x` and the local variable `x` will have different locations. In the inner block we can only directly access the location of the local variable but the procedure body for `p` may only access the location of the global variable.

Stores and variable environments

So far states in **State** have been used to associate values with variables. We shall now replace states with *stores* that map locations to values and with *variable environments* that map variables to locations. We introduce the domain

$$\mathbf{Loc} = \mathbf{Z}$$

of locations which for the sake of simplicity has been identified with the integers. We shall need an operation

$$\text{new}: \mathbf{Loc} \to \mathbf{Loc}$$

on locations that given a location will give the next one; since **Loc** is **Z** we may take 'new' to be the successor function on the integers.

We can now define a store, *sto*, as an element of

$$\mathbf{Store} = \mathbf{Loc} \cup \{\text{next}\} \to \mathbf{Z}$$

where 'next' is a special token used to hold the *next free location.* Note that since **Loc** is **Z** we have that '*sto* next' is a location.

A variable environment env_V is an element of

$$\mathbf{Env_V} = \mathbf{Var} \to \mathbf{Loc}$$

Thus the variable environment will assign a location to each variable.

So, rather than having a single mapping s from variables to values we have split it into two mappings env_V and *sto* and the idea is that $s = sto \circ env_V$. This motivates defining the function 'lookup' by

$$\mathcal{S}'_{\text{ds}}[\![x:=a]\!]env_V\ sto = sto[l \mapsto \mathcal{A}[\![a]\!](\text{lookup}\ env_V\ sto)]$$
$$\text{where } l = env_V\ x$$
$$\mathcal{S}'_{\text{ds}}[\![\texttt{skip}]\!]env_V = \text{id}$$
$$\mathcal{S}'_{\text{ds}}[\![S_1\ ;\ S_2]\!]env_V = (\mathcal{S}'_{\text{ds}}[\![S_2]\!]env_V) \circ (\mathcal{S}'_{\text{ds}}[\![S_1]\!]env_V)$$
$$\mathcal{S}'_{\text{ds}}[\![\texttt{if}\ b\ \texttt{then}\ S_1\ \texttt{else}\ S_2]\!]env_V =$$
$$\text{cond}(\mathcal{B}[\![b]\!]\circ(\text{lookup}\ env_V), \mathcal{S}'_{\text{ds}}[\![S_1]\!]env_V, \mathcal{S}'_{\text{ds}}[\![S_2]\!]env_V)$$
$$\mathcal{S}'_{\text{ds}}[\![\texttt{while}\ b\ \texttt{do}\ S]\!]env_V = \text{FIX } F$$
$$\text{where } F\ g = \text{cond}(\mathcal{B}[\![b]\!]\circ(\text{lookup}\ env_V), g \circ (\mathcal{S}'_{\text{ds}}[\![S]\!]env_V), \text{id})$$

Table 4.2: Denotational semantics for **While** using locations

$$\text{lookup}\ env_V\ sto = sto \circ env_V$$

so that 'lookup env_V' will transform a store to a state, that is

$$\text{lookup: } \mathbf{Env_V} \to \mathbf{Store} \to \mathbf{State}$$

Having replaced a one stage mapping with a two stage mapping we shall want to reformulate the semantic equations of Table 4.1 to use variable environments and stores. The new semantic function $\mathcal{S}'_{\text{ds}}$ has functionality

$$\mathcal{S}'_{\text{ds}}\text{: } \mathbf{Stm} \to \mathbf{Env_V} \to (\mathbf{Store} \hookrightarrow \mathbf{Store})$$

so that only the store is updated during the execution of statements. The clauses defining $\mathcal{S}'_{\text{ds}}$ are given in Table 4.2. Note that in the clause for assignment the variable environment is consulted to determine the location of the variable and this location is updated in the store. In the clauses for the conditional and the `while`-construct we use the auxiliary function 'cond' of functionality

$$\text{cond: } (\mathbf{Store} \to \mathbf{T}) \times (\mathbf{Store} \hookrightarrow \mathbf{Store}) \times (\mathbf{Store} \hookrightarrow \mathbf{Store})$$
$$\to (\mathbf{Store} \hookrightarrow \mathbf{Store})$$

and its definition is as in Section 4.1.

Exercise 4.62 We have to make sure that the clauses of Table 4.2 define a well-defined function $\mathcal{S}'_{\text{ds}}$. To do so

- equip **Store** $\hookrightarrow$ **Store** with a partial ordering such that it becomes a ccpo,
- show that $\circ$ is continuous in both of its arguments and that 'cond' is continuous in its second and third argument, and

- show that the fixed point operation is only applied to continuous functions.

Conclude that $\mathcal{S}'_{\text{ds}}$ is a well-defined function. □

Exercise 4.63 * Prove that the two semantic functions $\mathcal{S}_{\text{ds}}$ and $\mathcal{S}'_{\text{ds}}$ satisfy

$$\mathcal{S}_{\text{ds}}[\![S]\!] \circ (\text{lookup } env_V) = (\text{lookup } env_V) \circ (\mathcal{S}'_{\text{ds}}[\![S]\!] env_V)$$

for all statements S of **While** and for all env_V such that env_V is an injective mapping. □

Exercise 4.64 Having replaced a one stage mapping with a two stage mapping we might consider redefining the semantic functions $\mathcal{A}$ and $\mathcal{B}$. The new functionalities of $\mathcal{A}$ and $\mathcal{B}$ might be

$$\mathcal{A}'\text{: } \mathbf{Aexp} \to \mathbf{Env}_V \to (\mathbf{Store} \to \mathbf{Z})$$

$$\mathcal{B}'\text{: } \mathbf{Bexp} \to \mathbf{Env}_V \to (\mathbf{Store} \to \mathbf{T})$$

and the intended relationship is that

$$\mathcal{A}'[\![a]\!] env_V = \mathcal{A}[\![a]\!] \circ (\text{lookup } env_V)$$

$$\mathcal{B}'[\![b]\!] env_V = \mathcal{B}[\![b]\!] \circ (\text{lookup } env_V)$$

Give a compositional definition of the functions $\mathcal{A}'$ and $\mathcal{B}'$ such that this is the case. □

Updating the variable environment

The variable environment is updated whenever we enter a block containing local declarations. To express this we shall introduce a semantic function $\mathcal{D}^{\text{V}}_{\text{ds}}$ for the syntactic category of variable declarations. It has functionality

$$\mathcal{D}^{\text{V}}_{\text{ds}}\text{: } \mathbf{Dec}_V \to \mathbf{Env}_V \times \mathbf{Store} \to \mathbf{Env}_V \times \mathbf{Store}$$

The function $\mathcal{D}^{\text{V}}_{\text{ds}}[\![D_V]\!]$ will take a pair as arguments: the first component of that pair will be the current variable environment and the second component the current store. The function will return the updated variable environment as well as the updated store. The function is defined by the semantic clauses of Table 4.3. Note that we process the declarations from left to right and that we update the value of the token 'next' in the store.

In the case where there are *no* procedure declarations in a block we can extend the semantic function $\mathcal{S}'_{\text{ds}}$ of Table 4.2 with a clause like

$$\mathcal{S}'_{\text{ds}}[\![\texttt{begin } D_V \; S \texttt{ end}]\!] env_V \; sto = \mathcal{S}'_{\text{ds}}[\![S]\!] env'_V \; sto'$$

$$\text{where } \mathcal{D}^{\text{V}}_{\text{ds}}[\![D_V]\!](env_V, sto) = (env'_V, sto')$$

$$\mathcal{D}^{\mathrm{V}}_{\mathrm{ds}}[\![\texttt{var}\ x := a;\ D_V]\!](env_V,\ sto) =$$
$$\mathcal{D}^{\mathrm{V}}_{\mathrm{ds}}[\![D_V]\!](env_V[x\mapsto l],\ sto[l\mapsto v][\mathrm{next}\mapsto\mathrm{new}\ l])$$
$$\text{where } l = sto\ \mathrm{next} \text{ and } v = \mathcal{A}[\![a]\!](\mathrm{lookup}\ env_V\ sto)$$
$$\mathcal{D}^{\mathrm{V}}_{\mathrm{ds}}[\![\varepsilon]\!] = \mathrm{id}$$

Table 4.3: Denotational semantics for variable declarations

Thus we evaluate the body S in an updated variable environment and an updated store. We shall later modify the above clause to take the procedure declarations into account.

Exercise 4.65 Consider the following statement of **Proc**:

```
begin var y := 0; var x := 1;
        begin var x := 7; x := x+1 end;
        y := x
end
```

Use the semantic equations to show that the location for y is assigned the value **1** in the final store. □

Procedure environments

To cater for procedures we shall introduce the notion of a *procedure environment.* It will be a total function that will associate each procedure with the effect of executing its body. This means that a procedure environment, env_P, will be an element of

$$\mathbf{Env_P} = \mathbf{Pname} \rightarrow (\mathbf{Store} \hookrightarrow \mathbf{Store})$$

Remark This notion of procedure environment differs from that of the operational approach. □

The procedure environment is updated using the semantic function $\mathcal{D}^{\mathrm{P}}_{\mathrm{ds}}$ for procedure declarations. It has functionality

$$\mathcal{D}^{\mathrm{P}}_{\mathrm{ds}}\colon \mathbf{Dec_P} \rightarrow \mathbf{Env_V} \rightarrow \mathbf{Env_P} \rightarrow \mathbf{Env_P}$$

So given the current variable environment and the current procedure environment the function $\mathcal{D}^{\mathrm{P}}_{\mathrm{ds}}[\![D_P]\!]$ will update the procedure environment. The variable environment must be available because procedures must know the variables that have been declared so far. An example is the statement

$$\mathcal{D}^{\rm P}_{\rm ds}[\![\texttt{proc}\ p\ \texttt{is}\ S;\ D_P]\!]env_V\ env_P = \mathcal{D}^{\rm P}_{\rm ds}[\![D_P]\!]env_V\ (env_P[p\mapsto g])$$
$$\text{where } g = \mathcal{S}_{\rm ds}[\![S]\!]env_V\ env_P$$
$$\mathcal{D}^{\rm P}_{\rm ds}[\![\varepsilon]\!]env_V = \text{id}$$

Table 4.4: Denotational semantics for non-recursive procedure declarations

```
begin var x := 7; proc p is x := 0;
        begin var x := 5; call p end
end
```

where the body of p must know that a variable x has been declared in the outer block.

The semantic clauses defining $\mathcal{D}^{\rm P}_{\rm ds}$ in the case of *non-recursive procedures* are given in Table 4.4. In the clause for procedure declarations we use the semantic function $\mathcal{S}_{\rm ds}$ for statements (defined below) to determine the meaning of the body of the procedure using that env_V and env_P are the environments at the point of declaration. The variables occurring in the body S of p will therefore be bound to the locations of the variables as known at the time of declaration but the values of the locations will not be known until the time of call. In this way we ensure that we obtain static scope for variables. Also an occurrence of `call` p' in the body of the procedure will refer to a procedure p' mentioned in env_P, that is a procedure declared in an outer block or in the current block but preceding the present procedure. In this way we obtain static scope for procedures. This will be illustrated in Exercise 4.67 below.

The semantic function $\mathcal{S}_{\rm ds}$ for Proc

The meaning of a statement depends on the variables and procedures that have been declared. Therefore the semantic function $\mathcal{S}_{\rm ds}$ for statements in **Proc** will have functionality

$$\mathcal{S}_{\rm ds}\colon \textbf{Stm} \to \textbf{Env}_{\rm V} \to \textbf{Env}_{\rm P} \to (\textbf{Store} \hookrightarrow \textbf{Store})$$

The function is defined by the clauses of Table 4.5. In most cases the definition of $\mathcal{S}_{\rm ds}$ is a straightforward modification of the clauses of $\mathcal{S}'_{\rm ds}$. Note that the meaning of a procedure call is obtained by simply consulting the procedure environment.

Example 4.66 This example shows how we obtain static scope rules for the variables. Consider the application of the semantic function $\mathcal{S}_{\rm ds}$ to the statement

```
begin var x := 7; proc p is x := 0;
        begin var x := 5; call p end
end
```

$$\mathcal{S}_{\text{ds}}[\![x\text{:=}a]\!]env_V\ env_P\ sto = sto[l \mapsto \mathcal{A}[\![a]\!](\text{lookup}\ env_V\ sto)]$$
$$\text{where } l = env_V\ x$$
$$\mathcal{S}_{\text{ds}}[\![\texttt{skip}]\!]env_V\ env_P = \text{id}$$
$$\mathcal{S}_{\text{ds}}[\![S_1\ ;\ S_2]\!]env_V\ env_P = (\mathcal{S}_{\text{ds}}[\![S_2]\!]env_V\ env_P) \circ (\mathcal{S}_{\text{ds}}[\![S_1]\!]env_V\ env_P)$$
$$\mathcal{S}_{\text{ds}}[\![\texttt{if}\ b\ \texttt{then}\ S_1\ \texttt{else}\ S_2]\!]env_V\ env_P = \text{cond}(\mathcal{B}[\![b]\!]\circ(\text{lookup}\ env_V),\ \mathcal{S}_{\text{ds}}[\![S_1]\!]env_V\ env_P,\ \mathcal{S}_{\text{ds}}[\![S_2]\!]env_V\ env_P)$$
$$\mathcal{S}_{\text{ds}}[\![\texttt{while}\ b\ \texttt{do}\ S]\!]env_V\ env_P = \text{FIX}\ F$$
$$\text{where } F\ g = \text{cond}(\mathcal{B}[\![b]\!]\circ(\text{lookup}\ env_V),\ g \circ (\mathcal{S}_{\text{ds}}[\![S]\!]env_V\ env_P),\ \text{id})$$
$$\mathcal{S}_{\text{ds}}[\![\texttt{begin}\ D_V\ D_P\ S\ \texttt{end}]\!]env_V\ env_P\ sto = \mathcal{S}_{\text{ds}}[\![S]\!]env'_V\ env'_P\ sto'$$
$$\text{where } \mathcal{D}^{\text{V}}_{\text{ds}}[\![D_V]\!](env_V,\ sto) = (env'_V,\ sto')$$
$$\text{and } \mathcal{D}^{\text{P}}_{\text{ds}}[\![D_P]\!]env'_V\ env_P = env'_P$$
$$\mathcal{S}_{\text{ds}}[\![\texttt{call}\ p]\!]env_V\ env_P = env_P\ p$$

Table 4.5: Denotational semantics for **Proc**

Assume that the initial environments are env_V and env_P and that the initial store sto has sto next $=$ **12**. Then the first step will be to update the variable environment with the declarations of the outer block:

$$\begin{aligned}
&\mathcal{D}^{\text{V}}_{\text{ds}}[\![\texttt{var x} := 7;]\!](env_V,\ sto)\\
&\quad = \mathcal{D}^{\text{V}}_{\text{ds}}[\![\varepsilon]\!](env_V[\texttt{x}\mapsto\mathbf{12}],\ sto[\mathbf{12}\mapsto\mathbf{7}][\text{next}\mapsto\mathbf{13}])\\
&\quad = (env_V[\texttt{x}\mapsto\mathbf{12}],\ sto[\mathbf{12}\mapsto\mathbf{7}][\text{next}\mapsto\mathbf{13}])
\end{aligned}$$

Next we update the procedure environment:

$$\begin{aligned}
&\mathcal{D}^{\text{P}}_{\text{ds}}[\![\texttt{proc p is x} := 0;]\!](env_V[\texttt{x}\mapsto\mathbf{12}])\ env_P\\
&\quad = \mathcal{D}^{\text{P}}_{\text{ds}}[\![\varepsilon]\!](env_V[\texttt{x}\mapsto\mathbf{12}])\ (env_P[\texttt{p}\mapsto g])\\
&\quad = env_P[\texttt{p}\mapsto g]
\end{aligned}$$

where

$$\begin{aligned}
g\ sto &= \mathcal{S}_{\text{ds}}[\![\texttt{x} := \texttt{0}]\!](env_V[\texttt{x}\mapsto\mathbf{12}])\ env_P\ sto\\
&= sto[\mathbf{12}\mapsto\mathbf{0}]
\end{aligned}$$

because x is to be found in location **12** according to the variable environment. Then we get

$$\mathcal{S}_{\text{ds}}[\![\texttt{begin var x := 7; proc p is x := 0;}$$
$$\texttt{begin var x := 5; call p end end}]\!]\, env_V\ env_P\ sto$$
$$= \mathcal{S}_{\text{ds}}[\![\texttt{begin var x := 5; call p end}]\!]\ (env_V[\texttt{x}\mapsto\mathbf{12}])\ (env_P[\texttt{p}\mapsto g])$$
$$(sto[\mathbf{12}\mapsto\mathbf{7}][\text{next}\mapsto\mathbf{13}])$$

For the variable declarations of the inner block we have

$$\mathcal{D}^{\text{V}}_{\text{ds}}[\![\texttt{var x := 5;}]\!](env_V[\texttt{x}\mapsto\mathbf{12}],\ sto[\mathbf{12}\mapsto\mathbf{7}][\text{next}\mapsto\mathbf{13}])$$
$$= \mathcal{D}^{\text{V}}_{\text{ds}}[\![\varepsilon]\!](env_V[\texttt{x}\mapsto\mathbf{13}],\ sto[\mathbf{12}\mapsto\mathbf{7}][\mathbf{13}\mapsto\mathbf{5}][\text{next}\mapsto\mathbf{14}])$$
$$= (env_V[\texttt{x}\mapsto\mathbf{13}],\ sto[\mathbf{12}\mapsto\mathbf{7}][\mathbf{13}\mapsto\mathbf{5}][\text{next}\mapsto\mathbf{14}])$$

and

$$\mathcal{D}^{\text{P}}_{\text{ds}}[\![\varepsilon]\!](env_V[\texttt{x}\mapsto\mathbf{13}])\ (env_P[\texttt{p}\mapsto g]) = env_P[\texttt{p}\mapsto g]$$

Thus we get

$$\mathcal{S}_{\text{ds}}[\![\texttt{begin var x := 5; call p end}]\!]\ (env_V[\texttt{x}\mapsto\mathbf{12}])\ (env_P[\texttt{p}\mapsto g])$$
$$(sto[\mathbf{12}\mapsto\mathbf{7}][\text{next}\mapsto\mathbf{13}])$$
$$= \mathcal{S}_{\text{ds}}[\![\texttt{call p}]\!](env_V[\texttt{x}\mapsto\mathbf{13}])\ (env_P[\texttt{p}\mapsto g])$$
$$(sto[\mathbf{12}\mapsto\mathbf{7}][\mathbf{13}\mapsto\mathbf{5}][\text{next}\mapsto\mathbf{14}])$$
$$= g\ (sto[\mathbf{12}\mapsto\mathbf{7}][\mathbf{13}\mapsto\mathbf{5}][\text{next}\mapsto\mathbf{14}])$$
$$= sto[\mathbf{12}\mapsto\mathbf{0}][\mathbf{13}\mapsto\mathbf{5}][\text{next}\mapsto\mathbf{14}]$$

so we see that in the final store the location for the local variable has the value **5** and the one for the global variable has the value **0**. □

Exercise 4.67 Consider the following statement in **Proc**:

```
begin var x := 0;
        proc p is x := x+1;
        proc q is call p;
        begin proc p is x := 7;
                call q
        end
end
```

Use the semantic clauses of **Proc** to illustrate that procedures have static scope, that is show that the final store will associate the location of x with the value **1** (rather than **7**). □

$\mathcal{D}^{\mathrm{P}}_{\mathrm{ds}}[\![\texttt{proc}\ p\ \texttt{is}\ S;\ D_P]\!]env_V\ env_P = \mathcal{D}^{\mathrm{P}}_{\mathrm{ds}}[\![D_P]\!]env_V\ (env_P[p\mapsto \mathrm{FIX}\ F])$ where $F\ g = \mathcal{S}_{\mathrm{ds}}[\![S]\!]env_V\ (env_P[p\mapsto g])$
$\mathcal{D}^{\mathrm{P}}_{\mathrm{ds}}[\![\varepsilon]\!]env_V = \mathrm{id}$

Table 4.6: Denotational semantics for recursive procedure declarations

Recursive procedures

In the case where procedures are allowed to be *recursive* we shall be interested in a function g in **Store** $\hookrightarrow$ **Store** satisfying

$$g = \mathcal{S}_{\mathrm{ds}}[\![S]\!]env_V\ (env_P[p\mapsto g])$$

since this will ensure that the meaning of all the recursive calls is the same as that of the procedure being defined. For this only the clause for $\mathcal{D}^{\mathrm{P}}_{\mathrm{ds}}[\![\texttt{proc}\ p\ \texttt{is}\ S]\!]$ needs to be modified and the new clause is given in Table 4.6. We shall see in Exercise 4.69 that this is a permissible definition, that is F of Table 4.6 is indeed continuous.

Remark Let us briefly compare the above semantics with the operational semantics given in Section 2.5 for the same language. In the operational semantics the possibility of recursion is handled by updating the environment *each time the procedure is called* and, except for recording the declaration, no action takes place when the procedure is declared. In the denotational approach, the situation is very different. The possibility of recursion is handled *once and for all*, namely *when the procedure is declared.* □

Exercise 4.68 Consider the declaration of the factorial procedure

```
proc fac is begin var z := x;
                  if x = 1 then skip
                  else (x := x − 1; call fac; y := z ⋆ y)
            end;
```

Assume that the initial environments are env_V and env_P and that $env_V\ \mathtt{x} = l_{\mathtt{x}}$ and $env_V\ \mathtt{y} = l_{\mathtt{y}}$. Determine the updated procedure environment. □

As for **While** we must ensure that the semantic clauses define a total function $\mathcal{S}_{\mathrm{ds}}$. We leave the details to the exercise below.

Exercise 4.69 ** To ensure that the clauses for $\mathcal{S}_{\mathrm{ds}}$ define a total function we must show that FIX is only applied to continuous functions. In the case of recursive procedures this is a rather laborious task. First one may use structural induction to show that $\mathcal{D}^{\mathrm{V}}_{\mathrm{ds}}$ is indeed a well-defined function. Secondly one may define

$$env_P \sqsubseteq' env'_P \text{ if and only if } env_P\ p \sqsubseteq env'_P\ p \text{ for all } p \in \mathbf{Pname}$$

and show that ($\mathbf{Env}_P$, $\sqsubseteq'$) is a ccpo. Finally, one may use Exercise 4.41 (with D being **Store** $\hookrightarrow$ **Store**) to show that for all $env_V \in \mathbf{Env}_V$ the clauses of Tables 4.3, 4.5 and 4.6 do define continuous functions

$$\mathcal{S}_{\text{ds}}[\![S]\!]env_V\text{: } \mathbf{Env}_P \to (\mathbf{Store} \hookrightarrow \mathbf{Store})$$

$$\mathcal{D}^{\text{P}}_{\text{ds}}[\![D_P]\!]env_V\text{: } \mathbf{Env}_P \to \mathbf{Env}_P$$

This is performed using mutual structural induction on statements S and declarations D_P. □

Exercise 4.70 Modify the syntax of procedures so that they take two *call-by-value* parameters:

$$D_P ::= \texttt{proc}\ p(x_1,x_2)\ \texttt{is}\ S;\ D_P \mid \varepsilon$$

$$S ::= \cdots \mid \texttt{call}\ p(a_1,a_2)$$

The meaning of a procedure will now depend upon the values of its parameters as well as the state in which it is executed. We therefore change the definition of $\mathbf{Env}_P$ to be

$$\mathbf{Env}_P = \mathbf{Pname} \to ((\mathbf{Z} \times \mathbf{Z}) \to (\mathbf{Store} \hookrightarrow \mathbf{Store}))$$

so that given a pair of values and a store we can determine the final store. Modify the definition of $\mathcal{S}_{\text{ds}}$ to use this procedure environment. Also provide semantic clauses for $\mathcal{D}^{\text{P}}_{\text{ds}}$ in the case of non-recursive as well as recursive procedures. Construct statements that illustrate how the new clauses are used. □

Exercise 4.71 * Modify the semantics of **Proc** so that dynamic scope rules are employed for variables as well as procedures. □

The concept of continuations

Another important concept from denotational semantics is that of *continuations*. To illustrate it we shall consider an extension of **While** where exceptions can be raised and handled. The new language is called **Exc** and its syntax is:

$$\begin{aligned} S \ ::= \ & x := a \mid \texttt{skip} \mid S_1\ ;\ S_2 \mid \texttt{if}\ b\ \texttt{then}\ S_1\ \texttt{else}\ S_2 \\ \mid\ & \texttt{while}\ b\ \texttt{do}\ S \mid \texttt{begin}\ S_1\ \texttt{handle}\ e\text{: } S_2\ \texttt{end} \mid \texttt{raise}\ e \end{aligned}$$

The meta-variable e ranges over the syntactic category **Exception** of exceptions. The statement `raise` e is a kind of jump instruction: when it is encountered, the execution of the encapsulating block is stopped and the flow of control is given to the statement declaring the exception e. An example is the statement

```
begin while true do if x≤0
                    then raise exit
                    else x := x−1
     handle exit: y := 7
end
```

Assume that s_0 is the initial state and that s_0 $\mathtt{x} > \mathbf{0}$. Then the false branch of the conditional will be chosen and the value of `x` decremented. Eventually, `x` gets the value **0** and the true branch of the conditional will raise the exception `exit`. This will cause the execution of the `while`-loop to be terminated and control will be transferred to the handler for `exit`. Thus the statement will terminate in a state where `x` has the value **0** and `y` the value **7**.

The meaning of an exception will be the effect of *executing the remainder of the program* starting from the handler. Consider a statement of the form

$$(\texttt{if } b \texttt{ then } S_1 \texttt{ else } S_2)\ ;\ S_3$$

In the language **While** it is evident that independently of whether we execute S_1 or S_2 we have to continue with S_3. When we introduce exceptions this does not hold any longer: if one of the branches raises an exception not handled inside that branch, then we will certainly not execute S_3. It is therefore necessary to rewrite the semantics of **While** to make the "effect of executing the remainder of the program" more explicit.

Continuation style semantics for While

In a *continuation style semantics* the continuations describe the *effect of executing the remainder of the program.* For us a *continuation* c is an element of the domain

$$\mathbf{Cont} = \mathbf{State} \hookrightarrow \mathbf{State}$$

and is thus a partial function from **State** to **State**. Sometimes one uses partial functions from **State** to a "simpler" set **Ans** of answers but in all cases the purpose of a continuation is to express the "outcome" of the remainder of the program when started in a given state.

Consider a statement of the form $\cdots;\ S\ ;\ \cdots$ and let us explain the meaning of S in terms of the effect of executing the remainder of the program. The starting point will be the continuation c determining the effect of executing the part of the program *after* S, that is $c\ s$ is the state obtained when the remainder of the program is executed from state s. We shall then determine the effect of executing S and the remainder of the program, that is we shall determine a continuation c' such that $c'\ s$ is the state obtained when executing S and the part of the program following S from state s. Pictorially, from

$$\mathcal{S}'_{\text{cs}}[\![x{:=}a]\!]c\ s = c\ (s[x{\mapsto}\mathcal{A}[\![a]\!]s])$$
$$\mathcal{S}'_{\text{cs}}[\![\texttt{skip}]\!] = \text{id}$$
$$\mathcal{S}'_{\text{cs}}[\![S_1\ ;\ S_2]\!] = \mathcal{S}'_{\text{cs}}[\![S_1]\!] \circ \mathcal{S}'_{\text{cs}}[\![S_2]\!]$$
$$\mathcal{S}'_{\text{cs}}[\![\texttt{if}\ b\ \texttt{then}\ S_1\ \texttt{else}\ S_2]\!]c = \text{cond}(\mathcal{B}[\![b]\!], \mathcal{S}'_{\text{cs}}[\![S_1]\!]c, \mathcal{S}'_{\text{cs}}[\![S_2]\!]c)$$
$$\mathcal{S}'_{\text{cs}}[\![\texttt{while}\ b\ \texttt{do}\ S]\!] = \text{FIX}\ G$$
$$\text{where } (G\ g)\ c = \text{cond}(\mathcal{B}[\![b]\!], \mathcal{S}'_{\text{cs}}[\![S]\!](g\ c), c)$$

Table 4.7: Continuation style semantics for **While**

$$\cdots \quad ; \quad S \quad ; \underbrace{\quad \cdots \quad}_{c}$$

we want to obtain

$$\cdots \quad ; \underbrace{\quad S \quad ; \quad \cdots \quad}_{c'}$$

We shall define a semantic function $\mathcal{S}'_{\text{cs}}$ for **While** that achieves this. It has functionality

$$\mathcal{S}'_{\text{cs}}\text{: } \textbf{Stm} \to (\textbf{Cont} \to \textbf{Cont})$$

and is defined in Table 4.7. The clauses for assignment and `skip` are straightforward; however, note that we now use id as the identity function on **Cont**, that is id $c\ s = c\ s$. In the clause for composition the order of the functional composition is *reversed* compared with the direct style semantics of Table 4.1. Intuitively, the reason is that the continuations are "pulled backwards" through the two statements. So assuming that c is the continuation for the remainder of the program we shall first determine a continuation for S_2 followed by the remainder of the program and next for S_1 followed by S_2 *and* the remainder of the program.

The clause for the conditional is straightforward as the continuation applies to both branches. In the clause for the `while`-construct we use the fixed point operator as in the direct style semantics. If the test of `while` b `do` S evaluates to **ff** then we return the continuation c for the remainder of the program. If the test evaluates to **tt** then $g\ c$ denotes the effect of executing the remainder of the loop followed by the remainder of the program and is the continuation to be used for the first unfolding of the loop.

Example 4.72 Consider the statement `z := x; x := y; y := z` of Chapter 1. Let id be the identity function on **State**. Then we have

$$\begin{aligned}
&\mathcal{S}'_{\text{cs}}[\![\texttt{z := x; x := y; y := z}]\!]\text{id}\\
&\quad = (\mathcal{S}'_{\text{cs}}[\![\texttt{z := x}]\!] \circ \mathcal{S}'_{\text{cs}}[\![\texttt{x := y}]\!] \circ \mathcal{S}'_{\text{cs}}[\![\texttt{y := z}]\!])\ \text{id}\\
&\quad = (\mathcal{S}'_{\text{cs}}[\![\texttt{z := x}]\!] \circ \mathcal{S}'_{\text{cs}}[\![\texttt{x := y}]\!])\ g_1\\
&\qquad\qquad \text{where } g_1\ s = \text{id}(s[\texttt{y}\mapsto(s\ \texttt{z})])\\
&\quad = \mathcal{S}'_{\text{cs}}[\![\texttt{z := x}]\!] g_2\\
&\qquad\qquad \text{where } g_2\ s = g_1(s[\texttt{x}\mapsto(s\ \texttt{y})])\\
&\qquad\qquad\qquad\qquad = \text{id}(s[\texttt{x}\mapsto(s\ \texttt{y})][\texttt{y}\mapsto(s\ \texttt{z})])\\
&\quad = g_3\\
&\qquad\qquad \text{where } g_3\ s = g_2(s[\texttt{z}\mapsto(s\ \texttt{x})])\\
&\qquad\qquad\qquad\qquad = \text{id}(s[\texttt{z}\mapsto(s\ \texttt{x})][\texttt{x}\mapsto(s\ \texttt{y})][\texttt{y}\mapsto(s\ \texttt{x})])
\end{aligned}$$

Note that the semantic function is constructed in a "backwards" manner. □

As in the case of the direct style semantics we must ensure that the semantic clauses define a total function $\mathcal{S}'_{\text{cs}}$. We leave the details to the exercise below.

Exercise 4.73 ** To ensure that the clauses for $\mathcal{S}'_{\text{cs}}$ define a total function we must show that FIX is only applied to continuous functions. First one may define

$$g_1 \sqsubseteq' g_2 \text{ if and only if } g_1\ c \sqsubseteq g_2\ c \text{ for all } c \in \textbf{Cont}$$

and show that ($\textbf{Cont} \to \textbf{Cont}$, $\sqsubseteq'$) is a ccpo. Secondly, one may define

$$[\textbf{Cont} \to \textbf{Cont}] = \{\ g\text{: } \textbf{Cont} \to \textbf{Cont} \mid g \text{ is continuous } \}$$

and show that ($[\textbf{Cont} \to \textbf{Cont}]$, $\sqsubseteq'$) is a ccpo. Finally, one may use Exercise 4.41 (with $D = [\textbf{Cont} \to \textbf{Cont}]$) to show that the clauses of Table 4.7 define a function

$$\mathcal{S}'_{\text{cs}}\text{: } [\textbf{Cont} \to \textbf{Cont}]$$

using structural induction on S. □

Exercise 4.74 * Prove that the two semantic functions $\mathcal{S}_{\text{ds}}$ and $\mathcal{S}'_{\text{cs}}$ satisfy

$$\mathcal{S}'_{\text{cs}}[\![S]\!]c = c \circ \mathcal{S}_{\text{ds}}[\![S]\!]$$

for all statements S of **While** and for all continuations c. □

Exercise 4.75 Extend the language **While** with the construct `repeat` S `until` b and give the new (compositional) clause for $\mathcal{S}'_{\text{cs}}$. □

$$\mathcal{S}_{cs}[\![x{:=}a]\!]env_E\ c\ s = c\ (s[x \mapsto \mathcal{A}[\![a]\!]s])$$

$$\mathcal{S}_{cs}[\![\texttt{skip}]\!]env_E = \text{id}$$

$$\mathcal{S}_{cs}[\![S_1\ ;\ S_2]\!]env_E = (\mathcal{S}_{cs}[\![S_1]\!]env_E) \circ (\mathcal{S}_{cs}[\![S_2]\!]env_E)$$

$$\mathcal{S}_{cs}[\![\texttt{if}\ b\ \texttt{then}\ S_1\ \texttt{else}\ S_2]\!]env_E\ c = \text{cond}(\mathcal{B}[\![b]\!],\ \mathcal{S}_{cs}[\![S_1]\!]env_E\ c,\ \mathcal{S}_{cs}[\![S_2]\!]env_E\ c)$$

$$\mathcal{S}_{cs}[\![\texttt{while}\ b\ \texttt{do}\ S]\!]env_E = \text{FIX}\ G$$
$$\text{where } (G\ g)\ c = \text{cond}(\mathcal{B}[\![b]\!],\ \mathcal{S}_{cs}[\![S]\!]env_E\ (g\ c),\ c)$$

$$\mathcal{S}_{cs}[\![\texttt{begin}\ S_1\ \texttt{handle}\ e\texttt{:}\ S_2\ \texttt{end}]\!]env_E\ c = \mathcal{S}_{cs}[\![S_1]\!](env_E[e \mapsto \mathcal{S}_{cs}[\![S_2]\!]env_E\ c])\ c$$

$$\mathcal{S}_{cs}[\![\texttt{raise}\ e]\!]env_E\ c = env_E\ e$$

Table 4.8: Continuation style semantics for **Exc**

The semantic function $\mathcal{S}_{cs}$ for Exc

In order to keep track of the exceptions that have been introduced we shall use an *exception environment*. It will be an element, env_E, of

$$\mathbf{Env_E} = \mathbf{Exception} \to \mathbf{Cont}$$

Given an exception environment env_E and an exception e, the effect of executing the remainder of the program starting from the handler for e will then be $env_E\ e$.

The semantic function $\mathcal{S}_{cs}$ for the statements of the language **Exc** has functionality

$$\mathcal{S}_{cs}\text{: } \mathbf{Stm} \to \mathbf{Env_E} \to (\mathbf{Cont} \to \mathbf{Cont})$$

The function is defined by the clauses of Table 4.8. Most of the clauses are straightforward extensions of those given for **While** in Table 4.7. The meaning of the block construct is to execute the body in the updated environment. Therefore the environment is updated so that e is bound to the effect of executing the remainder of the program starting from the handler for e and this is the continuation obtained by executing first S_2 and then the remainder of the program, that is $\mathcal{S}_{cs}[\![S_2]\!]env_E\ c$. Finally, in the clause for `raise` e we *ignore* the continuation that is otherwise supplied. So rather than using c we choose to use $env_E\ e$.

Example 4.76 Let env_E be an initial environment and assume that the initial continuation is the identity function, id. Then we have

$$\begin{aligned}&\mathcal{S}_{cs}[\![\texttt{begin while true do if x}\leq\texttt{0 then raise exit else x := x}-\texttt{1}\\&\qquad\texttt{handle exit: y := 7 end}]\!]\,env_E\ \text{id}\\&= (\text{FIX } G)\ \text{id}\end{aligned}$$

where G is defined by

$$\begin{aligned}G\ g\ c\ s &= \text{cond}(\mathcal{B}[\![\texttt{true}]\!],\\&\qquad\qquad \text{cond}(\mathcal{B}[\![\texttt{x}\leq\texttt{0}]\!],\ c_{\text{exit}},\ \mathcal{S}_{cs}[\![\texttt{x := x}-\texttt{1}]\!]env_E\ (g\ c)),\ c)\ s\\&= \begin{cases} c_{\text{exit}}\ s & \text{if } s\ \texttt{x} \leq \mathbf{0}\\ (g\ c)\ (s[\texttt{x}\mapsto(s\ \texttt{x})-\mathbf{1}]) & \text{if } s\ \texttt{x} > \mathbf{0}\end{cases}\end{aligned}$$

and the continuation c_{exit} associated with the exception **exit** is given by

$$c_{\text{exit}}\ s = \text{id}\ (s[\texttt{y}\mapsto\mathbf{7}]) = s[\texttt{y}\mapsto\mathbf{7}]$$

Note that G may choose to use the "default" continuation c or the continuation c_{exit} associated with the exception, as appropriate. We then get

$$(\text{FIX } G)\ \text{id}\ s = \begin{cases} s[\texttt{y}\mapsto\mathbf{7}] & \text{if } s\ \texttt{x}\leq\mathbf{0}\\ s[\texttt{x}\mapsto\mathbf{0}][\texttt{y}\mapsto\mathbf{7}] & \text{if } s\ \texttt{x} > \mathbf{0}\end{cases}$$ □

Exercise 4.77 Show that FIX G as specified in the above example is indeed the least fixed point, that is construct the iterands $G^n\ \bot$ and show that their least upper bound is as specified. □

Exercise 4.78 ** Extend Exercise 4.73 to show the well-definedness of the function $\mathcal{S}_{cs}$ defined by the clauses of Table 4.8. □

Exercise 4.79 Suppose that there is a distinguished output variable $\texttt{out} \in \textbf{Var}$ and that only the final value of this variable is of interest. This might motivate defining

$$\textbf{Cont} = \textbf{Store} \hookrightarrow \textbf{Z}$$

Define the initial continuation $c_0 \in \textbf{Cont}$. What changes to $\textbf{Env}_E$, the functionality of $\mathcal{S}_{cs}$ and Table 4.8 are necessary? □

Chapter 5

Static Program Analysis

When implementing a programming language it is crucial that the implementation is faithful to the semantics of the language and in Chapter 3 we saw how the operational semantics could be used to prove this formally. However, it is also important that the implementation is reasonably efficient and it is therefore common to combine the code generation with various analyses collecting information about the programs. In this chapter we shall develop one such analysis in detail but let us first consider a couple of example analyses.

Constant propagation is an analysis that determines whether an expression always evaluates to a constant value and if so determines that value. The analysis is the basis for an optimization called *constant folding* where the expression is replaced by the constant. As an example the analysis will detect that the value of y in the statement

```
x := 5; y := x ⋆ x + 25
```

will always be **50**. It is therefore safe to replace the statement by

```
x := 5; y := 50
```

and more efficient code can be generated.

Another example is the *detection of signs analysis* where the idea is to determine the sign of expressions. So it will for example determine that the value of y in

```
y := x ⋆ x + 25
```

always will be positive (independently of the value assigned to x). This information will be useful for an optimization known as *code elimination*: in a statement as

```
y := x ⋆ x + 25; while y ≤ 0 do ···
```

there is no need to generate code for the `while`-loop because it will never be executed.

The example analysis to be developed in this chapter is a *dependency analysis*. Here the idea is to regard some of the variables as *input* variables and others as *output* variables. The analysis will then determine whether or not the final values of the output variables only depend upon the initial values of the input variables. If so we shall say that there is a *functional dependency* between the input and output variables of the statement. As an example consider once more the statement

$$\mathtt{y} := \mathtt{x} \star \mathtt{x} + 25$$

and assume that `x` is an input variable and `y` an output variable. Then the analysis will conclude that there is indeed a functional dependency between the input and output variables for the above statement. However, if `x` is *not* an input variable then the analysis will determine that the value of `y` is dubious as it does not solely depend on the values of the input variables. In that case the compiler might choose to issue a warning as this probably is not the intention of the programmer.

A more interesting example program is the factorial statement:

$$\mathtt{y} := 1;\ \mathtt{while}\ \neg\ (\mathtt{x} = 1)\ \mathtt{do}\ (\mathtt{y} := \mathtt{y} \star \mathtt{x};\ \mathtt{x} := \mathtt{x} - 1)$$

Again assume that `x` is an input variable and that `y` is an output variable. Then the final value of `y` only depends upon the initial value of `x`. However, if we drop the initialization of `y` (and assume that `y` is not an input variable) and consider the statement

$$\mathtt{while}\ \neg\ (\mathtt{x} = 1)\ \mathtt{do}\ (\mathtt{y} := \mathtt{y} \star \mathtt{x};\ \mathtt{x} := \mathtt{x} - 1)$$

then the final value of `y` does not only depend on the initial value of the input variable `x`, but also on the initial value of `y`, so it is *not* the case that the final values of the output variables only depend on the initial values of the input variables.

The kind of analyses exemplified above can be specified by defining so-called *non-standard semantics* of the programming language. These semantics will be patterned after the denotational semantics of Chapter 4 but they differ in that they do *not* operate on the exact values of variables and expressions but rather on *properties* of the exact values. For the constant propagation analysis we may use properties like

ANY, CONST-0, CONST-1, CONST-2, $\cdots$

For the detection of signs analysis we may use properties like

ANY, POS, NEG, and ZERO

and for the dependency analysis we may use properties

D? (meaning dubious) and OK (meaning proper)

Usually, the analyses will be part of a compiler and it is therefore important that they always terminate even for programs that loop when executed. The price we pay for always getting answers is that we occasionally get imprecise answers. So in the case of constant propagation the property ANY means that the analysis was not able to detect that the value always would be constant. Similarly, the property ANY for the detection of signs analysis means that the analysis was not able to detect a unique sign for the value. For the dependency analysis the property D? means that the analysis was not able to detect that the value only depends on the input variables. Note that an analysis that always returns these "fail-safe" properties will be a safe analysis although not a very informative one. Also note that in the case of the dependency analysis we could always expect the answer OK if all variables were regarded as input variables but again this is not what we are interested in.

The analysis we shall develop will detect whether or not a statement *definitely* has a functional dependency between its input and output variables. The overall algorithm operates as follows: initially all input variables have the property OK and all other variables the property D?. Then the analysis is performed and when it has terminated the properties of the output variables are inspected. If they are all OK then the analysis returns the answer YES and otherwise NO?. The analysis is guaranteed to give an answer within a finite amount of time (depending upon the statement) but the answer will not be precise in all cases. However, it will always be *safe* in the sense that

- if the analysis says YES then there is indeed a functional dependency between input and output, but
- if the analysis says NO? then there may or may not be a functional dependency between input and output.

The analysis will be specified *compositionally* just as the denotational semantics of Chapter 4. As mentioned above the main difference between the analysis and the denotational semantics is that the analysis does not operate on exact values but rather on *properties* of exact values. Because of the close correspondence between the specification of the analysis and the denotational semantics we shall prove the safety of the analysis with respect to the denotational semantics.

5.1 Properties and property states

For the dependency analysis we shall be interested in two properties:

- OK meaning that the value *definitely* only depends on the initial values of the input variables, and

- D? meaning that the value *may* depend on the initial values of non-input variables, that is the value may be dubious.

We shall write

$$\mathbf{P} = \{\text{OK}, \text{D?}\}$$

for this set of properties and we use p as a meta-variable ranging over $\mathbf{P}$. It is more informative to know that an expression has the property OK than D?. As a record of this we define a partial order $\sqsubseteq_{\text{P}}$ on $\mathbf{P}$:

$$\text{OK} \sqsubseteq_{\text{P}} \text{D?}, \quad \text{OK} \sqsubseteq_{\text{P}} \text{OK}, \quad \text{D?} \sqsubseteq_{\text{P}} \text{D?}$$

and depicted as

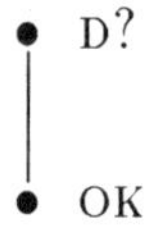

Thus the more informative property is at the bottom of the ordering! We have

---

Fact 5.1 $(\mathbf{P}, \sqsubseteq_{\text{P}})$ is a complete lattice. If Y is a subset of $\mathbf{P}$ then

$$\bigsqcup_{\text{P}} Y = \text{D?} \text{ if and only if } \text{D?} \in Y$$

Proof: The proof is straightforward using the definition of complete lattices given in Chapter 4. □

It is convenient to write $p_1 \sqcup_{\text{P}} p_2$ instead of $\bigsqcup_{\text{P}}\{p_1, p_2\}$. It follows from Fact 5.1 that the binary operation $\sqcup_{\text{P}}$ may be given by the table

$\sqcup_{\text{P}}$	OK	D?
OK	OK	D?
D?	D?	D?

When reasoning about the safety of the analysis we need to be a bit more precise about the meaning of the properties with respect to the values of the denotational semantics. While it may be intuitively clear whether or not the value of a variable only depends on the input variables, it turns out to be impossible to inspect a specific value, for example **27**, and decide whether or not this is indeed the case. The reason is that we lose the context in which the value arises. We shall solve this difficulty in Section 5.3 and to prepare for the solution we shall define the following parameterized relations:

$$\underline{\text{rel}}_{\text{Aexp}}\colon \mathbf{P} \to (\mathbf{Z} \times \mathbf{Z} \to \mathbf{T})$$

$$\underline{\text{rel}}_{\text{Bexp}}\colon \mathbf{P} \to (\mathbf{T} \times \mathbf{T} \to \mathbf{T})$$

For arithmetic expressions the relation is defined by:

$$\underline{\text{rel}}_{\text{Aexp}}(p)(v_1, v_2) = \begin{cases} \textbf{tt} & p = \text{D?} \text{ or } v_1 = v_2 \\ \textbf{ff} & \text{otherwise} \end{cases}$$

and similarly for boolean expression:

$$\underline{\text{rel}}_{\text{Bexp}}(p)(v_1, v_2) = \begin{cases} \textbf{tt} & p = \text{D?} \text{ or } v_1 = v_2 \\ \textbf{ff} & \text{otherwise} \end{cases}$$

We shall often omit the subscript when no confusion is likely to result. Each of the relations take a property and two values as parameters. Intuitively, the property expresses how much the two values are allowed to differ. Thus D? puts no requirements on the values whereas OK requires that the two values are equal. As an aid to readability we shall often write

$$v_1 \equiv v_2 \ \underline{\text{rel}} \ p$$

instead of $\underline{\text{rel}}(p)(v_1, v_2)$ and we shall say that *v_1 and v_2 are equal as far as p is concerned* (or relative to p).

Property states

In the operational and denotational semantics a state maps variables to their values. In the analysis the counterpart of this will be a *property state* which maps variables to properties, that is essentially a function in **Var** → **P**. The idea is that the initial property state will only map the input variables to OK and that if the final property state is acceptable and maps all output variables to OK then the output of the statement will definitely be functionally dependent on the input.

To make this idea work we have to extend the property state to model one additional phenomenon, namely the "flow of control". We shall illustrate this in Example 5.3 below but let us first introduce some notation that will handle the problem. The set **PState** of property states ranged over by the meta-variable *ps*, is defined by

$$\textbf{PState} = (\textbf{Var} \cup \{\text{on-track}\}) \to \textbf{P}$$

where 'on-track' is a special token used to model the "flow of control". If 'on-track' is mapped to OK this means that the "flow of control" only depends upon the values of the input variables; if it is mapped to D? this need not be the case. For a property state $ps \in$ **PState** we define the set

$$\text{OK}(ps) = \{\ x \in \textbf{Var} \cup \{\text{on-track}\} \mid ps\ x = \text{OK}\ \}$$

of "variables" mapped to OK and we say that

ps is *proper* if and only if $ps(\text{on-track}) = \text{OK}$.

If ps is not proper we shall sometimes say that it is improper.

The relationship between property states and states is given by the parameterized relation:

$$\underline{\text{rel}}_{\text{Stm}}\text{: } \mathbf{PState} \to (\mathbf{State} \times \mathbf{State} \to \mathbf{T})$$

defined by

$$\underline{\text{rel}}_{\text{Stm}}(ps)(s_1, s_2) = \begin{cases} \mathbf{tt} & \text{if } ps \text{ on-track} = \text{D?} \\ & \text{or } \forall\, x \in \mathbf{Var} \cap \text{OK}(ps)\text{: } s_1\, x = s_2\, x \\ \mathbf{ff} & \text{otherwise} \end{cases}$$

and again we may omit the subscript when no confusion is likely to occur. The relation expresses the extent to which two states are allowed to differ as far as a given property state is concerned. If ps is not proper then $\underline{\text{rel}}(ps)$ will hold on any two states. However, if ps is proper then $\underline{\text{rel}}(ps)$ will hold on two states if they are equal on the variables in $\text{OK}(ps)$. Phrased differently, we may view ps as a pair of glasses that only allows us to see part of the states and $\underline{\text{rel}}(ps)(s_1, s_2)$ means that s_1 and s_2 look the same when viewed through that pair of glasses. Again we shall write

$$s_1 \equiv s_2 \ \underline{\text{rel}}\ ps$$

for $\underline{\text{rel}}(ps)(s_1, s_2)$.

Example 5.2 Let s_1, s_2 and ps be given by

$$s_1\ \mathtt{x} = \mathbf{1} \text{ and } s_1\ y = \mathbf{0} \text{ for } y \in \mathbf{Var}\backslash\{\mathtt{x}\}$$

$$s_2\ \mathtt{x} = \mathbf{2} \text{ and } s_2\ y = \mathbf{0} \text{ for } y \in \mathbf{Var}\backslash\{\mathtt{x}\}$$

$$ps\ \mathtt{x} = \text{D?} \text{ and } ps\ y = \text{OK} \text{ for } y \in (\mathbf{Var} \cup \{\text{on-track}\})\backslash\{\mathtt{x}\}$$

Then $s_1 \equiv s_2\ \underline{\text{rel}}\ ps$. □

Example 5.3 To motivate the need for improper property states, that is the need for 'on-track', consider the following statements:

S_1: `x := 1`

S_2: `x := 2`

It would be natural to expect that the analysis of S_1 will map any property state ps to the property state $ps[\mathtt{x}\mapsto\text{OK}]$ since a constant value cannot depend on the value of any (non-input) variable. A similar argument holds for S_2. Now consider the statements

S_{11}: `if x = 1 then` S_1 `else` S_1

S_{12}: `if x = 1 then` S_1 `else` S_2

Again we may expect that the analysis of S_{11} will map any property state ps to the property state $ps[\mathtt{x}\mapsto\text{OK}]$, since S_{11} is semantically equivalent to S_1.

Concerning S_{12} it will not always be correct for the analysis to map a property state ps to $ps[\mathtt{x}\mapsto\text{OK}]$. For an example suppose that ps, s_1 and s_2 are such that

$$ps\ \mathtt{x} = \text{D?} \text{ and } ps\ y = \text{OK for } y \in (\mathbf{Var} \cup \{\text{on-track}\})\backslash\{\mathtt{x}\}$$

$$s_1\ \mathtt{x} = \mathbf{1} \text{ and } s_1\ y = \mathbf{0} \text{ for } y \in \mathbf{Var}\backslash\{\mathtt{x}\}$$

$$s_2\ \mathtt{x} = \mathbf{2} \text{ and } s_2\ y = \mathbf{0} \text{ for } y \in \mathbf{Var}\backslash\{\mathtt{x}\}$$

Then Example 5.2 gives

$$s_1 \equiv s_2\ \underline{\text{rel}}\ ps$$

but $\mathcal{S}_{\text{ds}}[\![S_{12}]\!]s_1 \equiv \mathcal{S}_{\text{ds}}[\![S_{12}]\!]s_2\ \underline{\text{rel}}\ ps[\mathtt{x}\mapsto\text{OK}]$ *fails* because $\mathcal{S}_{\text{ds}}[\![S_{12}]\!]s_1 = s_1$ and $\mathcal{S}_{\text{ds}}[\![S_{12}]\!]s_2 = s_2$ and $s_1\ \mathtt{x} \neq s_2\ \mathtt{x}$.

However, from the point of view of the *analysis* there is no difference between S_1 and S_2 because neither the value of `1` nor `2` depends on the values of the input variables. Since the analysis is compositionally defined this means that there can be no difference between S_{11} and S_{12} from the point of view of the analysis. Therefore we have to accept that also the analysis of S_{11} should *not* allow mapping an arbitrary property state ps to $ps[\mathtt{x}\mapsto\text{OK}]$.

The difference between S_1 and S_2 arises when the "flow of control" does not depend on the input variables and it is here the need for the special token 'on-track' comes in. We shall transform a property state into an improper one, by mapping 'on-track' to D?, whenever the "flow of control" is not "functionally dependent" on the input variables. Thus if $ps\ \mathtt{x} = \text{D?}$ then it is the test, `x = 1`, in S_{11} and S_{12} that will be responsible for mapping ps into the improper property state $ps[\text{on-track}\mapsto\text{D?}]$ and then the effect of analysing S_1 and S_2 does not matter as long as an improper property state is not mapped into a proper one. □

Our next task will be to endow **PState** with some partially ordered structure and to investigate the properties of $\underline{\text{rel}}_{\text{Stm}}$. Concerning the former this will be an instance of a general procedure:

Lemma 5.4 Assume that S is a non-empty set and that $(D, \sqsubseteq)$ is a partially ordered set. Let $\sqsubseteq'$ be the ordering on the set $S \to D$ defined by

$$f_1 \sqsubseteq' f_2 \text{ if and only if } f_1\ x \sqsubseteq f_2\ x \text{ for all } x \in S$$

Then $(S \to D, \sqsubseteq')$ is a partially ordered set. Furthermore, $(S \to D, \sqsubseteq')$ is a ccpo if D is and it is a complete lattice if D is. In both cases we have

$$(\bigsqcup' Y)\ x = \bigsqcup \{\ f\ x \mid f \in Y\ \}$$

so that least upper bounds are determined pointwise.

Proof: It is straightforward to verify that $\sqsubseteq'$ is a partial order so we omit the details. We shall first prove the lemma in the case where D is a complete lattice so let Y be a subset of $S \to D$. Then the formula

$$(\bigsqcup' Y)\ x = \bigsqcup \{\ f\ x \mid f \in Y\ \}$$

defines an element $\bigsqcup' Y$ of $S \to D$ because D being a complete lattice means that $\bigsqcup\{\ f\ x \mid f \in Y\ \}$ exists for all x of S. This shows that $\bigsqcup' Y$ is a *well-defined* element of $S \to D$. To see that $\bigsqcup' Y$ is an *upper bound* of Y let $f_0 \in Y$ and we shall show that $f_0 \sqsubseteq' \bigsqcup' Y$. This amounts to considering an arbitrary x in S and showing

$$f_0\ x \sqsubseteq \bigsqcup\{\ f\ x \mid f \in Y\ \}$$

and this is immediate because $\bigsqcup$ is the least upper bound operation in D. To see that $\bigsqcup' Y$ is the *least* upper bound of Y let f_1 be an upper bound of Y and we shall show that $\bigsqcup' Y \sqsubseteq' f_1$. This amounts to showing

$$\bigsqcup\{\ f\ x \mid f \in Y\ \} \sqsubseteq f_1\ x$$

for an arbitrary $x \in S$. However, this is immediate because $f_1\ x$ must be an upper bound of $\{\ f\ x \mid f \in Y\ \}$ and because $\bigsqcup$ is the least upper bound operation in D.

To prove the other part of the lemma assume that D is a ccpo and that Y is a chain in $S \to D$. The formula

$$(\bigsqcup' Y)\ x = \bigsqcup \{\ f\ x \mid f \in Y\ \}$$

defines an element $\bigsqcup' Y$ of $S \to D$: each $\{\ f\ x \mid f \in Y\ \}$ will be a chain in D because Y is a chain and hence each $\bigsqcup\{\ f\ x \mid f \in Y\ \}$ exists because D is a ccpo. That $\bigsqcup' Y$ is the least upper bound of Y in $S \to D$ follows as above. □

Instantiating S to be **Var** ∪ {on-track} and D to be **P** we get:

Corollary 5.5 Let $\sqsubseteq_{\text{PS}}$ be the ordering on **PState** defined by

$$ps_1 \sqsubseteq_{\text{PS}} ps_2 \text{ if and only if } ps_1\ x \sqsubseteq_{\text{P}} ps_2\ x \text{ for all } x \in \mathbf{Var} \cup \{\text{on-track}\}$$

Then (**PState**, $\sqsubseteq_{\text{PS}}$) is a complete lattice. In particular, the least upper bound $\bigsqcup_{\text{PS}} Y$ of a subset Y of **PState** is characterized by

$$(\bigsqcup_{\text{PS}} Y)\ x = \bigsqcup_{\text{P}}\ \{\ ps\ x \mid ps \in Y\ \}$$

We shall write LOST for the property state ps that maps all variables to D? and that maps 'on-track' to D?. Similarly, we shall write INIT for the property state that maps all variables to OK and that maps 'on-track' to OK. Note that INIT is the *least element* of **PState**.

Exercise 5.6 (Essential) Show that

$$ps_1 \sqsubseteq_{\text{PS}} ps_2 \text{ if and only if } \text{OK}(ps_1) \supseteq \text{OK}(ps_2)$$

Next show that

$$\text{OK}(\bigsqcup_{\text{PS}} Y) = \bigcap\{\ \text{OK}(ps) \mid ps \in Y\ \}$$

whenever Y is a non-empty subset of **PState**. □

Properties of rel

To study the properties of the parameterized relation rel we need a notion of an equivalence relation. A relation

$$R\colon E \times E \to \mathbf{T}$$

is an *equivalence relation* on a set E if and only if

$R(e_1, e_1)$	(reflexivity)
$R(e_1, e_2)$ and $R(e_2, e_3)$ imply $R(e_1, e_3)$	(transitivity)
$R(e_1, e_2)$ implies $R(e_2, e_1)$	(symmetry)

for all e_1, e_2 and e_3 of E.

Exercise 5.7 Show that $\underline{\text{rel}}_{\text{Aexp}}(p)$, $\underline{\text{rel}}_{\text{Bexp}}(p)$ and $\underline{\text{rel}}_{\text{Stm}}(ps)$ are equivalence relations for all choices of $p \in \mathbf{P}$ and $ps \in$ **PState**. □

Each of $\underline{\text{rel}}_{\text{Aexp}}$, $\underline{\text{rel}}_{\text{Bexp}}$ and $\underline{\text{rel}}_{\text{Stm}}$ are examples of parameterized (equivalence) relations. In general a *parameterized relation* is of the form

$$\mathcal{R}\colon D \to (E \times E \to \mathbf{T})$$

where $(D, \sqsubseteq)$ is a partially ordered set, E is a set and each $\mathcal{R}(d)$ is a relation. We shall say that a parameterized relation $\mathcal{R}$ is a *Kripke-relation* if

$$d_1 \sqsubseteq d_2 \text{ implies that for all } e_1, e_2 \in E\text{:}$$
$$\text{if } \mathcal{R}(d_1)(e_1, e_2) \text{ then } \mathcal{R}(d_2)(e_1, e_2)$$

Note that this is a kind of monotonicity property.

Lemma 5.8 $\underline{\text{rel}}_{\text{Stm}}$ is a Kripke-relation.

Proof: Let ps_1 and ps_2 be such that $ps_1 \sqsubseteq_{\text{PS}} ps_2$ and assume that

$$s_1 \equiv s_2 \ \underline{\text{rel}}\ ps_1$$

holds for all states s_1 and s_2. We must show

$$s_1 \equiv s_2 \ \underline{\text{rel}}\ ps_2$$

If ps_2 on-track $= \text{D?}$ this is immediate from the definition of $\underline{\text{rel}}_{\text{Stm}}$. So assume that ps_2 on-track $= \text{OK}$. In this case we must show

$$\forall x \in \text{OK}(ps_2) \cap \textbf{Var}\text{: } s_1\ x = s_2\ x$$

Since $ps_1 \sqsubseteq_{\text{PS}} ps_2$ and ps_2 on-track $= \text{OK}$ it must be the case that ps_1 on-track is OK. From $s_1 \equiv s_2\ \underline{\text{rel}}\ ps_1$ we therefore get

$$\forall x \in \text{OK}(ps_1) \cap \textbf{Var}\text{: } s_1\ x = s_2\ x$$

From Exercise 5.6 and the assumption $ps_1 \sqsubseteq_{\text{PS}} ps_2$ we get $\text{OK}(ps_1) \supseteq \text{OK}(ps_2)$ and thereby we get the desired result. □

Exercise 5.9 (Essential) Show that $\underline{\text{rel}}_{\text{Aexp}}$ and $\underline{\text{rel}}_{\text{Bexp}}$ are Kripke-relations. □

5.2 The analysis

When specifying the analysis we shall be concerned with expressions as well as statements.

Expressions

The analysis of an arithmetic expression a will be specified by a (total) function $\mathcal{PA}[\![a]\!]$ from property states to properties:

$$\mathcal{PA}\text{: } \textbf{Aexp} \to (\textbf{PState} \to \textbf{P})$$

Similarly, the analysis of a boolean expression b will be defined by a (total) function $\mathcal{PB}[\![b]\!]$ from property states to properties:

$$\mathcal{PB}\text{: } \textbf{Bexp} \to (\textbf{PState} \to \textbf{P})$$

$$\mathcal{PA}[\![n]\!]ps = \begin{cases} \text{OK} & \text{if } ps \text{ on-track} = \text{OK} \\ \text{D?} & \text{otherwise} \end{cases}$$

$$\mathcal{PA}[\![x]\!]ps = \begin{cases} ps\ x & \text{if } ps \text{ on-track} = \text{OK} \\ \text{D?} & \text{otherwise} \end{cases}$$

$$\mathcal{PA}[\![a_1 + a_2]\!]ps = (\mathcal{PA}[\![a_1]\!]ps) \sqcup_P (\mathcal{PA}[\![a_2]\!]ps)$$

$$\mathcal{PA}[\![a_1 \star a_2]\!]ps = (\mathcal{PA}[\![a_1]\!]ps) \sqcup_P (\mathcal{PA}[\![a_2]\!]ps)$$

$$\mathcal{PA}[\![a_1 - a_2]\!]ps = (\mathcal{PA}[\![a_1]\!]ps) \sqcup_P (\mathcal{PA}[\![a_2]\!]ps)$$

$$\mathcal{PB}[\![\texttt{true}]\!]ps = \begin{cases} \text{OK} & \text{if } ps \text{ on-track} = \text{OK} \\ \text{D?} & \text{otherwise} \end{cases}$$

$$\mathcal{PB}[\![\texttt{false}]\!]ps = \begin{cases} \text{OK} & \text{if } ps \text{ on-track} = \text{OK} \\ \text{D?} & \text{otherwise} \end{cases}$$

$$\mathcal{PB}[\![a_1 = a_2]\!]ps = (\mathcal{PA}[\![a_1]\!]ps) \sqcup_P (\mathcal{PA}[\![a_2]\!]ps)$$

$$\mathcal{PB}[\![a_1 \leq a_2]\!]ps = (\mathcal{PA}[\![a_1]\!]ps) \sqcup_P (\mathcal{PA}[\![a_2]\!]ps)$$

$$\mathcal{PB}[\![\neg\, b]\!]ps = \mathcal{PB}[\![b]\!]ps$$

$$\mathcal{PB}[\![b_1 \wedge b_2]\!]ps = (\mathcal{PB}[\![b_1]\!]ps) \sqcup_P (\mathcal{PB}[\![b_2]\!]ps)$$

Table 5.1: Analysis of expressions

The defining clauses are given in Table 5.1. The clause for n reflects that the value of n in a proper property state ps does not depend on any variable and therefore it will have the property OK. The property of a variable x in a proper property state ps is the property bound to x in ps, that is $ps\ x$. Thus if ps is the initial property state then the intention is that $\mathcal{PA}[\![x]\!]ps$ is OK if and only if x is one of the input variables. For a composite expression, like $a_1 + a_2$, the idea is that it can only have the property OK if both subexpressions have that property. This is ensured by the binary operation $\sqcup_P$ introduced in Section 5.1.

Example 5.10 If ps **x** = OK and ps on-track = OK then $\mathcal{PA}[\![\mathtt{x} + \mathtt{1}]\!]ps$ = OK since $\mathcal{PA}[\![\mathtt{x}]\!]ps$ = OK and $\mathcal{PA}[\![\mathtt{1}]\!]ps$ = OK. On the other hand, if ps **x** = D? then $\mathcal{PA}[\![\mathtt{x} + \mathtt{1}]\!]ps$ = D? because $\mathcal{PA}[\![\mathtt{x}]\!]ps$ = D?.

Furthermore, $\mathcal{PB}[\![\mathtt{x} = \mathtt{x}]\!]ps$ = D? if ps **x** = D? even though the test **x** = **x** will evaluate to **tt** independently of whether or not **x** is initialized properly. □

The functions $\mathcal{PA}[\![a]\!]$ and $\mathcal{PB}[\![b]\!]$ are closely connected with the sets of free variables defined in Chapter 1:

$$\mathcal{PS}[\![x := a]\!]\ ps = ps[x \mapsto \mathcal{PA}[\![a]\!]ps]$$

$$\mathcal{PS}[\![\texttt{skip}]\!] = \text{id}$$

$$\mathcal{PS}[\![S_1;S_2]\!] = \mathcal{PS}[\![S_2]\!] \circ \mathcal{PS}[\![S_1]\!]$$

$$\mathcal{PS}[\![\texttt{if } b \texttt{ then } S_1 \texttt{ else } S_2]\!] = \text{cond}_{\text{P}}(\mathcal{PB}[\![b]\!], \mathcal{PS}[\![S_1]\!], \mathcal{PS}[\![S_2]\!])$$

$$\mathcal{PS}[\![\texttt{while } b \texttt{ do } S]\!] = \text{FIX } H$$
$$\text{where } H\ h = \text{cond}_{\text{P}}(\mathcal{PB}[\![b]\!], h \circ \mathcal{PS}[\![S]\!], \text{id})$$

Table 5.2: Analysis of statements in **While**

Exercise 5.11 (Essential) Prove that for every arithmetic expression a we have

$$\mathcal{PA}[\![a]\!]ps = \text{OK if and only if FV}(a) \cup \{\text{on-track}\} \subseteq \text{OK}(ps)$$

Formulate and prove a similar result for boolean expressions. Deduce that for all a of **Aexp** we get $\mathcal{PA}[\![a]\!]ps = \text{D?}$ if ps is improper, and that for all b of **Bexp** we get $\mathcal{PB}[\![b]\!]ps = \text{D?}$ if ps is improper. □

Statements

Turning to statements we shall specify their analysis by a function $\mathcal{PS}$ of functionality:

$$\mathcal{PS}\text{: } \mathbf{Stm} \rightarrow (\mathbf{PState} \rightarrow \mathbf{PState})$$

The totality of $\mathcal{PS}[\![S]\!]$ reflects that we shall be able to analyse *all* statements including a statement like `while true do skip` that loops. The definition of $\mathcal{PS}$ is given in Table 5.2 and the clauses for assignment, `skip` and composition are much as in the direct style denotational semantics of Chapter 4. The remaining clauses will be explained below.

Example 5.12 Consider the statement

y := x

First assume that ps is a proper property state with ps x = OK and ps y = D?. Then we have

$$(\mathcal{PS}[\![\texttt{y := x}]\!]ps)\ \texttt{x} = \text{OK}$$
$$(\mathcal{PS}[\![\texttt{y := x}]\!]ps)\ \texttt{y} = \text{OK}$$
$$(\mathcal{PS}[\![\texttt{y := x}]\!]ps)\ \text{on-track} = \text{OK}$$

Since $\mathcal{PS}[\![\texttt{y := x}]\!]ps$ is proper we conclude that both $\texttt{x}$ and $\texttt{y}$ only depend on the input variables after $\texttt{y}$ is assigned a value that only depends on the input variables.

Assume next that $ps\ \texttt{y} = \text{OK}$ but $ps\ \texttt{x} = \text{D?}$. Then

$$(\mathcal{PS}[\![\texttt{y := x}]\!]ps)\ \texttt{y} = \text{D?}$$

showing that when a dubious value is used in an assignment then the assigned variable will get a dubious value as well. □

Exercise 5.13 Consider the statements S_1 and S_2 of Example 5.3. Use Tables 5.1 and 5.2 to characterize the behaviour of $\mathcal{PS}[\![S_1]\!]$ and $\mathcal{PS}[\![S_2]\!]$ on proper and improper property states. Anticipating Section 5.3 show that

$$s_1 \equiv s_2\ \underline{\text{rel}}\ ps \text{ implies } \mathcal{S}_{\text{ds}}[\![S_{\text{i}}]\!]s_1 \equiv \mathcal{S}_{\text{ds}}[\![S_{\text{i}}]\!]s_2\ \underline{\text{rel}}\ \mathcal{PS}[\![S_{\text{i}}]\!]ps$$

for i = 1, 2 and for all $ps \in$ **PState**. □

In the clause for `if` b `then` S_1 `else` S_2 we use the auxiliary function cond$_{\text{P}}$ defined by

$$\text{cond}_{\text{P}}(f,\ h_1,\ h_2)\ ps = \begin{cases} (h_1\ ps) \sqcup_{\text{PS}} (h_2\ ps) & \text{if } f\ ps = \text{OK} \\ \text{LOST} & \text{if } f\ ps = \text{D?} \end{cases}$$

First consider the case where we are successful in analysing the condition, that is where $f\ ps = \text{OK}$. For each variable x we can determine the result of analysing each of the branches, namely $(h_1\ ps)\ x$ for the true branch and $(h_2\ ps)\ x$ for the false branch. The least upper bound of these two results will be the new property bound to x, that is the new property state will map x to

$$((h_1\ ps)\ x) \sqcup_{\text{P}} ((h_2\ ps)\ x)$$

If the analysis of the condition is not successful, that is $f\ ps = \text{D?}$, then the analysis of the conditional will fail and we shall therefore use the property state LOST.

Example 5.14 Consider now the statement

```
if x = x then z := y else y := z
```

Clearly, the final value of $\texttt{z}$ can be determined uniquely from the initial value of $\texttt{y}$. However, if $\texttt{z}$ is dubious then the analysis cannot give this result. To see this assume that ps is a proper property state such that $ps\ \texttt{x} = \text{OK}$, $ps\ \texttt{y} = \text{OK}$ and $ps\ \texttt{z} = \text{D?}$. Then

$$\begin{aligned}
&(\mathcal{PS}[\![\texttt{if x = x then z := y else y := z}]\!]ps)\ \texttt{z} \\
&\quad = (\text{cond}_{\text{P}}(\mathcal{PB}[\![\texttt{x = x}]\!],\ \mathcal{PS}[\![\texttt{z := y}]\!],\ \mathcal{PS}[\![\texttt{y := z}]\!])\ ps)\ \texttt{z} \\
&\quad = (\mathcal{PS}[\![\texttt{z := y}]\!]\ ps \sqcup_{\text{P}} \mathcal{PS}[\![\texttt{y := z}]\!]\ ps)\ \texttt{z} \\
&\quad = \text{D?}
\end{aligned}$$

because $\mathcal{PB}[\![\texttt{x = x}]\!]ps = \text{OK}$, $(\mathcal{PS}[\![\texttt{z := y}]\!]ps)\ \texttt{z} = \text{OK}$ but $(\mathcal{PS}[\![\texttt{y := z}]\!]ps)\ \texttt{z} = \text{D?}$. So even though the false branch never will be executed it will influence the result obtained by the analysis.

Similarly, even if y and z are not dubious but x is, the analysis cannot determine that the final value of z only depends on the value of y. To see this assume that ps is a proper property state such that $ps\ \texttt{x} = \text{D?}$, $ps\ \texttt{y} = \text{OK}$ and $ps\ \texttt{z} = \text{OK}$. We then get

$$\begin{aligned}
&\mathcal{PS}[\![\texttt{if x = x then z := y else y := z}]\!]ps\\
&\quad = \text{cond}_{\text{P}}(\mathcal{PB}[\![\texttt{x = x}]\!], \mathcal{PS}[\![\texttt{z := y}]\!], \mathcal{PS}[\![\texttt{y := z}]\!])ps\\
&\quad = \text{LOST}
\end{aligned}$$

because $\mathcal{PB}[\![\texttt{x = x}]\!]ps = \text{D?}$. These examples show that the result of the analysis is safe but usually somewhat imprecise. More complex analyses could do better (for example by trying to predict the outcome of tests) but in general no decidable analysis can provide exact results. □

Exercise 5.15 Consider the statements S_{11} and S_{12} of Example 5.3. Use Tables 5.1 and 5.2 to characterize the behaviour of $\mathcal{PS}[\![S_{11}]\!]$ and $\mathcal{PS}[\![S_{12}]\!]$ on proper and improper property states. Anticipating Section 5.3 show that

$$s_1 \equiv s_2\ \underline{\text{rel}}\ ps \text{ implies } \mathcal{S}_{\text{ds}}[\![S_{\text{i}}]\!]s_1 \equiv \mathcal{S}_{\text{ds}}[\![S_{\text{i}}]\!]s_2\ \underline{\text{rel}}\ \mathcal{PS}[\![S_{\text{i}}]\!]ps$$

for i = 11, 12 and for all $ps \in$ **PState**. Finally argue that it would *not* be sensible to use

$$\text{cond}'_{\text{P}}(f, h_1, h_2)\ ps = (h_1\ ps) \sqcup_{\text{PS}} (h_2\ ps)$$

instead of the cond_{P} defined above. □

In the clause for the `while`-loop we also use the function cond_{P} and otherwise the clause is as in the direct style denotational semantics of Chapter 4. In particular we use the fixed point operation FIX as it corresponds to unfolding the `while`-loop a number of times — once for each time the *analysis* traverses the loop. As in Chapter 4 the fixed point is defined by

$$\text{FIX } H = \bigsqcup\{\, H^{\text{n}}\ \bot \mid \text{n} \geq 0 \,\}$$

where the functionality of H is

$$H\colon (\textbf{PState} \to \textbf{PState}) \to (\textbf{PState} \to \textbf{PState})$$

and where **PState** → **PState** is the set of total functions from **PState** to **PState**. In order for this to make sense H must be a continuous function on a ccpo with $\bot$ as its least element. We shall shortly verify that this is indeed the case.

Example 5.16 We are now in a position where we can attempt the application of the analysis to the factorial statement:

$$\mathcal{PS}[\![\texttt{y := 1; while}\ \neg(\texttt{x=1})\ \texttt{do (y := y}\star\texttt{x; x := x}-\texttt{1)}]\!]$$

We shall apply this function to the proper property state ps_0 that maps `x` to OK and all other variables (including `y`) to D? as this corresponds to viewing `x` as the only input variable of the statement.

To do so we use the clauses of Tables 5.1 and 5.2 and get

$$\begin{aligned}&\mathcal{PS}[\![\texttt{y := 1; while}\ \neg(\texttt{x=1})\ \texttt{do (y := y}\star\texttt{x; x := x}-\texttt{1)}]\!]\ ps_0\\&\quad = (\text{FIX}\ H)\ (ps_0[\texttt{y}\mapsto\text{OK}])\end{aligned}$$

where

$$H\ h = \text{cond}_{\text{P}}(\mathcal{PB}[\![\neg(\texttt{x=1})]\!],\ h \circ \mathcal{PS}[\![\texttt{y := y}\star\texttt{x; x := x}-\texttt{1}]\!],\ \text{id})$$

We first simplify H and obtain

$$(H\ h)\ ps = \begin{cases}\text{LOST} & \text{if } ps\ \text{on-track} = \text{D?} \text{ or } ps\ \texttt{x} = \text{D?}\\ (h\ ps) \sqcup_{\text{PS}} ps & \text{if } ps\ \text{on-track} = \text{OK} \text{ and } ps\ \texttt{x} = \text{OK}\end{cases}$$

At this point we shall pretend that we have shown the following property of H (to be proved in Exercise 5.18):

$$\begin{aligned}&\text{if } H^{\text{n}}\ \bot = H^{\text{n}+1}\ \bot \text{ for some n}\\&\text{then FIX } H = H^{\text{n}}\ \bot\end{aligned}$$

where $\bot$ is the function $\bot\ ps = \text{INIT}$ for all ps. We can now calculate the iterands $H^0\ \bot$, $H^1\ \bot$, $\cdots$. We obtain

$$(H^0\ \bot)\ ps = \text{INIT}$$

$$(H^1\ \bot)\ ps = \begin{cases}\text{LOST} & \text{if } ps\ \texttt{x} = \text{D?} \text{ or } ps \text{ not proper}\\ ps & \text{if } ps\ \texttt{x} = \text{OK} \text{ and } ps \text{ proper}\end{cases}$$

$$(H^2\ \bot)\ ps = \begin{cases}\text{LOST} & \text{if } ps\ \texttt{x} = \text{D?} \text{ or } ps \text{ not proper}\\ ps & \text{if } ps\ \texttt{x} = \text{OK} \text{ and } ps \text{ proper}\end{cases}$$

where ps is an arbitrary property state. Since $H^1\ \bot = H^2\ \bot$ our assumption above ensures that we have found the least fixed point for H:

$$(\text{FIX}\ H)\ ps = \begin{cases}\text{LOST} & \text{if } ps\ \texttt{x} = \text{D?} \text{ or } ps \text{ not proper}\\ ps & \text{if } ps\ \texttt{x} = \text{OK} \text{ and } ps \text{ proper}\end{cases}$$

It is now straightforward to verify that $(\text{FIX}\ H)\ (ps_0[\texttt{y}\mapsto\text{OK}])\ \texttt{y} = \text{OK}$ and that $(\text{FIX}\ H)(ps_0[\texttt{y}\mapsto\text{OK}])$ is proper. We conclude that there *is* a functional dependency between the input variable `x` and the output variable `y`. □

Well-definedness of $\mathcal{PS}$

Having specified the analysis we shall now show that it is indeed well-defined. As in Chapter 4 there are three stages:

- First we introduce a partial order on **PState** → **PState** such that it becomes a ccpo.
- Then we show that certain auxiliary functions used in the definition of $\mathcal{PS}$ are continuous.
- Finally we show that the fixed point operator only is applied to continuous functions.

Thus our first task is to define a partial order on **PState** → **PState** and for this we use the approach developed in Lemma 5.4. Instantiating the non-empty set S to the set **PState** and the partially ordered set $(D, \sqsubseteq)$ to $(\mathbf{PState}, \sqsubseteq_{PS})$ we get:

Corollary 5.17 Let $\sqsubseteq$ be the ordering on **PState** → **PState** defined by

$h_1 \sqsubseteq h_2$ if and only if $h_1\ ps \sqsubseteq_{PS} h_2\ ps$ for all property states ps

Then $(\mathbf{PState} \to \mathbf{PState}, \sqsubseteq)$ is a complete lattice, and hence a ccpo, and the formula for least upper bounds is

$$(\bigsqcup Y)\ ps = \bigsqcup_{PS} \{\ h\ ps \mid h \in Y\ \}$$

for any subset Y of **PState** → **PState**.

Exercise 5.18 (Essential) Show that the assumption made in Example 5.16 is correct. That is first show that

$$H\colon (\mathbf{PState} \to \mathbf{PState}) \to (\mathbf{PState} \to \mathbf{PState})$$

as defined in Example 5.16 is indeed a monotone function. Next show that for any monotone function H of the above functionality if

$$H^{n}\ \bot = H^{n+1}\ \bot$$

for some n then $H^{n}\ \bot$ is the least fixed point of H. □

Our second task is to ensure that the function H used in Table 5.2 is a continuous function from **PState** → **PState** to **PState** → **PState**. For this we follow the approach of Section 4.3 and show that cond_P is continuous in its second argument and later that composition is continuous in its first argument.

Lemma 5.19 Let f: **PState** $\to$ **P**, h_0: **PState** $\to$ **PState** and define

$$H\ h = \mathrm{cond}_\mathrm{P}(f,\ h,\ h_0)$$

Then H: (**PState**$\to$**PState**) $\to$ (**PState**$\to$**PState**) is a continuous function.

Proof: We shall first prove that H is *monotone* so let h_1 and h_2 be such that $h_1 \sqsubseteq h_2$, that is $h_1\ ps \sqsubseteq_{\mathrm{PS}} h_2\ ps$ for all property states ps. We then have to show that $\mathrm{cond}_\mathrm{P}(f,\ h_1,\ h_0)\ ps \sqsubseteq_{\mathrm{PS}} \mathrm{cond}_\mathrm{P}(f,\ h_2,\ h_0)\ ps$. The proof is by cases on the value of $f\ ps$. If $f\ ps = \mathrm{OK}$ then the result follows since

$$(h_1\ ps) \sqcup_{\mathrm{PS}} (h_0\ ps) \sqsubseteq_{\mathrm{PS}} (h_2\ ps) \sqcup_{\mathrm{PS}} (h_0\ ps)$$

If $f\ ps = \mathrm{D?}$ then the result follows since $\mathrm{LOST} \sqsubseteq_{\mathrm{PS}} \mathrm{LOST}$.

To see that H is *continuous* let Y be a non-empty chain in **PState** $\to$ **PState**. Using the characterization of least upper bounds in **PState** given in Corollary 5.17 we see that we must show that

$$(H\ (\bigsqcup Y))\ ps = \bigsqcup_{\mathrm{PS}} \{\ (H\ h)\ ps \mid h \in Y\ \}$$

for all property states ps in **PState**. The proof is by cases on the value of $f\ ps$. If $f\ ps = \mathrm{D?}$ then we have $(H\ (\bigsqcup Y))\ ps = \mathrm{LOST}$ and

$$\begin{aligned}\bigsqcup_{\mathrm{PS}} \{\ (H\ h)\ ps \mid h \in Y\ \} &= \bigsqcup_{\mathrm{PS}} \{\ \mathrm{LOST} \mid h \in Y\ \}\\ &= \mathrm{LOST}\end{aligned}$$

where the last equality is because Y is not empty. Thus we have proved the required result in this case. If $f\ ps = \mathrm{OK}$ then the characterization of least upper bounds in **PState** gives:

$$\begin{aligned}(H\ (\bigsqcup Y))\ ps &= ((\bigsqcup Y)\ ps) \sqcup_{\mathrm{PS}} (h_0\ ps)\\ &= (\bigsqcup_{\mathrm{PS}} \{\ h\ ps \mid h \in Y\ \}) \sqcup_{\mathrm{PS}} (h_0\ ps)\\ &= \bigsqcup_{\mathrm{PS}} \{\ h\ ps \mid h \in Y \cup \{\ h_0\ \}\ \}\end{aligned}$$

and

$$\begin{aligned}\bigsqcup_{\mathrm{PS}} \{\ (H\ h)\ ps \mid h \in Y\ \} &= \bigsqcup_{\mathrm{PS}} \{\ (h\ ps) \sqcup_{\mathrm{PS}} (h_0\ ps) \mid h \in Y\ \}\\ &= \bigsqcup_{\mathrm{PS}} \{\ h\ ps \mid h \in Y \cup \{\ h_0\ \}\ \}\end{aligned}$$

where the last equality follows because Y is not empty. Thus the result follows in this case. □

Exercise 5.20 Let f: **PState** $\to$ **P**, h_0: **PState** $\to$ **PState** and define

$$H\ h = \text{cond}_P(f,\ h_0,\ h)$$

Show that H: (**PState** $\to$ **PState**) $\to$ (**PState** $\to$ **PState**) is a continuous function. □

Lemma 5.21 Let h_0: **PState** $\to$ **PState** and define

$$H\ h = h \circ h_0$$

Then H: (**PState**$\to$**PState**) $\to$ (**PState**$\to$**PState**) is a continuous function.

Proof: We shall first show that H is *monotone* so let h_1 and h_2 be such that $h_1 \sqsubseteq h_2$, that is $h_1\ ps \sqsubseteq_{PS} h_2\ ps$ for all property states ps. Clearly we then have $h_1(h_0\ ps) \sqsubseteq_{PS} h_2(h_0\ ps)$ for all property states ps and thereby we have proved the monotonicity of H.

To prove the *continuity* let Y be a non-empty chain in **PState** $\to$ **PState**. We must show that

$$(H\ (\bigsqcup Y))\ ps = (\bigsqcup\{\ H\ h \mid h \in Y\ \})\ ps$$

for all property states ps. Using the characterization of least upper bounds given in Corollary 5.17 we get

$$\begin{aligned}(H\ (\bigsqcup Y))\ ps &= ((\bigsqcup Y) \circ h_0)\ ps\\ &= (\bigsqcup Y)\ (h_0\ ps)\\ &= \bigsqcup_{PS}\ \{\ h\ (h_0\ ps) \mid h \in Y\ \}\end{aligned}$$

and

$$\begin{aligned}(\bigsqcup\{\ H\ h \mid h \in Y\ \})\ ps &= \bigsqcup_{PS}\ \{\ (H\ h)\ ps \mid h \in Y\ \}\\ &= \bigsqcup_{PS}\ \{\ (h \circ h_0)\ ps \mid h \in Y\ \}\end{aligned}$$

Hence the result follows. □

This suffices for showing the well-definedness of $\mathcal{PS}$:

Proposition 5.22 The semantic function $\mathcal{PS}[\![S]\!]$: **PState** $\to$ **PState** of Table 5.2 is a well-defined function for all statements S of the language **While**.

Proof: The proof is by structural induction on S and only the case of the `while`-loop is interesting. We note that the function H used in Table 5.2 is given by

$$H = H_1 \circ H_2$$

where

$$H_1\ h = \text{cond}_P(\mathcal{PB}[\![b]\!],\ h,\ \text{id})$$
$$H_2\ h = h \circ \mathcal{PS}[\![S]\!]$$

As H_1 and H_2 are continuous functions by Lemmas 5.19 and 5.21 we have that H is a continuous function by Lemma 4.35. Hence FIX H is well-defined and this completes the proof. □

Exercise 5.23 Consider the statement

$$\texttt{z := 0; while y}\leq\texttt{x do (z := z+1; x := x-y)}$$

where **x** and **y** are input variables and **z** is the output variable. Use the approach of Example 5.16 to show that there is a functional dependency between the input and output variables. □

Exercise 5.24 Apply the analysis $\mathcal{PS}$ to the statement `while true do skip` and explain why the analysis terminates. □

Exercise 5.25 Extend **While** with the statement `repeat` S `until` b and give the new (compositional) clause for $\mathcal{PS}$. Discuss your extension and validate the well-definedness. □

Exercise 5.26 Extend **While** with the statement `for` x := a_1 `to` a_2 `do` S and give the new (compositional) clause for $\mathcal{PS}$. Discuss your extension and validate the well-definedness. □

Exercise 5.27 (Essential) Show that for every statement S

$$ps \text{ on-track} \sqsubseteq (\mathcal{PS}[\![S]\!]ps) \text{ on-track}$$

so that ps must be proper if $\mathcal{PS}[\![S]\!]ps$ is. In the case of `while` b `do` S you should first prove that for all n $\geq$ 1:

$$ps \text{ on-track} \sqsubseteq ((H^{\text{n}}\ \bot)\ ps) \text{ on-track}$$

where $\bot\ ps' = \text{INIT}$ for all ps' and $H\ h = \text{cond}_P(\mathcal{PB}[\![b]\!],\ h \circ \mathcal{PS}[\![S]\!],\ \text{id})$. □

Exercise 5.28 Show that there exists h_0: **PState** → **PState** such that H defined by $H\ h = h_0 \circ h$ is *not even* a monotone function from **PState** → **PState** to **PState** → **PState**. □

Remark The example of the above exercise indicates a major departure from the secure world of Chapter 4. Luckily an insurance policy can be arranged. The premium is to replace all occurrences of

$$\mathbf{PState} \to \mathbf{PState} \quad \text{and} \quad \mathbf{PState} \to \mathbf{P}$$

by

$$[\mathbf{PState} \to \mathbf{PState}] \quad \text{and} \quad [\mathbf{PState} \to \mathbf{P}]$$

where $[D \to E] = \{ f\colon D \to E \mid f \text{ is continuous } \}$. One can then show that $[D \to E]$ is a ccpo if D and E are and that the characterization of least upper bounds given in Lemma 5.4 still holds. Furthermore, one can show that Exercise 5.6 ensures that $\mathcal{PA}[\![a]\!]$ and $\mathcal{PB}[\![b]\!]$ are continuous. Finally, the entire development in this section still carries through although there are additional proof obligations to be carried out. In this setting one gets that if h_0: $[\mathbf{PState} \to \mathbf{PState}]$ then H defined by $H\ h = h_0 \circ h$ is indeed a continuous function from $[\mathbf{PState} \to \mathbf{PState}]$ to $[\mathbf{PState} \to \mathbf{PState}]$. □

To summarize, the well-definedness of $\mathcal{PS}$ relies on the following results established above:

Proof Summary for While:

Well-definedness of Static Analysis

1: The set $\mathbf{PState} \to \mathbf{PState}$ equipped with an appropriate ordering $\sqsubseteq$ is a ccpo (Corollary 5.17).

2: Certain functions Ψ: $(\mathbf{PState} \to \mathbf{PState}) \to (\mathbf{PState} \to \mathbf{PState})$ are continuous (Lemmas 5.19 and 5.21).

3: In the definition of $\mathcal{PS}$ we only apply the fixed point operation to continuous functions (Proposition 5.22).

Our overall algorithm for determining whether or not there is a functional dependency between input and output variables then proceeds as follows:

INPUT:	a statement S of **While**
	a set $I \subseteq \mathbf{Var}$ of input variables
	a set $O \subseteq \mathbf{Var}$ of output variables
OUTPUT:	YES, if there *definitely* is a functional dependency
	NO?, if there *may not* be a functional dependency

METHOD: let ps_I be uniquely determined by $\text{OK}(ps_I) = I \cup \{\text{on-track}\}$

let $ps_O = \mathcal{PS}[\![S]\!]ps_I$

output YES if $\text{OK}(ps_O) \supseteq O \cup \{\text{on-track}\}$

output NO? otherwise

5.3 Safety of the analysis

In this section we shall show that the analysis functions $\mathcal{PA}$, $\mathcal{PB}$ and $\mathcal{PS}$ are correct with respect to the semantic functions $\mathcal{A}$, $\mathcal{B}$ and $\mathcal{S}_{\text{ds}}$. This amounts to a formalization of the considerations that were already illustrated in Exercises 5.13 and 5.15. We begin with the rather simple case of arithmetic expressions.

Expressions

Let g: **State** $\to$ **Z** be a function, perhaps of the form $\mathcal{A}[\![a]\!]$ for some arithmetic expression $a \in$ **Aexp**, and let h: **PState** $\to$ **P** be another function, perhaps of the form $\mathcal{PA}[\![a]\!]$ for some arithmetic expression $a \in$ **Aexp**. We shall introduce a relation

$$g \ \underline{\text{sat}}_{\text{Aexp}} \ h$$

for expressing when the analysis h is correct with respect to the semantics g. It is defined by

$$s_1 \equiv s_2 \ \underline{\text{rel}}_{\text{Stm}} \ ps \text{ implies } g\ s_1 \equiv g\ s_2 \ \underline{\text{rel}}_{\text{Aexp}} \ h\ ps$$

for all states s_1 and s_2 and property states ps. This condition says that the results of g will be suitably related provided that the arguments are. It is perhaps more intuitive when rephrased as

$$(s_1 \equiv s_2 \ \underline{\text{rel}}_{\text{Stm}} \ ps) \text{ and } (h\ ps = \text{OK}) \text{ imply } g\ s_1 = g\ s_2$$

The safety of the analysis $\mathcal{PA}$ is then expressed by

---

Fact 5.29 For all arithmetic expressions $a \in$ **Aexp** we have

$$\mathcal{A}[\![a]\!] \ \underline{\text{sat}}_{\text{Aexp}} \ \mathcal{PA}[\![a]\!]$$

Proof: This is an immediate consequence of Lemma 1.11 and Exercise 5.11. □

The analysis $\mathcal{PB}$ of boolean expressions is safe in the following sense:

Exercise 5.30 (Essential) Repeat the development for boolean expressions, that is define a relation $\underline{\text{sat}}_{\text{Bexp}}$ and show that

$$\mathcal{B}[\![b]\!] \ \underline{\text{sat}}_{\text{Bexp}} \ \mathcal{PB}[\![b]\!]$$

for all boolean expressions $b \in$ **Bexp**. □

Statements

The safety of the analysis of statements will express that if OK(ps) includes all the input variables and if OK($\mathcal{PS}[\![S]\!]ps$) includes 'on-track' and all the output variables then $\mathcal{S}_{\mathrm{ds}}[\![S]\!]$ determines a functional relationship between the input and output variables. This validation is important because although the intuition about OK meaning "depending only on input variables" goes a long way towards motivating the analysis, it is not perfect. As we already mentioned in Section 5.1 one cannot inspect a value, like **27**, and determine whether it has its value because it only depends on input variables or because it just happened to be **27**. To aid the intuition in determining that no errors have been made in the definition of the analysis it is *necessary* to give a formal statement of the relationship between computations in the standard (denotational) semantics and in the analysis.

Our key tool will be the relation $s_1 \equiv s_2\ \underline{\mathrm{rel}}\ ps$ and we shall show that if this relationship holds before the statement is executed and analysed then either the statement will loop on both states or the same relationship will hold between the final states and the final property state (provided that the analysis does not get "lost"). We shall formalize this by defining a relation

$$g\ \underline{\mathrm{sat}}_{\mathrm{Stm}}\ h$$

between a function g: **State** $\hookrightarrow$ **State**, perhaps of the form $\mathcal{S}_{\mathrm{ds}}[\![S]\!]$ for some S in **Stm**, and another function h: **PState** $\rightarrow$ **PState**, perhaps of the form $\mathcal{PS}[\![S]\!]$ for some S in **Stm**. The formal definition amounts to

$$(s_1 \equiv s_2\ \underline{\mathrm{rel}}\ ps) \text{ and } (h\ ps \text{ is proper})$$

imply

$$(g\ s_1 = \underline{\mathrm{undef}} \text{ and } g\ s_2 = \underline{\mathrm{undef}}) \text{ or}$$

$$(g\ s_1 \neq \underline{\mathrm{undef}} \text{ and } g\ s_2 \neq \underline{\mathrm{undef}} \text{ and } g\ s_1 \equiv g\ s_2\ \underline{\mathrm{rel}}\ h\ ps)$$

for all states s_1, $s_2 \in$ **State** and all property states $ps \in$ **PState**. To motivate this definition consider two states s_1 and s_2 that are equal relative to ps. If ps is proper this means that $s_1\ x = s_2\ x$ for all variables x in OK(ps). The analysis of the statement may get "lost" in which case $h\ ps$ is not proper and we cannot deduce anything about the behaviour of the statement. Alternatively, it may be the case that $h\ ps$ is proper and in that case the statement must behave in the same way whether executed from s_1 or from s_2. In particular

- the statement may enter a loop when executed from s_1 and s_2, that is $g\ s_1 = \underline{\mathrm{undef}}$ and $g\ s_2 = \underline{\mathrm{undef}}$, or

- the statement does not enter a loop when executed from s_1 and s_2, that is $g\ s_1 \neq \underline{\mathrm{undef}}$ and $g\ s_2 \neq \underline{\mathrm{undef}}$.

In the latter case the two final states $g\ s_1$ and $g\ s_2$ must be equal relative to the resulting property state $h\ ps$, that is $(g\ s_1)\ x = (g\ s_2)\ x$ for all variables x in $\mathrm{OK}(h\ ps)$.

We may then formulate the desired relationship between the semantics and the analysis as follows:

Theorem 5.31 For all statements S of **While** we have $\mathcal{S}_{\mathrm{ds}}[\![S]\!]\ \underline{\mathrm{sat}}_{\mathrm{Stm}}\ \mathcal{PS}[\![S]\!]$.

Before conducting the proof we need to establish some properties of the auxiliary operations composition and conditional.

Lemma 5.32 Let g_1, g_2: **State** $\hookrightarrow$ **State** and h_1, h_2: **PState** $\rightarrow$ **PState** and assume that

$$ps \text{ on-track} \sqsubseteq_{\mathrm{P}} (h_2\ ps) \text{ on-track} \qquad (*)$$

holds for all $ps \in$ **PState**. Then

$$g_1\ \underline{\mathrm{sat}}_{\mathrm{Stm}}\ h_1 \text{ and } g_2\ \underline{\mathrm{sat}}_{\mathrm{Stm}}\ h_2 \text{ imply } g_2 \circ g_1\ \underline{\mathrm{sat}}_{\mathrm{Stm}}\ h_2 \circ h_1$$

Proof: Let s_1, s_2 and ps be such that

$$s_1 \equiv s_2\ \underline{\mathrm{rel}}\ ps, \text{ and } (h_2 \circ h_1)\ ps \text{ is proper}$$

Using that $h_2\ (h_1\ ps)$ is proper we get from (*) that $h_1\ ps$ must be proper as well (by taking ps to be $h_1\ ps$). So from the assumption $g_1\ \underline{\mathrm{sat}}_{\mathrm{Stm}}\ h_1$ we get

$$g_1\ s_1 = \underline{\mathrm{undef}} \text{ and } g_1\ s_2 = \underline{\mathrm{undef}}, \text{ or}$$
$$g_1\ s_1 \neq \underline{\mathrm{undef}} \text{ and } g_1\ s_2 \neq \underline{\mathrm{undef}} \text{ and } g_1\ s_1 \equiv g_1\ s_2\ \underline{\mathrm{rel}}\ h_1\ ps$$

In the first case we are finished since it follows that $(g_2 \circ g_1)\ s_1 = \underline{\mathrm{undef}}$ and that $(g_2 \circ g_1)\ s_2 = \underline{\mathrm{undef}}$. In the second case we use that

$$g_1\ s_1 \equiv g_1\ s_2\ \underline{\mathrm{rel}}\ h_1\ ps, \text{ and } h_2(h_1\ ps) \text{ is proper}$$

The assumption $g_2\ \underline{\mathrm{sat}}_{\mathrm{Stm}}\ h_2$ then gives

$$g_2\ (g_1\ s_1) = \underline{\mathrm{undef}} \text{ and } g_2\ (g_1\ s_2) = \underline{\mathrm{undef}}, \text{ or}$$
$$g_2\ (g_1\ s_1) \neq \underline{\mathrm{undef}} \text{ and } g_2\ (g_1\ s_2) \neq \underline{\mathrm{undef}} \text{ and}$$
$$g_2(g_1\ s_1) \equiv g_2(g_1\ s_2)\ \underline{\mathrm{rel}}\ h_2(h_1\ ps)$$

In both cases we have completed the proof. □

Lemma 5.33 Assume that g_1, g_2: **State** $\hookrightarrow$ **State**, and g: **State** $\rightarrow$ **T** and that h_1, h_2: **PState** $\rightarrow$ **PState** and f: **PState** $\rightarrow$ **P**. Then

$$g \ \underline{\text{sat}}_{\text{Bexp}} \ f,\ g_1 \ \underline{\text{sat}}_{\text{Stm}} \ h_1 \text{ and } g_2 \ \underline{\text{sat}}_{\text{Stm}} \ h_2 \text{ imply}$$

$$\text{cond}(g,\ g_1,\ g_2) \ \underline{\text{sat}}_{\text{Stm}} \ \text{cond}_{\text{P}}(f,\ h_1,\ h_2)$$

Proof: Let s_1, s_2 and ps be such that

$$s_1 \equiv s_2 \ \underline{\text{rel}} \ ps \text{ and } \text{cond}_{\text{P}}(f,\ h_1,\ h_2) \ ps \text{ is proper}$$

First assume that $f\ ps$ = D?. This case turns out to be impossible since then $\text{cond}_{\text{P}}(f, h_1, h_2)\ ps$ = LOST so $\text{cond}_{\text{P}}(f, h_1, h_2)\ ps$ cannot be proper.

So we know that $f\ ps$ = OK. From $g \ \underline{\text{sat}}_{\text{Bexp}} \ f$ we then get $g\ s_1 = g\ s_2$. We also get that $\text{cond}_{\text{P}}(f, h_1, h_2)\ ps = (h_1\ ps) \sqcup_{\text{PS}} (h_2\ ps)$. Thus $h_1\ ps$ as well as $h_2\ ps$ must be proper since otherwise $\text{cond}_{\text{P}}(f, h_1, h_2)\ ps$ cannot be proper. Now let i denote the branch chosen by the test g. We then have

$$s_1 \equiv s_2 \ \underline{\text{rel}} \ ps \text{ and } h_{\text{i}}\ ps \text{ is proper}$$

From the assumption $g_{\text{i}} \ \underline{\text{sat}}_{\text{Stm}} \ h_{\text{i}}$ we therefore get

$$g_{\text{i}}\ s_1 = \underline{\text{undef}} \text{ and } g_{\text{i}}\ s_2 = \underline{\text{undef}}, \text{ or}$$

$$g_{\text{i}}\ s_1 \neq \underline{\text{undef}} \text{ and } g_{\text{i}}\ s_2 \neq \underline{\text{undef}} \text{ and } g_{\text{i}}\ s_1 \equiv g_{\text{i}}\ s_2 \ \underline{\text{rel}} \ h_{\text{i}}\ ps$$

In the first case we get

$$\text{cond}(g,\ g_1,\ g_2)\ s_1 = \underline{\text{undef}} \text{ and } \text{cond}(g,\ g_1,\ g_2)\ s_2 = \underline{\text{undef}}$$

and we are finished. In the second case we get

$$\text{cond}(g,\ g_1,\ g_2)\ s_1 \neq \underline{\text{undef}} \text{ and } \text{cond}(g,\ g_1,\ g_2)\ s_2 \neq \underline{\text{undef}}$$

Furthermore, we have

$$\text{cond}(p,\ g_1,\ g_2)\ s_1 \equiv \text{cond}(p,\ g_1,\ g_2)\ s_2 \ \underline{\text{rel}} \ h_{\text{i}}\ ps$$

Clearly $h_{\text{i}}\ ps \sqsubseteq h_1\ ps \sqcup_{\text{PS}} h_2\ ps$ and using the definition of cond_{P} and Lemma 5.8 we get

$$\text{cond}(g,\ g_1,\ g_2)\ s_1 \equiv \text{cond}(g,\ g_1,\ g_2)\ s_2 \ \underline{\text{rel}} \ \text{cond}_{\text{P}}(p,\ h_1,\ h_2)\ ps$$

as required. □

We now have the apparatus needed to show the safety of $\mathcal{PS}$:

Proof of Theorem 5.31: We shall show that $\mathcal{S}_{\text{ds}}[\![S]\!] \ \underline{\text{sat}}_{\text{Stm}} \ \mathcal{PS}[\![S]\!]$ and we proceed by structural induction on the statement S.

The case $x := a$: Let s_1, s_2 and ps be given such that

$$s_1 \equiv s_2 \ \underline{\text{rel}} \ ps \text{ and } \mathcal{PS}[\![x := a]\!]ps \text{ is proper}$$

It then follows from Exercise 5.27 that ps is proper because $\mathcal{PS}[\![x := a]\!]ps$ is. Also both $\mathcal{S}_{\text{ds}}[\![x := a]\!]s_1$ and $\mathcal{S}_{\text{ds}}[\![x := a]\!]s_2$ will be defined so we only have to show that

$$(\mathcal{S}_{\text{ds}}[\![x := a]\!]s_1)\ y = (\mathcal{S}_{\text{ds}}[\![x := a]\!]s_2)\ y$$

for all $y \in \textbf{Var} \cap \text{OK}(\mathcal{PS}[\![x := a]\!]ps)$. If $y \neq x$ then $y \in \text{OK}(ps)$ and it is immediate from the definition of $\mathcal{S}_{\text{ds}}$ that $(\mathcal{S}_{\text{ds}}[\![x := a]\!]s_1)\ y = (\mathcal{S}_{\text{ds}}[\![x := a]\!]s_2)\ y$. If $y = x$ and x is in $\text{OK}(\mathcal{PS}[\![x := a]\!]ps)$ then we use the assumption $s_1 \equiv s_2$ $\underline{\text{rel}}$ ps together with $(\mathcal{PS}[\![x := a]\!]ps)\ x = \text{OK}$ to get

$$\mathcal{A}[\![a]\!]s_1 = \mathcal{A}[\![a]\!]s_2$$

by Fact 5.29. Hence $(\mathcal{S}_{\text{ds}}[\![x := a]\!]s_1)\ y = (\mathcal{S}_{\text{ds}}[\![x := a]\!]s_2)\ y$ follows also in this case. This proves the required relationship.

The case `skip`: Straightforward.

The case S_1;S_2: The induction hypothesis applied to S_1 and S_2 gives

$$\mathcal{S}_{\text{ds}}[\![S_1]\!] \ \underline{\text{sat}}_{\text{Stm}} \ \mathcal{PS}[\![S_1]\!] \text{ and } \mathcal{S}_{\text{ds}}[\![S_2]\!] \ \underline{\text{sat}}_{\text{Stm}} \ \mathcal{PS}[\![S_2]\!]$$

It follows from Exercise 5.27 that ps on-track $\sqsubseteq_{\text{P}}$ $(\mathcal{PS}[\![S_2]\!]ps)$ on-track holds for all property states ps. The desired result

$$\mathcal{S}_{\text{ds}}[\![S_2]\!] \circ \mathcal{S}_{\text{ds}}[\![S_1]\!] \ \underline{\text{sat}}_{\text{Stm}} \ \mathcal{PS}[\![S_2]\!] \circ \mathcal{PS}[\![S_1]\!]$$

then follows from Lemma 5.32.

The case `if` b `then` S_1 `else` S_2: From Exercise 5.30 we have

$$\mathcal{B}[\![b]\!] \ \underline{\text{sat}}_{\text{Bexp}} \ \mathcal{PB}[\![b]\!]$$

and the induction hypothesis applied to S_1 and S_2 gives

$$\mathcal{S}_{\text{ds}}[\![S_1]\!] \ \underline{\text{sat}}_{\text{Stm}} \ \mathcal{PS}[\![S_1]\!] \text{ and } \mathcal{S}_{\text{ds}}[\![S_2]\!] \ \underline{\text{sat}}_{\text{Stm}} \ \mathcal{PS}[\![S_2]\!]$$

The desired result

$$\text{cond}(\mathcal{B}[\![b]\!], \mathcal{S}_{\text{ds}}[\![S_1]\!], \mathcal{S}_{\text{ds}}[\![S_2]\!]) \ \underline{\text{sat}}_{\text{Stm}} \ \text{cond}_{\text{P}}(\mathcal{PB}[\![b]\!], \mathcal{PS}[\![S_1]\!], \mathcal{PS}[\![S_2]\!])$$

then follows from Lemma 5.33.

The case `while` b `do` S: We must prove that

$$\text{FIX}(G) \ \underline{\text{sat}}_{\text{Stm}} \ \text{FIX}(H)$$

where

$$G\ g = \text{cond}\ (\mathcal{B}[\![b]\!],\ g \circ \mathcal{S}_{\text{ds}}[\![S]\!],\ \text{id})$$
$$H\ h = \text{cond}_{\text{P}}\ (\mathcal{PB}[\![b]\!],\ h \circ \mathcal{PS}[\![S]\!],\ \text{id})$$

To do this we recall the definition of the least fixed points:

$$\text{FIX}\ G = \bigsqcup\{ G^{\text{n}}\ g_0 \mid \text{n} \geq 0 \}\ \text{where}\ g_0\ s = \underline{\text{undef}}\ \text{for all}\ s$$
$$\text{FIX}\ H = \bigsqcup\{ H^{\text{n}}\ h_0 \mid \text{n} \geq 0 \}\ \text{where}\ h_0\ ps = \text{INIT}\ \text{for all}\ ps$$

The proof proceeds in two stages. We begin by proving that

$$G^{\text{n}}\ g_0\ \underline{\text{sat}}_{\text{Stm}}\ \text{FIX}\ H\ \text{for all n} \qquad (*)$$

and then

$$\text{FIX}\ G\ \underline{\text{sat}}_{\text{Stm}}\ \text{FIX}\ H \qquad (**)$$

We prove (*) by induction on n. For the base case we observe that

$$g_0\ \underline{\text{sat}}_{\text{Stm}}\ \text{FIX}\ H$$

holds trivially since $g_0\ s = \underline{\text{undef}}$ for all states s. For the induction step we assume that

$$G^{\text{n}}\ g_0\ \underline{\text{sat}}_{\text{Stm}}\ \text{FIX}\ H$$

and we shall prove the result for n+1. We have

$$\mathcal{B}[\![b]\!]\ \underline{\text{sat}}_{\text{Bexp}}\ \mathcal{PB}[\![b]\!]$$

from Exercise 5.30,

$$\mathcal{S}_{\text{ds}}[\![S]\!]\ \underline{\text{sat}}_{\text{Stm}}\ \mathcal{PS}[\![S]\!]$$

from the induction hypothesis applied to the body of the `while`-loop, and it is clear that

$$\text{id}\ \underline{\text{sat}}_{\text{Stm}}\ \text{id}$$

By Exercise 5.27 we also have

$$ps\ \text{on-track} \sqsubseteq_{\text{P}} ((\text{FIX}\ H)\ ps)\ \text{on-track}$$

for all property states ps. We then obtain

$$\text{cond}(\mathcal{B}[\![b]\!],\ (G^{\text{n}}\ g_0)\circ\mathcal{S}_{\text{ds}}[\![S]\!],\ \text{id})\ \underline{\text{sat}}_{\text{Stm}}\ \text{cond}_{\text{P}}(\mathcal{PB}[\![b]\!],\ (\text{FIX}\ H)\circ\mathcal{PS}[\![S]\!],\ \text{id})$$

from Lemmas 5.32 and 5.33 and this is indeed the desired result since the right-hand side amounts to H (FIX H) which equals FIX H.

Finally we must show (**). This amounts to showing

$$\bigsqcup Y\ \underline{\text{sat}}_{\text{Stm}}\ \text{FIX}\ H$$

where $Y = \{ G^n\ g_0 \mid n \geq 0 \}$. So assume that

$$s_1 \equiv s_2\ \underline{\text{rel}}\ ps \text{ and } (\text{FIX } H)\ ps \text{ is proper}$$

Since g $\underline{\text{sat}}_{\text{Stm}}$ FIX H holds for all $g \in Y$ by (*) we get that either

$$g\ s_1 = \underline{\text{undef}} \text{ and } g\ s_2 = \underline{\text{undef}}, \text{ or}$$

$$g\ s_1 \neq \underline{\text{undef}} \text{ and } g\ s_2 \neq \underline{\text{undef}} \text{ and } g\ s_1 \equiv g\ s_2\ \underline{\text{rel}}\ (\text{FIX } H)\ ps$$

If $(\bigsqcup Y)\ s_1 = \underline{\text{undef}}$ then $g\ s_1 = \underline{\text{undef}}$ for all $g \in Y$ and thereby $g\ s_2 = \underline{\text{undef}}$ for all $g \in Y$ so that $(\bigsqcup Y)\ s_2 = \underline{\text{undef}}$. Similarly $(\bigsqcup Y)\ s_2 = \underline{\text{undef}}$ will imply that $(\bigsqcup Y)\ s_1 = \underline{\text{undef}}$. So consider now the case where $(\bigsqcup Y)\ s_1 \neq \underline{\text{undef}}$ as well as $(\bigsqcup Y)\ s_2 \neq \underline{\text{undef}}$ and let $x \in \textbf{Var} \cap \text{OK}((\text{FIX } H)\ ps)$. By Lemma 4.25 we have

$$\text{graph}(\bigsqcup Y) = \bigcup \{ \text{graph } g \mid g \in Y \}$$

and $(\bigsqcup Y)\ s_i \neq \underline{\text{undef}}$ therefore shows the existence of an element g_i in Y such that $g_i\ s_i \neq \underline{\text{undef}}$ and $(\bigsqcup Y)\ s_i = g_i\ s_i$ (for i = 1, 2). Since Y is a chain either $g_1 \sqsubseteq g_2$ or $g_2 \sqsubseteq g_1$ so let g be the larger of the two. We then have

$$\begin{aligned}
((\textstyle\bigsqcup Y)\ s_1)\ x &= (g_1\ s_1)\ x && \text{as } (\textstyle\bigsqcup Y)\ s_1 = g_1\ s_1 \\
&= (g\ s_1)\ x && \text{as } g_1 \sqsubseteq g \text{ and } g_1\ s_1 \neq \underline{\text{undef}} \\
&= (g\ s_2)\ x && \text{as } g\ s_1 \equiv g\ s_2\ \underline{\text{rel}}\ (\text{FIX } H)\ ps \\
&= (g_2\ s_2)\ x && \text{as } g_2 \sqsubseteq g \text{ and } g_2\ s_2 \neq \underline{\text{undef}} \\
&= ((\textstyle\bigsqcup Y)\ s_2)\ x && \text{as } (\textstyle\bigsqcup Y)\ s_2 = g_2\ s_2
\end{aligned}$$

as required. This finishes the proof of the theorem. □

It follows from this theorem that the algorithm listed at the end of Section 5.2 is indeed correct. The proof of safety of the analysis can be summarized as follows:

Proof Summary for While: **Safety of Static Analysis**	
1:	Define a relation $\underline{\text{sat}}_{\text{Stm}}$ expressing the relationship between the functions of **State** $\hookrightarrow$ **State** and **PState** $\to$ **PState**.
2:	Show that the relation is preserved by certain pairs of auxiliary functions used in the denotational semantics and the static analysis (Lemmas 5.32 and 5.33).
3:	Use *structural induction* on the statements S to show that the relation holds between the semantics and the analysis of S.

Exercise 5.34 Extend the proof of the theorem to incorporate the analysis developed for `repeat` S `until` b in Exercise 5.25. □

Exercise 5.35 When specifying $\mathcal{PS}$ in the previous section we rejected the possibility of using

$$\text{cond}'_\text{P}(f,\ h_1,\ h_2)\ ps = (h_1\ ps) \sqcup_\text{PS} (h_2\ ps)$$

rather than cond_P. Formally show that the analysis obtained by using cond'_P rather than cond_P cannot be correct in the sense of Theorem 5.31. Hint: Consider the statement S_{12} of Example 5.3. □

Exercise 5.36 In the above exercise we saw that cond_P could not be simplified so as to ignore the test for whether the condition is dubious or not. Now consider the following remedy

$$\text{cond}'_\text{P}(f,\ h_1,\ h_2)\ ps = \begin{cases} (h_1\ ps) \sqcup_\text{PS} (h_2\ ps) & \text{if } f\ ps = \text{OK} \\ ((h_1\ (ps[\text{on-track}\mapsto\text{D?}])) \sqcup_\text{PS} (h_2\ (ps[\text{on-track}\mapsto\text{D?}])))[\text{on-track}\mapsto\text{OK}] & \\ & \text{if } f\ ps = \text{D?} \end{cases}$$

Give an example statement where cond'_P is preferable to cond_P. Does the safety proof carry through when cond_P is replaced by cond'_P? If not, suggest how to weaken the safety predicate such that another safety result may be proved. □

5.4 Bounded iteration

In Example 5.16 we analysed the factorial statement and saw that the fixed point computation stabilizes after a finite number of unfoldings, irrespective of the property state that is supplied as argument. This is quite unlike what was the case for the denotational semantics of Chapter 4, where the number of unfoldings depended on the state and was unbounded. A similar example was studied in Exercise 5.24 where we saw that the analysis would terminate upon a statement that never terminated in the denotational semantics of Chapter 4.

This is an instance of a general phenomenon and we shall show two propositions about this. The first proposition says that for each statement `while` b `do` S there is a constant k such that the kth unfolding will indeed be the fixed point. The second proposition is considerably harder and says that it is possible to take k to be $(\text{m}+1)^2$ where m is the number of distinct variables in `while` b `do` S.

To prepare for the first proposition we need an inductive definition of the set $\text{FV}(S)$ of free variables in the statement S:

$$\begin{array}{lcl}
\mathrm{FV}(x := a) & = & \mathrm{FV}(a) \cup \{x\} \\
\mathrm{FV}(\texttt{skip}) & = & \emptyset \\
\mathrm{FV}(S_1;S_2) & = & \mathrm{FV}(S_1) \cup \mathrm{FV}(S_2) \\
\mathrm{FV}(\texttt{if } b \texttt{ then } S_1 \texttt{ else } S_2) & = & \mathrm{FV}(b) \cup \mathrm{FV}(S_1) \cup \mathrm{FV}(S_2) \\
\mathrm{FV}(\texttt{while } b \texttt{ do } S) & = & \mathrm{FV}(b) \cup \mathrm{FV}(S)
\end{array}$$

Our first observation is that we can repeat the development of the previous sections if we restrict the property states to consider only variables that are free in the overall program. So let $X \subseteq \mathbf{Var}$ be a finite set of variables and define $\mathbf{PState}_X$ to be

$$\mathbf{PState}_X = (X \cup \{\text{on-track}\}) \to \mathbf{P}$$

Exercise 5.37 (Essential) Define $\mathbf{Aexp}_X$ to be the set of arithmetic expressions a of $\mathbf{Aexp}$ with $\mathrm{FV}(a) \subseteq X$ and let $\mathbf{Bexp}_X$ and $\mathbf{Stm}_X$ be defined similarly. Modify Tables 5.1 and 5.2 to define analysis functions

$$\mathcal{PA}_X\colon \mathbf{Aexp}_X \to \mathbf{PState}_X \to \mathbf{P}$$

$$\mathcal{PB}_X\colon \mathbf{Bexp}_X \to \mathbf{PState}_X \to \mathbf{P}$$

$$\mathcal{PS}_X\colon \mathbf{Stm}_X \to \mathbf{PState}_X \to \mathbf{PState}_X$$

□

The connection between the analysis functions of the above exercise and those of Tables 5.1 and 5.2 should be intuitively clear. Formally the connection may be worked out as follows:

Exercise 5.38 * Define

$$\mathrm{extend}_X\colon \mathbf{PState}_X \to \mathbf{PState}$$

by

$$(\mathrm{extend}_X\ ps)\ x = \begin{cases} ps\ x & \text{if } x \in X \cup \{\text{on-track}\} \\ ps\ \text{on-track} & \text{otherwise} \end{cases}$$

Show that

$$\begin{array}{lcl}
\mathcal{PA}[\![a]\!] \circ \mathrm{extend}_X & = & \mathcal{PA}_X[\![a]\!] \\
\mathcal{PB}[\![b]\!] \circ \mathrm{extend}_X & = & \mathcal{PB}_X[\![b]\!] \\
\mathcal{PS}[\![S]\!] \circ \mathrm{extend}_X & = & \mathrm{extend}_X \circ \mathcal{PS}_X[\![S]\!]
\end{array}$$

whenever $\mathrm{FV}(a) \subseteq X$, $\mathrm{FV}(b) \subseteq X$ and $\mathrm{FV}(S) \subseteq X$. □

The property states of $\mathbf{PState}_X$ are only defined on a finite number of arguments because X is a finite set. This is the key to showing:

Proposition 5.39 For each statement `while` b `do` S of **While** there exists a constant k such that

$$\mathcal{PS}_X[\![\texttt{while}\ b\ \texttt{do}\ S]\!] = H^{\mathrm{k}}\ \bot$$

where $H\ h = \mathrm{cond_P}(\mathcal{PB}_X[\![b]\!],\ h \circ \mathcal{PS}_X[\![S]\!],\ \mathrm{id})$ and $\mathrm{FV}(\texttt{while}\ b\ \texttt{do}\ S) \subseteq X$.

Note that using the result of Exercise 5.38 we could dispense with X altogether.

Proof: Let m be the cardinality of X. Then there will be $2^{\mathrm{m}+1}$ *different* property states in $\mathbf{PState}_X$. This means that $\mathbf{PState}_X \to \mathbf{PState}_X$ will contain

$$\mathrm{k} = (2^{\mathrm{m}+1})^{2^{\mathrm{m}+1}}$$

different functions. It follows that there can be at most k different iterands $H^{\mathrm{n}}\ \bot$ of H. Since H is monotone Exercise 5.18 gives that $H^{\mathrm{k}}\ \bot$ must be equal to the fixed point FIX H. This concludes the proof of the Proposition. □

Making it practical

The constant k determined above is a safe upper bound but is rather large even for small statements. As an example it says that the 16,777,216th iteration of the functional will suffice for the factorial statement and this is quite useless for practical purposes. In the remainder of this section we shall show that a much smaller constant can be used:

Proposition 5.40 For each statement `while` b `do` S of **While** we have

$$\mathcal{PS}_X[\![\texttt{while}\ b\ \texttt{do}\ S]\!] = H^{\mathrm{k}}\ \bot$$

where $H\ h = \mathrm{cond_P}(\mathcal{PB}_X[\![b]\!],\ h \circ \mathcal{PS}_X[\![S]\!],\ \mathrm{id})$, $\mathrm{k} = (\mathrm{m}+1)^2$, and m is the cardinality of the set $X = \mathrm{FV}(\texttt{while}\ b\ \texttt{do}\ S)$.

Note that using the result of Exercise 5.38 we could dispense with X altogether.

For the factorial statement this will imply that FIX $H = H^9\ \bot$ so only nine iterands need to be constructed. This may be compared with the observation made in Example 5.16 that already $H^1\ \bot$ is the least fixed point.

The proof of Proposition 5.40 requires some preliminary results. To motivate these consider why the upper bound determined in Proposition 5.39 is so imprecise. The reason is that we consider *all* functions in $\mathbf{PState}_X \to \mathbf{PState}_X$ and do not exploit any special properties of the functions $H^{\mathrm{n}}\ \bot$, such as monotonicity or continuity. To obtain a better bound we shall exploit properties of the $\mathcal{PS}_X[\![S]\!]$ analysis functions. Recall that a function

$$h\colon \mathbf{PState}_X \to \mathbf{PState}_X$$

is *strict* if and only if

$$h\ \text{INIT}_X = \text{INIT}_X$$

where INIT_X is the least element of $\mathbf{PState}_X$. It is an *additive* function if and only if

$$h\ (ps_1 \sqcup_{\text{PS}} ps_2) = (h\ ps_1) \sqcup_{\text{PS}} (h\ ps_2)$$

holds for all property states ps_1 and ps_2 of $\mathbf{PState}_X$.

Exercise 5.41 (Essential) Give a formal definition of what it means for a function

$$h\colon \mathbf{PState}_X \to \mathbf{P}$$

to be strict and additive. Use Exercise 5.11 to show that $\mathcal{PA}_X[\![a]\!]$ and $\mathcal{PB}_X[\![b]\!]$ are strict and additive. (We tacitly assume that $\text{FV}(a) \subseteq X$ and $\text{FV}(b) \subseteq X$.) □

We shall first show that the auxiliary functions for composition and conditional preserve strictness and additivity and next we shall prove that the analysis function $\mathcal{PS}_X[\![S]\!]$ is strict and additive for all statements S.

Exercise 5.42 (Essential) Show that if h_1 and h_2 are strict and additive functions in $\mathbf{PState}_X \to \mathbf{PState}_X$ then so is $h_1 \circ h_2$. □

Exercise 5.43 (Essential) Assume that f in $\mathbf{PState}_X \to \mathbf{P}$ is strict and additive and that h_1 and h_2 in $\mathbf{PState}_X \to \mathbf{PState}_X$ are strict and additive. Show that $\text{cond}_{\text{P}}(f, h_1, h_2)$ is a strict and additive function. Hint: if $f\ (ps_1 \sqcup_{\text{PS}} ps_2) = \text{D?}$ then $f\ ps_{\text{i}} = \text{D?}$ for i = 1 or i = 2. □

Lemma 5.44 For all statements S of **While**, $\mathcal{PS}_X[\![S]\!]$ is a strict and additive function whenever $\text{FV}(S) \subseteq X$.

Proof: We proceed by structural induction on S and assume that $\text{FV}(S) \subseteq X$.

The case $x := a$: We have

$$\mathcal{PS}_X[\![x := a]\!]\ \text{INIT}_X = \text{INIT}_X$$

because Exercise 5.41 gives that $\mathcal{PA}_X[\![a]\!]$ is strict so $\mathcal{PA}_X[\![a]\!]\ \text{INIT}_X = \text{OK}$. Next we show that $\mathcal{PS}_X[\![x := a]\!]$ is additive:

$$\begin{aligned}
&\mathcal{PS}_X[\![x := a]\!](ps_1 \sqcup_{\rm PS} ps_2)\\
&\quad= (ps_1 \sqcup_{\rm PS} ps_2)[x \mapsto \mathcal{PA}_X[\![a]\!](ps_1 \sqcup_{\rm PS} ps_2)]\\
&\quad= (ps_1 \sqcup_{\rm PS} ps_2)[x \mapsto \mathcal{PA}_X[\![a]\!]ps_1 \sqcup_{\rm P} \mathcal{PA}_X[\![a]\!]ps_2]\\
&\quad= ps_1[x \mapsto \mathcal{PA}_X[\![a]\!]ps_1] \sqcup_{\rm PS} ps_2[x \mapsto \mathcal{PA}_X[\![a]\!]ps_2]\\
&\quad= \mathcal{PS}_X[\![x := a]\!]ps_1 \sqcup_{\rm PS} \mathcal{PS}_X[\![x := a]\!]ps_2
\end{aligned}$$

where the second equality follows from $\mathcal{PA}_X[\![a]\!]$ being additive (Exercise 5.41).

The case `skip` is immediate.

The case S_1; S_2 follows from Exercise 5.42 and the induction hypothesis applied to S_1 and S_2.

The case `if` b `then` S_1 `else` S_2 follows from Exercise 5.43, the induction hypothesis applied to S_1 and S_2 and Exercise 5.41.

The case `while` b `do` S: Define

$$H\ h = \mathrm{cond_P}(\mathcal{PB}_X[\![b]\!],\ h \circ \mathcal{PS}_X[\![S]\!],\ \mathrm{id})$$

Our first claim is that

$$H^{\rm n}\ \bot$$

is strict and additive for all n. This is proved by numerical induction and the base case, n = 0, is immediate. The induction step follows from the induction hypothesis of the structural induction, the induction hypothesis of the numerical induction, Exercises 5.42, 5.41 and 5.43 and that id is strict and additive. Our second claim is that

$$\mathrm{FIX}\ H = \bigsqcup_{\rm PS} \{\ H^{\rm n}\ \bot \mid {\rm n} \geq 0\ \}$$

is strict and additive. For strictness we calculate

$$\begin{aligned}
(\mathrm{FIX}\ H)\ \mathrm{INIT}_X &= \bigsqcup_{\rm PS} \{\ (H^{\rm n}\ \bot)\ \mathrm{INIT}_X \mid {\rm n} \geq 0\ \}\\
&= \mathrm{INIT}_X
\end{aligned}$$

where the last equality follows from $H^{\rm n}\ \bot$ being strict for all n. For additivity we calculate

$$\begin{aligned}
&(\mathrm{FIX}\ H)(ps_1 \sqcup_{\rm PS} ps_2)\\
&\quad= \bigsqcup_{\rm PS} \{\ (H^{\rm n}\ \bot)(ps_1 \sqcup_{\rm PS} ps_2) \mid {\rm n} \geq 0\ \}\\
&\quad= \bigsqcup_{\rm PS} \{\ (H^{\rm n}\ \bot)ps_1 \sqcup_{\rm PS} (H^{\rm n}\ \bot)ps_2 \mid {\rm n} \geq 0\ \}\\
&\quad= \bigsqcup_{\rm PS} \{\ (H^{\rm n}\ \bot)ps_1 \mid {\rm n} \geq 0\ \} \sqcup_{\rm PS} \bigsqcup_{\rm PS} \{\ (H^{\rm n}\ \bot)ps_2 \mid {\rm n} \geq 0\ \}\\
&\quad= (\mathrm{FIX}\ H)ps_1 \sqcup_{\rm PS} (\mathrm{FIX}\ H)ps_2
\end{aligned}$$

The second equality uses the additivity of $H^n \perp$ for all n. This concludes the proof of the lemma. □

Strict and additive functions have a number of interesting properties:

Exercise 5.45 (Essential) Show that if h: $\mathbf{PState}_X \rightarrow \mathbf{PState}_X$ is additive then h is monotone. □

The next result expresses that when two distinct analysis functions h_1 and h_2 are strict and additive and satisfies $h_1 \sqsubseteq h_2$ then it will be the property assigned to just one of the "variables" that accounts for the difference between h_1 and h_2.

Lemma 5.46 Consider strict and additive functions

$$h_1,\ h_2\text{: } \mathbf{PState}_X \rightarrow \mathbf{PState}_X$$

such that $h_1 \sqsubseteq h_2$ and $h_1 \neq h_2$. Then there exist "variables" x, $y \in X \cup \{\text{on-track}\}$ such that

$$(h_1\ (\text{INIT}_X[y\mapsto\text{D?}]))\ x = \text{OK but}$$

$$(h_2\ (\text{INIT}_X[y\mapsto\text{D?}]))\ x = \text{D?}$$

Proof: Since $h_1 \sqsubseteq h_2$ and $h_1 \neq h_2$ there exists a property state ps such that

$$h_1\ ps \sqsubseteq_{\text{PS}} h_2\ ps$$

$$h_1\ ps \neq h_2\ ps$$

It follows that there exists a "variable" $x \in X \cup \{\text{on-track}\}$ such that

$$(h_1\ ps)\ x = \text{OK}$$

$$(h_2\ ps)\ x = \text{D?}$$

Consider now the set OK(ps). It is finite because OK(ps) $\subseteq X \cup \{\text{on-track}\}$. First assume that OK($ps$) $= X \cup \{\text{on-track}\}$. Then $ps = \text{INIT}_X$ and since we know that h_1 and h_2 are strict we have $h_1\ \text{INIT}_X = \text{INIT}_X$ and $h_2\ \text{INIT}_X = \text{INIT}_X$. Therefore $h_1\ ps = h_2\ ps$ which contradicts the way ps was chosen.

Therefore OK(ps) is a true subset of $X \cup \{\text{on-track}\}$. Now let $\{y_1, \cdots, y_n\}$ be the "variables" of $X \cup \{\text{on-track}\}$ that do not occur in OK(ps). This means that

$$ps = \text{INIT}_X[y_1\mapsto\text{D?}]\cdots[y_n\mapsto\text{D?}]$$

which is equivalent to

$$ps = \text{INIT}_X[y_1\mapsto\text{D?}] \sqcup_{\text{PS}} \cdots \sqcup_{\text{PS}} \text{INIT}_X[y_n\mapsto\text{D?}]$$

Since h_2 is additive we have

$$h_2\ ps = h_2(\text{INIT}_X[y_1 \mapsto \text{D?}]) \sqcup_{\text{PS}} \cdots \sqcup_{\text{PS}} h_2(\text{INIT}_X[y_n \mapsto \text{D?}])$$

We have assumed that $(h_2\ ps)\ x = \text{D?}$ and now it follows that for some i $(1 \leq i \leq n)$

$$h_2(\text{INIT}_X[y_i \mapsto \text{D?}])\ x = \text{D?}$$

Since $\text{INIT}_X[y_i \mapsto \text{D?}] \sqsubseteq_{\text{PS}} ps$ and h_1 is monotone (Exercise 5.45) we get that

$$h_1\ (\text{INIT}_X[y_i \mapsto \text{D?}]) \sqsubseteq_{\text{PS}} h_1\ ps$$

and thereby

$$h_1\ (\text{INIT}_X[y_i \mapsto \text{D?}])\ x = \text{OK}$$

So the lemma follows by taking y to be y_i. □

The next step will be to generalize this result to sequences of strict and additive functions.

Corollary 5.47 Consider a sequence

$$h_0 \sqsubseteq h_1 \sqsubseteq \cdots \sqsubseteq h_n$$

of strict and additive functions

$$h_i\text{: } \mathbf{PState}_X \rightarrow \mathbf{PState}_X$$

that are all distinct, that is $h_i \neq h_j$ if $i \neq j$. Then $n \leq (m+1)^2$ where m is the cardinality of X.

Proof: For each $i \in \{0,1,\cdots,n-1\}$ the previous lemma applied to h_i and h_{i+1} gives that there are "variables"

$$x_i,\ y_i \in X \cup \{\text{on-track}\}$$

such that

$$h_i(\text{INIT}_X[y_i \mapsto \text{D?}])\ x_i = \text{OK}$$

$$h_{i+1}(\text{INIT}_X[y_i \mapsto \text{D?}])\ x_i = \text{D?}$$

First assume that all $(x_i,\ y_i)$ are distinct. Since the cardinality of X is m there can at most be $(m+1)^2$ such pairs and we have shown $n \leq (m+1)^2$.

Next assume that there exists $i < j$ such that $(x_i,\ y_i) = (x_j,\ y_j)$. We then have

$$h_{i+1}(\text{INIT}_X[y_i \mapsto \text{D?}])\ x_i = \text{D?}$$

and

$$h_j(\mathrm{INIT}_X[y_i \mapsto \mathrm{D?}])\ x_i = \mathrm{OK}$$

Since i+1 ≤ j we have $h_{i+1} \sqsubseteq h_j$ and therefore

$$h_{i+1}\ (\mathrm{INIT}_X[y_i \mapsto \mathrm{D?}])\ x_i \sqsubseteq_P h_j\ (\mathrm{INIT}_X[y_i \mapsto \mathrm{D?}])\ x_i$$

This is a contradiction as it is *not* the case that D? $\sqsubseteq_P$ OK. Thus it cannot be the case that some of the pairs (x_i, y_i) obtained from Lemma 5.46 coincide and we have proved the corollary. □

We shall now turn towards the proof of the main result:

Proof of Proposition 5.40. Consider the construct `while` b `do` S and let H be given by

$$H\ h = \mathrm{cond}_P(\mathcal{PB}_X[\![b]\!],\ h \circ \mathcal{PS}_X[\![S]\!],\ \mathrm{id})$$

We shall then prove that

$$\mathcal{PS}_X[\![\texttt{while}\ b\ \texttt{do}\ S]\!] = H^k\ \bot$$

where $k = (m+1)^2$ and m is the cardinality of X = FV(`while` b `do` S). To do that consider the sequence

$$H^0\ \bot \sqsubseteq H^1\ \bot \sqsubseteq \cdots \sqsubseteq H^k\ \bot \sqsubseteq H^{k+1}\ \bot$$

It follows from Lemma 5.44 that each $H^i\ \bot$ is a strict and additive function. It now follows from Corollary 5.47 that not all $H^i\ \bot$, for i ≤ k+1, are distinct. If i<j satisfies

$$H^i\ \bot = H^j\ \bot$$

then we also have

$$H^i\ \bot = H^n\ \bot \text{ for } n \geq i$$

and in particular

$$H^k\ \bot = H^{k+1}\ \bot$$

Hence FIX $H = H^k\ \bot$ as desired because of Exercise 5.18. □

Exercise 5.48 * Show that the bound exhibited in Corollary 5.47 is tight. That is describe how to construct a sequence

$$h_0 \sqsubseteq h_1 \sqsubseteq \cdots \sqsubseteq h_n$$

of strict and additive functions h_i: $\mathbf{PState}_X \to \mathbf{PState}_X$ such that all h_i are distinct and n = $(m+1)^2$ where m is the cardinality of X. Hint: Begin by considering m = 0, m = 1, m = 2 and then try to generalize. □

To summarize, the quadratic upper bound on the required number of iterands is obtained as follows:

Proof Summary for While:

Bounding the Number of Iterations in the Static Analysis

1:	The analysis is modified to use the set $\mathbf{PState}_X$ rather than **PState** (Exercise 5.37).
2:	A proof by *structural induction* on the statements shows that the analysis functions $\mathcal{PS}_X[\![S]\!]$ are strict and additive (Lemma 5.44).
3:	Sequences of strict and additive functions in $\mathbf{PState}_X \to \mathbf{PState}_X$ can at most have length $(m+1)^2$ where m is the cardinality of X (Corollary 5.47).

Using the result of Proposition 5.40 we get that at most 9 iterations are needed to compute the fixed point present in the analysis of the factorial statement. Since we know that already the first iterand will equal the fixed point one may ask whether one can obtain an even better bound on the number of iterations. The following exercise shows that the quadratic upper bound can be replaced by a linear upper bound:

Exercise 5.49 ** Show that for each statement `while` b `do` S of **While** we have

$$\mathcal{PS}_X[\![\texttt{while } b \texttt{ do } S]\!] = H^k \perp$$

where $H\ h = \text{cond}_P(\mathcal{PB}_X[\![b]\!], h \circ \mathcal{PS}_X[\![S]\!], \text{id})$, k = m+1, and m is the cardinality of the set $X = \text{FV}(\texttt{while } b \texttt{ do } S)$. □

For the factorial statement this result will give that at most 3 iterations are needed to determine the fixed point. The next exercise shows that this is almost the best upper bound we can hope for:

Exercise 5.50 * Show that for each m ≥ 1 there is a statement `while` b `do` S of **While** such that

$$\mathcal{PS}_X[\![\texttt{while } b \texttt{ do } S]\!] \neq H^k \perp$$

where $H\ h = \text{cond}_P(\mathcal{PB}_X[\![b]\!], h \circ \mathcal{PS}_X[\![S]\!], \text{id})$, k = m−1, and m is the cardinality of the set $X = \text{FV}(\texttt{while } b \texttt{ do } S)$. □

Chapter 6

Axiomatic Program Verification

The kinds of semantics we have seen so far specify the meaning of programs although they may also be used to prove that given programs possess certain properties. We may distinguish between several classes of properties: *partial correctness properties* are properties expressing that *if* a given program terminates *then* there will be a certain relationship between the initial and the final values of the variables. Thus a partial correctness property of a program need *not* ensure that it terminates. This is contrary to *total correctness properties* which express that the program *will* terminate *and* that there will be a certain relationship between the initial and the final values of the variables. Thus we have

partial correctness + termination = total correctness

Yet another class of properties is concerned with the *resources* used when executing the program. An example is the *time* used to execute the program on a particular machine.

6.1 Direct proofs of program correctness

In this section we shall give some examples that prove partial correctness of statements based directly on the operational and denotational semantics. We shall prove that the factorial statement

```
y := 1; while ¬(x=1) do (y := y⋆x; x := x−1)
```

is partially correct, that is *if* the statement terminates *then* the final value of y will be the factorial of the initial value of x.

Natural semantics

Using *natural semantics* the partial correctness of the factorial statement can be formalized as follows:

For all states s and s', if

$$\langle \texttt{y := 1; while } \neg(\texttt{x=1}) \texttt{ do (y := y}\star\texttt{x; x := x}-\texttt{1)}, s\rangle \to s'$$

then $s'\ \texttt{y} = (s\ \texttt{x})!$ and $s\ \texttt{x} > \mathbf{0}$

This is indeed a partial correctness property because the statement does not terminate if the initial value $s\ \texttt{x}$ of $\texttt{x}$ is non-positive.

The proof proceeds in three stages:

Stage 1: We prove that the body of the `while` loop satisfies:

$$\begin{array}{l} \text{if } \langle \texttt{y := y}\star\texttt{x; x := x}-\texttt{1}, s\rangle \to s'' \text{ and } s''\ \texttt{x} > \mathbf{0} \\ \text{then } (s\ \texttt{y}) \star (s\ \texttt{x})! = (s''\ \texttt{y}) \star (s''\ \texttt{x})! \text{ and } s\ \texttt{x} > \mathbf{0} \end{array} \qquad (*)$$

Stage 2: We prove that the `while` loop satisfies:

$$\begin{array}{l} \text{if } \langle \texttt{while } \neg(\texttt{x=1}) \texttt{ do (y := y}\star\texttt{x; x := x}-\texttt{1)}, s\rangle \to s'' \\ \text{then } (s\ \texttt{y}) \star (s\ \texttt{x})! = s''\ \texttt{y} \text{ and } s''\ \texttt{x} = \mathbf{1} \text{ and } s\ \texttt{x} > \mathbf{0} \end{array} \qquad (**)$$

Stage 3: We prove the partial correctness property for the complete program:

$$\begin{array}{l} \text{if } \langle \texttt{y := 1; while } \neg(\texttt{x=1}) \texttt{ do (y := y}\star\texttt{x; x := x}-\texttt{1)}, s\rangle \to s' \\ \text{then } s'\ \texttt{y} = (s\ \texttt{x})! \text{ and } s\ \texttt{x} > \mathbf{0} \end{array} \qquad (***)$$

In each of the three stages the derivation tree of the given transition is inspected in order to prove the property.

In the *first stage* we consider the transition

$$\langle \texttt{y := y}\star\texttt{x; x := x}-\texttt{1}, s\rangle \to s''$$

According to [comp_{ns}] there will be transitions

$$\langle \texttt{y := y}\star\texttt{x}, s\rangle \to s' \text{ and } \langle \texttt{x := x}-\texttt{1}, s'\rangle \to s''$$

for some s'. From the axiom [ass_{ns}] we then get that $s' = s[\texttt{y}\mapsto\mathcal{A}[\![\texttt{y}\star\texttt{x}]\!]s]$ and that $s'' = s'[\texttt{x}\mapsto\mathcal{A}[\![\texttt{x}-\texttt{1}]\!]s']$. Combining these results we have

$$s'' = s[\texttt{y}\mapsto(s\ \texttt{y})\star(s\ \texttt{x})][\texttt{x}\mapsto(s\ \texttt{x})-\mathbf{1}]$$

Assuming that $s''\ \texttt{x} > \mathbf{0}$ we can then calculate

$$(s''\ \texttt{y}) \star (s''\ \texttt{x})! = ((s\ \texttt{y}) \star (s\ \texttt{x})) \star ((s\ \texttt{x})-\mathbf{1})! = (s\ \texttt{y}) \star (s\ \texttt{x})!$$

and since $s\ \texttt{x} = (s''\ \texttt{x}) + \mathbf{1}$ this shows that (*) does indeed hold.

In the *second stage* we proceed by induction on the shape of the derivation tree for

$$\langle \texttt{while } \neg(\texttt{x=1}) \texttt{ do (y := y}\star\texttt{x; x := x}-\texttt{1)}, s\rangle \to s'$$

One of two axioms and rules could have been used to construct this derivation. If $[\text{while}^{\text{ff}}_{\text{ns}}]$ has been used then $s' = s$ and $\mathcal{B}[\![\neg(\mathtt{x}=1)]\!]s = \mathbf{ff}$. This means that $s'\ \mathtt{x} = \mathbf{1}$ and since $\mathbf{1}! = \mathbf{1}$ we get the required $(s\ \mathtt{y}) \star (s\ \mathtt{x})! = s\ \mathtt{y}$ and $s\ \mathtt{x} > \mathbf{0}$. This proves (**).

Next assume that $[\text{while}^{\text{tt}}_{\text{ns}}]$ is used to construct the derivation. Then it must be the case that $\mathcal{B}[\![\neg(\mathtt{x}=1)]\!]s = \mathbf{tt}$ and

$$\langle \mathtt{y := y\star x;\ x := x-1},\ s\rangle \to s''$$

and

$$\langle \mathtt{while}\ \neg(\mathtt{x}=1)\ \mathtt{do}\ (\mathtt{y := y\star x;\ x := x-1}),\ s''\rangle \to s'$$

for some state s''. The induction hypothesis applied to the latter derivation gives that

$$(s''\ \mathtt{y}) \star (s''\ \mathtt{x})! = s'\ \mathtt{y} \text{ and } s'\ \mathtt{x} = \mathbf{1} \text{ and } s''\ \mathtt{x} > \mathbf{0}$$

From (*) we get that

$$(s\ \mathtt{y}) \star (s\ \mathtt{x})! = (s''\ \mathtt{y}) \star (s''\ \mathtt{x})! \text{ and } s\ \mathtt{x} > \mathbf{0}$$

Putting these results together we get

$$(s\ \mathtt{y}) \star (s\ \mathtt{x})! = s'\ \mathtt{y} \text{ and } s'\ \mathtt{x} = \mathbf{1} \text{ and } s\ \mathtt{x} > \mathbf{0}$$

This proves (**) and thereby the second stage of the proof is completed.

Finally, consider the *third stage* of the proof and the derivation

$$\langle \mathtt{y := 1;\ while}\ \neg(\mathtt{x}=1)\ \mathtt{do}\ (\mathtt{y := y\star x;\ x := x-1}),\ s\rangle \to s'$$

According to $[\text{comp}_{\text{ns}}]$ there will be a state s'' such that

$$\langle \mathtt{y} := \mathbf{1},\ s\rangle \to s''$$

and

$$\langle \mathtt{while}\ \neg(\mathtt{x}=1)\ \mathtt{do}\ (\mathtt{y := y\star x;\ x := x-1}),\ s''\rangle \to s'$$

From axiom $[\text{ass}_{\text{ns}}]$ we see that $s'' = s[\mathtt{y}\mapsto\mathbf{1}]$ and from (**) we get that $s''\ \mathtt{x} > \mathbf{0}$ and therefore $s\ \mathtt{x} > \mathbf{0}$. Hence $(s\ \mathtt{x})! = (s''\ \mathtt{y}) \star (s''\ \mathtt{x})!$ holds and using (**) we get

$$(s\ \mathtt{x})! = (s''\ \mathtt{y}) \star (s''\ \mathtt{x})! = s'\ \mathtt{y}$$

as required. This proves the partial correctness of the factorial statement.

Exercise 6.1 Use the natural semantics to prove the partial correctness of the statement

$\texttt{z := 0; while y}\leq\texttt{x do (z := z+1; x := x-y)}$

that is prove that *if* the statement terminates in s' when executed from a state s with $s\ \texttt{x} > \mathbf{0}$ and $s\ \texttt{y} > \mathbf{0}$, *then* $s'\ \texttt{z} = (s\ \texttt{x})\ \mathbf{div}\ (s\ \texttt{y})$ and $s'\ \texttt{x} = (s\ \texttt{x})\ \mathbf{mod}\ (s\ \texttt{y})$ where **div** is integer division and **mod** is the modulo operation. □

Exercise 6.2 Use the natural semantics to prove the following *total correctness* property for the factorial program: for all states s

if $s\ \texttt{x} > \mathbf{0}$ then there exists a state s' such that

$$\langle \texttt{y := 1; while }\neg\texttt{(x=1) do (y := y}\star\texttt{x; x := x}-\texttt{1)}, s\rangle \to s'$$

and $s'\ \texttt{y} = (s\ \texttt{x})!$ □

Structural operational semantics

The partial correctness of the factorial statement can also be established using the *structural operational semantics*. The property is then reformulated as:

For all states s and s', if

$$\langle \texttt{y := 1; while }\neg\texttt{(x=1) do (y := y}\star\texttt{x; x := x}-\texttt{1)}, s\rangle \Rightarrow^* s'$$

then $s'\ \texttt{y} = (s\ \texttt{x})!$ and $s\ \texttt{x} > \mathbf{0}$

Again it is worthwhile to approach the proof in stages:

Stage 1: We prove by induction on the length of derivation sequences that

if $\langle \texttt{while }\neg\texttt{(x=1) do (y := y}\star\texttt{x; x := x}-\texttt{1)}, s\rangle \Rightarrow^{\mathrm{k}} s'$

then $s'\ \texttt{y} = (s\ \texttt{y}) \star (s\ \texttt{x})!$ and $s'\ \texttt{x} = \mathbf{1}$ and $s\ \texttt{x} > \mathbf{0}$

Stage 2: We prove that

if $\langle \texttt{y := 1; while }\neg\texttt{(x=1) do (y := y}\star\texttt{x; x := x}-\texttt{1)}, s\rangle \Rightarrow^* s'$

then $s'\ \texttt{y} = (s\ \texttt{x})!$ and $s\ \texttt{x} > \mathbf{0}$

Exercise 6.3 Complete the proof of stages 1 and 2. □

Denotational semantics

We shall now use the denotational semantics to prove partial correctness properties of statements. The idea is to formulate the property as a *predicate* ψ on the ccpo $(\mathbf{State} \hookrightarrow \mathbf{State}, \sqsubseteq)$, that is

$$\psi\colon (\mathbf{State} \hookrightarrow \mathbf{State}) \to \mathbf{T}$$

As an example, the partial correctness of the factorial statement will be written as

$$\psi_{fac}(\mathcal{S}_{\rm ds}[\![\texttt{y := 1; while } \neg(\texttt{x=1}) \texttt{ do (y := y}\star\texttt{x; x := x}-\texttt{1)}]\!]) = \textbf{tt}$$

where the predicate ψ_{fac} is defined by

$\psi_{fac}(g) = \textbf{tt}$

if and only if

for all states s and s', if $g\ s = s'$ then $s'\ \texttt{y} = (s\ \texttt{x})!$ and $s\ \texttt{x} > \textbf{0}$

A predicate ψ: $D \to \textbf{T}$ defined on a ccpo $(D,\sqsubseteq)$ is called an *admissible predicate* if and only if we have

$$\text{if } \psi\ d = \textbf{tt} \text{ for all } d \in Y \text{ then } \psi(\bigsqcup Y) = \textbf{tt}$$

for every chain Y in D. Thus if ψ holds on all the elements of the chain then it also holds on the least upper bound of the chain.

Example 6.4 Consider the predicate ψ'_{fac} defined on **State** $\hookrightarrow$ **State** by

$\psi'_{fac}(g) = \textbf{tt}$

if and only if

for all states s and s', if $g\ s = s'$

then $s'\ \texttt{y} = (s\ \texttt{y}) \star (s\ \texttt{x})!$ and $s\ \texttt{x} > \textbf{0}$

Then ψ'_{fac} is an admissible predicate. To see this assume that Y is a chain in **State** $\hookrightarrow$ **State** and assume that $\psi'_{fac}\ g = \textbf{tt}$ for all $g \in Y$. We shall then prove that $\psi'_{fac}(\bigsqcup Y) = \textbf{tt}$, that is

$(\bigsqcup Y)\ s = s'$

implies

$s'\ \texttt{y} = (s\ \texttt{y}) \star (s\ \texttt{x})!$ and $s\ \texttt{x} > \textbf{0}$

From Lemma 4.25 we have $\text{graph}(\bigsqcup Y) = \bigcup\{\ \text{graph}(g) \mid g \in Y\ \}$. We have assumed that $(\bigsqcup Y)\ s = s'$ so Y cannot be empty and $\langle s,\ s'\rangle \in \text{graph}(g)$ for some $g \in Y$. But then

$s'\ \texttt{y} = (s\ \texttt{y}) \star (s\ \texttt{x})!$ and $s\ \texttt{x} > \textbf{0}$

as $\psi'_{fac}\ g = \textbf{tt}$ for all $g \in Y$. This proves that ψ'_{fac} is an admissible predicate. □

For admissible predicates we have the following induction principle called *fixed point induction*:

Theorem 6.5 Let $(D,\sqsubseteq)$ be a ccpo and let f: $D \rightarrow D$ be a continuous function and let ψ be an admissible predicate on D. If for all $d \in D$

$$\psi\ d = \mathbf{tt} \text{ implies } \psi(f\ d) = \mathbf{tt}$$

then $\psi(\text{FIX } f) = \mathbf{tt}$.

Proof: We shall first note that

$$\psi\ \bot = \mathbf{tt}$$

holds by admissibility of ψ (applied to the chain $Y = \emptyset$). By induction on n we can then show that

$$\psi(f^{\text{n}}\ \bot) = \mathbf{tt}$$

using the assumptions of the theorem. By admissibility of ψ (applied to the chain $Y = \{\ f^{\text{n}}\ \bot \mid \text{n} \geq 0\ \}$) we then have

$$\psi(\text{FIX } f) = \mathbf{tt}$$

This completes the proof. □

We are now in a position where we can prove the partial correctness of the factorial statement. The first observation is that

$$\mathcal{S}_{\text{ds}}[\![\texttt{y} := 1;\ \texttt{while}\ \neg(\texttt{x}=1)\ \texttt{do}\ (\texttt{y} := \texttt{y}\star\texttt{x};\ \texttt{x} := \texttt{x}-1)]\!]s = s'$$

if and only if

$$\mathcal{S}_{\text{ds}}[\![\texttt{while}\ \neg(\texttt{x}=1)\ \texttt{do}\ (\texttt{y} := \texttt{y}\star\texttt{x};\ \texttt{x} := \texttt{x}-1)]\!](s[\texttt{y}\mapsto\mathbf{1}]) = s'$$

Thus it is sufficient to prove that

$$\psi'_{fac}(\mathcal{S}_{\text{ds}}[\![\texttt{while}\ \neg(\texttt{x}=1)\ \texttt{do}\ (\texttt{y} := \texttt{y}\star\texttt{x};\ \texttt{x} := \texttt{x}-1)]\!]) = \mathbf{tt} \qquad (*)$$

(where ψ'_{fac} is defined in Example 6.4) as this will imply that

$$\psi_{fac}(\mathcal{S}_{\text{ds}}[\![\texttt{y} := \texttt{1};\ \texttt{while}\ \neg(\texttt{x}=1)\ \texttt{do}\ (\texttt{y} := \texttt{y}\star\texttt{x};\ \texttt{x} := \texttt{x}-1)]\!]) = \mathbf{tt}$$

We shall now reformulate (*) slightly to bring ourselves in a position where we can use fixed point induction. Using the definition of $\mathcal{S}_{\text{ds}}$ in Table 4.1 we have

$$\mathcal{S}_{\text{ds}}[\![\texttt{while}\ \neg(\texttt{x}=1)\ \texttt{do}\ (\texttt{y} := \texttt{y}\star\texttt{x};\ \texttt{x} := \texttt{x}-1)]\!] = \text{FIX } F$$

where the functional F is defined by

$$F\ g = \text{cond}(\mathcal{B}[\![\neg(\texttt{x}=1)]\!],\ g \circ \mathcal{S}_{\text{ds}}[\![\texttt{y} := \texttt{y}\star\texttt{x};\ \texttt{x} := \texttt{x}-1]\!],\ \text{id})$$

Using the semantic equations defining $\mathcal{S}_{\text{ds}}$ we can rewrite this definition as

$$(F\ g)\ s = \begin{cases} s & \text{if } s\ x = \mathbf{1} \\ g(s[\mathtt{y}{\mapsto}(s\ \mathtt{y}){\star}(s\ \mathtt{x})][\mathtt{x}{\mapsto}(s\ \mathtt{x}){-}\mathbf{1}]) & \text{otherwise} \end{cases}$$

We have already seen that F is a continuous function (for example in the proof of Proposition 4.47) and from Example 6.4 we have that ψ'_{fac} is an admissible predicate. Thus we see from Theorem 6.5 that (*) follows if we show that

$$\psi'_{fac}\ g = \mathbf{tt} \text{ implies } \psi'_{fac}(F\ g) = \mathbf{tt}$$

To prove this implication assume that $\psi'_{fac}\ g = \mathbf{tt}$, that is for all states s and s'

$$\text{if } g\ s = s' \text{ then } s'\ \mathtt{y} = (s\ \mathtt{y}) \star (s\ \mathtt{x})! \text{ and } s\ \mathtt{x} > \mathbf{0}$$

We shall prove that $\psi'_{fac}(F\ g) = \mathbf{tt}$, that is for all states s and s'

$$\text{if } (F\ g)\ s = s' \text{ then } s'\ \mathtt{y} = (s\ \mathtt{y}) \star (s\ \mathtt{x})! \text{ and } s\ \mathtt{x} > \mathbf{0}$$

Inspecting the definition of F we see that there are two cases. First assume that $s\ \mathtt{x} = \mathbf{1}$. Then $(F\ g)\ s = s$ and clearly $s\ \mathtt{y} = (s\ \mathtt{y}) \star (s\ \mathtt{x})!$ and $s\ \mathtt{x} > \mathbf{0}$. Next assume that $s\ \mathtt{x} \neq \mathbf{1}$. Then

$$(F\ g)\ s = g(s[\mathtt{y}{\mapsto}(s\ \mathtt{y}){\star}(s\ \mathtt{x})][\mathtt{x}{\mapsto}(s\ \mathtt{x}){-}\mathbf{1}])$$

From the assumptions about g we then get that

$$s'\ \mathtt{y} = ((s\ \mathtt{y}){\star}(s\ \mathtt{x})) \star ((s\ \mathtt{x}){-}\mathbf{1})! \text{ and } (s\ \mathtt{x}){-}\mathbf{1} > \mathbf{0}$$

so that the desired result

$$s'\ \mathtt{y} = (s\ \mathtt{y}) \star (s\ \mathtt{x})! \text{ and } s\ \mathtt{x} > \mathbf{0}$$

follows.

Exercise 6.6 Repeat Exercise 6.1 using the denotational semantics. □

6.2 Partial correctness assertions

One may argue that the above proofs are too detailed to be practically useful; the reason is that they are too closely connected with the semantics of the programming language. One may therefore want to capture the *essential properties* of the various constructs so that it would be less demanding to conduct proofs about given programs. Of course the choice of "essential properties" will determine the sort of properties that we may accomplish proving. In this section we shall be interested in partial correctness properties and therefore the "essential properties" of the various constructs will not include termination.

The idea is to specify properties of programs as *assertions*, or claims, about them. An assertion is a triple of the form

$$\{ P \} \; S \; \{ Q \}$$

where S is a statement and P and Q are predicates. Here P is called the *precondition* and Q is called the *postcondition*. Intuitively, the meaning of $\{ P \} \; S \; \{ Q \}$ is that

> *if* P holds in the initial state, and
>
> *if* the execution of S terminates when started in that state,
>
> *then* Q will hold in the state in which S halts

Note that for $\{ P \} \; S \; \{ Q \}$ to hold we do *not* require that S halts when started in states satisfying P — merely that *if* it does halt *then* Q holds in the final state.

Logical variables

As an example we may write

$$\{ \texttt{x=n} \} \; \texttt{y := 1; while} \; \neg(\texttt{x=1}) \; \texttt{do (y := x}\star\texttt{y; x := x}-\texttt{1)} \; \{ \texttt{y=n!} \wedge \texttt{n>0} \}$$

to express that if the value of `x` is equal to the value of `n` *before* the factorial program is executed then the value of `y` will be equal to the factorial of the value of `n` *after* the execution of the program has terminated (if indeed it terminates). Here `n` is a special variable called a *logical* variable and these logical variables must not appear in any statement considered. The role of these variables is to "remember" the initial values of the program variables. Note that if we replace the postcondition $\texttt{y=n!} \wedge \texttt{n>0}$ by the new postcondition $\texttt{y=x!} \wedge \texttt{x>0}$ then the assertion above will express a relationship between the final value of `y` and the final value of `x` and this is not what we want. The use of logical variables solves the problem because it allows us to refer to initial values of variables.

We shall thus distinguish between two kinds of variables:

- program variables, and
- logical variables.

The states will determine the values of both kinds of variables and since logical variables do not occur in programs their values will always be the same. In case of the factorial program we know that the value of `n` is the same in the initial state and in the final state. The precondition $\texttt{x} = \texttt{n}$ expresses that `n` has the same value as `x` in the initial state. Since the program will not change the value of `n` the postcondition $\texttt{y} = \texttt{n!}$ will express that the final value of `y` is equal to the factorial of the initial value of `x`.

The assertion language

There are two approaches concerning how to specify the preconditions and postconditions of the assertions:

- the intensional approach, versus
- the extensional approach.

In the *intensional approach* the idea is to introduce an explicit language called an *assertion language* and then the conditions will be formulae of that language. This assertion language is in general much more powerful than the boolean expressions, **Bexp**, introduced in Chapter 1. In fact the assertion language has to be very powerful indeed in order to be able to express all the preconditions and postconditions we may be interested in; we shall return to this in the next section. The approach we shall follow is the *extensional approach* and it is a kind of shortcut. The idea is that the conditions are predicates, that is functions in **State** $\rightarrow$ **T**. Thus the meaning of $\{ P \} S \{ Q \}$ may be reformulated as saying that if P holds on a state s and if S executed from state s results in the state s' then Q holds on s'. We can write any predicates we like and therefore the expressiveness problem mentioned above does not arise.

Each boolean expression b defines a predicate $\mathcal{B}[\![b]\!]$. We shall feel free to let b include logical variables as well as program variables so the precondition $\mathtt{x} = \mathtt{n}$ used above is an example of a boolean expression. To ease the readability, we introduce the following notation

$P_1 \wedge P_2$	for	P where $P\ s = (P_1\ s)$ and $(P_2\ s)$
$P_1 \vee P_2$	for	P where $P\ s = (P_1\ s)$ or $(P_2\ s)$
$\neg P$	for	P' where $P'\ s = \neg(P\ s)$
$P[x \mapsto \mathcal{A}[\![a]\!]]$	for	P' where $P'\ s = P\ (s[x \mapsto \mathcal{A}[\![a]\!]s])$
$P_1 \Rightarrow P_2$	for	$\forall s \in$ **State**: $P_1\ s$ implies $P_2\ s$

When it is convenient, but not when defining formal inference rules, we shall allow to dispense with $\mathcal{B}[\![\cdots]\!]$ and $\mathcal{A}[\![\cdots]\!]$ inside brackets *and* preconditions and postconditions.

Exercise 6.7 Show that

- $\mathcal{B}[\![b[x \mapsto a]]\!] = \mathcal{B}[\![b]\!][x \mapsto \mathcal{A}[\![a]\!]]$ for all b and a,
- $\mathcal{B}[\![b_1 \wedge b_2]\!] = \mathcal{B}[\![b_1]\!] \wedge \mathcal{B}[\![b_2]\!]$ for all b_1 and b_2, and
- $\mathcal{B}[\![\neg b]\!] = \neg \mathcal{B}[\![b]\!]$ for all b. □

$[\text{ass}_\text{p}]$	$\{\ P[x\mapsto\mathcal{A}[\![a]\!]]\ \}\ x := a\ \{\ P\ \}$
$[\text{skip}_\text{p}]$	$\{\ P\ \}\ \texttt{skip}\ \{\ P\ \}$
$[\text{comp}_\text{p}]$	$\dfrac{\{\ P\ \}\ S_1\ \{\ Q\ \},\quad \{\ Q\ \}\ S_2\ \{\ R\ \}}{\{\ P\ \}\ S_1;\ S_2\ \{\ R\ \}}$
$[\text{if}_\text{p}]$	$\dfrac{\{\ \mathcal{B}[\![b]\!] \wedge P\ \}\ S_1\ \{\ Q\ \},\quad \{\ \neg\mathcal{B}[\![b]\!] \wedge P\ \}\ S_2\ \{\ Q\ \}}{\{\ P\ \}\ \texttt{if}\ b\ \texttt{then}\ S_1\ \texttt{else}\ S_2\ \{\ Q\ \}}$
$[\text{while}_\text{p}]$	$\dfrac{\{\ \mathcal{B}[\![b]\!] \wedge P\ \}\ S\ \{\ P\ \}}{\{\ P\ \}\ \texttt{while}\ b\ \texttt{do}\ S\ \{\ \neg\mathcal{B}[\![b]\!] \wedge P\ \}}$
$[\text{cons}_\text{p}]$	$\dfrac{\{\ P'\ \}\ S\ \{\ Q'\ \}}{\{\ P\ \}\ S\ \{\ Q\ \}}$ if $P \Rightarrow P'$ and $Q' \Rightarrow Q$

Table 6.1: Axiomatic system for partial correctness

The inference system

The partial correctness assertions will be specified by an inference system consisting of a set of axioms and rules. The formulae of the inference system have the form

$$\{\ P\ \}\ S\ \{\ Q\ \}$$

where S is a statement in the language **While** and P and Q are predicates. The axioms and rules are summarized in Table 6.1 and will be explained below. The inference system specifies an *axiomatic semantics* for **While**.

The axiom for assignment statements is

$$\{\ P[x\mapsto\mathcal{A}[\![a]\!]]\ \}\ x := a\ \{\ P\ \}$$

This axiom assumes that the execution of $x := a$ starts in a state s that satisfies $P[x\mapsto\mathcal{A}[\![a]\!]]$, that is in a state s where $s[x\mapsto\mathcal{A}[\![a]\!]s]$ satisfies P. The axiom expresses that if the execution of $x := a$ terminates (which will always be the case) then the final state will satisfy P. From the earlier definitions of the semantics of **While** we know that the final state will be $s[x\mapsto\mathcal{A}[\![a]\!]s]$ so it is easy to see that the axiom is plausible.

For `skip` the axiom is

$$\{\ P\ \}\ \texttt{skip}\ \{\ P\ \}$$

Thus if P holds before `skip` is executed then it also holds afterwards. This is clearly plausible as `skip` does nothing.

Axioms [ass$_p$] and [skip$_p$] are really *axiom schemes* generating separate axioms for each choice of predicate P. The meaning of the remaining constructs are given by rules of inference rather than axiom schemes. Each such rule specifies a way of deducing an assertion about a compound construct from assertions about its constituents. For composition the rule is:

$$\frac{\{ P \}\ S_1\ \{ Q \},\quad \{ Q \}\ S_2\ \{ R \}}{\{ P \}\ S_1;\ S_2\ \{ R \}}$$

This says that if P holds prior to the execution of S_1; S_2 and if the execution terminates then we can conclude that R holds in the final state provided that there is a predicate Q for which we can deduce that

- if S_1 is executed from a state where P holds and if it terminates then Q will hold for the final state, and that
- if S_2 is executed from a state where Q holds and if it terminates then R will hold for the final state.

The rule for the conditional is

$$\frac{\{ \mathcal{B}[\![b]\!] \wedge P \}\ S_1\ \{ Q \},\quad \{ \neg\mathcal{B}[\![b]\!] \wedge P \}\ S_2\ \{ Q \}}{\{ P \}\ \texttt{if}\ b\ \texttt{then}\ S_1\ \texttt{else}\ S_2\ \{ Q \}}$$

The rule says that if `if` b `then` S_1 `else` S_2 is executed from a state where P holds and if it terminates then Q will hold for the final state provided that we can deduce that

- if S_1 is executed from a state where P and b hold and if it terminates then Q holds on the final state, and that
- if S_2 is executed from a state where P and $\neg b$ hold and if it terminates then Q holds on the final state.

The rule for the iterative statement is

$$\frac{\{ \mathcal{B}[\![b]\!] \wedge P \}\ S\ \{ P \}}{\{ P \}\ \texttt{while}\ b\ \texttt{do}\ S\ \{ \neg\mathcal{B}[\![b]\!] \wedge P \}}$$

The predicate P is called an *invariant* for the `while`-loop and the idea is that it will hold *before* and *after* each execution of the body S of the loop. The rule says that if additionally b is true before each execution of the body of the loop then $\neg b$ will be true when the execution of the `while`-loop has terminated.

To complete the inference system we need one more rule of inference

$$\frac{\{ P' \}\ S\ \{ Q' \}}{\{ P \}\ S\ \{ Q \}} \quad \text{if } P \Rightarrow P' \text{ and } Q' \Rightarrow Q$$

This rule says that we can strengthen the precondition P' and weaken the post-condition Q'. This rule is often called the *rule of consequence*.

Note that Table 6.1 specifies a set of axioms and rules just as the tables defining the operational semantics in Chapter 2. The analogue of a derivation tree will now be called an *inference tree* since it shows how to infer that a certain property holds. Thus the leaves of an inference tree will be instances of axioms and the internal nodes will correspond to instances of rules. We shall say that the inference tree gives a *proof* of the property expressed by its root. We shall write

$$\vdash_{\rm p} \{ P \}\ S\ \{ Q \}$$

for the provability of the assertion $\{ P \}\ S\ \{ Q \}$. An inference tree is called *simple* if it is an instance of one of the axioms and otherwise it is called *composite*.

Example 6.8 Consider the statement `while true do skip`. From [$\text{skip}_{\rm p}$] we have (omitting the $\mathcal{B}[\![\cdots]\!]$)

$$\vdash_{\rm p} \{ \texttt{true} \}\ \texttt{skip}\ \{ \texttt{true} \}$$

Since ($\texttt{true} \wedge \texttt{true}$) $\Rightarrow$ `true` we can apply the rule of consequence [$\text{cons}_{\rm p}$] and get

$$\vdash_{\rm p} \{ \texttt{true} \wedge \texttt{true} \}\ \texttt{skip}\ \{ \texttt{true} \}$$

Hence by the rule [$\text{while}_{\rm p}$] we get

$$\vdash_{\rm p} \{ \texttt{true} \}\ \texttt{while true do skip}\ \{ \neg\texttt{true} \wedge \texttt{true} \}$$

We have that $\neg\texttt{true} \wedge \texttt{true} \Rightarrow \texttt{true}$ so by applying [$\text{cons}_{\rm p}$] once more we get

$$\vdash_{\rm p} \{ \texttt{true} \}\ \texttt{while true do skip}\ \{ \texttt{true} \}$$

The inference above can be summarized by the following inference tree:

$$\cfrac{\cfrac{\cfrac{\{ \texttt{true} \}\ \texttt{skip}\ \{ \texttt{true} \}}{\{ \texttt{true} \wedge \texttt{true} \}\ \texttt{skip}\ \{ \texttt{true} \}}}{\{ \texttt{true} \}\ \texttt{while true do skip}\ \{ \neg\texttt{true} \wedge \texttt{true} \}}}{\{ \texttt{true} \}\ \texttt{while true do skip}\ \{ \texttt{true} \}}$$

It is now easy to see that we cannot claim that $\{ P \}\ S\ \{ Q \}$ means that S will terminate in a state satisfying Q when it is started in a state satisfying P. For the assertion $\{ \texttt{true} \}$ `while true do skip` $\{ \texttt{true} \}$ this reading would mean that the program would always terminate and clearly this is not the case. □

Example 6.9 To illustrate the use of the axiomatic semantics for verification we shall prove the assertion

$$\{\ \mathtt{x} = \mathtt{n}\ \}$$
$$\mathtt{y} := \mathtt{1};\ \mathtt{while}\ \neg(\mathtt{x}{=}\mathtt{1})\ \mathtt{do}\ (\mathtt{y} := \mathtt{y}{\star}\mathtt{x};\ \mathtt{x} := \mathtt{x}{-}\mathtt{1})$$
$$\{\ \mathtt{y} = \mathtt{n}!\ \wedge\ \mathtt{n} > \mathtt{0}\ \}$$

where, for the sake of readability, we write $\mathtt{y} = \mathtt{n}!\ \wedge\ \mathtt{n} > \mathtt{0}$ for the predicate

$$P \text{ where } P\ s = (s\ \mathtt{y} = (s\ \mathtt{n})!\ \wedge\ s\ \mathtt{n} > \mathbf{0})$$

The inference of this assertion proceeds in a number of stages. First we define the predicate *INV* that is going to be the invariant of the `while`-loop:

$$\mathit{INV}\ s = (s\ \mathtt{x} > \mathbf{0} \text{ implies } ((s\ \mathtt{y}) \star (s\ \mathtt{x})! = (s\ \mathtt{n})! \text{ and } s\ \mathtt{n} \geq s\ \mathtt{x}))$$

We shall then consider the body of the loop. Using [$\mathrm{ass_p}$] we get

$$\vdash_{\mathrm{p}} \{\ \mathit{INV}[\mathtt{x}{\mapsto}\mathtt{x}{-}\mathtt{1}]\ \}\ \mathtt{x} := \mathtt{x}{-}\mathtt{1}\ \{\ \mathit{INV}\ \}$$

Similarly, we get

$$\vdash_{\mathrm{p}} \{\ (\mathit{INV}[\mathtt{x}{\mapsto}\mathtt{x}{-}\mathtt{1}])[\mathtt{y}{\mapsto}\mathtt{y}{\star}\mathtt{x}]\ \}\ \mathtt{y} := \mathtt{y} \star \mathtt{x}\ \{\ \mathit{INV}[\mathtt{x}{\mapsto}\mathtt{x}{-}\mathtt{1}]\ \}$$

We can now apply the rule [$\mathrm{comp_p}$] to the two assertions above and get

$$\vdash_{\mathrm{p}} \{\ (\mathit{INV}[\mathtt{x}{\mapsto}\mathtt{x}{-}\mathtt{1}])[\mathtt{y}{\mapsto}\mathtt{y}{\star}\mathtt{x}]\ \}\ \mathtt{y} := \mathtt{y} \star \mathtt{x};\ \mathtt{x} := \mathtt{x}{-}\mathtt{1}\ \{\ \mathit{INV}\ \}$$

It is easy to verify that

$$(\neg(\mathtt{x}{=}\mathtt{1})\ \wedge\ \mathit{INV}) \Rightarrow (\mathit{INV}[\mathtt{x}{\mapsto}\mathtt{x}{-}\mathtt{1}])[\mathtt{y}{\mapsto}\mathtt{y}{\star}\mathtt{x}]$$

so using the rule [$\mathrm{cons_p}$] we get

$$\vdash_{\mathrm{p}} \{\ \neg(\mathtt{x} = \mathtt{1})\ \wedge\ \mathit{INV}\ \}\ \mathtt{y} := \mathtt{y} \star \mathtt{x};\ \mathtt{x} := \mathtt{x}{-}\mathtt{1}\ \{\ \mathit{INV}\ \}$$

We are now in a position to use the rule [$\mathrm{while_p}$] and get

$$\vdash_{\mathrm{p}} \{\ \mathit{INV}\ \}$$
$$\mathtt{while}\ \neg(\mathtt{x}{=}\mathtt{1})\ \mathtt{do}\ (\mathtt{y} := \mathtt{y}{\star}\mathtt{x};\ \mathtt{x} := \mathtt{x}{-}\mathtt{1})$$
$$\{\neg(\neg(\mathtt{x} = \mathtt{1}))\ \wedge\ \mathit{INV}\ \}$$

Clearly we have

$$\neg(\neg(\mathtt{x} = \mathtt{1}))\ \wedge\ \mathit{INV} \Rightarrow \mathtt{y} = \mathtt{n}!\ \wedge\ \mathtt{n} > \mathtt{0}$$

so applying rule [cons_p] we get

$$\vdash_p \{\ INV\ \}\ \texttt{while}\ \neg(\texttt{x=1})\ \texttt{do}\ (\texttt{y := y}\star\texttt{x; x := x}-\texttt{1})\ \{\ \texttt{y} = \texttt{n!} \wedge \texttt{n} > \texttt{0}\ \}$$

We shall now apply the axiom [ass_p] to the statement y := 1 and get

$$\vdash_p \{\ INV[\texttt{y}\mapsto\texttt{1}]\ \}\ \texttt{y := 1}\ \{\ INV\ \}$$

Using that

$$\texttt{x} = \texttt{n} \Rightarrow INV[\texttt{y}\mapsto\texttt{1}]$$

together with [cons_p] we get

$$\vdash_p \{\ \texttt{x} = \texttt{n}\ \}\ \texttt{y := 1}\ \{\ INV\ \}$$

Finally, we can use the rule [comp_p] and get

$$\vdash_p \{\ \texttt{x} = \texttt{n}\ \}$$
$$\texttt{y := 1; while}\ \neg(\texttt{x=1})\ \texttt{do}\ (\texttt{y := y}\star\texttt{x; x := x}-\texttt{1})$$
$$\{\ \texttt{y} = \texttt{n!} \wedge \texttt{n} > \texttt{0}\ \}$$

as required. □

Exercise 6.10 Specify a formula expressing the partial correctness property of the program of Exercise 6.1. Construct an inference tree giving a proof of this property using the inference system of Table 6.1. □

Exercise 6.11 Suggest an inference rule for `repeat` S `until` b. You are not allowed to rely on the existence of a `while`-construct in the language. □

Exercise 6.12 Suggest an inference rule for `for` x := a_1 `to` a_2 `do` S. You are not allowed to rely on the existence of a `while`-construct in the language. □

Properties of the semantics

In the operational and denotational semantics we defined a notion of two programs being semantically equivalent. We can define a similar notion for the axiomatic semantics: Two programs S_1 and S_2 are *provably equivalent* according to the axiomatic semantics of Table 6.1 if for all preconditions P and postconditions Q we have

$$\vdash_p \{\ P\ \}\ S_1\ \{\ Q\ \} \quad \text{if and only if} \quad \vdash_p \{\ P\ \}\ S_2\ \{\ Q\ \}$$

Exercise 6.13 Show that the following statements of **While** are provably equivalent in the above sense:

- S; `skip` and S
- S_1; (S_2; S_3) and (S_1; S_2); S_3 □

Proofs of properties of the axiomatic semantics will often proceed by *induction on the shape of the inference tree*:

Induction on the Shape of Inference Trees	
1:	Prove that the property holds for all the simple inference trees by showing that it holds for the *axioms* of the inference system.
2:	Prove that the property holds for all composite inference trees: For each *rule* assume that the property holds for its premises (this is called the *induction hypothesis*) and that the conditions of the rule are satisfied and then prove that it also holds for the conclusion of the rule.

Exercise 6.14 ** Using the inference rule for `repeat` S `until` b given in Exercise 6.11 show that `repeat` S `until` b is provably equivalent to S; `while` $\neg b$ `do` S. Hint: it is not too hard to show that what is provable about `repeat` S `until` b is also provable about S; `while` $\neg b$ `do` S. □

Exercise 6.15 Show that $\vdash_p \{ P \}\ S\ \{ \texttt{true} \}$ for all statements S and properties P. □

6.3 Soundness and completeness

We shall now address the relationship between the inference system of Table 6.1 and the operational and denotational semantics of the previous chapters. We shall prove that

- the inference system is *sound*: if some partial correctness property can be proved using the inference system then it does indeed hold according to the semantics, and
- the inference system is *complete*: if some partial correctness property does hold according to the semantics then we can also find a proof for it using the inference system.

The completeness result can only be proved because we use the extensional approach where preconditions and postconditions are arbitrary predicates. In the intensional approach we only have a weaker result; we shall return to this later in this section.

As the operational and denotational semantics are equivalent we only need to consider one of them here and we shall choose the natural semantics. The partial correctness assertion $\{ P \} S \{ Q \}$ is said to be *valid* if and only if

$$\text{for all states } s \text{, if } P\ s = \mathbf{tt} \text{ and } \langle S, s \rangle \to s' \text{ for some } s' \text{ then } Q\ s' = \mathbf{tt}$$

and we shall write this as

$$\models_{\mathrm{p}} \{ P \} S \{ Q \}$$

The soundness property is then expressed by

$$\vdash_{\mathrm{p}} \{ P \} S \{ Q \} \text{ implies } \models_{\mathrm{p}} \{ P \} S \{ Q \}$$

and the completeness property is expressed by

$$\models_{\mathrm{p}} \{ P \} S \{ Q \} \text{ implies } \vdash_{\mathrm{p}} \{ P \} S \{ Q \}$$

We have

Theorem 6.16 For all partial correctness assertions $\{ P \} S \{ Q \}$ we have

$$\models_{\mathrm{p}} \{ P \} S \{ Q \} \text{ if and only if } \vdash_{\mathrm{p}} \{ P \} S \{ Q \}$$

It is customary to prove the soundness and completeness results separately.

Soundness

We shall first prove:

Lemma 6.17 The inference system of Table 6.1 is sound, that is for every partial correctness formula $\{ P \} S \{ Q \}$ we have

$$\vdash_{\mathrm{p}} \{ P \} S \{ Q \} \text{ implies } \models_{\mathrm{p}} \{ P \} S \{ Q \}$$

Proof: The proof is by induction on the shape of the inference tree used to infer $\vdash_{\mathrm{p}} \{ P \} S \{ Q \}$. This amounts to nothing but a formalization of the intuitions we gave when introducing the axioms and rules.

The case $[\mathrm{ass}_{\mathrm{p}}]$: We shall prove that the axiom is valid, so suppose that

$$\langle x := a,\ s \rangle \to s'$$

and $(P[x\mapsto\mathcal{A}[\![a]\!]])\ s = \mathbf{tt}$. We shall then prove that $P\ s' = \mathbf{tt}$. From [ass$_{\rm ns}$] we get that $s' = s[x\mapsto\mathcal{A}[\![a]\!]s]$ and from $(P[x\mapsto\mathcal{A}[\![a]\!]])\ s = \mathbf{tt}$ we get that $P\ (s[x\mapsto\mathcal{A}[\![a]\!]s])$ $= \mathbf{tt}$. Thus $P\ s' = \mathbf{tt}$ as was to be shown.

The case [skip$_{\rm p}$]: This case is immediate using the clause [skip$_{\rm ns}$].

The case [comp$_{\rm p}$]: We assume that

$$\models_{\rm p} \{\ P\ \}\ S_1\ \{\ Q\ \} \text{ and } \models_{\rm p} \{\ Q\ \}\ S_2\ \{\ R\ \}$$

and we have to prove that $\models_{\rm p} \{\ P\ \}\ S_1;\ S_2\ \{\ R\ \}$. So consider arbitrary states s and s'' such that $P\ s = \mathbf{tt}$ and

$$\langle S_1;S_2,\ s\rangle \rightarrow s''$$

From [comp$_{\rm ns}$] we get that there is a state s' such that

$$\langle S_1,\ s\rangle \rightarrow s' \quad \text{and} \quad \langle S_2,\ s'\rangle \rightarrow s''$$

From $\langle S_1,\ s\rangle \rightarrow s'$, $P\ s = \mathbf{tt}$ and $\models_{\rm p} \{\ P\ \}\ S_1\ \{\ Q\ \}$ we get $Q\ s' = \mathbf{tt}$. From $\langle S_2,\ s'\rangle \rightarrow s''$, $Q\ s' = \mathbf{tt}$ and $\models_{\rm p} \{\ Q\ \}\ S_2\ \{\ R\ \}$ it follows that $R\ s'' = \mathbf{tt}$ as was to be shown.

The case [if$_{\rm p}$]: Assume that

$$\models_{\rm p} \{\ \mathcal{B}[\![b]\!] \wedge P\ \}\ S_1\ \{\ Q\ \} \text{ and } \models_{\rm p} \{\ \neg\mathcal{B}[\![b]\!] \wedge P\ \}\ S_2\ \{\ Q\ \}$$

To prove $\models_{\rm p} \{\ P\ \}$ `if` b `then` S_1 `else` S_2 $\{\ Q\ \}$ consider arbitrary states s and s' such that $P\ s = \mathbf{tt}$ and

$$\langle \texttt{if}\ b\ \texttt{then}\ S_1\ \texttt{else}\ S_2,\ s\rangle \rightarrow s'$$

There are two cases. If $\mathcal{B}[\![b]\!]s = \mathbf{tt}$ then we get $(\mathcal{B}[\![b]\!] \wedge P)\ s = \mathbf{tt}$ and from [if$_{\rm ns}$] we have

$$\langle S_1,\ s\rangle \rightarrow s'$$

From the first assumption we therefore get $Q\ s' = \mathbf{tt}$. If $\mathcal{B}[\![b]\!]s = \mathbf{ff}$ the result follows in a similar way from the second assumption.

The case [while$_{\rm p}$]: Assume that

$$\models_{\rm p} \{\ \mathcal{B}[\![b]\!] \wedge P\ \}\ S\ \{\ P\ \}$$

To prove $\models_{\rm p} \{\ P\ \}$ `while` b `do` S $\{\ \neg\mathcal{B}[\![b]\!] \wedge P\ \}$ consider arbitrary states s and s'' such that $P\ s = \mathbf{tt}$ and

$$\langle \texttt{while}\ b\ \texttt{do}\ S,\ s\rangle \rightarrow s''$$

and we shall show that $(\neg\mathcal{B}[\![b]\!]\wedge P)\ s'' = \mathbf{tt}$. We shall now proceed by induction on the shape of the derivation tree in the natural semantics. One of two cases apply. If $\mathcal{B}[\![b]\!]s = \mathbf{ff}$ then $s'' = s$ according to [while$^{\mathrm{ff}}_{\mathrm{ns}}$] and clearly $(\neg\mathcal{B}[\![b]\!] \wedge P)\ s'' = \mathbf{tt}$ as required. Next consider the case where $\mathcal{B}[\![b]\!]s = \mathbf{tt}$ and

$$\langle S,\ s\rangle \to s' \quad \text{and} \quad \langle \texttt{while}\ b\ \texttt{do}\ S,\ s'\rangle \to s''$$

for some state s'. Thus $(\mathcal{B}[\![b]\!] \wedge P)\ s = \mathbf{tt}$ and we can then apply the assumption $\models_{\mathrm{P}} \{\ \mathcal{B}[\![b]\!] \wedge P\ \}\ S\ \{\ P\ \}$ and get that $P\ s' = \mathbf{tt}$. The induction hypothesis can now be applied to the derivation $\langle \texttt{while}\ b\ \texttt{do}\ S,\ s'\rangle \to s''$ and gives that $(\neg\mathcal{B}[\![b]\!] \wedge P)\ s'' = \mathbf{tt}$. This completes the proof of this case.

The case [cons$_{\mathrm{p}}$]: Suppose that

$$\models_{\mathrm{P}} \{\ P'\ \}\ S\ \{\ Q'\ \} \text{ and } P \Rightarrow P' \text{ and } Q' \Rightarrow Q$$

To prove $\models_{\mathrm{P}} \{\ P\ \}\ S\ \{\ Q\ \}$ consider states s and s' such that $P\ s = \mathbf{tt}$ and

$$\langle S,\ s\rangle \to s'$$

Since $P\ s = \mathbf{tt}$ and $P \Rightarrow P'$ we also have $P'\ s = \mathbf{tt}$ and the assumption then gives us that $Q'\ s' = \mathbf{tt}$. From $Q' \Rightarrow Q$ we therefore get $Q\ s' = \mathbf{tt}$ as required. □

Exercise 6.18 Show that the inference rule for `repeat` S `until` b suggested in Exercise 6.11 preserves validity. Argue that this means that the entire proof system consisting of the axioms and rules of Table 6.1 together with the rule of Exercise 6.11 is sound. □

Exercise 6.19 Define $\models' \{\ P\ \}\ S\ \{\ Q\ \}$ to mean that

> for all states s such that $P\ s = \mathbf{tt}$ there exists a state s' such that $Q\ s' = \mathbf{tt}$ and $\langle S,\ s\rangle \to s'$

Show that it is *not* the case that $\vdash_{\mathrm{p}} \{\ P\ \}\ S\ \{\ Q\ \}$ implies $\models' \{\ P\ \}\ S\ \{\ Q\ \}$ and conclude that the proof system of Table 6.1 cannot be sound with respect to this definition of validity. □

Completeness (in the extensional approach)

Before turning to the proof of the completeness result we shall consider a special predicate wlp(S, Q) defined for each statement S and predicate Q:

$$\mathrm{wlp}(S,\ Q)\ s = \mathbf{tt}$$

if and only if for all states s',

$$\text{if } \langle S,\ s\rangle \to s' \text{ then } Q\ s' = \mathbf{tt}$$

The predicate is called the *weakest liberal precondition* for Q and it satisfies:

Fact 6.20 For every statement S and predicate Q we have

- $\models_p \{ \text{wlp}(S, Q) \} \ S \ \{ Q \}$ (*)
- if $\models_p \{ P \} \ S \ \{ Q \}$ then $P \Rightarrow \text{wlp}(S, Q)$ (**)

meaning that $\text{wlp}(S, Q)$ is the weakest possible precondition for S and Q.

Proof: To verify that (*) holds let s and s' be states such that $\langle S, s\rangle \to s'$ and $\text{wlp}(S, Q)\ s = \mathbf{tt}$. From the definition of $\text{wlp}(S, Q)$ we get that $Q\ s' = \mathbf{tt}$ as required. To verify that (**) holds assume that $\models_p \{ P \} \ S \ \{ Q \}$ and let $P\ s = \mathbf{tt}$. If $\langle S, s\rangle \to s'$ then $Q\ s' = \mathbf{tt}$ (because $\models_p \{ P \} \ S \ \{ Q \}$) so clearly $\text{wlp}(S,Q)\ s = \mathbf{tt}$. □

Exercise 6.21 Prove that the predicate INV of Example 6.9 satisfies

$$INV = \text{wlp}(\texttt{while}\ \neg(\texttt{x}=1)\ \texttt{do}\ (\texttt{y} := \texttt{y}\star\texttt{x};\ \texttt{x} := \texttt{x}-1),\ \texttt{y} = \texttt{n}! \wedge \texttt{n} > 0)$$ □

Exercise 6.22 Another interesting predicate called the *strongest postcondition* for S and P can be defined by

$$\text{sp}(P, S)\ s' = \mathbf{tt}$$

if and only if

there exists s such that $\langle S, s\rangle \to s'$ and $P\ s = \mathbf{tt}$

Prove that

- $\models_p \{ P \} \ S \ \{ \text{sp}(P, S) \}$
- if $\models_p \{ P \} \ S \ \{ Q \}$ then $\text{sp}(P, S) \Rightarrow Q$

Thus $\text{sp}(P, S)$ is the strongest possible postcondition for P and S. □

Lemma 6.23 The inference system of Table 6.1 is complete, that is for every partial correctness formula $\{ P \} \ S \ \{ Q \}$ we have

$$\models_p \{ P \} \ S \ \{ Q \} \text{ implies } \vdash_p \{ P \} \ S \ \{ Q \}$$

Proof: The completeness result follows if we can infer

$$\vdash_{\mathrm{p}} \{ \text{wlp}(S,\ Q) \}\ S\ \{ Q \} \qquad (*)$$

for all statements S and predicates Q. To see this suppose that

$$\models_{\mathrm{p}} \{ P \}\ S\ \{ Q \}$$

Then Fact 6.20 gives that

$$P \Rightarrow \text{wlp}(S,Q)$$

so that (*) and [cons$_{\mathrm{p}}$] give

$$\vdash_{\mathrm{p}} \{ P \}\ S\ \{ Q \}$$

as required.

To prove (*) we proceed by structural induction on the statement S.

The case $x := a$: Based on the natural semantics it is easy to verify that

$$\text{wlp}(x := a,\ Q) = Q[x \mapsto \mathcal{A}[\![a]\!]]$$

so the result follows directly from [ass$_{\mathrm{p}}$].

The case `skip`: Since wlp(`skip`, Q) = Q the result follows from [skip$_{\mathrm{p}}$].

The case $S_1;S_2$: The induction hypothesis applied to S_1 and S_2 gives

$$\vdash_{\mathrm{p}} \{ \text{wlp}(S_2,\ Q) \}\ S_2\ \{ Q \}$$

and

$$\vdash_{\mathrm{p}} \{ \text{wlp}(S_1,\ \text{wlp}(S_2,\ Q)) \}\ S_1\ \{ \text{wlp}(S_2,\ Q) \}$$

so that [comp$_{\mathrm{p}}$] gives

$$\vdash_{\mathrm{p}} \{ \text{wlp}(S_1,\ \text{wlp}(S_2,\ Q)) \}\ S_1;S_2\ \{ Q \}$$

We shall now prove that

$$\text{wlp}(S_1;S_2,\ Q) \Rightarrow \text{wlp}(S_1,\ \text{wlp}(S_2,\ Q))$$

as then [cons$_{\mathrm{p}}$] will give the required proof in the inference system. So assume that wlp($S_1;S_2$, Q) s = **tt** and we shall show that wlp(S_1, wlp(S_2, Q)) s = **tt**. This is obvious unless there is a state s' such that $\langle S_1,\ s\rangle \to s'$ and then we must prove that wlp(S_2, Q) s' = **tt**. However, this is obvious too unless there is a state s'' such that $\langle S_2,\ s'\rangle \to s''$ and then we must prove that $Q\ s''$ = **tt**. But by [comp$_{\mathrm{ns}}$] we have $\langle S_1;S_2,\ s\rangle \to s''$ so that $Q\ s''$ = **tt** follows from wlp($S_1;S_2$, Q) s = **tt**.

The case `if` b `then` S_1 `else` S_2: The induction hypothesis applied to S_1 and S_2 give

$$\vdash_p \{ \text{wlp}(S_1, Q) \} \; S_1 \; \{ Q \} \text{ and } \vdash_p \{ \text{wlp}(S_2, Q) \} \; S_2 \; \{ Q \}$$

Define the predicate P by

$$P = (\mathcal{B}[\![b]\!] \wedge \text{wlp}(S_1, Q)) \vee (\neg\mathcal{B}[\![b]\!] \wedge \text{wlp}(S_2, Q))$$

Then we have

$$(\mathcal{B}[\![b]\!] \wedge P) \Rightarrow \text{wlp}(S_1, Q) \text{ and } (\neg\mathcal{B}[\![b]\!] \wedge P) \Rightarrow \text{wlp}(S_2, Q)$$

so $[\text{cons}_\text{p}]$ can be applied twice and gives

$$\vdash_p \{ \mathcal{B}[\![b]\!] \wedge P \} \; S_1 \; \{ Q \} \text{ and } \vdash_p \{ \neg\mathcal{B}[\![b]\!] \wedge P \} \; S_2 \; \{ Q \}$$

Using $[\text{if}_\text{p}]$ we therefore get

$$\vdash_p \{ P \} \; \texttt{if } b \texttt{ then } S_1 \texttt{ else } S_2 \; \{ Q \}$$

To see that this is the desired result it suffices to show that

$$\text{wlp}(\texttt{if } b \texttt{ then } S_1 \texttt{ else } S_2, Q) \Rightarrow P$$

and this is straightforward by cases on the value of b.

The case `while` b `do` S: Define the predicate P by

$$P = \text{wlp}(\texttt{while } b \texttt{ do } S, Q)$$

We first show that

$$(\neg\mathcal{B}[\![b]\!] \wedge P) \Rightarrow Q \qquad (**)$$

$$(\mathcal{B}[\![b]\!] \wedge P) \Rightarrow \text{wlp}(S,P) \qquad (***)$$

To verify (**) let s be such that $(\neg\mathcal{B}[\![b]\!] \wedge P)\; s = \mathbf{tt}$. Then it must be the case that $\langle \texttt{while } b \texttt{ do } S, s\rangle \to s$ so we have $Q\; s = \mathbf{tt}$. To verify (***) let s be such that $(\mathcal{B}[\![b]\!] \wedge P)\; s = \mathbf{tt}$ and we shall show that $\text{wlp}(S,P)\; s = \mathbf{tt}$. This is obvious unless there is a state s' such that $\langle S, s\rangle \to s'$ in which case we shall prove that $P\; s' = \mathbf{tt}$. We have two cases. First we assume that $\langle \texttt{while } b \texttt{ do } S, s'\rangle \to s''$ for some s''. Then $[\text{while}^{\text{tt}}_{\text{ns}}]$ gives us that $\langle \texttt{while } b \texttt{ do } S, s\rangle \to s''$ and since $P\; s = \mathbf{tt}$ we get that $Q\; s'' = \mathbf{tt}$ using Fact 6.20. But this means that $P\; s' = \mathbf{tt}$ as was required. In the second case we assume that $\langle \texttt{while } b \texttt{ do } S, s'\rangle \to s''$ does *not* hold for any state s''. But this means that $P\; s' = \mathbf{tt}$ holds vacuously and we have finished the proof of (***).

The induction hypothesis applied to the body S of the `while`-loop gives

$$\vdash_p \{ \text{wlp}(S,P) \} \; S \; \{ P \}$$

and using (***) together with $[\text{cons}_\text{p}]$ we get

$$\vdash_p \{ \mathcal{B}[\![b]\!] \wedge P \} \; S \; \{ P \}$$

We can now apply the rule [while$_{\mathrm{p}}$] and get

$$\vdash_{\mathrm{p}} \{\ P\ \}\ \texttt{while}\ b\ \texttt{do}\ S\ \{\ \neg\mathcal{B}[\![b]\!] \wedge P\ \}$$

Finally, we use (**) together with [cons$_{\mathrm{p}}$] and get

$$\vdash_{\mathrm{p}} \{\ P\ \}\ \texttt{while}\ b\ \texttt{do}\ S\ \{\ Q\ \}$$

as required. □

Exercise 6.24 Prove that the inference system for the `while`-language extended with `repeat` S `until` b as in Exercise 6.11 is complete. (If not you should improve your rule for `repeat` S `until` b.) □

Exercise 6.25 * Prove the completeness of the inference system of Table 6.1 using the *strongest postconditions* of Exercise 6.22 rather than the weakest liberal preconditions as used in the proof of Lemma 6.23. □

Exercise 6.26 Define a notion of validity based on the denotational semantics of Chapter 4 and prove the soundness of the inference system of Table 6.1 using this definition, that is without using the equivalence between the denotational semantics and the operational semantics. □

Exercise 6.27 Use the definition of validity of Exercise 6.26 and prove the completeness of the inference system of Table 6.1. □

Expressiveness problems (in the intensional approach)

So far we have only considered the extensional approach where the preconditions and postconditions of the formulae are predicates. In the *intensional approach* they are formulae of some assertion language $\mathcal{L}$. The axioms and rules of the inference system will be as in Table 6.1, the only difference being that the preconditions and postconditions are formulae of $\mathcal{L}$ and that operations such as $P[x\mapsto\mathcal{A}[\![a]\!]]$, $P_1 \wedge P_2$ and $P_1 \Rightarrow P_2$ are operations on formulae of $\mathcal{L}$.

It will be natural to let $\mathcal{L}$ include the boolean expressions of **While**. The soundness proof of Lemma 6.17 then carries directly over to the intensional approach. Unfortunately, this is not the case for the completeness proof of Lemma 6.23. The reason is that the predicates wlp(S, Q) used as preconditions now have to be represented as formulae of $\mathcal{L}$ and that this may not be possible.

To illustrate the problems let S be a statement, for example a universal program in the sense of recursion theory, that has an undecidable Halting problem. Further, suppose that $\mathcal{L}$ only contains the boolean expressions of **While**. Finally, assume that there is a formula b_S of $\mathcal{L}$ such that for all states s

$$\mathcal{B}[\![b_S]\!]\ s = \mathbf{tt} \text{ if and only if } \mathrm{wlp}(S, \mathtt{false})\ s = \mathbf{tt}$$

Then also $\neg b_S$ is a formula of $\mathcal{L}$. We have

$$\mathcal{B}[\![b_S]\!]\ s = \mathbf{tt} \text{ if and only if the computation of } S \text{ on } s \text{ loops}$$

and hence

$$\mathcal{B}[\![\neg b_S]\!]\ s = \mathbf{tt} \text{ if and only if the computation of } S \text{ on } s \text{ terminates}$$

We now have a contradiction: the assumptions about S ensure that $\mathcal{B}[\![\neg b_S]\!]$ must be an undecidable function; on the other hand Table 1.2 suggests an obvious algorithm for evaluating $\mathcal{B}[\![\neg b_S]\!]$. Hence our assumption about the existence of b_S must be mistaken. Consequently we cannot mimic the proof of Lemma 6.23.

The obvious remedy is to extend $\mathcal{L}$ to be a much more powerful language that allows quantification as well. A central concept is that $\mathcal{L}$ must be *expressive* with respect to **While** and its semantics, and one then shows that Table 6.1 is *relatively complete* (in the sense of Cook). It is beyond the scope of this book to go deeper into these matters but we provide references in Chapter 7.

6.4 Extensions of the axiomatic system

In this section we shall consider two extensions of the inference system for partial correctness assertions. The first extension shows how the approach can be modified to prove *total correctness assertions* thereby allowing us to reason about termination properties. In the second extension we consider how to extend the inference systems to more language constructs, in particular recursive procedures.

Total correctness assertions

We shall now consider formulae of the form

$$\{\ P\ \}\ S\ \{\ \Downarrow Q\ \}$$

The idea is that

if the precondition P is fulfilled

then S is guaranteed to terminate (as recorded by the symbol $\Downarrow$)

and the final state will satisfy the postcondition Q.

This is formalized by defining validity of $\{\ P\ \}\ S\ \{\ \Downarrow Q\ \}$ by

$$\models_t \{\ P\ \}\ S\ \{\ \Downarrow Q\ \}$$

$[\mathrm{ass_t}]$	$\{\ P[x\mapsto\mathcal{A}[\![a]\!]]\ \}\ x := a\ \{\ \Downarrow P\ \}$
$[\mathrm{skip_t}]$	$\{\ P\ \}\ \texttt{skip}\ \{\ \Downarrow P\ \}$
$[\mathrm{comp_t}]$	$\dfrac{\{\ P\ \}\ S_1\ \{\ \Downarrow Q\ \},\quad \{\ Q\ \}\ S_2\ \{\ \Downarrow R\ \}}{\{\ P\ \}\ S_1;\ S_2\ \{\ \Downarrow R\ \}}$
$[\mathrm{if_t}]$	$\dfrac{\{\ \mathcal{B}[\![b]\!] \wedge P\ \}\ S_1\ \{\ \Downarrow Q\ \},\quad \{\ \neg\mathcal{B}[\![b]\!] \wedge P\ \}\ S_2\ \{\ \Downarrow Q\ \}}{\{\ P\ \}\ \texttt{if}\ b\ \texttt{then}\ S_1\ \texttt{else}\ S_2\ \{\ \Downarrow Q\ \}}$
$[\mathrm{while_t}]$	$\dfrac{\{\ P(\mathbf{z}{+}\mathbf{1})\ \}\ S\ \{\ \Downarrow P(\mathbf{z})\ \}}{\{\ \exists \mathbf{z}.P(\mathbf{z})\ \}\ \texttt{while}\ b\ \texttt{do}\ S\ \{\ \Downarrow P(\mathbf{0})\ \}}$ where $P(\mathbf{z}{+}\mathbf{1}) \Rightarrow \mathcal{B}[\![b]\!]$, $P(\mathbf{0}) \Rightarrow \neg\mathcal{B}[\![b]\!]$ and $\mathbf{z}$ ranges over natural numbers (that is $\mathbf{z}\geq\mathbf{0}$)
$[\mathrm{cons_t}]$	$\dfrac{\{\ P'\ \}\ S\ \{\ \Downarrow Q'\ \}}{\{\ P\ \}\ S\ \{\ \Downarrow Q\ \}}$ where $P \Rightarrow P'$ and $Q' \Rightarrow Q$

Table 6.2: Axiomatic system for total correctness

if and only if

for all states s, if $P\ s = \mathbf{tt}$ then there exists s' such that

$Q\ s' = \mathbf{tt}$ and $\langle S,\ s\rangle \rightarrow s'$

The inference system for total correctness assertions is very similar to that for partial correctness assertions, the only difference being that the rule for the `while`-construct has changed. The complete set of axioms and rules is given in Table 6.2. We shall write

$$\vdash_{\mathrm{t}} \{\ P\ \}\ S\ \{\ \Downarrow Q\ \}$$

if there exists an inference tree with the formula $\{\ P\ \}\ S\ \{\ \Downarrow Q\ \}$ as root, that is if the formula is provably in the inference system.

In the rule $[\mathrm{while_t}]$ we use a parameterized family $P(\mathbf{z})$ of predicates for the invariant. The idea is that $\mathbf{z}$ is the number of unfoldings of the `while`-loop that will be necessary. So if the `while`-loop does not have to be unfolded at all then $P(\mathbf{0})$ holds and it must imply that b is false. If the `while`-loop has to be unfolded $\mathbf{z}{+}\mathbf{1}$ times then $P(\mathbf{z}{+}\mathbf{1})$ holds and b must hold *before* the body of the loop is executed; then $P(\mathbf{z})$ will hold *afterwards* so that we have decreased the total number of times the loop remains to be unfolded. The precondition of the conclusion of the rule expresses that there exists a bound on the number of times the loop has to be unfolded and the postcondition expresses that when the `while`-loop has terminated then no more unfoldings are necessary.

Example 6.28 The total correctness of the factorial statement can be expressed by the following assertion:

$$\{ \texttt{x} > \texttt{0} \land \texttt{x} = \texttt{n} \}$$
$$\texttt{y := 1; while } \neg(\texttt{x=1}) \texttt{ do (y := y}\star\texttt{x; x := x}-\texttt{1)}$$
$$\{ \Downarrow \texttt{y} = \texttt{n!} \}$$

where $\texttt{y} = \texttt{n!}$ is an abbreviation for the predicate

$$P \text{ where } P\ s = (s\ \texttt{y} = (s\ \texttt{n})!)$$

In addition to expressing that the final value of `y` is the factorial of the initial value of `x` the assertion also expresses that the program does indeed terminate on all states satisfying the precondition. The inference of this assertion proceeds in a number of stages. First we define the predicate $INV(\texttt{z})$ that is going to be the invariant of the `while`-loop

$$INV(\texttt{z})\ s = (s\ \texttt{x} > \mathbf{0} \text{ and } (s\ \texttt{y}) \star (s\ \texttt{x})! = (s\ \texttt{n})! \text{ and } s\ \texttt{x} = \texttt{z} + \mathbf{1})$$

We shall first consider the body of the loop. Using $[\text{ass}_t]$ we get

$$\vdash_t \{ INV(\texttt{z})[\texttt{x}\mapsto\texttt{x}-\texttt{1}] \}\ \texttt{x := x}-\texttt{1}\ \{ \Downarrow INV(\texttt{z}) \}$$

Similarly, we get

$$\vdash_t \{ (INV(\texttt{z})[\texttt{x}\mapsto\texttt{x}-\texttt{1}])[\texttt{y}\mapsto\texttt{y}\star\texttt{x}] \}\ \texttt{y := y} \star \texttt{x}\ \{ \Downarrow INV(\texttt{z})[\texttt{x}\mapsto\texttt{x}-\texttt{1}] \}$$

We can now apply the rule $[\text{comp}_t]$ to the two assertions above and get

$$\vdash_t \{ (INV(\texttt{z})[\texttt{x}\mapsto\texttt{x}-\texttt{1}])[\texttt{y}\mapsto\texttt{y}\star\texttt{x}] \}\ \texttt{y := y} \star \texttt{x; x := x}-\texttt{1}\ \{ \Downarrow INV(\texttt{z}) \}$$

It is easy to verify that

$$INV(\texttt{z}+\mathbf{1}) \Rightarrow (INV(\texttt{z})[\texttt{x}\mapsto\texttt{x}-\texttt{1}])[\texttt{y}\mapsto\texttt{y}\star\texttt{x}]$$

so using the rule $[\text{cons}_t]$ we get

$$\vdash_t \{ INV(\texttt{z}+\mathbf{1}) \}\ \texttt{y := y} \star \texttt{x; x := x}-\texttt{1}\ \{ \Downarrow INV(\texttt{z}) \}$$

It is straightforward to verify that

$$INV(\mathbf{0}) \Rightarrow \neg(\neg(\texttt{x=1})), \text{ and}$$
$$INV(\texttt{z}+\mathbf{1}) \Rightarrow \neg(\texttt{x=1})$$

Therefore we can use the rule $[\text{while}_t]$ and get

$$\vdash_t \{ \exists \texttt{z}.INV(\texttt{z}) \}\ \texttt{while } \neg(\texttt{x=1}) \texttt{ do (y := y}\star\texttt{x; x := x}-\texttt{1)}\ \{ \Downarrow INV(\mathbf{0}) \}$$

We shall now apply the axiom $[\text{ass}_t]$ to the statement `y := 1` and get

$\vdash_t \{ (\exists z.INV(z))[y \mapsto 1] \}$ y := 1 $\{ \Downarrow \exists z.INV(z) \}$

so using [comp$_t$] we get

$\vdash_t \{ (\exists z.INV(z))[y \mapsto 1] \}$

y := 1; while ¬(x=1) do (y := y⋆x; x := x−1)

$\{ \Downarrow INV(\mathbf{0}) \}$

Clearly we have

$x > 0 \land x = n \Rightarrow (\exists z.INV(z))[y \mapsto \mathbf{1}]$, and

$INV(\mathbf{0}) \Rightarrow y = n!$

so applying rule [cons$_t$] we get

$\vdash_t \{ x > 0 \land x = n \}$

y := 1; while ¬(x=1) do (y := y⋆x; x := x−1)

$\{ \Downarrow y = n! \}$

as required. □

Exercise 6.29 Suggest a total correctness inference rule for `repeat` S `until` b. You are not allowed to rely on the existence of a `while`-construct in the programming language. □

Lemma 6.30 The total correctness system of Table 6.2 is sound, that is for every total correctness formula $\{ P \}\ S\ \{ \Downarrow Q \}$ we have

$$\vdash_t \{ P \}\ S\ \{ \Downarrow Q \} \text{ implies } \models_t \{ P \}\ S\ \{ \Downarrow Q \}$$

Proof: The proof proceeds by induction on the shape of the inference tree just as in the proof of Lemma 6.17.

The case [ass$_t$]: We shall prove that the axiom is valid, so assume that s is such that $(P[x \mapsto \mathcal{A}[\![a]\!]])\ s = \mathbf{tt}$ and let $s' = s[x \mapsto \mathcal{A}[\![a]\!]s]$. Then [ass$_{ns}$] gives

$$\langle x := a,\ s \rangle \to s'$$

and from $(P[x \mapsto \mathcal{A}[\![a]\!]])\ s = \mathbf{tt}$ we get $P\ s' = \mathbf{tt}$ as was to be shown.

The case [skip$_t$]: This case is immediate.

The case [comp$_t$]: We assume that

$$\models_t \{ P \}\ S_1\ \{ \Downarrow Q \}, \text{ and} \qquad (*)$$

$$\models_t \{ Q \}\ S_2\ \{ \Downarrow R \} \qquad (**)$$

and we have to prove that $\models_t \{ P \}\ S_1;\ S_2\ \{ \Downarrow R \}$. So let s be such that $P\ s = \mathbf{tt}$. From (*) we get that there exists a state s' such that $Q\ s' = \mathbf{tt}$ and

$$\langle S_1, s\rangle \to s'$$

Since $Q\ s' = \mathbf{tt}$ we get from (**) that there exists a state s'' such that $R\ s'' = \mathbf{tt}$ and

$$\langle S_2, s'\rangle \to s''$$

Using [comp$_{\rm ns}$] we therefore get

$$\langle S_1;\ S_2, s\rangle \to s''$$

and since $R\ s'' = \mathbf{tt}$ we have finished this case.

The case [if$_{\rm t}$]: Assume that

$$\models_{\rm t} \{\ \mathcal{B}[\![b]\!] \wedge P\ \}\ S_1\ \{\ \Downarrow Q\ \}, \text{ and} \qquad (*)$$
$$\models_{\rm t} \{\ \neg\mathcal{B}[\![b]\!] \wedge P\ \}\ S_2\ \{\ \Downarrow Q\ \}$$

To prove $\models_{\rm t} \{\ P\ \}\ \texttt{if}\ b\ \texttt{then}\ S_1\ \texttt{else}\ S_2\ \{\ \Downarrow Q\ \}$ consider a state s such that $P\ s = \mathbf{tt}$. We have two cases. If $\mathcal{B}[\![b]\!]s = \mathbf{tt}$ then $(\mathcal{B}[\![b]\!] \wedge P)\ s = \mathbf{tt}$ and from (*) we get that there is a state s' such that $Q\ s' = \mathbf{tt}$ and

$$\langle S_1, s\rangle \to s'$$

From [if$_{\rm ns}$] we then get

$$\langle \texttt{if}\ b\ \texttt{then}\ S_1\ \texttt{else}\ S_2, s\rangle \to s'$$

as was to be proved. If $\mathcal{B}[\![b]\!]s = \mathbf{ff}$ the result follows in a similar way from the second assumption.

The case [while$_{\rm t}$]: Assume that

$$\models_{\rm t} \{\ P(\mathbf{z}{+}\mathbf{1})\ \}\ S\ \{\ \Downarrow P(\mathbf{z})\ \}, \qquad (*)$$
$$P(\mathbf{z}{+}\mathbf{1}) \Rightarrow \mathcal{B}[\![b]\!], \text{ and}$$
$$P(\mathbf{0}) \Rightarrow \neg\mathcal{B}[\![b]\!]$$

To prove $\models_{\rm t} \{\ \exists \mathbf{z}.P(\mathbf{z})\ \}\ \texttt{while}\ b\ \texttt{do}\ S\ \{\ \Downarrow P(\mathbf{0})\ \}$ it is sufficient to prove that for all natural numbers $\mathbf{z}$

$$\text{if } P(\mathbf{z})\ s = \mathbf{tt} \text{ then there exists a state } s' \text{ such that}$$
$$P(\mathbf{0})\ s' = \mathbf{tt} \text{ and } \langle \texttt{while}\ b\ \texttt{do}\ S, s\rangle \to s' \qquad (**)$$

So consider a state s such that $P(\mathbf{z})\ s = \mathbf{tt}$. The proof is now by numerical induction on $\mathbf{z}$.

First assume that $\mathbf{z} = \mathbf{0}$. The assumption $P(\mathbf{0}) \Rightarrow \neg\mathcal{B}[\![b]\!]$ gives that $\mathcal{B}[\![b]\!]s = \mathbf{ff}$ and from [while$^{\rm ff}_{\rm ns}$] we get

$$\langle \texttt{while}\ b\ \texttt{do}\ S, s\rangle \to s$$

Since $P(\mathbf{0})\ s = \mathbf{tt}$ this proves the base case.

For the induction step assume that (**) holds for all states satisfying $P(\mathbf{z})$ and that $P(\mathbf{z}{+}\mathbf{1})\ s = \mathbf{tt}$. From (*) we get that there is a state s' such that $P(\mathbf{z})\ s' = \mathbf{tt}$ and

$$\langle S,\ s\rangle \to s'$$

The numerical induction hypothesis applied to s' gives that there is some state s'' such that $P(\mathbf{0})\ s'' = \mathbf{tt}$ and

$$\langle \texttt{while}\ b\ \texttt{do}\ S,\ s'\rangle \to s''$$

Furthermore, the assumption $P(\mathbf{z}{+}\mathbf{1}) \Rightarrow \mathcal{B}[\![b]\!]$ gives $\mathcal{B}[\![b]\!]s = \mathbf{tt}$. We can therefore apply [$\text{while}^{\text{tt}}_{\text{ns}}$] and get that

$$\langle \texttt{while}\ b\ \texttt{do}\ S,\ s\rangle \to s''$$

Since $P(\mathbf{0})\ s'' = \mathbf{tt}$ this completes the proof of (**).

The case [cons_{t}]: Suppose that

$$\models_{\text{t}} \{\ P'\ \}\ S\ \{\ \Downarrow Q'\ \},$$
$$P \Rightarrow P', \text{ and}$$
$$Q' \Rightarrow Q$$

To prove $\models_{\text{t}} \{\ P\ \}\ S\ \{\ \Downarrow Q\ \}$ consider a state s such that $P\ s = \mathbf{tt}$. Then $P'\ s = \mathbf{tt}$ and there is a state s' such that $Q'\ s' = \mathbf{tt}$ and

$$\langle S,\ s\rangle \to s'$$

However, we also have that $Q\ s' = \mathbf{tt}$ and this proves the result. □

Exercise 6.31 Show that the inference rule for `repeat` S `until` b suggested in Exercise 6.29 preserves validity. Argue that this means that the entire proof system consisting of the axioms and rules of Table 6.2 together with the rule of Exercise 6.29 is sound. □

Exercise 6.32 * Prove that the inference system of Table 6.2 is complete, that is

$$\models_{\text{t}} \{\ P\ \}\ S\ \{\ \Downarrow Q\ \} \text{ implies } \vdash_{\text{t}} \{\ P\ \}\ S\ \{\ \Downarrow Q\ \}$$ □

Exercise 6.33 * Prove that

$$\text{if } \vdash_{\text{t}} \{\ P\ \}\ S\ \{\ \Downarrow Q\ \} \text{ then } \vdash_{\text{p}} \{\ P\ \}\ S\ \{\ Q\ \}$$

Does the converse result hold? □

Extensions of While

We conclude by considering an extension of **While** with non-determinism and (parameterless) procedures. The syntax of the extended language is given by

$$\begin{array}{rcl} S & ::= & x := a \mid \texttt{skip} \mid S_1 \texttt{ ; } S_2 \mid \texttt{if } b \texttt{ then } S_1 \texttt{ else } S_2 \\ & \mid & \texttt{while } b \texttt{ do } S \mid S_1 \texttt{ or } S_2 \\ & \mid & \texttt{begin proc } p \texttt{ is } S_1\texttt{; } S_2 \texttt{ end} \mid \texttt{call } p \end{array}$$

Note that in $\texttt{begin proc } p \texttt{ is } S_1\texttt{; } S_2 \texttt{ end}$ the body of p is S_1 and the remainder of the program is S_2.

Non-determinism

It is straightforward to handle non-determinism (in the sense of Section 2.4) in the axiomatic approach. The idea is that an assertion holds for $S_1 \texttt{ or } S_2$ if the similar assertion holds for S_1 as well as for S_2. The motivation for this is that when reasoning about the statement we have no way of influencing whether S_1 or S_2 is chosen. For partial correctness we thus extend Table 6.1 with the rule

$$[\mathrm{or_p}] \quad \frac{\{\ P\ \}\ S_1\ \{\ Q\ \},\ \{\ P\ \}\ S_2\ \{\ Q\ \}}{\{\ P\ \}\ S_1 \texttt{ or } S_2\ \{\ Q\ \}}$$

For total correctness we extend Table 6.2 with the rule

$$[\mathrm{or_t}] \quad \frac{\{\ P\ \}\ S_1\ \{\ \Downarrow Q\ \},\ \{\ P\ \}\ S_2\ \{\ \Downarrow Q\ \}}{\{\ P\ \}\ S_1 \texttt{ or } S_2\ \{\ \Downarrow Q\ \}}$$

When dealing with soundness and completeness of these rules one must be careful in using a semantics that models "non-deterministic choice" in the proper manner. We saw in Section 2.4 that this is the case for structural operational semantics but not for natural semantics. With respect to the structural operational semantics one can show that the above rules are sound and that the resulting inference systems are complete. If one insists on using the natural semantics the `or`-construct would model a kind of "angelic choice" and both rules would be sound. However, only the partial correctness inference system will be complete.

Non-recursive procedures

For the sake of simplicity we shall restrict our attention to statements with at most one procedure declaration. For non-recursive procedures the idea is that an assertion that holds for the body of the procedure also holds for the calls of the procedure. This motivates extending the partial correctness inference system of Table 6.1 with the rule

$$[\text{call}_\text{p}] \quad \frac{\{\ P\ \}\ S\ \{\ Q\ \}}{\{\ P\ \}\ \texttt{call}\ p\ \{\ Q\ \}} \quad \text{where } p \text{ is defined by } \texttt{proc}\ p\ \texttt{is}\ S$$

Similarly the inference system for total correctness in Table 6.2 can be extended with the rule

$$[\text{call}_\text{t}] \quad \frac{\{\ P\ \}\ S\ \{\ \Downarrow Q\ \}}{\{\ P\ \}\ \texttt{call}\ p\ \{\ \Downarrow Q\ \}} \quad \text{where } p \text{ is defined by } \texttt{proc}\ p\ \texttt{is}\ S$$

In both cases the resulting inference system can be proved sound and complete.

Recursive procedures

The above rules turn out to be insufficient when procedures are allowed to be recursive: in order to prove an assertion for `call` p one has to prove the assertion for the body of the procedure and this implies that one has to prove an assertion about each occurrence of `call` p inside the body and so on.

Consider first the case of *partial correctness* assertions. In order to prove some property $\{\ P\ \}$ `call` p $\{\ Q\ \}$ we shall prove the similar property for the body of the procedure but *under the assumption that* $\{\ P\ \}$ `call` p $\{\ Q\ \}$ holds for the recursive calls of p. Often this is expressed by a rule of the form

$$[\text{call}_\text{p}^\text{rec}] \quad \frac{\{\ P\ \}\ \texttt{call}\ p\ \{\ Q\ \} \vdash_\text{p} \{\ P\ \}\ S\ \{\ Q\ \}}{\{\ P\ \}\ \texttt{call}\ p\ \{\ Q\ \}}$$

where p is defined by `proc` p `is` S

The premise of the rule expresses that $\{\ P\ \}\ S\ \{\ Q\ \}$ is provable under the assumption that $\{\ P\ \}$ `call` p $\{\ Q\ \}$ can be proved for the recursive calls present in S. The conclusion expresses that $\{\ P\ \}$ `call` p $\{\ Q\ \}$ holds for all calls of p.

Example 6.34 Consider the following statement

```
begin proc fac is (if x = 1 then skip
                   else (y := x⋆y; x := x−1; call fac));
      y := 1; call fac
end
```

We want to prove that the final value of `y` is the factorial of the initial value of `x`. We shall prove that

$$\{\ \texttt{x} > 0 \land \texttt{n} = \texttt{y} \star \texttt{x}!\ \}\ \texttt{call fac}\ \{\ \texttt{y} = \texttt{n}\ \}$$

where $\texttt{x} > 0 \land \texttt{n} = \texttt{y} \star \texttt{x}!$ is an abbreviation for the predicate P defined by

$$P\ s = (s\ \texttt{x} > \mathbf{0} \text{ and } s\ \texttt{n} = s\ \texttt{y} \star (s\ \texttt{x})!)$$

We assume that

$$\vdash_p \{ \mathtt{x} > 0 \land \mathtt{n} = \mathtt{y} \star \mathtt{x}! \} \ \mathtt{call\ fac} \ \{ \mathtt{y} = \mathtt{n} \} \qquad (*)$$

holds for the recursive calls of fac. We shall then construct a proof of

$$\{ \mathtt{x} > 0 \land \mathtt{n} = \mathtt{y} \star \mathtt{x}! \}$$
$$\mathtt{if\ x = 1\ then\ skip\ else\ (y := x{\star}y;\ x := x{-}1;\ call\ fac)} \qquad (**)$$
$$\{ \mathtt{y} = \mathtt{n} \}$$

and, using $[\text{call}_p^{\text{rec}}]$ we obtain a proof of (*) for all occurrences of call fac. To prove (**) we first use the assumption (*) to get

$$\vdash_p \{ \mathtt{x} > 0 \land \mathtt{n} = \mathtt{y} \star \mathtt{x}! \} \ \mathtt{call\ fac} \ \{ \mathtt{y} = \mathtt{n} \}$$

Then we apply $[\text{ass}_p]$ and $[\text{comp}_p]$ twice and get

$$\vdash_p \{ ((\mathtt{x} > 0 \land \mathtt{n} = \mathtt{y} \star \mathtt{x}!)[\mathtt{x}{\mapsto}\mathtt{x}{-}1])[\mathtt{y}{\mapsto}\mathtt{x}{\star}\mathtt{y}] \}$$
$$\mathtt{y := x{\star}y;\ x := x{-}1;\ call\ fac}$$
$$\{ \mathtt{y} = \mathtt{n} \}$$

We have

$$\neg(\mathtt{x}{=}1) \land (\mathtt{x} > 0 \land \mathtt{n} = \mathtt{y} \star \mathtt{x}!) \Rightarrow ((\mathtt{x} > 0 \land \mathtt{n} = \mathtt{y} \star \mathtt{x}!)[\mathtt{x}{\mapsto}\mathtt{x}{-}1])[\mathtt{y}{\mapsto}\mathtt{x}{\star}\mathtt{y}]$$

so using $[\text{cons}_p]$ we get

$$\vdash_p \{ \neg(\mathtt{x}{=}1) \land (\mathtt{x} > 0 \land \mathtt{n} = \mathtt{y} \star \mathtt{x}!) \}$$
$$\mathtt{y := x{\star}y;\ x := x{-}1;\ call\ fac}$$
$$\{ \mathtt{y} = \mathtt{n} \}$$

Using that

$$\mathtt{x}{=}1 \land \mathtt{x} > 0 \land \mathtt{n} = \mathtt{y} \star \mathtt{x}! \Rightarrow \mathtt{y} = \mathtt{n}$$

it is easy to prove

$$\vdash_p \{ \mathtt{x}{=}1 \land \mathtt{x} > 0 \land \mathtt{n} = \mathtt{y} \star \mathtt{x}! \} \ \mathtt{skip} \ \{ \mathtt{y} = \mathtt{n} \}$$

so $[\text{if}_p]$ can be applied and gives a proof of (**). □

Table 6.1 extended with the rule $[\text{call}_p^{\text{rec}}]$ can be proved to be sound. However, in order to get a completeness result the inference system has to be extended with additional rules. To illustrate why this is necessary consider the following version of the factorial program:

```
begin proc fac is if x=1 then y := 1
                  else (x := x-1; call fac; x := x+1; y := x*y);
      call fac
end
```

Assume that we want to prove that this program does not change the value of **x**, that is

$$\{ \texttt{x} = \texttt{n} \} \ \texttt{call fac} \ \{ \texttt{x} = \texttt{n} \} \qquad (*)$$

In order to do that we assume that we have a proof of (*) for the recursive call of `fac` and we have to construct a proof of the property for the body of the procedure. It seems that in order to do so we must construct a proof of

$$\{ \texttt{x} = \texttt{n}-1 \} \ \texttt{call fac} \ \{ \texttt{x} = \texttt{n}-1 \}$$

and there are no axioms and rules that allow us to obtain such a proof from (*). However, we shall not go further into this.

The case of *total correctness* is slightly more complicated because we have to bound the number of recursive calls. The rule adopted is

$$[\text{call}_t^{\text{rec}}] \quad \frac{\{ P(\mathbf{z}) \} \ \texttt{call}\ p \ \{ \Downarrow Q \} \vdash_t \{ P(\mathbf{z}+\mathbf{1}) \} \ S \ \{ \Downarrow Q \}}{\{ \exists \mathbf{z}.P(\mathbf{z}) \} \ \texttt{call}\ p \ \{ \Downarrow Q \}}$$

where $\neg P(\mathbf{0})$ holds

and $\mathbf{z}$ ranges over the natural numbers (that is $\mathbf{z}>\mathbf{0}$)

and where p is defined by $\texttt{proc}\ p\ \texttt{is}\ S$

The premise of this rule expresses that if we assume that we have a proof of $\{ P(\mathbf{z}) \} \ \texttt{call}\ p \ \{ \Downarrow Q \}$ for all recursive calls of p of depth at most $\mathbf{z}$ then we can prove $\{ P(\mathbf{z}+\mathbf{1}) \} \ S \ \{ \Downarrow Q \}$. The conclusion expresses that for any depth of recursive calls we have a proof of $\{ \exists \mathbf{z}.P(\mathbf{z}) \} \ \texttt{call}\ p \ \{ \Downarrow Q \}$.

The inference system of Table 6.2 extended with the rule $[\text{call}_t^{\text{rec}}]$ can be proved to be sound. If it is extended with additional rules (as discussed above) it can also be proved to be complete.

6.5 Assertions for execution time

A proof system for total correctness can be used to prove that a program does indeed terminate but it does not say how many resources it needs in order to terminate. We shall now show how to extend the total correctness proof system of Table 6.2 to prove *the order of magnitude of the execution time* of a statement.

It is easy to give some informal guidelines for how to determine the order of magnitude of execution time:

assignment: the execution time is $\mathcal{O}(\mathbf{1})$, that is, it is bounded by a constant,

skip: the execution time is $\mathcal{O}(\mathbf{1})$,

composition: the execution time is, to within a constant factor, the sum of the execution times of each of the statements,

conditional: the execution time is, to within a constant factor, the largest of the execution times of the two branches, and

iteration: the execution time of the loop is, to within a constant factor, the sum, over all iterations round the loop, of the time to execute the body.

The idea now is to formalize these rules by giving an inference system for reasoning about execution times. To do so we shall proceed in three stages:

- first we specify the exact time needed to evaluate arithmetic and boolean expressions,
- next we extend the natural semantics of Chapter 2 to count the exact execution time, and
- finally we extend the total correctness proof system to prove the order of magnitude of the execution time of statements.

However, before addressing these issues we have to fix a *computational model*, that is we have to determine how to count the cost of the various operations. The actual choice is not so important but for the sake of simplicity we have based it upon the abstract machine of Chapter 3. The idea is that each instruction of the machine takes one time unit and the time required to execute an arithmetic expression, a boolean expression or a statement will be the time required to execute the generated code. However, no knowledge of Chapter 3 is required in the sequel.

Exact execution times for expressions

The time needed to evaluate an arithmetic expression is given by a function

$$\mathcal{TA}\text{: } \mathbf{Aexp} \to \mathbf{Z}$$

so $\mathcal{TA}[\![a]\!]$ is the number of time units required to evaluate a in any state. Similarly, the function

$$\mathcal{TB}\text{: } \mathbf{Bexp} \to \mathbf{Z}$$

determines the number of time units required to evaluate a boolean expression. These functions are defined in Table 6.3.

$\mathcal{TA}[\![n]\!]$	$=$	$\mathbf{1}$
$\mathcal{TA}[\![x]\!]$	$=$	$\mathbf{1}$
$\mathcal{TA}[\![a_1 + a_2]\!]$	$=$	$\mathcal{TA}[\![a_1]\!] + \mathcal{TA}[\![a_2]\!] + \mathbf{1}$
$\mathcal{TA}[\![a_1 \star a_2]\!]$	$=$	$\mathcal{TA}[\![a_1]\!] + \mathcal{TA}[\![a_2]\!] + \mathbf{1}$
$\mathcal{TA}[\![a_1 - a_2]\!]$	$=$	$\mathcal{TA}[\![a_1]\!] + \mathcal{TA}[\![a_2]\!] + \mathbf{1}$
$\mathcal{TB}[\![\texttt{true}]\!]$	$=$	$\mathbf{1}$
$\mathcal{TB}[\![\texttt{false}]\!]$	$=$	$\mathbf{1}$
$\mathcal{TB}[\![a_1 = a_2]\!]$	$=$	$\mathcal{TA}[\![a_1]\!] + \mathcal{TA}[\![a_2]\!] + \mathbf{1}$
$\mathcal{TB}[\![a_1 \leq a_2]\!]$	$=$	$\mathcal{TA}[\![a_1]\!] + \mathcal{TA}[\![a_2]\!] + \mathbf{1}$
$\mathcal{TB}[\![\neg b]\!]$	$=$	$\mathcal{TB}[\![b]\!] + \mathbf{1}$
$\mathcal{TB}[\![b_1 \wedge b_2]\!]$	$=$	$\mathcal{TB}[\![b_1]\!] + \mathcal{TB}[\![b_2]\!] + \mathbf{1}$

Table 6.3: Exact execution times for expressions

Exact execution times for statements

Turning to the execution time for statements we shall extend the natural semantics of Table 2.1 to specify the time requirements. This is done by extending the transitions to have the form

$$\langle S, s\rangle \to^t s'$$

meaning that if S is executed from state s then it will terminate in state s' and exactly t time units will be required for this. The extension of Table 2.1 is fairly straightforward and is given in Table 6.4.

The inference system

The inference system for proving the order of magnitude of the execution time of statements will have assertions of the form

$$\{\ P\ \}\ S\ \{\ e \Downarrow Q\ \}$$

where P and Q are predicates as in the previous inference systems and e is an arithmetic expression (that is $e \in \mathbf{Aexp}$). The idea is that

if the execution of S is started in a state satisfying P

then it terminates in a state satisfying Q

and the required execution time is $\mathcal{O}(e)$, that is has order of magnitude e.

So for example

$[\text{ass}_{\text{tns}}]$	$\langle x := a,\ s\rangle \to^{\mathcal{TA}[\![a]\!]+1} s[x\mapsto\mathcal{A}[\![a]\!]s]$
$[\text{skip}_{\text{tns}}]$	$\langle \texttt{skip},\ s\rangle \to^{1} s$
$[\text{comp}_{\text{tns}}]$	$\dfrac{\langle S_1,s\rangle \to^{t_1} s',\ \langle S_2,s'\rangle \to^{t_2} s''}{\langle S_1;S_2,\ s\rangle \to^{t_1+t_2} s''}$
$[\text{if}^{\text{tt}}_{\text{tns}}]$	$\dfrac{\langle S_1,s\rangle \to^{t} s'}{\langle \texttt{if}\ b\ \texttt{then}\ S_1\ \texttt{else}\ S_2,\ s\rangle \to^{\mathcal{TB}[\![b]\!]+t+1} s'}$ if $\mathcal{B}[\![b]\!]s = \mathbf{tt}$
$[\text{if}^{\text{ff}}_{\text{tns}}]$	$\dfrac{\langle S_2,s\rangle \to^{t} s'}{\langle \texttt{if}\ b\ \texttt{then}\ S_1\ \texttt{else}\ S_2,\ s\rangle \to^{\mathcal{TB}[\![b]\!]+t+1} s'}$ if $\mathcal{B}[\![b]\!]s = \mathbf{ff}$
$[\text{while}^{\text{tt}}_{\text{tns}}]$	$\dfrac{\langle S,s\rangle \to^{t} s',\ \langle \texttt{while}\ b\ \texttt{do}\ S,\ s'\rangle \to^{t'} s''}{\langle \texttt{while}\ b\ \texttt{do}\ S,\ s\rangle \to^{\mathcal{TB}[\![b]\!]+t+t'+2} s''}$ if $\mathcal{B}[\![b]\!]s = \mathbf{tt}$
$[\text{while}^{\text{ff}}_{\text{tns}}]$	$\langle \texttt{while}\ b\ \texttt{do}\ S,\ s\rangle \to^{\mathcal{TB}[\![b]\!]+3} s$ if $\mathcal{B}[\![b]\!]s = \mathbf{ff}$

Table 6.4: Natural semantics for **While** with exact execution times

$$\{\ \texttt{x} = 3\ \}\ \texttt{y := 1; while}\ \neg(\texttt{x=1})\ \texttt{do (y := y}\star\texttt{x; x := x}-\texttt{1)}\ \{\ \texttt{1} \Downarrow \texttt{true}\ \}$$

expresses that the execution of the factorial statement from a state where x has the value **3** has order of magnitude 1, that is it is bounded by a constant. Similarly,

$$\{\ \texttt{x} > 0\ \}\ \texttt{y := 1; while}\ \neg(\texttt{x=1})\ \texttt{do (y := y}\star\texttt{x; x := x}-\texttt{1)}\ \{\ \texttt{x} \Downarrow \texttt{true}\ \}$$

expresses that the execution of the factorial statement on a state where x is positive has order of magnitude x.

Formally, *validity* of the formula $\{\ P\ \}\ S\ \{\ e \Downarrow Q\ \}$ is defined by

$$\models_{\mathrm{e}} \{\ P\ \}\ S\ \{\ e \Downarrow Q\ \}$$

if and only if

> there exists a natural number **k** such that for all states s,
>
> if $P\ s = \mathbf{tt}$ then there exists a state s' and a number t such that
>
> $Q\ s' = \mathbf{tt}$, $\langle S,\ s\rangle \to^{t} s'$, and $t \le \mathbf{k} \star (\mathcal{A}[\![e]\!]s)$

Note that the expression e is evaluated in the initial state rather than the final state.

The axioms and rules of the inference system are given in Table 6.5. Provability of the assertion $\{\ P\ \}\ S\ \{\ e \Downarrow Q\ \}$ in the inference system is written

$$\vdash_{\mathrm{e}} \{\ P\ \}\ S\ \{\ e \Downarrow Q\ \}$$

[ass$_e$]	$\{ P[x\mapsto\mathcal{A}[\![a]\!]] \}\ x := a\ \{ 1 \Downarrow P \}$
[skip$_e$]	$\{ P \}$ skip $\{ 1 \Downarrow P \}$
[comp$_e$]	$\dfrac{\{ P \land \mathcal{B}[\![e_2'=\mathtt{u}]\!] \}\ S_1\ \{ e_1 \Downarrow Q \land \mathcal{B}[\![e_2\leq \mathtt{u}]\!] \},\ \ \{ Q \}\ S_2\ \{ e_2 \Downarrow R \}}{\{ P \}\ S_1;\ S_2\ \{ e_1+e_2' \Downarrow R \}}$ where u is an unused logical variable
[if$_e$]	$\dfrac{\{ \mathcal{B}[\![b]\!] \land P \}\ S_1\ \{ e \Downarrow Q \},\ \ \{ \neg\mathcal{B}[\![b]\!] \land P \}\ S_2\ \{ e \Downarrow Q \}}{\{ P \}\ \texttt{if}\ b\ \texttt{then}\ S_1\ \texttt{else}\ S_2\ \{ e \Downarrow Q \}}$
[while$_e$]	$\dfrac{\{ P(\mathtt{z}+1) \land \mathcal{B}[\![e'=\mathtt{u}]\!] \}\ S\ \{ e_1 \Downarrow P(\mathtt{z}) \land \mathcal{B}[\![e\leq \mathtt{u}]\!] \}}{\{ \exists \mathtt{z}.P(\mathtt{z}) \}\ \texttt{while}\ b\ \texttt{do}\ S\ \{ e \Downarrow P(0) \}}$ where $P(\mathtt{z}+1) \Rightarrow \mathcal{B}[\![b]\!] \land \mathcal{B}[\![e\geq e_1+e']\!]$, $P(0) \Rightarrow \neg\mathcal{B}[\![b]\!] \land \mathcal{B}[\![1\leq e]\!]$ and u is an unused logical variable and z ranges over natural numbers (that is $\mathtt{z}\geq 0$)
[cons$_e$]	$\dfrac{\{ P' \}\ S\ \{ e' \Downarrow Q' \}}{\{ P \}\ S\ \{ e \Downarrow Q \}}$ where (for some natural number k) $P \Rightarrow P' \land \mathcal{B}[\![e'\leq \mathtt{k}\star e]\!]$ and $Q' \Rightarrow Q$

Table 6.5: Axiomatic system for order of magnitude of execution time

The assignment statement and the skip statement can be executed in constant time and therefore we use the arithmetic expression 1.

The rule [comp$_e$] assumes that we have proofs showing that e_1 and e_2 are the order of magnitudes of the execution times for the two statements. However, e_1 expresses the time requirements of S_1 relative to the initial state of S_1 and e_2 expresses the time requirements relative to the initial state of S_2. This means that we cannot simply use $e_1 + e_2$ as the time requirement for S_1; S_2. We have to replace e_2 with an expression e_2' such that e_2' evaluated in the initial state of S_1 will bound the value of e_2 in the initial state of S_2 (which is the final state of S_1). This is expressed by the extended precondition and postcondition of S_1 using the logical variable u.

The rule [if$_e$] is fairly straightforward since the time required for the test is constant.

In the rule for the while-construct we assume that the execution time is e_1 for the body and is e for the loop itself. As in the rule [comp$_e$] we cannot just use $e_1 + e$ as the total time required because e_1 refers to the state before the body of the loop is executed and e to the state after the body is executed once. We shall therefore require that there is an expression e' such that e' evaluated before the body will bound e evaluated after the body. Then it must be the case that e satisfies $e \geq e_1 + e'$ because e has to bound the time for executing the `while`-loop independently of the number of times it is unfolded. As we shall see in Example 6.36, this corresponds to the *recurrence equations* that often have to be solved when analysing the execution time of programs. Finally, the rule [cons_e] should be straightforward.

Example 6.35 We shall now prove that the execution time of the factorial statement has order of magnitude x. This can be expressed by the following assertion:

$$\{ \texttt{x} > \texttt{0} \}\ \texttt{y := 1; while}\ \neg(\texttt{x=1})\ \texttt{do (y := y}\star\texttt{x; x := x}-\texttt{1)}\ \{ \texttt{x} \Downarrow \texttt{true} \}$$

The inference of this assertion proceeds in a number of stages. First we define the predicate $\mathit{INV}(\texttt{z})$ that is to be the invariant of the `while`-loop

$$\mathit{INV}(\texttt{z})\ s = (s\ \texttt{x} > \mathbf{0}\ \&\ s\ \texttt{x} = \texttt{z} + \mathbf{1})$$

The logical variables $\texttt{u}_1$ and $\texttt{u}_2$ are used for the `while`-loop and the body of the `while`-loop, respectively. We shall first consider the body of the loop. Using [ass_e] we get

$$\vdash_\text{e} \{ (\mathit{INV}(\texttt{z}) \wedge \texttt{x}{\leq}\texttt{u}_1)[\texttt{x}{\mapsto}\texttt{x}-\texttt{1}] \}\ \texttt{x := x} - \texttt{1}\ \{ \texttt{1} \Downarrow \mathit{INV}(\texttt{z}) \wedge \texttt{x}{\leq}\texttt{u}_1 \}$$

Similarly, we get

$$\vdash_\text{e} \{ ((\mathit{INV}(\texttt{z}) \wedge \texttt{x}{\leq}\texttt{u}_1)[\texttt{x}{\mapsto}\texttt{x}-\texttt{1}] \wedge \texttt{1}{\leq}\texttt{u}_2)[\texttt{y}{\mapsto}\texttt{y}\star\texttt{x}] \}$$
$$\texttt{y := y} \star \texttt{x}$$
$$\{ \texttt{1} \Downarrow (\mathit{INV}(\texttt{z}) \wedge \texttt{x}{\leq}\texttt{u}_1)[\texttt{x}{\mapsto}\texttt{x}-\texttt{1}] \wedge \texttt{1}{\leq}\texttt{u}_2 \}$$

Before applying the rule [comp_e] we have to modify the precondition of the above assertion. We have

$$\mathit{INV}(\texttt{z+}\mathbf{1}) \wedge \texttt{x}-\texttt{1}{=}\texttt{u}_1 \wedge \texttt{1}{=}\texttt{u}_2$$
$$\Rightarrow ((\mathit{INV}(\texttt{z}) \wedge \texttt{x}{\leq}\texttt{u}_1)[\texttt{x}{\mapsto}\texttt{x}-\texttt{1}] \wedge \texttt{1}{\leq}\texttt{u}_2)[\texttt{y}{\mapsto}\texttt{y}\star\texttt{x}]$$

so using [cons_e] we get

$$\vdash_\text{e} \{ \mathit{INV}(\texttt{z+}\mathbf{1}) \wedge \texttt{x}-\texttt{1}{=}\texttt{u}_1 \wedge \texttt{1}{=}\texttt{u}_2 \}$$
$$\texttt{y := y} \star \texttt{x}$$
$$\{ \texttt{1} \Downarrow (\mathit{INV}(\texttt{z}) \wedge \texttt{x}{\leq}\texttt{u}_1)[\texttt{x}{\mapsto}\texttt{x}-\texttt{1}] \wedge \texttt{1}{\leq}\texttt{u}_2 \}$$

We can now apply [comp_e] and get

$$\vdash_e \{\ INV(\mathtt{z}+\mathbf{1}) \land \mathtt{x}-1=\mathtt{u}_1\ \}$$
$$\mathtt{y} := \mathtt{y} \star \mathtt{x};\ \mathtt{x} := \mathtt{x}-1$$
$$\{\ 1+1 \Downarrow INV(\mathtt{z}) \land \mathtt{x}\leq\mathtt{u}_1\ \}$$

and using [cons$_e$] we get

$$\vdash_e \{\ INV(\mathtt{z}+\mathbf{1}) \land \mathtt{x}-1=\mathtt{u}_1\ \}$$
$$\mathtt{y} := \mathtt{y} \star \mathtt{x};\ \mathtt{x} := \mathtt{x}-1$$
$$\{\ 1 \Downarrow INV(\mathtt{z}) \land \mathtt{x}\leq\mathtt{u}_1\ \}$$

It is easy to verify that

$$INV(\mathtt{z}+\mathbf{1}) \Rightarrow \neg(\mathtt{x} = 1) \land \mathtt{x}\geq 1+(\mathtt{x}-1), \text{ and}$$
$$INV(\mathbf{0}) \Rightarrow \neg(\neg(\mathtt{x} = 1)) \land 1\leq\mathtt{x}$$

Therefore we can use the rule [while$_e$] and get

$$\vdash_e \{\ \exists\mathtt{z}.INV(\mathtt{z})\ \}\ \mathtt{while}\ \neg(\mathtt{x}=1)\ \mathtt{do}\ (\mathtt{y} := \mathtt{y}\star\mathtt{x};\ \mathtt{x} := \mathtt{x}-1)\ \{\ \mathtt{x} \Downarrow INV(\mathbf{0})\ \}$$

We shall now apply the axiom [ass$_e$] to the statement $\mathtt{y} := 1$ and get

$$\vdash_e \{\ (\exists\mathtt{z}.INV(\mathtt{z}) \land 1\leq\mathtt{u}_3)[\mathtt{y}\mapsto 1]\ \}\ \mathtt{y} := 1\ \{\ 1 \Downarrow \exists\mathtt{z}.INV(\mathtt{z}) \land 1\leq\mathtt{u}_3\ \}$$

We have

$$\mathtt{x}>0 \land 1=\mathtt{u}_3 \Rightarrow (\exists\mathtt{z}.INV(\mathtt{z}) \land 1\leq\mathtt{u}_3)[\mathtt{y}\mapsto 1]$$

so using [cons$_e$] we get

$$\vdash_e \{\ \mathtt{x}>0 \land 1=\mathtt{u}_3\ \}\ \mathtt{y} := 1\ \{\ 1 \Downarrow \exists\mathtt{z}.INV(\mathtt{z}) \land 1\leq\mathtt{u}_3\ \}$$

The rule [comp$_e$] now gives

$$\vdash_e \{\ \mathtt{x}>0\ \}$$
$$\mathtt{y} := 1;\ \mathtt{while}\ \neg(\mathtt{x}=1)\ \mathtt{do}\ (\mathtt{y} := \mathtt{y}\star\mathtt{x};\ \mathtt{x} := \mathtt{x}-1)$$
$$\{\ 1+\mathtt{x} \Downarrow INV(\mathbf{0})\ \}$$

Clearly we have

$$\mathtt{x}>0 \Rightarrow 1+\mathtt{x} \leq \mathbf{2}\star\mathtt{x}, \text{ and}$$
$$INV(\mathbf{0}) \Rightarrow \mathtt{true}$$

so applying rule [cons$_e$] we get

$$\vdash_e \{\ \mathtt{x} > 0\ \}$$
$$\mathtt{y} := 1;\ \mathtt{while}\ \neg(\mathtt{x}=1)\ \mathtt{do}\ (\mathtt{y} := \mathtt{y}\star\mathtt{x};\ \mathtt{x} := \mathtt{x}-1)$$
$$\{\ \mathtt{x} \Downarrow \mathtt{true}\ \}$$

as required. □

Example 6.36 Assume now that we want to determine an arithmetic expression e_{fac} such that

$$\vdash_e \{\ \mathtt{x} > 0\ \}$$
$$\mathtt{y := 1;\ while\ \neg(x=1)\ do\ (y := y\star x;\ x := x-1)}$$
$$\{\ e_{\text{fac}} \Downarrow \mathtt{true}\ \}$$

In other words we want to determine the order of magnitude of the time required to execute the factorial statement. We can then attempt constructing a proof of the above assertion using the inference system of Table 6.5 with e_{fac} being an unspecified arithmetic expression. The various side conditions of the rules will then specify a set of (in)equations that have to be fulfilled by e_{fac} in order for the proof to exist.

We shall first consider the body of the loop. Very much as in the previous example we get

$$\vdash_e \{\ \mathit{INV}(\mathtt{z}+\mathbf{1}) \wedge e[\mathtt{x}\mapsto\mathtt{x}-1]=\mathtt{u}_1\ \}$$
$$\mathtt{y := y \star x;\ x := x-1}$$
$$\{\ 1 \Downarrow \mathit{INV}(\mathtt{z}) \wedge e\leq\mathtt{u}_1\ \}$$

where e is the execution time of the `while`-construct. We can now apply the rule [while$_e$] if e fulfils the conditions

$$\begin{aligned} &\mathit{INV}(\mathtt{z}+\mathbf{1}) \Rightarrow e\geq 1+e[\mathtt{x}\mapsto\mathtt{x}-1] \\ &\mathit{INV}(\mathbf{0}) \Rightarrow 1\leq e \end{aligned} \qquad (*)$$

and we will get

$$\vdash_e \{\ \exists\mathtt{z}.\mathit{INV}(\mathtt{z})\ \}\ \mathtt{while}\ \neg(\mathtt{x=1})\ \mathtt{do}\ (\mathtt{y := y\star x;\ x := x-1})\ \{\ e \Downarrow \mathit{INV}(\mathbf{0})\ \}$$

The requirement (*) corresponds to the recurrence equation

$$T(\mathtt{x}) = 1 + T(\mathtt{x}-1)$$
$$T(1) = 1$$

obtained by the standard techniques from execution time analysis. If we take e to be `x` then (*) is fulfilled. The remainder of the proof is very much as in Exercise 6.35 and we get that e_{fac} must satisfy

$$\mathtt{x} > 0 \Rightarrow \mathtt{x}+1 \leq \mathbf{k}\star e_{\text{fac}} \text{ for some constant } \mathbf{k}$$

so e_{fac} may be taken to be `x`. □

Exercise 6.37 Modify the proof of Lemma 6.30 to show that the inference system of Table 6.5 is sound. □

Exercise 6.38 ** Suggest an alternative rule for `while` b `do` S that expresses that its execution time, neglecting constant factors, is the product of the number of times the loop is executed and the maximal execution time for the body of the loop. □

Exercise 6.39 Suggest an inference rule for `repeat` S `until` b. You are not allowed to rely on the existence of a `while`-construct in the language. □

Chapter 7

Further Reading

In this book we have covered the basic ingredients in three approaches to semantics:

- operational semantics,
- denotational semantics, and
- axiomatic semantics.

We have concentrated on a rather simple language of `while`-programs and have studied the underlying theories and the formal relationships between the various approaches. The power of the three approaches have been illustrated by various extensions of **While**: non-determinism, parallelism, recursive procedures and exceptions.

We believe that formal semantics is an important tool for reasoning about many aspects of the behaviour of programs and programming languages. To support this belief we have given three examples, one for each approach to semantics:

- a simple compiler,
- a static program analysis, and
- an inference system for execution time.

In conclusion we shall provide a few pointers to the literature (mainly textbooks) where a more comprehensive treatment of language features or theoretical aspects may be found. We do not reference the vast number of research publications in the area but rely on the references in the books mentioned.

Operational semantics

Structural operational semantics was introduced by Gordon Plotkin in [14]. This is a standard reference and covers a number of features from imperative and functional languages whereas features from parallel languages are covered in [15]. A more introductory treatment of structural operational semantics is given in [9]. *Natural semantics* is derived from structural operational semantics and the basic ideas are presented in [6] for a functional language.

Although we have covered many of the essential ideas behind operational semantics we should like to mention three techniques that have had to be omitted.

A technique that is often used when specifying a structural operational semantics is to extend the syntactic component of the configurations with special notation for recording *partially processed constructs.* The inference system will then contain axioms and rules that handle these "extended" configurations. This technique may be used to specify a structural operational semantics of the languages **Block** and **Proc** in Section 2.5 and to specify a structural operational semantics of expressions.

Both kinds of operational semantics can easily be extended to cope explicitly with *dynamic errors* (as e.g. division by zero). The idea is to extend the set of configurations with special error-configurations and then augment the inference system with extra axioms and rules for how to handle these configurations.

Often programs have to fulfil certain conditions in order to be *statically well-formed* and hence preclude certain dynamic errors. These conditions can be formulated using inductively defined predicates and may be integrated with the operational semantics.

Provably correct implementation

The *correctness of the implementation* of Chapter 3 was a relatively simple proof because it was based on an abstract machine designed for the purpose. In general, when more realistic machines or larger languages are considered, proofs easily become unwieldy and perhaps for this reason there is no ideal textbook in this area. We therefore only reference two research papers: [7] for an approach based on natural semantics and [13] for an approach based on denotational semantics.

Denotational semantics

A general introduction to *denotational semantics* (as developed by C. Strachey and D. Scott) may be found in [16]. It covers denotational semantics for (mainly) imperative languages and covers the fundamentals of domain theory (including reflexive domains). Another good reference for imperative languages is [8] but it does not cover the domain theory. We should also mention a classic in the field [17] even though the domain theory is based on the (by now obsolete) approach of complete lattices.

We have restricted the treatment of domain theory to what is needed for specifying the denotational semantics of the `while`-language. The benefit of this is that we can restrict ourselves to partial functions between states and thereby obtain a relatively simple theoretical development. The drawback is that it becomes rather cumbersome to verify the existence of semantic specifications for other languages (as evidenced in Section 4.5).

The traditional solution is to develop a *meta-language* for expressing denotational definitions. The theoretical foundation of this language will then ensure that the semantic functions do exist as long as one only uses domains and operations from the meta-language. The benefit of this is obvious; the drawback is that one has to prove a fair amount of results but the efforts are greatly rewarded in the long run. Both [16] and [17] contain such a development.

The denotational approach can handle *abortion* and *non-determinism* using a kind of powersets called power-domains. Certain kinds of *parallelism* can be handled as well but for many purposes it is better to use a structural operational semantics instead.

Static program analysis

A selection of *static program analysis* techniques for imperative languages (as well as techniques for implementations on realistic machines) is given in [3]; but unfortunately, no considerations of correctness are given. Treatments of correctness are often based on abstract interpretation and [1] surveys a number of approaches.

Axiomatic program verification

A general introduction to *program verification*, and in particular *axiomatic semantics* may be found in [11]. The presentation covers a flowchart language, a `while`-language and a (first order) functional language and also includes a study of expressiveness (as needed for the intensional approach to axiomatic semantics). Many books, including [10], develop axiomatic program verification together with practically motivated examples. A good introduction to the analysis of *resource requirements* of programs is [2] and the formulation as formal inference systems may be found in [12]. We should also mention a classic [5] that studies soundness and completeness properties with respect to a denotational semantics. Rules for procedures may be found in [4].

We should point out that we have used the extensional approach to specifying the assertions of the inference systems. This allows us to concentrate on the *formulation* of the inference systems without having to worry about the *existence* of the assertions in an explicit assertion language. However, it is more common to use the intensional approach as is done in [11].

Appendix A

Review of Notation

We use the following notation:

$\exists$	there exists
$\forall$	for all
$\{ x \mid \ldots x \ldots \}$	the set of those x such that $\ldots x \ldots$ holds
$x \in X$	x is a member of the set X
$X \subseteq Y$	set X is contained in set Y
$X \cup Y$	$\{ z \mid z \in X$ or $z \in Y \}$ (union)
$X \cap Y$	$\{ z \mid z \in X$ and $z \in Y \}$ (intersection)
$X \setminus Y$	$\{ z \mid z \in X$ and $z \notin Y \}$ (set difference)
$X \times Y$	$\{ \langle x, y \rangle \mid x \in X$ and $y \in Y \}$ (Cartesian product)
$\mathcal{P}(X)$	$\{ Z \mid Z \subseteq X \}$ (powerset)
$\bigcup \mathcal{Y}$	$\{ y \mid \exists Y \in \mathcal{Y}\colon y \in Y \}$ (so that $\bigcup \{ Y_1, Y_2 \} = Y_1 \cup Y_2$)
$\emptyset$	the empty set
$\mathbf{T}$	$\{ \mathbf{tt}, \mathbf{ff} \}$ (truth values $\mathbf{tt}$ (true) and $\mathbf{ff}$ (false))
$\mathbf{N}$	$\{ \mathbf{0}, \mathbf{1}, \mathbf{2}, \ldots \}$ (natural numbers)
$\mathbf{Z}$	$\{ \ldots, \mathbf{-2}, \mathbf{-1}, \mathbf{0}, \mathbf{1}, \mathbf{2}, \ldots \}$ (integers)
$f{:}X \rightarrow Y$	f is a total function from X to Y
$X \rightarrow Y$	$\{ f \mid f{:}X \rightarrow Y \}$
$f{:}X \hookrightarrow Y$	f is a partial function from X to Y
$X \hookrightarrow Y$	$\{ f \mid f{:}X \hookrightarrow Y \}$

In addition to this we have special notations for functions, relations, predicates and transition systems.

Functions

The effect of a function $f{:}X \to Y$ is expressed by its *graph*:

$$\text{graph}(f) = \{ \langle x, y\rangle \in X \times Y \mid f\ x = y \}$$

which is merely an element of $\mathcal{P}(X \times Y)$. The graph of f has the following properties

- $\langle x, y\rangle \in \text{graph}(f)$ and $\langle x, y'\rangle \in \text{graph}(f)$ imply $y = y'$, and
- $\forall x \in X$: $\exists y \in Y$: $\langle x, y\rangle \in$ graph(f)

This expresses the single-valuedness of f and the totality of f. We say that f is *injective* if $f\ x = f\ x'$ implies that $x = x'$.

A *partial* function $g{:}X \hookrightarrow Y$ is a function from a subset X_g of X to Y, that is $g{:}X_g \to Y$. Again one may define

$$\text{graph}(g) = \{ \langle x, y\rangle \in X \times Y \mid g\ x = y \text{ and } x \in X_g \}$$

but now only an analogue of the single-valuedness property above is satisfied. We shall write $g\ x = y$ whenever $\langle x, y\rangle \in \text{graph}(g)$ and $g\ x = \underline{\text{undef}}$ whenever $x \notin X_g$, that is whenever $\neg\exists y \in Y$: $\langle x, y\rangle \in \text{graph}(g)$. To distinguish between a function f and a partial function g one often calls f a *total* function. We shall view the partial functions as encompassing the total functions.

For total functions f_1 and f_2 we define their composition $f_2 \circ f_1$ by

$$(f_2 \circ f_1)\ x = f_2(f_1\ x)$$

(Note that the opposite order is sometimes used in the literature.) For partial functions g_1 and g_2 we define $g_2 \circ g_1$ similarly:

$$\begin{array}{ll} (g_2 \circ g_1)\ x = z & \text{if there exists } y \text{ such that } g_1\ x = y \text{ and } g_2\ y = z \\ (g_2 \circ g_1)\ x = \underline{\text{undef}} & \text{if } g_1\ x = \underline{\text{undef}} \text{ or} \\ & \text{if there exists } y \text{ such that } g_1\ x = y \\ & \text{but } g_2\ y = \underline{\text{undef}} \end{array}$$

The identity function $\text{id}{:}X \to X$ is defined by

$$\text{id}\ x = x$$

Finally, if $f{:}X \to Y$, $x \in X$ and $y \in Y$ then the function $f[x \mapsto y]{:}X \to Y$ is defined by

$$f[x \mapsto y]\ x' = \begin{cases} y & \text{if } x = x' \\ f\ x' & \text{otherwise} \end{cases}$$

A similar notation may be used when f is a partial function.

The function f is of *order of magnitude* g, written $\mathcal{O}(g)$, if there exists a natural number $\mathbf{k}$ such that $\forall x.\ f\ x \leq \mathbf{k} \star (g\ x)$.

Relations

A *relation from X to Y* is a subset of $X \times Y$ (that is an element of $\mathcal{P}(X \times Y)$). A relation *on* X is a subset of $X \times X$. If $f{:}X \to Y$ or $f{:}X \hookrightarrow Y$ then the graph of f is a relation. (Sometimes a function is identified with its graph but we shall keep the distinction.) The *identity relation* on X is the relation

$$\mathrm{I}_X = \{ \langle x, x \rangle \mid x \in X \}$$

from X to X. When X is clear from the context we shall omit the subscript X and simply write I.

If $R_1 \subseteq X \times Y$ and $R_2 \subseteq Y \times Z$ the *composition* of R_1 followed by R_2, which we denote by $R_1 \diamond R_2$, is defined by

$$R_1 \diamond R_2 = \{ \langle x, z \rangle \mid \exists y \in Y{:}\ \langle x, y \rangle \in R_1 \text{ and } \langle y, z \rangle \in R_2 \}$$

Note that the order of composition differs from that used for functions,

$$\mathrm{graph}(f_2 \circ f_1) = \mathrm{graph}(f_1) \diamond \mathrm{graph}(f_2)$$

and that we have the equation

$$\mathrm{I} \diamond R = R \diamond \mathrm{I} = R$$

If R is a relation on X then the *reflexive transitive closure* is the relation R^* on X defined by

$$R^* = \{ \langle x, x' \rangle \mid \exists \mathrm{n} \geq 1{:}\ \exists x_1, \ldots, x_\mathrm{n}{:}\ x = x_1 \text{ and } x' = x_\mathrm{n} \text{ and } \forall \mathrm{i} < \mathrm{n}{:}\ \langle x_\mathrm{i}, x_{\mathrm{i}+1} \rangle \in R \}$$

Note that by taking n=1 and $x = x' = x_1$ it follows that $\mathrm{I} \subseteq R^*$. In a similar way it follows that $R \subseteq R^*$. Finally, we define

$$R^+ = R \diamond R^*$$

and observe that $R \subseteq R^+ \subseteq R^*$.

Predicates

A *predicate* on X is a function from X to $\mathbf{T}$. If $p{:}X \to \mathbf{T}$ is a predicate on X, the relation I_p on X is defined by

$$\mathrm{I}_p = \{ \langle x, x \rangle \mid x \in X \text{ and } p\ x = \mathbf{tt} \}$$

Note that $\mathrm{I}_p \subseteq \mathrm{I}$ and that

$$\mathrm{I}_p \diamond R = \{ \langle x, y \rangle \mid p\ x = \mathbf{tt} \text{ and } \langle x, y \rangle \in R \}$$

$$R \diamond \mathrm{I}_q = \{ \langle x, y \rangle \mid \langle x, y \rangle \in R \text{ and } q\ y = \mathbf{tt} \}$$

Transition systems

A *transition system* is a triple of the form

$$(\Gamma,\mathrm{T},\ \triangleright)$$

where Γ is a set of *configurations*, T is a subset of Γ called the *terminal* (or *final*) configurations and $\triangleright$ is a relation on Γ called a *transition relation.* The relation $\triangleright$ must satisfy

$$\forall\gamma\in\mathrm{T}\colon \forall\gamma'\in\Gamma\colon \neg(\gamma \triangleright \gamma')$$

Any configuration γ in $\Gamma\backslash\mathrm{T}$ such that the transition $\gamma \triangleright \gamma'$ holds for no γ' is called *stuck.*

Appendix B

Introduction to Miranda Implementations

In this appendix we give the basic definitions needed to implement the various semantic definitions in **Miranda**. Essentially, this amounts to an implementation of the material of Chapter 1.

B.1 Abstract syntax

For **Num** we choose the primitive type `num` of **Miranda**. For **Var** we choose strings of characters and so define the type synonym:

```
> var == [char]
```

For each of the syntactic categories **Aexp**, **Bexp** and **Stm** we define an algebraic data type taking into account the various possibilities mentioned by the BNF syntax of Section 1.2:

```
> aexp ::= N num | V var | Add aexp aexp |
>          Mult aexp aexp | Sub aexp aexp

> bexp ::= TRUE | FALSE | Eq aexp aexp | Le aexp aexp |
>          Neg bexp | And bexp bexp

> stm  ::= Ass var aexp | Skip | Comp stm stm |
>          If bexp stm stm | While bexp stm
```

Example B.1 The factorial statement of Example 1.1 is represented by

```
>  factorial = Comp (Ass "y" (N 1))
>                    (While (Neg (Eq (V "x") (N 1)))
>                      (Comp (Ass "y" (Mult (V "y") (V "x")))
>                            (Ass "x" (Sub (V "x") (N 1)))))
```

Note that this is a representation of the *abstract syntax* of the statement. One may be interested in a parser that would translate the more readable form

y := 1; while ¬(x = 1) do (y := y * x; x := x − 1)

into the above representation. However, we shall refrain from undertaking the task of implementing a parser as we are mainly concerned with semantics. □

Exercise B.2 Specify an element of `stm` that represents the statement constructed in Exercise 1.2 for computing n to the power of m. □

B.2 Evaluation of expressions

We shall first be concerned with the representation of values and states. The natural numbers **Z** will be represented by the type `num` meaning that the semantic function $\mathcal{N}$ becomes trivial. The truth values **T** will be represented by the type `bool` of booleans. So we define the type synonyms:

```
>  z == num
>  t == bool
```

The set **State** is defined as the set of functions from variables to natural numbers so we define:

```
>  state == var -> z
```

Example B.3 The state `s_init` that maps all variables except `x` to **0** and that maps `x` to **3** can be defined by

```
>  s_init "x" = 3
>  s_init y   = 0
```

Note that we encapsulate the specific variable name `x` in quotes whereas `y` can be any variable. □

The functions $\mathcal{A}$ and $\mathcal{B}$ will be called `a_val` and `b_val` in the implementation and they are defined by directly translating Tables 1.1 and 1.2 into **Miranda**:

```
> a_val :: aexp -> state -> z
> b_val :: bexp -> state -> t

> a_val (N n) s         = n
> a_val (V x) s         = s x
> a_val (Add a1 a2) s  = (a_val a1 s) + (a_val a2 s)
> a_val (Mult a1 a2) s = (a_val a1 s) * (a_val a2 s)
> a_val (Sub a1 a2) s  = (a_val a1 s) - (a_val a2 s)

> b_val TRUE s          = True
> b_val FALSE s         = False
> b_val (Eq a1 a2) s    = True,  if a_val a1 s = a_val a2 s
>                       = False, if a_val a1 s ~= a_val a2 s
> b_val (Le a1 a2) s    = True,  if a_val a1 s <= a_val a2 s
>                       = False, if a_val a1 s > a_val a2 s
> b_val (Neg b) s       = True,  if b_val b s = False
>                       = False, if b_val b s = True
> b_val (And b1 b2) s   = True,  if b_val b1 s = True &
>                                   b_val b2 s = True
>                       = False, if b_val b1 s = False \/
>                                   b_val b2 s = False
```

Exercise B.4 Construct an algebraic data type for the binary numerals considered in Section 1.3. Define a function `n_val` that associates a number (in the decimal system) to each numeral. □

Exercise B.5 Define functions

```
> fv_aexp :: aexp -> [var]
> fv_bexp :: bexp -> [var]
```

computing the set of free variables occurring in an expression. Ensure that each variable occurs at most once in the resulting lists. □

Exercise B.6 Define functions

```
> subst_aexp :: aexp -> var -> aexp -> aexp
> subst_bexp :: bexp -> var -> aexp -> bexp
```

implementing the substitution operations, that is `subst_aexp` $a\ y\ a_0$ constructs $a[y \mapsto a_0]$ and `subst_bexp` $b\ y\ a_0$ constructs $b[y \mapsto a_0]$. □

Appendix C

Operational Semantics in Miranda

In this appendix we implement the natural semantics and the structural operational semantics of Chapter 2 in **Miranda** and show how similar techniques can be used to implement an interpreter for the abstract machine and the code generation of Chapter 3.

We shall need the definitions from Appendix B so we begin by including these:

```
> %include "appB"
```

In Chapter 2 we distinguish between two kinds of configurations, intermediate configurations and final configurations. This is captured by the algebraic data type:

```
> config ::= Inter stm state | Final state
```

In the next section we shall show how the natural semantics can be implemented and after that we shall turn to the structural operational semantics.

C.1 Natural semantics

Corresponding to the relation $\rightarrow$ in Section 2.1 we shall introduce a function `ns_stm` of type

```
> ns_stm :: config -> config
```

The argument of this function corresponds to the left-hand side of $\rightarrow$ whereas the result produced will correspond to the right-hand side of the relation. This is possible because Theorem 2.9 shows that the relation is deterministic. The definition of `ns_stm` follows closely the definition of $\rightarrow$ in Table 2.1:

```
> ns_stm (Inter (Ass x a) s)
>        = Final (update s x (a_val a s))
>          where
>          update s x v y = v, if x = y
>                         = s y, otherwise

> ns_stm (Inter (Skip) s) = Final s

> ns_stm (Inter (Comp ss1 ss2) s)
>        = Final s''
>          where
>          Final s' = ns_stm (Inter ss1 s)
>          Final s'' = ns_stm (Inter ss2 s')

> ns_stm (Inter (If b ss1 ss2) s)
>        = Final s', if b_val b s
>          where
>          Final s' = ns_stm (Inter ss1 s)

> ns_stm (Inter (If b ss1 ss2) s)
>        = Final s', if ~b_val b s
>          where
>          Final s' = ns_stm (Inter ss2 s)

> ns_stm (Inter (While b ss) s)
>        = Final s'', if b_val b s
>          where
>          Final s' = ns_stm (Inter ss s)
>          Final s'' = ns_stm (Inter (While b ss) s')

> ns_stm (Inter (While b ss) s)
>        = Final s, if ~b_val b s
```

Note that in the axiom for assignment update s x v corresponds to $s[x \mapsto v]$.

The semantic function $\mathcal{S}_{\mathrm{ns}}$ can now be defined by

```
> s_ns ss s = s'
>             where
>             Final s' = ns_stm (Inter ss s)
```

Example C.1 We can execute the factorial statement (see Example B.1) from the state `s_init` mapping `x` to **3** and all other variables to **0** (see Example B.3). The final state `s_fac` is obtained as follows:

```
> s_fac = s_ns factorial s_init
```

To get the final value of `y` we evaluate `s_fac "y"`. □

Exercise C.2 Extend the definition of `stm` and `ns_stm` to include the `repeat`-construct. □

Exercise C.3 Define an algebraic data type `deriv_tree` representing the derivation trees of the natural semantics. Construct a variant of the function `s_ns` of type

```
s_ns :: stm -> state -> deriv_tree
```

that constructs the *derivation tree* for a given statement and state rather than just the final state. Apply the function to some example statements. □

C.2 Structural operational semantics

When specifying the structural operational semantics we shall need to test whether $\Rightarrow$ produces an intermediate configuration or a final configuration. So we shall introduce the function `is_Final` defined by:

```
>  is_Final (Inter ss s) = False
>  is_Final (Final s) = True
```

Corresponding to the relation $\Rightarrow$ we define the function `sos_stm` of type:

```
>  sos_stm :: config -> config
```

As in the previous section the argument of this function will correspond to the configuration on the left-hand side of the relation $\Rightarrow$ and the result will correspond to the right-hand side. Again this implementation technique is only possible because the semantics is deterministic (Exercise 2.22). The definition of `sos_stm` follows Table 2.2 closely:

```
>  sos_stm (Inter (Ass x a) s)
>          = Final (update s x (a_val a s))
>            where
>            update s x v y = v, if x = y
>                           = s y, otherwise

>  sos_stm (Inter Skip s) = Final s

>  sos_stm (Inter (Comp ss1 ss2) s)
>          = Inter (Comp ss1' ss2) s',
>                 if ~is_Final(sos_stm (Inter ss1 s))
>            where
>            Inter ss1' s' = sos_stm (Inter ss1 s)

>  sos_stm (Inter (Comp ss1 ss2) s)
>          = Inter ss2 s',
>                 if is_Final(sos_stm (Inter ss1 s))
>            where
>            Final s' = sos_stm (Inter ss1 s)

>  sos_stm (Inter (If b ss1 ss2) s)
>          = Inter ss1 s, if b_val b s

>  sos_stm (Inter (If b ss1 ss2) s)
>          = Inter ss2 s, if ~b_val b s

>  sos_stm (Inter (While b ss) s)
>          = Inter (If b (Comp ss (While b ss)) Skip) s
```

The function `sos_stm` implements one step of the computation. The function `deriv_seq` defined below will determine the complete derivation sequence (*even if it is infinite!*).

```
>  deriv_seq (Inter ss s)
>          = (Inter ss s) : (deriv_seq (sos_stm (Inter ss s)))
>  deriv_seq (Final s) = [Final s]
```

The semantic function $\mathcal{S}_{\text{sos}}$ can now be defined by the **Miranda** function `s_sos`:

```
> s_sos ss s = s'
>              where
>              Final s' = last (deriv_seq (Inter ss s))
```

Example C.4 The derivation sequence obtained by executing the factorial statement on the state `s_init` of Example B.3 can now be obtained as follows:

```
> fac_seq = deriv_seq (Inter factorial s_init)
```

We may want to inspect this in more detail and in particular we may be interested in the values of the variables `x` and `y` in the various intermediate states. To facilitate this we use the function

```
> show_seq fv l = lay (map show_config l)
>                 where
>                 show_config (Final s) =
>                   "final state:\n"++lay (map (show_val s) fv)
>                 show_config (Inter ss s) =
>                   show ss++"\n"++lay (map (show_val s) fv)
>                 show_val s x = " s("++x++")="++shownum (s x)
```

The function call `show_seq ["x","y"] fac_seq` will for each configuration in the derivation sequence `fac_seq` list the statement part and the values of `x` and `y` in the state part.

The final state of the derivation sequence can be obtained from

```
> s_fac' = s_sos factorial s_init
```

and the value obtained for `y` is obtained by executing `s_fac' "y"`. □

Exercise C.5 Extend the definition of `stm` and `sos_stm` to include the `repeat`-construct. □

C.3 Extensions of While

The implementation of the natural semantics of **While** in Section C.1 will now be extended to the procedure language **Proc** of of Section 2.5. Rather than presenting a fully worked out implementation we shall give detailed instructions for how to construct it. We shall pay special attention to the semantics of **Proc** with static scope rules for variables as well as procedures.

Exercise C.6 The first step will be to define the datatypes needed to represent the syntax and the semantics of **Proc**.

- Extend the abstract datatype `stm` with the new forms of statements and define abstract datatypes `dec_V` and `dec_P` for variable declarations and procedure declarations.

- Define the algebraic type `loc` to be `num` such that locations will be numbers. Define the function

```
new :: loc -> loc
```

  such that `new` increments its argument by one.

- Define algebraic types `env_V` and `env_P` corresponding to $\mathbf{Env}_V$ and $\mathbf{Env}_P$. Define the function

```
upd_P :: (dec_P, env_V, env_P) -> env_P
```

  corresponding to upd_P.

- Finally, we need a type `store` corresponding to **Store**. There are at least three possibilities: One possibility is to define

```
loc' ::= Loc loc | Next

store == loc' -> z
```

  as this will correspond closely to the definition of **Store**. Alternatively, one may identify the special token 'next' with location **0** and then simply define

```
store == loc -> z
```

  The third possibility is to define

```
store == (loc -> z, loc)
```

  where the second component corresponds to the value of 'next'.

  Choose a method that seems appropriate to you. □

Exercise C.7 Finally we turn towards the transition systems. We begin by implementing the transition system for variable declarations:

- Define an abstract datatype `config_D` for the configurations of the transition system for variable declarations.

- Then define a function

```
ns_dec_V :: config_D -> config_D
```

corresponding to the relation $\to_D$.

Now we turn to the transition relation for statements:

- Define an abstract datatype `config_P` corresponding to the configurations $\langle S, sto \rangle$ and *sto* of the transition system.
- Next define a function

  ```
  ns_stm :: (env_V, env_P) -> config_P -> config_P
  ```

  corresponding to the transition relation $\to$.

Finally define a function

```
s_ns :: stm -> store -> store
```

that calls `ns_stm` with appropriately initialized environments. Use the function on various example statements in order to ensure that the implementation works as intended. □

Exercise C.8 Modify the implementation above to use dynamic scope rules for variable declarations as well as procedure declarations. □

It is more problematic to extend the implementation to handle the constructs of Section 2.4:

Exercise C.9 Discuss how to extend the implementation of the natural semantics in Section C.1 to incorporate the constructs considered in Section 2.4. □

Exercise C.10 Discuss how to extend the implementation of the structural operational semantics of Section C.2 to incorporate the constructs considered in Section 2.4. □

C.4 Provably correct implementation

Rather than presenting a fully worked out **Miranda** script we shall provide exercises showing how to develop an implementation corresponding to Chapter 3.

Exercise C.11 We need some data types to represent the configurations of the machine:

- Define an algebraic data type `am_ins` for representing instructions and define the type synonym

```
am_code == [am_ins]
```

for representing code.

- Define an algebraic data type `stack_values` representing the elements that may be on the evaluation stack and define the type synonym

```
stack == [stack_values]
```

- Define a type `storage` representing the storage.

Finally define

```
am_config == (am_code, stack, storage)
```

for the configurations of **AM**. □

Exercise C.12 We can then turn to the semantics of the machine instructions. For this we proceed in three stages:

- First define a function `am_step` of type

```
am_step :: am_config -> am_config
```

implementing Table 3.1.

- We shall also be interested in the computation sequences of **AM** so define a function

```
am_comp_seq :: am_code -> storage -> [am_config]
```

that given a sequence of instructions and an initial storage will construct the corresponding computation sequence.

- Finally define a function `run` corresponding to the function $\mathcal{M}$ of Chapter 3.

This provides us with an interpreter for **AM**. What happens if we enter a stuck configuration? □

Exercise C.13 Finally, we implement the code generation functions:

- Define functions corresponding to $\mathcal{CA}$, $\mathcal{CB}$ and $\mathcal{CS}$.

- Define a function `am_stm` corresponding to the function $\mathcal{S}_{\mathrm{am}}$.

Apply the construction to a couple of examples to verify that everything works as expected. □

Exercise C.14 Modify the implementation to use the abstract machine $\mathbf{AM}_2$ of Exercises 3.8 and 3.17 rather than **AM**. □

Appendix D

Denotational Semantics in Miranda

In this appendix we implement the denotational semantics of Chapter 4 in **Miranda** and show how similar techniques can be used to implement the static program analysis of Chapter 5.

We shall need the definitions from Appendix B so we begin by including these:

```
> %include "appB"
```

D.1 Direct style semantics

In the implementation we shall rely on some of the built-in functions of **Miranda**. In particular, `id` is the identity function and '.' is function composition. The auxiliary function `cond` is defined by

```
> cond (p, g1, g2) s = g1 s, if p s
>                    = g2 s, if ~p s
```

The theoretical foundation of **Miranda** is closely related to the theory developed in Chapter 4 (although it is outside the scope of this book to go further into this). One of the consequences of this is that the fixed point operation can be implemented in a very simple way:

```
> fix ff = ff (fix ff)
```

The function $\mathcal{S}_{\mathrm{ds}}$ can now be implemented by the function

```
> s_ds :: stm -> state -> state
```

A straightforward rewriting of Table 4.1 gives:

```
> s_ds (Ass x a) s = update s (a_val a s) x
>                    where
>                    update s v x y = v, if x = y
>                                   = s y, otherwise

> s_ds Skip = id

> s_ds (Comp ss1 ss2) = (s_ds ss2) . (s_ds ss1)

> s_ds (If b ss1 ss2) = cond (b_val b, s_ds ss1, s_ds ss2)

> s_ds (While b ss) = fix ff
>                     where
>                     ff g = cond (b_val b, g . s_ds ss, id)
```

Example D.1 Returning to the factorial statement we can apply its denotation to the initial state `s_init` as follows:

```
> s_final = s_ds factorial s_init
```
□

Exercise D.2 We may be interested in the various iterands of the fixed point. Rewrite the semantic equations above so that each fixed point is unfolded at most n times where n is an additional parameter to the functions. Give examples showing that if the value of n is sufficiently large then we get the same result as above. □

Exercise D.3 Extend the definition above to handle the `repeat`-construct. □

D.2 Extensions of While

It is fairly straightforward to extend the implementation to handle the procedure language and the exception language of Section 4.5.

Exercise D.4 Modify the above implementation to use environments and stores and extend it to implement the semantics of the language **Proc** of Section 4.5. □

Exercise D.5 Modify the above implementation to use continuations and extend it to handle the language **Exc** of Section 4.5. □

D.3 Static program analysis

Rather than presenting a fully worked out **Miranda** script performing the dependency analysis we shall provide a rather detailed list of instructions for how to develop such an implementation.

Exercise D.6 The first step will be to implement the complete lattices **P** and **PState** and the operations on them:

- Define an algebraic data type `property` representing the set **P** of properties and define a function `p_lub` corresponding to $\sqcup_P$.

- Define a type synonym `pstate` representing the property states. Define the special property states INIT and LOST. Define a function `pstate_lub` corresponding to $\sqcup_{PS}$. □

Exercise D.7 We can then turn to the semantic equations defining the analysis:

- Define the functions

  ```
  p_aexp :: aexp -> pstate -> property
  ```

  corresponding to $\mathcal{PA}$ and

  ```
  p_bexp :: bexp -> pstate -> property
  ```

  corresponding to $\mathcal{PB}$.

- Define the auxiliary function `cond_P` corresponding to cond_P.

- Define the function

  ```
  p_stm :: stm -> pstate -> pstate
  ```

  corresponding to $\mathcal{PS}$ of Table 5.2. (You may use the results of Section 5.4 for this.) □

Exercise D.8 Implement the algorithm of Section 5.2 and apply the implementation to a couple of examples to verify that everything works as expected. □

Bibliography

[1] S. Abramsky, C. Hankin: *Abstract Interpretation of Declarative Languages*, Ellis Horwood (1987).

[2] A. V. Aho, J. E. Hopcroft, J. D. Ullman: *Data Structures and Algorithms*, Addison–Wesley (1982).

[3] A. V. Aho, R. Sethi, J. D. Ullman: *Compilers: Principles, Techniques and Tools*, Addison–Wesley (1986).

[4] K. R. Apt: *Ten Years of Hoare's Logic: A Survey — Part 1*, ACM Toplas **3** 4 (1981).

[5] J. W. de Bakker: *Mathematical Theory of Program Correctness*, Prentice-Hall (1980).

[6] D. Clément, J. Despeyroux, T. Despeyroux, G. Kahn: A simple applicative language: Mini-ML, *Proceedings of the 1986 ACM Conference on Lisp and Functional Programming* (1986).

[7] J. Despeyroux: Proof of translation in natural semantics, *Proceedings of Symposium on Logic in Computer Science*, Cambridge, Massachusetts, USA (1986).

[8] M. J. C. Gordon: *The Denotational Description of Programming Languages, An Introduction*, Springer-Verlag (1979).

[9] M. Hennessy: *The Semantics of Programming Languages: An Elementary Introduction using Structural Operational Semantics*, Wiley (1991).

[10] C. B. Jones: *Software Development: A Rigorous Approach*, Prentice-Hall (1980).

[11] J. Loeckx, K. Sieber: *The Foundations of Program Verification*, Wiley–Teubner Series in Computer Science (1984).

[12] H. R. Nielson: A Hoare-like proof system for run-time analysis of programs, *Science of Computer Programming*, vol 9 (1987).

[13] F. Nielson, H. R. Nielson: Two-level semantics and code generation, *Theoretical Computer Science*, vol 56 (1988).

[14] G. D. Plotkin: *Structural Operational Semantics*, Lecture notes, DAIMI FN-19, Aarhus University, Denmark (1981, reprinted 1991).

[15] G. D. Plotkin: An operational semantics for CSP, in: *Formal Description of Programming Concepts II*, Proceedings of TC-2 Work. Conf. (ed. D. Bjørner), North–Holland (1982).

[16] D. A. Schmidt: *Denotational Semantics: a Methodology for Language Development*, Allyn & Bacon, Inc. (1986).

[17] J. E. Stoy: *Denotational Semantics: The Scott–Strachey Approach to Programming Language Theory*, MIT Press (1977).

Index of Symbols

Index